*Lester
Pearson
and the
Dream
of Unity*

PETER STURSBERG

Lester Pearson and the Dream of Unity

DOUBLEDAY CANADA LIMITED
Toronto, Ontario
DOUBLEDAY AND COMPANY, INC.
Garden City, New York
1978

ISBN No. 0-385-13478-9
Library of Congress Catalog Card No. 77-16951

All photographs are from the Duncan
Cameron Collection in the Public
Archives, Ottawa.

First Edition

Printed and bound in Canada by The Bryant Press Limited
Book design by Robert Garbutt

Canadian Cataloguing in Publication Data
Stursberg, Peter, 1915-
   Lester Pearson and the dream of unity

Includes index.
ISBN 0-385-13478-9

1. Canada — Politics and government — 1963-
2. Pearson, Lester B., 1897-1972. I. Title.

FC620.S78   971.06'43   C78-001352-2
F1034.2.S78

Preface

THIS IS THE first volume of my oral or living history project on Lester B. Pearson, and it deals mainly with his work as Prime Minister; the second volume will be concerned with his activities as a diplomat and world statesman. The books on Pearson follow my two-volume work on John G. Diefenbaker, the only Conservative Prime Minister of Canada in more than forty years, *Diefenbaker: Leadership Gained: 1956-62* and *Diefenbaker: Leadership Lost: 1962-67,* were more or less a chronological account of the rise and fall of the prairie politician. However, in Mike Pearson's case, there seemed to be a natural division in his career between the part that he played in international affairs and his role in national affairs. Hence, *Lester Pearson and the Dream of Unity* details his struggle to keep Quebec in Confederation, while the second volume will concentrate on his relations with the United States but will go into his endeavours and achievements at the United Nations and in peacekeeping generally.

It is not a hard and fast division. There was bound to be a certain amount of over-lapping of foreign affairs on the domestic scene. For instance, the question of nuclear warheads, and whether or not Canada should accept them — I deal with that fairly fully in the first volume because it is an important part in the story of how Pearson became Prime Minister; in fact, some of his associates believed that his decision to reverse the Liberal Party's anti-nuclear policy led to his winning the 1963 election. However, there were other matters with domestic repercussions, such as the Canada-United States auto pact and Canadian-American economic relations that I am relegating to the second volume. All the agonising over the Vietnam War and the many attempts that Prime Minister Pearson and his External Affairs Minister, Paul Martin, made to resolve that conflict, have a more obvious place in my next book. The state visit of President Charles de Gaulle in 1967 could be classified as an international event, but the way that he encouraged the separatists with his cry of *"Vive le Québec libre"* made it a subject for the first volume, which is concerned with the attempt to settle the French Canadian problem.

As a diplomat and foreign minister, Lester Pearson was involved in most of the momentous events of the mid-century, and his activities then, before becoming Liberal Party Leader or Prime Minister, will, of course, be dealt with in the second volume. He joined the newly formed Department of External Affairs in 1928, the year before the stock market crash and the beginning of the Great Depression. His first posting abroad was to Canada House in London, England, and from this vantage point, he watched the Nazi drive in Europe which culminated in the Second World War. He was the Canadian representative in Washington when the Nuclear Age began with the destruction of Hiroshima and Nagasaki; among the conferences that he attended was the first conference on atomic energy between the three powers responsible for the bomb, the United States, Great Britain, and Canada. The Second World War was succeeded not by peace but by the Cold War, and Pearson was one of the architects of the North Atlantic Alliance. At the United Nations, he helped in the creation of Israel and in the settlement of the Korean War by means of an armistice. His crowning achievement, for which he received the Nobel Peace Prize, was the creation of the United Nations Emergency Force, the first peacekeeping force, which went far toward resolving the Suez Crisis and kept the peace in the Middle East for a decade.

This book is based on more than sixty interviews with close associates of Mr. Pearson as Liberal Party Leader and Prime Minister, and these included not only his Cabinet colleagues but also political opponents. I expect to record the recollections of another thirty people, mostly diplomats and former public servants, for the second volume. Some of those quoted in this first volume were interviewed originally for the Diefenbaker work, but the careers of the two Prime Ministers of the tenth decade of Confederation (1957-67) were so inter-twined that one could hardly consider one without referring to the other. Most of the men and women whose memories of Mike Pearson I sought gave of them freely; a few were reluctant but were persuaded that their views should be recorded for the benefit of posterity, at least. I wish to thank all of them for their contributions. There are, however, two important persons whose recollections are missing—Guy Favreau's life was cut tragically short in July 1967, and Robert Winters collapsed and died while on a visit to California in October 1969. These deaths are examples of living history's limitations. However, I interviewed enough people to assure that their stories would be fully told.

As in the case of my Diefenbaker books, *The Dream of Unity* is a departure of the oral or living history technique in that those quoted are identified; they are not the anonymous ordinary folk but the main actors, the movers and shakers of the times. Thus, the history of the Pearson Government's attempt to grapple with the Quebec problem is told by those who were involved in making the decisions; and Lester Pearson himself is seen by friend and foe as a much more complex character than he seemed to be. Direct excerpts from the transcripts of the interviews have been used; they have had to be edited in order to make the spoken word readable but every precaution has been taken not to change the meaning or intent of what was said or to take it out of context. The challenge of this book is in the editing, to convert the spoken word into the written word without losing its sense of spontaneity and emotional involvement, so that it seems, in the mind's eye of the reader, that the person is actually talking and explaining in his or her own way the history that he or she made. I hope I have been successful. There is a surprising candour about the comments of those who were interviewed, and I have found that politicians are much more forthcoming when they are speaking, even though they know they are being taped, than when writing. This may be because we use the telephone much more than the pen. Certainly, oral or living history takes advantage of the latest electronic means of communication.

Altogether, there were more than 120 hours of interviews, amounting to a million words—needless to say, only a small percentage of this abundant verbiage was used in this book. However, there had to be full transcripts made, and I am grateful to the Public Archives of Canada and the Parliamentary Library in Ottawa for undertaking this onerous task. Among those I should like to thank for their assistance are: Leo LaClare who was the real initiator of this project, and his successor as head of the historical sound recording section, Ernest J. Dick; Dr. W. I. Smith, the Dominion Archivist, who has been a strong supporter from the beginning; and Eric Spicer, the Parliamentary Librarian and a living history enthusiast. A grant from the Canada Council's Explorations Program helped to pay for travel and other expenses. Sylvia Carriere did most of the transcripts; others were done by Ethel Greene and Shirley Moulton. Richard Huyda helped in expediting the pictures of the period, which are all from the Duncan Cameron Collection in the Public Archives. As editing is the essence of this kind of work, I owe a debt of gratitude to my editor at Doubleday, Betty Jane Corson. I should like to say how much I appreciate my wife Jessamy's help and understanding.

Peter Stursberg
Ottawa, Ontario
June 1978

Prologue

LESTER PEARSON WAS one of the few Canadians who was a world figure. He was a career diplomat, External Affairs Minister, one of the architects of the North Atlantic Treaty Organisation, and president of the seventh session of the United Nations General Assembly in 1952-53. He won the Nobel Peace Prize in 1957 for his work at the time of the Suez Crisis in organising the first United Nations peace force (UNEF).

It was in 1957 that the Liberal government of Prime Minister Louis St. Laurent, in which Pearson served as External Affairs Minister, was turned out of office by the Progressive Conservatives under their new Western Leader, John Diefenbaker. It was an extraordinary political upset because the Liberals had been in power for twenty-two years. St. Laurent, who was seventy-five years old, retired, and Pearson was elected Leader in the month after he received the Nobel Prize in Oslo. However, the great world statesman was no match for the prairie politician, who was considered by many to be the finest stump orator and campaigner in Canadian history. In the election held on March 31, 1958, the Liberals were wiped out of six of the ten provinces, and all that Pearson was able to salvage was forty-eight seats, more than half of them from Quebec. The Conservatives won a record number, 208 of the 265 seats in the Canadian House of Commons, and Prime Minister Diefenbaker had the largest majority in history.

The extraordinary feature of Diefenbaker's overwhelming victory was the fact that he got fifty seats in Quebec; not even Sir John A. Macdonald, the old Conservative chieftain and founding father of Confederation, had ever won that number, although the forty-eight seats he got in 1882 represented a higher percentage because there were fewer seats in those days. This triumph was largely due to Premier Maurice Duplessis of Quebec, who realised that Diefenbaker was going to sweep the country, and decided to join in; he ordered his powerful Union Nationale machine into action and most of the fifty Conservatives elected federally had been members of the provincial Union Nationale party.

Duplessis, who came from a well-to-do family in the St. Lawrence River port of Trois-Rivières, had been elected as a Conservative member of the Quebec legislature back in the '20s and was chosen the provincial party's leader in 1933. However, he came to the conclusion that he could never become premier with the Conservatives and so he formed the Union Nationale Party, which was a mixture of old "Bleus," as the Quebec Tories were called, nationalists and disaffected Liberals, and was swept into office in the 1936 provincial election. He was defeated at the polls in the fall of 1939, but that was his last loss and he returned to power in 1944 and was the undisputed ruler of Quebec until his death in 1959.

Although Maurice Le Noblet Duplessis was no separatist, he was a French Canadian nationalist and a champion of provincial autonomy who refused to co-operate with Ottawa on cost-sharing programs or in any other way and turned down federal grants even when they were badly needed. His regime was called authoritarian and reactionary. During the early '50s Quebec was considered to be more Catholic and priest-ridden than Ireland or Spain. Duplessis's attitude was that of the *grand seigneur:* he looked on the *habitant* farmers of Quebec as the guardian of French Canada's virtues and a bulwark against the vices of the English-speaking cities and of the international unions. Yet "le Chef," as he was called by his followers, wanted the province to become industrialised; he opposed any increase in the Quebec minimum wage because he believed that low wages would attract

American capital. While Duplessis used the English-speaking businessmen as whipping boys, he made no demands on them, and the English-language press generally stayed on the sidelines; the Montreal *Star* had more foreign news than any other Canadian paper of its size, and its editor, George Ferguson, explained that this was because the newspaper did not feel it should be involved in provincial politics. The French-language press suffered from no such inhibition, and André Laurendeau, the editor of *Le Devoir*, called Duplessis "Le Roi Nègre," the black king who ran the colony on behalf of its white masters.

One of Prime Minister Diefenbaker's first acts was to introduce simultaneous translation of the deliberations of Parliament. This was acknowledged to be a great boon because before that, whenever a Member spoke in French, the House of Commons emptied since most of the English-speaking Members didn't understand French. There was also a provision for bilingual cheques but the long-drawn-out struggle in the Cabinet to get them approved made the Conservative Prime Minister hesitate about proceeding any further with bilingualism. He was proud of the fact that he had appointed the first French Canadian Governor-General, Georges Philias Vanier. Whenever there was criticism that he hadn't gone far enough, Mr. Diefenbaker always asserted that he had lived up to the Constitution as far as this issue was concerned. Then, there was no pressure from Quebec about this—Maurice Duplessis was interested in provincial rights, not language rights.

On September 7, 1959, Premier Maurice Duplessis died at Schefferville in northern Quebec while visiting the operations of the Iron Ore Company of Canada. He was succeeded by Paul Sauvé, a long-time political associate but a very different kind of man. Although Sauvé was as determined as Duplessis to protect Quebec's culture and autonomy, he went about it in a positive manner; he looked for ways to co-operate with Ottawa and found a formula whereby Quebec could accept federal grants for its universities. The changes he made delighted the Diefenbaker Tories: not only did they get along well with this genial, easygoing man who had commanded the Fusiliers Mont Royal during the war and been decorated in Normandy, but they regarded him as one of their own kind of Conservative because he was the son of a

Bennett Cabinet Minister. Furthermore, there seemed to be no doubt now that the Union Nationale Party could beat off the Liberal challenge and win re-election in the province. However, a little more than a hundred days from the time he was sworn in as premier, Paul Sauvé died. There was no one to succeed him.

The Union Nationale Party began to break up. Antonio Barrette, a Duplessis minister, had been the compromise selection as leader but he did not have the authority or the stature to hold the organisation together. An election was called for June 22, and, after a vigorous campaign with the slogan that it was "time for a change," the Liberals won. They were led by Jean Lesage, a former federal Cabinet Minister and colleague of Lester Pearson. The repressive Union Nationale government of Maurice Duplessis which Paul Sauvé had not had time to reform had been ousted after sixteen years in power. There was dancing in the streets of Montreal, and, according to Maurice Sauvé, one of the organisers of the victory, there was as much excitement among the young people as there was on November 15, 1976, when the Parti Québécois won. Lesage's success in Quebec was the first good news that Pearson had had since the 1958 debacle and he began to feel that his fortunes were on the rise.

It was a bad blow for John Diefenbaker, who was to say some years later that, had Paul Sauvé lived (which would have meant that the Union Nationale would have won), his government would have retained its majority in the 1962 election. He went on to assert that, had Paul Sauvé lived, he might have become Prime Minister of Canada, presumably as Diefenbaker's successor. However, it was not really the Quebec problem or bilingualism that brought the Conservatives down, but economic conditions. There had been a recession with accompanying heavy unemployment which had hurt the Tories badly. Then their own mismanagement of affairs, the devaluation of the dollar in the midst of the 1962 election campaign, lost them most of the seats along the United States border. Finally, the minority Diefenbaker Government of 1962-63 disintegrated over the failure to come to grips with the issue of having American nuclear warheads in Canada.

Just a few days before the 1963 election, which put Lester Pearson and the Liberals in power, a bomb exploded on the railway track near Lemieux, Quebec, a few hours before Prime Minister Diefenbaker was to have travelled over it; the Conservative leader's campaign train had to be rerouted. This was the work of an urban guerrilla group known as the "Front de Liberation du Québec" (FLQ). There had been acts of vandalism and arson before that—"FLQ" and "Québec Libre" had been daubed on federal buildings and mailboxes and on the Wolfe monument in Quebec City — but this was the first of the bomb blasts that were to punctuate the early days of the Pearson government; they resulted in the death of a night watchman and the serious injury of an army sergeant belonging to a bomb disposal unit. These terrorist acts merely served to dramatise the discontent in Quebec. The FLQ itself was an insignificant factor, but the separatists, who included many young people, had been active for years in the province, and the so-called "Quiet Revolution" had been turning things inside out since 1960. Ottawa's relations with French Canada were in a turmoil, and the English-language press was asking, "What does Quebec want?"

It was to satisfy what were considered to be Quebec's demands that Prime Minister Pearson introduced bilingualism, in the federal public service as a first step, and began the spending of vast sums of money on teaching middle-aged officials to speak French. He accepted the concept that Canada was a bilingual country, that Confederation was a compact between the two founding peoples, the British and the French, and that a French Canadian should have the same rights throughout the country that he enjoyed in Quebec, including the right to have his children educated in French. Although a renowned internationalist, Pearson proposed a maple leaf flag as an emblem of national unity and national identity and had it accepted after a long and bitter debate in Parliament. The doctrine of "co-operative federalism" was devised to meet Quebec's claims and the greatest example of this was the way that the Pearson government changed the Canada Pension Plan and made it fit in with the Quebec Pension Plan.

By the time Lester Pearson became Prime Minister in 1963 the "new wave" of Liberals had been running Quebec for almost three years. They had moved quickly to modernise the province and bring it into line with Ontario and other parts of the country. They instituted a wide variety of social and educational reforms, which resulted in the Roman Catholic Church's losing a lot of its prestige and influence. One of the first acts of the Lesage government was to establish a system of hospital insurance and thus take advantage of the federal cost-sharing grants for such a program. There was a bold scheme to expropriate all the private power companies, which was being pressed by René Lévesque, Quebec Minister of Natural Resources, but Lesage didn't want to go ahead with it until he had got a mandate from the people. The 1962 provincial election resulted in a Liberal landslide. Quebec Hydro was set up as a publicly owned monoply similar to Ontario Hydro.

The fact that Lester Pearson had been a diplomat, representing Canada, supposedly a bilingual country, and could only speak English, made him more conscious of bilingualism than most of his contempories in English Canada. He relied on the advice of French Canadian confidantes in formulating policy with regard to the Quebec problem. A man who had great influence was Maurice Lamontagne, who joined Pearson shortly after he became Leader of the Liberal Party and Leader of the Opposition. Guy Favreau was his first Quebec lieutenant when he became Prime Minister. Lamontagne was one of the first French Canadian economists and set up the faculty of Social Sciences at Laval University, Quebec City; he became part of the Ottawa establishment in the early '50s and was an aide to Prime Minister St. Laurent for a short time. Guy Favreau had worked on a number of federal commissions and was Associate Deputy Minister of Justice before becoming a Liberal M.P. and Cabinet Minister.

Both Lamontagne and Favreau were supporters of the Quiet Revolution, but they were not on the ground when such people as Jean Lesage and Paul Gérin-Lajoie and René Lévesque were attacking the bastions of reaction. While Favreau had been a lawyer in Montreal, Lamontagne had spent most of the past decade in Ottawa, and neither of them, according to Gérard Pelletier, was a very well-known figure in French Canada. As premier, Lesage was just as determined as Maurice Duplessis had been to protect Quebec's autonomy, only he didn't call it that. When he was asked what Quebec wanted, he said that the province wanted its constitutional rights. Although he had some angry confrontations at federal-provincial conferences, Lesage felt that Prime Minister Pearson did understand Quebec's needs and had gone a long way to meet them with the policy of co-operative federalism.

One of the organisers of the Quiet Revolution, Maurice Sauvé, went to Ottawa; he was elected to Parliament in 1962, the year before Guy Favreau was elected, but he was not appointed to the first Cabinet, and never became one of Pearson's close advisors, although he was instrumental in resolving the Canada Pension Plan crisis. When Favreau and Lamontagne fell from grace, Lester Pearson turned not to Maurice Sauvé but to Jean Marchand and Pierre Trudeau, who had come to Ottawa as a result of the 1965 election. Jean Marchand succeeded Guy Favreau as the head of the Quebec caucus and Mr. Pearson's Quebec lieutenant.

While Marchand and Trudeau and the other member of the Quebec triumvirate, Pelletier, were connected with the Quiet Revolution—they had been attacking Duplessis long before Lesage left federal politics or René Lévesque the Canadian Broadcasting Corporation—they were federalists. They were against yielding any more power to the provinces and believed that decentralisation would loosen the ties of Confederation and lead to the break-up of Canada. As Lester Pearson came to rely more and more on their advice, there was a down-playing of co-operative federalism until it became a dead document and an up-grading of bilingualism.

Contents

The Cast

GOVERNOR-GENERAL OF CANADA
Roland Michener

GOVERNMENT
Lester Bowles Pearson
PRIME MINISTER, 1963-68
LEADER OF THE OPPOSITION, 1958-63

Liberal Cabinet Ministers

E. J. Benson
Léo Cadieux
Lucien Cardin
Lionel Chevrier
Jean Chrétien
John Connolly
C. M. Drury
Yvon Dupuis
Walter Gordon
J. J. Greene
Harry Hays
Paul Hellyer
Judy LaMarsh
Maurice Lamontagne

Allan MacEachen
Bryce Mackasey
Jean Marchand
Paul Martin
George McIlraith
J. R. Nicholson
Lawrence Pennell
Jean-Luc Pepin
J. W. Pickersgill
Maurice Sauvé
Mitchell Sharp
Pierre Trudeau
John Turner

Liberal M.P.s

Ralph Cowan
Pauline Jewett
John Matheson

Gérard Pelletier
James Walker

Liberal Party Organiser

Keith Davey

Speaker of the House

Alan Macnaughton

OPPOSITION

John George Diefenbaker

LEADER OF THE OPPOSITION, 1963-67
PRIME MINISTER, 1957-63

Progressive Conservative Party

Gordon Churchill
Alvin Hamilton
George Hees
Erik Nielsen
Pierre Sévigny

New Democratic Party

T. C. Douglas
Douglas Fisher
Stanley Knowles
David Lewis

Social Credit Party (including Quebec Créditistes)

Réal Caouette
Raymond Langlois
Dr. Guy Marcoux
Robert Thompson

OTHERS

Executive Assistants, Reporters, Etc.

Florence Bird
Jim Coutts
Robert Fowler
Bruce Hutchison
Stuart Keate
Tom Kent
Eric Kierans
Mary Macdonald

Victor Mackie
A. H. McDonald
John Nichol
Richard O'Hagan
Maurice Wright
Christopher Young
Lubor Zink

Provincial Premiers

Jean Lesage
PREMIER OF QUEBEC

J. R. Smallwood
PREMIER OF NEWFOUNDLAND

John Robarts
PREMIER OF ONTARIO

Robert Stanfield
PREMIER OF NOVA SCOTIA
LEADER OF THE OPPOSITION, 1967

*Lester
Pearson
and the
Dream
of Unity*

I The Bilingual Pledge

WHEN THE LIBERAL *Party Leader and Leader of the Opposition, Lester B. Pearson, rose to speak on Tuesday afternoon, December 17, 1962, the galleries were full and more than the usual number of Members were in their seats for a supply debate (a time for the Opposition to raise issues). Attendance had been high since the opening of the Twenty-fifth Parliament of Canada on September 27 because the fall of the minority Diefenbaker government was expected daily. There was an atmosphere of clamorous excitement in the Green Chamber. The Progressive Conservatives, who had had more than two hundred seats only a few months before, were reduced to 116 Members in the June 18, 1962, election, and had to share the government side, on Mr. Speaker's right, with nineteen New Democrats, while the one hundred Liberals and thirty Social Crediters filled the Opposition side. That was the "House of Minorities," as Robert Thompson, the new Social Credit Leader, liked to call it, before which Mr. Pearson made his bilingual pledge.*

It was no ringing declaration. But that was not Mike Pearson's style, although he had improved as an orator and debater since becoming Liberal Leader in 1958. He started off by noting that preparations were being made to celebrate the centenary of Confederation in little more than four years' time (1967) but that there was anxiety and uncertainty about the country's future. "Recent events," he said, "have shown clearly that we are going through another crisis of national unity, and I do not think it is an exaggeration to call it this."

3

There were two different interpretations of Confederation in Canada, and Mr. Pearson asserted that they had brought about confusion, frustration, and even conflict. To the French-speaking Canadians, Confederation meant a bilingual and bicultural nation, with their rights protected across the whole country and with equal opportunities to share in Canadian development, whereas most English-speaking Canadians felt that the only part of the country that could be called bilingual and bicultural was Quebec and that French-language rights were protected by the Constitution (British North America Act) in that province, Parliament, and the federal courts. As long as there were only marginal contacts between the language groups, the "two solitudes" got along well enough together. However, Quebec's industrial revolution, which had given rise to a social revolution, had changed all that, and now French-speaking Canadians were "determined to become directors of their economic and cultural destiny."

"This means, I believe," Mr. Pearson went on, "that we have now reached a stage when we should seriously and collectively review the bicultural and bilingual situation in our country; our experience in the teaching of English and French, and in the relations existing generally between our two founding racial groups. In this review there should also be, in my view, every opportunity and every encouragement for Canadians, individually or in their associations and organisations, to express their ideas on this situation. If they find it unsatisfactory they should suggest concrete measures to meet it and to reach a better, more balanced participation of our two founding groups in our national affairs."

Then he asked a series of rhetorical questions: "Are we ready, for instance, to give to all young Canadians a real opportunity to become truly bilingual?" "What further contributions to this end have we the right to expect from radio, from television, and from films in both languages?" "What are the reasons why there are so few French-speaking Canadians in the professional and administrative jobs of the federal civil service, including crown corporations and federal agencies? How can that situation be improved? Would it be desirable, for instance, to have a bilingual school of public administration operated by the federal government in Ottawa?"

Despite its somewhat academic approach—and both Lester Pearson and Maurice Lamontagne, his chief Quebec advisor and author of the bilingual pledge, were former professors—the political import of the speech was immediately recognised. The Liberal Leader had accepted what he himself said was the French Canadian view that Canada was a bilingual and bicultural nation. When he became Prime Minister—and few doubted that he would after the next election—he would appoint a commission to carry out the sort of enquiry that André Laurendeau, publisher of Le Devoir, *had been demanding in his paper, and would take the first steps toward national bilingualism in the federal civil service.*

The fact that he was not bilingual was a matter of regret to Lester Pearson. He himself admitted that he had not much facility for languages, and he marvelled at the way that Jean Chrétien, who came to Ottawa speaking only French, could teach himself English and could become so fluent that he could give speeches in English during the 1965 election campaign. He confessed to Chrétien, whom he appointed his Parliamentary Secretary before making him the youngest Minister in more than half a century, that he hadn't thought it necessary to learn French when he was young.

In this regard, Pearson was no different from so many English-speaking Canadians of the period; even those who grew up in Montreal and went to McGill University didn't bother to learn French. However, he was more conscious of this inadequacy in his education than most, in the view of Jean-Luc Pepin, another bright young Québécois whom he promoted to the Cabinet.

JEAN CHRÉTIEN

Pearson said, "I was a student in history at the University of Toronto and I had to take a course in language." And he was a bit like me, you know. Sports were more important than studies. He said, "I would take the easiest subject I could think of." So he had to take a language, and he had the choice between Spanish, French, and German. "I took German because I was told that it was easier to learn for an Anglophone than French."

"It was crazy," he said. "They should have told me that here in Canada you learn French, and after that you learn German."

JEAN-LUC PEPIN

Here he was, a top Canadian diplomat, who had gone through life without being bilingual, representing a bilingual country abroad. You know, there may have been a bit of remorse in his (later) dedication to bilingualism. But I always conceived of it as a very generous disposition on the part of Mr. Pearson. He understood the country; he understood that French-speaking people had to be given equal status, if you want to put it this way, linguistically. They had to be able to associate with the federal government as well as people from other provinces. And he realised that a very great move had to be made in this area.

Paul Martin, the veteran Liberal M.P., recalled a discussion with Mr. Pearson about the French-English problem while they were attending a United Nations meeting in New York, long before Mike became Leader of the Liberal Party.

PAUL MARTIN

One day at the United Nations he and I went to a baseball game together, as we often did, and during that game—it wasn't one of the most exciting ones, although he found every game exciting—I suggested to him that, important as our foreign policy was, the really big question in Canada was the problem between the French and the English, and how to resolve this. And I found him surprisingly interested.

His foreign policy, the foreign policy that he recommended as Undersecretary or that he practised as Secretary of State for External Affairs, was not predicated in any way on the "French Fact," as it later became known. So I was very surprised this day to find that he was intensely interested in the French-English problem and that he recognised that the unity of the country depended on these two groups getting along well together. He said, "We really have to do something about this."

"Well," I said, "this surprises me because you don't show that in your friendships; you don't show that in what you say at the United Nations and elsewhere."

"I know," he said. "But we're not going to hold Canada together unless we do find some way of accommodation. Do you know what I think we should do?" he went on. "We should bring home to the people of Canada generally the facts of this problem, an understanding of this problem. They don't all realise the extent to which Quebec and English-speaking Canada must get along together if we're going to hold the unity of the country. They don't understand that. I think we ought to really have a royal commission on this. I think we ought to have a public exposure of the facts."

However, there was a certain ambivalence in Pearson's attitude toward French Canadians; while he could not speak the language and, according to Paul Martin, his old friend and rival, was never very comfortable in the presence of French people, he was sympathetic to Francophone aspirations and, in the view of his colleagues, had a better grasp of the Quebec situation in relation to the rest of the country than other English-speaking politicians. Yet he was reluctant to make the speech on bilingualism during the supply debate. There were the pressures of the Liberal caucus, according to Vic Mackie, the correspondent of the Winnipeg Free Press, and the contrary advice that he was receiving. In fact, Maurice Lamontagne had to threaten to quit before Pearson would decide to go ahead, and Walter Gordon, who was the architect of the Liberal revival, emphasised Lamontagne's great contribution.

MAURICE LAMONTAGNE

I began to prepare the speech, and I proposed that it should be made before the election was declared—we were pretty sure at that time that we would defeat the Diefenbaker government in the House because the situation was getting completely out of hand. We were in the last month of the fiscal year, and no credits had been voted yet.

There was a small fight between ourselves. I remember that we had a supply motion coming, and Tom Kent [one of Pearson's advisors] was of the view that we should have the motion on the collapse of the government, on the inefficiency of the government. He thought it was very important to put that on the record, and make the Conservatives ill at ease over this, and help them to further divide. I was about to lose my proposal, so I told Mr. Pearson, "Well, I'll go back home for a few days and whenever you've decided to make that speech, I'll come back."

It was not opposition to the speech. It was opposition to the strategy, and it came mainly from Tom [Kent] and to some extent from Walter [Gordon]. They didn't see this as a big issue. They didn't see this as helping us very much. As soon as Mr. Pearson decided to make the speech, I went to Montreal and I showed my notes to [Gérard] Pelletier, who was the editor of *La Presse* at that time, and to [André] Laurendeau. Of course, they were very enthusiastic about it. However, they didn't believe that the speech would ever be made.

When Mr. Pearson made the speech, we got tremendous support throughout the country—the Toronto *Star* and most of the English-speaking press and the French-speaking press. That put the Quebec Conservatives very much on the defensive. [Pierre] Sévigny [Associate Defence Minister] told me afterward that he tried to convince Diefenbaker to agree with the proposal to set up a Royal Commission on Bilingualism and, of course, he didn't succeed. So I think that the speech helped us during the campaign, but more importantly, I think, it was the beginning of a new era in Canada.

WALTER GORDON

I don't think anybody has emphasised Lamontagne's real contribution, not only to Pearson and the Liberal Party, but also to the country. He has been a thinker from the beginning, from the days when he was a young professor at Laval, and I think he is a very wise fellow. He was the one who sold Pearson on this speech, and it was the most effective speech that was made during that session. It received a great deal of acclaim in Quebec and Laurendeau said never before had an English-speaking politician showed that he had any understanding of Quebec, that this was something new.

So that it not only helped Pearson a great deal personally in Quebec, but it gave the Liberal Party a great lift there. Pearson didn't do it for that reason. He did it because he thought this was vital to the country. I don't think there was any politics in that speech. The political repercussions were great, but it wasn't done for that reason.

VIC MACKIE

I remember thinking that Mike had fallen into the same pattern as his predecessors in the Liberal Party and become the captive of the majority in the caucus. Every Liberal Prime Minister has to understand that if he's going to continue to be Prime Minister, he has to live with the fact that he gets tremendous support from Quebec, from French Canada. And he must appease Quebec. He must make concessions to Quebec, and whenever he goes into that caucus he's facing a huge phalanx of Quebec Members, and because of that the Liberal Party always has to make major concessions to Quebec, and this is what has antagonised Western Canada and the Maritimes. Ontario seems to have a guilt complex and feels that they have got to go along with Quebec and see to it that Quebec has a special place in Confederation. I think it's the Ontario vote that decides the elections.

TOM KENT

I remember very clearly a meeting of the Advisory Committee in Mr. Pearson's office with Maurice Lamontagne, who, of course, had drafted that speech. Jack Pickersgill, Paul Martin, and I think Lionel Chevrier [former Liberal Cabinet Ministers] were also there. I expressed some doubts but was converted as to the wisdom of that speech.

J. W. PICKERSGILL

We knew that Pearson had decided to support this proposal for a commission. One is sometimes a little hazy about recollections about what happened. I think I was rather sceptical about it. It wasn't that I was opposed to the objectives in the least, but I was rather unsure about whether this was the most effective approach to it. But I certainly didn't oppose it. But I don't think we had much discussion of it. I think he pretty much decided himself that this was what he wanted to do. He was undoubtedly influenced enormously by Maurice Lamontagne about this.

And I was always a little afraid that Pearson was too much influenced by what I would describe as the French Canadian intellectuals, and that he really needed a few people with their feet on the ground and their heads not too high up as well to advise him about French Canada because I have never really believed that most French Canadians care very much about bilingualism outside the area where they'd like anyone to be bilingual if they can't speak English very well. I don't think it was a grievance that was very widespread in the country. But I think it's a proper thing to do, to have a functionally bilingual public service. I've always thought that.

As Mr. Pearson said in his December 17, 1962, speech, English-speaking Canadians considered that the Articles of Confederation guaranteed the language rights of French Canadians in Parliament and the federal courts, as well as in the province of Quebec. That was the overwhelming view in the country, and it seemed to be borne out by Section 133 of the BNA Act. In other words, Canada, as far as most Canadians were concerned, was English-speaking and only Quebec was bilingual. Certainly, the federal civil service was English-speaking; the only bilingual officials were the few French Canadians in Ottawa and they had to work in English. There were usually enough French-speaking judges to hear cases argued in French before the Supreme Court of Canada and the Exchequer Court.

However, until 1957 an M.P. could speak French in the House but it would be to a largely uncomprehending audience. The Member speaking French could not even be sure that he was being understood by the Speaker because, in the old days, as Stanley Knowles, the veteran NDP Member and procedural expert, said, the Speaker didn't have to be bilingual, and some were not.

STANLEY KNOWLES

Let me discuss the Speakership a bit further, just to show how things have changed. In '57 Diefenbaker could offer it to me, and Pearson could offer it a bit later.* Nobody could take that Chair today unless he was fluent in both languages. You just couldn't handle the House of Commons today.

Now Diefenbaker said to me in August '57, that one of the reasons he was letting me know well in advance was so I could go somewhere and get enough French to handle the odds and ends. I had to be able to read the prayer in French every second day and say *Adopté* and *D'accord*. But you didn't need to have French. Mind you, there wasn't even simultaneous translation in the House at that point. That was installed by Diefenbaker later. But things change around this place. The onerous responsibilities of the Speaker have grown too.

*See Chapter 6, page 173.

If things changed around Parliament, as Stanley Knowles said they did, they reflected changes in the country at large, and the most significant of them was the overthrow of the reactionary Union Nationale regime in Quebec by a rejuvenated provincial Liberal Party on June 22, 1960. It was the beginning of the Quiet Revolution. Although the new premier, Jean Lesage, had been a federal Cabinet Minister and a colleague of Pearson's, he was as much a French Canadian nationalist as the late Premier Maurice Duplessis. However, he was a modern man and was ready to co-operate with Ottawa in shared-cost programs, if only on a temporary basis. But he kept insisting on provincial rights. Lesage warned the largely Anglophone owners of Quebec industry that his government planned to take a very active part in the economic life of the province. René Lévesque, the broadcaster-turned-politician who was one of Lesage's ministers, was beating the drum for the nationalisation of the hydro-electric power companies. That was the meaning of the Liberal slogan of "Maître Chez Nous." *There were charges that the new Quebec government was undermining the Roman Catholic Church and moving toward socialism.*

Yet, as late as 1961, a book could be published entitled Canadian Issues *which made no mention of bilingualism or what Paul Martin called the French-English problem. In fact, one of the contributors, James A. Corry, who was then vice-principal of Queen's University, wrote that "the relations of French speaking and English speaking Canadians had improved immensely in recent years." He put down "the decline in recrimination and the rise in generosity" to "the meeting each year in national associations of one kind and another of relatively small numbers of persons of the two language groups who reach not only understanding but friendship. They recognize themselves and one another as Canadians." Another contributor—the book was brought out in honour of Professor Henry F. Angus of the University of British Columbia on his retirement—was John Turner, who wrote an essay on "The Senate of Canada—Political Conundrum" in which he argued for the abolition of the Upper House as "it no longer plays a useful part in the government of Canada."*

It was a Defence Research Board scientist, Dr. Marcel Chaput, who brought the language issue to the attention of the politicians and powers-that-be in Ottawa. He had written a book, Pourquoi Je Suis Séparatiste, *which was widely read in Quebec and, in the spring of 1961, began actively campaigning for the province's secession with speeches in Montreal and across the river from Ottawa in Hull. The Conservative government regarded his behaviour as little short of treasonous, and when Dr. Chaput attended a conference in Quebec City on "The Canadian Experiment—Success or Failure" despite the fact that he had been refused leave, he was suspended by the DRB. His suspension was upheld by the Defence Minister, Douglas Harkness. On December 4, 1961, Dr. Chaput resigned, vowing never to speak English again. He returned to Montreal to be given a hero's welcome by the RIN (Le Rassemblement pour l'Indépendance Nationale), an early separatist organisation.*

Meanwhile, there was increasing publicity about separatism in the French-language press which made little or no impression on English Canada since it was not very well reported in the English-language newspapers. In March 1961 La Presse *said that 45 percent of 11,000 people who answered a questionnaire in the paper favoured separatism.* Le Devoir *ran a series of fifteen articles on the independence issue and followed that up with a plebiscite which, it said, showed that more than 75 percent believed that a separate state was desirable. It was on January 19, 1962, that André Laurendeau came out with his call for an enquiry into bilingualism and biculturalism in a* Le Devoir *editorial.*

However, the one incident that probably had as much effect as any on Pearson making his bilingual pledge in Parliament was Donald Gordon's appearance before the Commons Railway Committee on November 20, 1962. The president of the state-owned Canadian National Railway admitted that there were no French Canadians on the railway's board and few if any in the upper levels of management. He went further and suggested that the reason for this was that there were none who were qualified. The Créditistes, as the Social Credit members from Quebec were known, were furious, and Donald Gordon was burned in effigy by student demonstrators when he returned to Montreal.

The Quiet Revolution was becoming noisier, and the newspapers in English Canada were asking the question: "What does Quebec want?" In the fall of 1962 Lesage decided that he needed a new mandate on the question of nationalisation. A second election was held on November 14, 1962, and the Liberals increased their seats from fifty-four to sixty-three, or more than double the number of the Union Nationale. On December 28 of that year the Quebec government bought out the power companies.

But was bilingualism what Quebec really wanted? Lionel Chevrier, who was Mr. Pearson's Quebec lieutenant (chief advisor on Quebec) during the years in Opposition and the first year of his government, was sure that it was. He said that the Liberal Leader's December 17, 1962, speech was meant to offset the threat of separatism. Maurice Lamontagne was inclined to agree. However, he chose to emphasise its effect on the recruitment of French Canadians into the federal civil service.

MAURICE LAMONTAGNE

There are really two things involved. The average French Canadian couldn't care less. A man from Rimouski, where I come from, will never hear any word of English there; so he didn't even know really that he could not be served in French in Ottawa. Insofar as his daily life was concerned, it didn't affect him really. But it gave him a pride of being a Canadian if this kind of thing were to be settled.

And there's the other element, the elite or the new university graduates, who would not have come to Ottawa to the extent that they have. And remember, in those years, starting in 1960, Jean Lesage was trying to build up rapidly the provincial civil service because there was no professional civil service under Mr. Duplessis. He never hired one of our graduates from Laval University in the field of the social sciences.

When I went to Quebec City to help Jean Lesage prepare the speech that he gave at the first federal-provincial conference that he attended as premier [July 25, 1960]—that was when he spoke of the "opening of Quebec"—we discussed the matter [of the civil service]. I was at the Maison Montmorency with Father Lévesque, preparing the speech, and Jean Lesage and René Lévesque would come every evening. I had a number of [Laval] graduates in Ottawa, and we'd talk and I would say, "Well, you need this man."

That was how Michel Delanger left the federal civil service to go to Quebec and become René Lévesque's deputy minister. Also Marier went as Deputy Minister of Health and Welfare—Marier had been a teacher at Laval and specialised in social work. You see how intricate and difficult the situation was, because then we were beginning to compete with the provincial people. So we had to make this kind of a gesture [bilingualism] because otherwise we would not have got anyone here in Ottawa.

When Jean Lesage was asked whether bilingualism was the right answer to the question of what Quebec wanted, he answered bluntly.

JEAN LESAGE

Not the way I saw it. The way I saw it was that Quebec should have full exercise of its powers under the Constitution. That's the fight I had with Ottawa, that in the social field, first in the social and educational field, Ottawa should be out. I was against the grants to universities; I asked for income tax points; same with hospitalisation insurance . . .

It was all part of the same basic policy of giving to Quebec all its exclusive rights under the Constitution. As a matter of fact, I still think that Ottawa should give us all the powers in the social and educational and cultural fields, and in the field of communications when it is communications inside the province. This is a fight which is going on and on. I cannot accept Mr. Trudeau's view on this.

This has been my thinking all along. Of course, I clashed with the Ottawa government, first with Diefenbaker from '60 to '63 and then with Mr. Pearson. They knew about my views, which had been expressed at federal-provincial conferences. The Liberal Party in Ottawa was aware of my thinking and my policy, our Quebec policy. Mr. Pearson understood it. I don't recall having talked about languages in federal-provincial conferences or to Mr. Pearson, although he talked to me about them.

As for Maurice Sauvé, he felt that the main purpose of Mr. Pearson's December 17 speech was to bring more French Canadians to Ottawa; otherwise he believed that it was misguided and based on the wrong analysis of the situation in Quebec.

MAURICE SAUVÉ

Pearson thought that was one of the means to bring more Quebeckers in the [federal] civil service, and if there were more Quebeckers in the civil service, then the Quebeckers would have more stake in Canada. But he didn't believe that this was the only method. On the contrary, he was very strong on giving the provinces more autonomy, more fiscal freedom. He wanted the federal government to get out of some of the programs which were in the provincial jurisdiction. But he thought—and in this I have no quarrel at all with him—that if Canada were more bilingual the French Canadian would feel happier. He had the wrong interpretation of the situation, and this was mostly given to him by Maurice Lamontagne who, like most other French Canadian political leaders, always interpreted the difficult political relations between Quebec or the French Canadians and the Anglophones as being a cultural problem. I'm not saying it's not cultural, but it's not mainly cultural; it's mainly economic. Maurice and Trudeau and the others have all that same interpretation, and as long as the political leadership from Quebec maintains that the difficult problem of political relations between the Francophone and the Anglophone is linguistic or cultural, we'll go nowhere. The problem in Canada is fundamentally a problem of economic domination of the French Canadians by the Anglophones. And if you resolve that problem of economic domination, then you might be able to bring a better political adjustment in this country.

But this is a subject on which I could talk for hours because much of the situation—and the interpretation of this problem— rests with the French Canadian bourgeoisie, who since the Conquest have been able to make their peace with the Anglophones at the expense of the vast majority of the French Canadian population on the basis that if they were treated fairly then it didn't matter if the rest of the population was living in difficult economic conditions, as long as they were well treated.

One of the problems we're now facing is that the bourgeoisie in the province of Quebec since 1960 is increasing very fast, and their share of the economic pie is not large enough to satisfy them. We know that the separatist and nationalist forces are mainly in the bourgeois groups, which explains why the elites are all in favour of the strong nationalist view, or separatism. As I've said, I don't think that the solution is bilingualism. It's something else.

The proposal that Lester Pearson should make this promise in Parliament to begin bilingualism was discussed at the Liberal caucuses, and Maurice Sauvé was aware of this. However, he had agreed to help Premier Lesage in the provincial election campaign and was away from the House much of the time before the speech was made. As a result, he wasn't able to argue effectively against the idea of a bilingual and bicultural commission to which he was totally opposed. The Liberals were split on the issue, with most Quebeckers agitating in favour while the Anglophones were against or were apathetic, dismissing it as another election gimmick. Bryce Mackasey, a newly elected English-speaking member from Quebec, was active behind the scenes.

BRYCE MACKASEY

I found myself appalled at the lack of understanding in the national caucus about Quebec problems. Since I was bilingual and active, I was taking one stand in the Quebec caucus and another one in the national caucus, trying to be the bridge between the two cultures.

The fact that Mr. Pearson was slowly but surely identifying with bilingualism, and endorsing Quebec and a new role for Quebec, was making some other parts of the country a little uneasy. Not that he didn't know what he was doing, because he told me one day that this was a calculated risk, but imperative. He saw, as far back as when I was first elected, the threat of separation.

When we were in the Opposition in '62 there was the very unfortunate statement of Donald Gordon's on the CNR—the inability to get a French-speaking Canadian who could be a director of the railway. This upset him [Mr. Pearson] and I recall a pretty rough caucus on that subject. The French-speaking Canadians were very angry, as he was. And I suppose that's when he first framed that speech of his, promising bilingualism.

I remember participating in that caucus and ticking off one member, who later on went into the Cabinet. This fellow said, "Now, you fellows from Quebec go home this weekend and tell these people that they've got to stop all this agitation. It's not good for the country." In other words, "Go back to your secondary role." We weren't taking that, the Quebec Members. I was particularly vocal about it. I was as insulted as anybody, and had a lot to say.

C. M. "Bud" Drury, who represented Westmount, the wealthy Anglophone suburb of Montreal, confessed that he didn't have much interest in bilingualism at that time, which was typical of the attitude of the English-speaking elite in Canada, the real rulers of the country. Lester Pearson belonged to that elite and the fact that he had concerned himself with this issue, which the others had ignored, was the measure of the man. In his December 17, 1962, speech, he declared that Confederation was Canada's "declaration of independence from the United States." Not only had this country rejected political and economic annexation by the great neighbour to the south "but also the American melting-pot concept of national unity." Instead of that, Mr. Pearson said that Confederation had put forward "an understanding or a settlement between the two founding races of Canada made on the basis of an acceptable and equal partnership." National unity would be achieved without cultural or linguistic uniformity. The only way in which an equal partnership could be assured, in the Liberal Leader's view, would be by making bilingualism gradually a reality.

The December 17, 1962, speech could be described as a Declaration of French Canadian Rights and, whatever Pearson's motives might have been, it was an extraordinary utterance for a man who was not naturally a crusader. In fact, his career from history professor to diplomat to minister of the crown to political leader seemed to be the result of chance and charm.

2 The Making of the Leader

LESTER BOWLES PEARSON was born on April 23, 1897, in Newtonbrook, Ontario, now part of metropolitan Toronto. He was the second son of the Reverend Edwin Arthur Pearson, a Methodist minister, and Annie Sarah Bowles; he was of Irish descent on both sides of his family, the Pearsons having come to Toronto by way of New York from Dublin in 1849, and the Bowleses to York, as Toronto was then known, from Tipperary in 1824. He was educated at various schools in Aurora, Toronto, Peterborough, and Hamilton, wherever his father had a pulpit.

Pearson recalled that parsonage life in those days was simple and reasonably serene; the parsonage was usually a big brick house with trees, a lawn, and a backyard where vegetables were grown and where he played games with his older brother, Marmaduke, who was called "Duke," and Vaughan, his younger brother. As a minister's son he had to go to church four times on Sundays and once at midweek; growing up, however, was a healthy, happy, and relatively untroubled process. There was not much money but the family lacked for nothing important, although he said that he longed for a bicycle, a Boy Scout uniform, and a pair of genuine tube hockey skates. From an early age he had a passion for sports, but he didn't seem to have any particular ambition, and certainly never dreamed of becoming Prime Minister.

Of his later political associates, only Ralph Cowan knew him as a boy—which was ironical since Cowan became the one Liberal M.P. who

18

was virulent in his criticism of Pearson's policies as Prime Minister, and especially the bilingual policy. Cowan said that everybody knew the Pearson family in Peterborough as the father was the minister of the biggest Methodist church there. He remembered Lester, or Les, as he called him, entering the ten-mile road race, a famous sporting event in those days, and, although only twelve years old, finishing this long and exhausting run.

In 1915, when he was at the University of Toronto and had just turned eighteen, Pearson enlisted as a private in the army medical corps; he was sent overseas almost immediately and spent much of the war as a hospital orderly at Salonika. After more than a year and a half of this, he was able to get himself transferred to England and an officer-training course —the course was given at an Oxford college, which so enchanted him that he determined to return someday. Because there was a need for airmen, he joined the Royal Flying Corps, and it was there that he acquired the nickname "Mike" from his commanding officer, who felt that Lester was not a fitting name for a fighter pilot. The nickname stuck. While on a training flight he had a minor accident landing his plane and was given a few days off for his cuts and bruises to mend. It was then that he was struck by a London bus in the blackout, and, as a result of the injuries suffered, invalided home.

He returned to the University of Toronto where he got his degree (B.A. honours history) and played hockey and football; he played semi-pro baseball with the Guelph Maple Leafs for one summer. After a brief stab at law, which he found appallingly dull, he tried business and got a job with Armour and Company through his uncle, who was president of the meat-packing concern. However, this was not for him, and he left Chicago to return to the academic life and the study of history; he was fortunate enough to win a Vincent Massey Fellowship and thus realise his dream of returning to Oxford. There was a young Rhodes Scholar at the university named Roland Michener, with whom Mike became friendly and whom he later appointed Governor-General of Canada.

ROLAND MICHENER

There were quite a number of Canadians at Oxford and I suppose more as a rag than anything else, we called our group the Colonial Club. We used to have our meetings at the Cadina Café. And that's where I first met Pearson in 1921.

Then we began to exchange visits between colleges. He'd come to dinner at Hertford in the Junior Common Room where we got all dressed up in white ties and went through a tremendous meal with wines and toasts afterwards. It was just a rag, a good time, with a couple of dons and fifteen or twenty students.

Pearson was a member of quite a famous club at St. John's called the Archery Club. St. John's had very nice gardens, and the members of the Archery Club, which I suppose goes back to the time of Charles I, used to set up their butts in a rather splendid garden, and they'd take their bows and arrows and fire at them. That was the excuse for their being. But they were quite a serious-minded club, as were many of the Oxford clubs.

So I went there, and I met quite a number of his friends. One of them was the poet Robert Graves, who lived in college with Pearson. Another was Malcolm MacDonald, whose subsequent career is well known, the son of Ramsay MacDonald. Then there was the son of a famous Canadian, Bonar Law, Richard Law — Dick Law he was called. He was at St. John's with him.

Mike was a very delightful companion and personality. He was informal, approachable, not aged by his war experience particularly. He was sort of carefree. He didn't give the impression of being too much interested in his studies, you know, but he did them well and got a good degree. He was very sociable and very intelligent and interested both in his studies and other pursuits of the undergraduate, the intellectual kind. And, of course, very much interested in sport.

At Oxford Pearson played hockey and lacrosse and did so well at the latter game that he made a couple of transatlantic tours and was picked for the South of England team. In his book Stephen Leacock, *David Legate remarked on the visit of the lacrosse team to Orillia, Ontario, in the summer of 1923, and that one of the players was Lester B. Pearson. It was an important enough event, he wrote, to attract Prime Minister W. L. Mackenzie King, who threw out the first ball. Hockey, or ice hockey as it was called in Britain to distinguish it from field hockey, was played during the winter vacations in Switzerland, and Michener recalled the championship Oxford teams of 1922 and 1923, the games against Cambridge, and the fun they had playing at resort hotels and living the life of luxury.*

ROLAND MICHENER

It was a Canadian show. All our team was Canadian except the captain, who was former captain of the Harvard ice hockey team, named Mack Bacon. He became a financial man in New York. All the rest were Canadians. The Cambridge team was all Canadian except the goalkeeper; he was an Englishman named Anderson. I remember he couldn't skate, and when he got far out of goal we always had to stop the game and get him back in again. However, that wasn't a measure of the kind of hockey we played. It was pretty good intermediate hockey, at the level of the university play here, because we'd all been on university teams.

Mike played defence and I played either centre or left wing. We had seven to a team then.

Mike was a very good player. He was a good stick-handler. When I saw these Russians playing here recently, they didn't appear to be trying to score, but they were trying to keep the puck, stick-handling, getting ready for a dash. That's typical of Mike's play. He would swerve back and forth across the rink—he often started from defence position. So the Swiss in their sport columns called him Herr Zigzag, which was typical of his play.

The hotels invited us to stay with them after we were through with our Oxford-Cambridge affair, which took about ten days and was at Mürren. We played any teams that came along, mostly the Swiss teams. It was a vigorous, healthy life—the games were outdoors—and we enjoyed it. And we were courted by the guests of the hotels. They all wanted to meet us, and they used to entertain us.

We were in St. Moritz one Christmas, and I remember we had a great party at Davos, a New Year's party, which almost got us into trouble because one of the Canadians dressed himself up as a girl and went to the ball. He was so convincing and so beautiful that he attracted the attention of a French officer, who pursued him all through the dance until midnight when he took off his wig. The Frenchman was so angry and humiliated that he was ready to fight.

Mike Pearson got to know what runaway inflation was like when he and Michener and another Canadian student, Dick Bonnycastle, who was to become chairman of Metropolitan Winnipeg, spent a summer vacation in Heidelberg.

ROLAND MICHENER

It was a rather unusual opportunity to live beyond one's means because we could have dinner in the Stottgarten in the evening with a bottle of champagne that had cost twenty-five cents, and go over to the coffeehouse afterward and have coffee and liqueur. We couldn't spend more than ten dollars a week if we tried.

There was 400 percent inflation in the six weeks we were there, which indicates the acceleration of inflation when it gets going. When we bought our first Marks we got 2,500 Marks for the pound sterling—we were using pounds—and when we cashed our last money, it was 10,000 Marks for the pound. Prices didn't keep pace with that inflation, so that it was a very good time for tourists in Germany or visitors, and a very tough time for the Germans.

After a couple of blissful years at Oxford, Pearson returned to Canada to take up an appointment as lecturer in modern history at the University of Toronto. Once again he became active in sports, and was the coach of the Varsity football and hockey teams and the playing coach of the lacrosse team. However, it was as a result of his teaching that, as he was to say, by far the most important event of all his years occurred: he fell in love and married one of his students, Maryon Moodie. The wedding, in Winnipeg on August 22, 1925, was a double ceremony with Maryon's elder sister, Grace, marrying Norman Young. Norman's son, Christopher, who was to become editor of the Ottawa Citizen, *recalled Mike as every child's favourite uncle.*

CHRISTOPHER YOUNG

He was the type of uncle that got down on his hands and knees and crawled around on the floor and played silly games with children, and bought them jelly beans and generally was very amusing and friendly. He was like a big teddy bear with them. He also liked physical activity.

Even when he was in his seventies, he would never sit still for very long in a chair just chatting, which I suppose is the way most adults proceed when they're visiting. He would do that for five or ten minutes. Then he'd be up and around—"let's go out and play some ball" or something, whatever the season required. He would get on his outdoor clothes in the wintertime and go for a walk or a skate. So that again appealed to children, the action and the activity that surrounded him.

During the summer following their wedding the Pearsons went to Ottawa so that Mike could do research work at the Public Archives—he wanted to write a book on the United Empire Loyalists. It was in the nation's capital that he met Dr. O. D. Skelton whom Prime Minister Mackenzie King had appointed to take over the administration of foreign relations from the British government at Westminster. Dr. Skelton spoke to the youthful professor about the possibility of his joining the new Department of External Affairs, which he was in the process of forming, but Pearson enjoyed the academic life and had no intention of leaving the university at that time. He did show an interest in politics, and Paul Martin, who knew him as a professor and was to become one of his closest colleagues, recalled how Pearson insisted on their attending a debate in the House of Commons.

PAUL MARTIN

In 1926 I was going home at the end of the academic year to Pembroke, where my father and mother lived and where I had spent my boyhood. The train journey took you from Toronto to Ottawa, and then you'd wait for an hour and a half in the Ottawa Central Station, and go on to Pembroke on the morning train. When I got off the train from Toronto, who should be getting off the neighbouring coach but Mike Pearson, who said to me, "Where are you going, Martin?" That is the form of address of a professor to a student. I said, "I'm on my way home to Pembroke for the summer."

"Well," he said, "I'm here to do some work in the Archives." And he said to me, "You know, this is a very important day in Canadian parliamentary political history." Mr. King had asked for a dissolution of Parliament. The Governor-General, Lord Byng, refused, and Mr. King was to announce his dispute with the Governor-General and the circumstances connected with it in Parliament that afternoon.

So Mike, knowing that I had some political interest on the campus—had been president of the University of Toronto Liberal Club—he suggested that I stay in Ottawa that day instead of going to Pembroke and go with him and listen to the debate in Parliament that afternoon. I didn't know, as a matter of fact, that you could go to Parliament. I had never been around the Parliament Buildings, even though I'd been in Ottawa visiting my grandmother from time to time as a young man. That intrigued me, and the result is that he and I sat in the House of Commons in what is now the diplomatic gallery, almost right behind the clock—I can remember it as though it was yesterday—and we heard Mackenzie King announce why he did not get a dissolution, the position that he would take as a result, which led to the general elections. This was a very exciting day, for me to be introduced to the House of Commons by a man who was later to become Prime Minister, who was to become a colleague of mine in the Cabinet. We have often thought, both of us, particularly as we sat in the House of Commons, of that day.

I didn't know any Members of Parliament, and the only one he knew was J. S. Woodsworth. At six o'clock we went up to Woodsworth's room to get his diagnosis of the political situation as revealed that day by Mr. Mackenzie King. We stayed and had dinner with Mr. Woodsworth in his room. It was a dinner consisting, I remember so well, of brown bread and some good cheese and some good tea. I mention Mr. Woodsworth because it is rather curious that it was to Woodsworth that Mike Pearson directed me. Woodsworth was a graduate of Victoria College, so was Mike. And that was their meeting ground.

In the winter of 1927 Dr. Skelton wrote Professor Pearson saying that there were to be examinations for positions in the new Department of External Affairs and suggesting that he might like to be a candidate. The following spring the application forms and the examination papers arrived, and, while Pearson said that he felt no urge to leave the university, he decided to fill them out. There was no French paper, nor any question as to whether or not the candidate had any facility in the French language, which was surprising since, aside from the fact of French Canada, French was supposed to be the language of diplomacy. On August 10, 1928, Pearson received a telegram informing him that he had

come first in the competition for the post of first secretary and asking him to
report to Ottawa on the following Monday, which he did.

He had joined the Canadian diplomatic service in its embryo stage, and
it was not surprising that in his first enthusiasm he should consider it an
"elite" service—the Department of External Affairs came under the
Prime Minister. As first secretary, Lester Pearson could not fail to be
noticed by those in power. When the government changed in 1930, and the
Conservatives took office, Prime Minister R. B. Bennett gave him some
domestic assignments. He was made secretary of the Royal Commission
on Grain Futures; for the first time he travelled across the prairies and was
shocked by what he saw for, as he said, 1932 was a year of drought, dust,
depression, and despair. He must have done a competent job because Mr.
Bennett made him secretary of the Royal Commission on Price Spreads
and Mass Buying, which was nothing less than an investigation into the
causes and effects of the Great Depression. The commission, which was
under the chairmanship of H. H. Stevens, got so carried away with its
task that it seemed to be attacking the capitalist system. Pearson said that
he never worked harder than in bringing out the commission's report. A
young chartered accountant, Walter Gordon, served on this commission
and remembered what Pearson was like in those early days.

WALTER GORDON

By 1934 the Stevens Commission was getting out of hand and
Mr. Bennett called on Pearson, who at that time was a young
member of the Department of External Affairs, to take over as
secretary, and his instructions were to get a report written and
wind up the commission as soon as possible. That was when I first
met him.

Pearson made an impression on me at the time, and on
everybody else, with the way he went at it. He showed his usual
good humour. He worked very hard and he was extremely
tactful, and he finished the job with a minimum of fuss. I thought
at the time, and I still do in retrospect, that considering what he
had to move into and take over, it was a remarkably able piece of
work on his part, and I think it is fair to say that he won the
admiration of everybody who knew what he was responsible for.

We had no occasion to talk about politics or Quebec or any
matters other than the economic situation at the time and the

particular work of the Commission. We were all fully conscious of the conditions in the depression years and the fact that there were a lot of people out of work, and that was one of the purposes of the commission—to see if they could spot any reasons for this. But it was a way to allow people to let off steam at a time when everybody was suffering and they did this by taking it out on the business community, which I don't suppose did the business community a great deal of harm. It pleased everybody else.

I saw quite a bit of Mike from time to time. I think it is fair to say that he was my closest friend, but I can't speak for him...I doubt if he thought I was his closest friend. I just don't know. I never asked him. We were obviously close friends, but when you say closest that puts an emphasis on it that you would have to ask him about.

Shortly after the Price-Spreads Commission, I was in Europe doing a job for the government and at one stage my wife and I were staying at the Connaught Hotel in London. Mr. Bennett had come over for the Jubilee celebrations and had brought Pearson with him as his main advisor as a kind of reward for the job he had done on the commission, and they were staying at Claridge's. As I said, I had met Pearson through the Stevens Commission but he had known my wife before that. So he used to come and see us at the Connaught, which is just about two hundred yards away, say a couple of times a day. We had a lot of fun together.

Then after that I used to see him periodically whenever our paths crossed. He was away a lot. We got along well together and hit it off.

Mitchell Sharp, who eventually succeeded Walter Gordon as Finance Minister, was a junior colleague of Pearson in the civil service.

MITCHELL SHARP

He [Pearson] was very free and easy. This was the main impression I had of him. He was a man who didn't like the restrictions of the civil service and he tried to avoid them wherever possible. He had views about things, and he expressed them freely. He was, at the time that I knew him, less concerned with the details than he was with the general over-all picture.

I can well understand how it was that Mr. Mackenzie King looked upon him as a potential politician. He was much readier to express his views than other civil servants whom I encountered at that time. He was the antithesis of a stuffy bureaucrat. That was his reputation. His nickname is an indication of that—Mike, just the way you address people that are not stuffy. He was much easier to address than people like Arnold Heeney or Norman Robertson [senior officials with External Affairs]. He was different. His approach was a very general one, and it went to the heart of the matter. And he would express his views quite easily and quite forthrightly.

While he was a diplomat and civil servant Pearson's main sport was tennis. He played with his old Oxford friend, Roland Michener, and with John Connolly, who was to become a Senator and a member of his Cabinet. Florence Bird, whom he was to name chairman of the Royal Commission on the Status of Women, remembered meeting him for the first time on the tennis court. He was as good at tennis as at other sports, and there is a plaque at the Rockcliffe Lawn Tennis Club that lists him as the singles champion in 1933 and 1935. John Turner, who was young enough to be his son and went to school with his son, Geoffrey, told a story that showed what a competitor Mike could be.

JOHN TURNER

I remember running into Georges LeClair, who was at one time nonplaying captain of our Davis Cup team, and Georges had a good game. He asked me about Mr. Pearson and he said, "You know that I once got beaten by Mr. Pearson in a tennis match."

Georges LeClair is a phenomenal character in the tennis world in Canada. He kept a written record of every set he's played, with the people he's played, and the scores by set, and I've seen the book. And he leafed through this book and it was sometime around the mid-'30s, and there it was. Mr. Pearson had beaten him—I forget the scores—in two sets.

So I, in a relaxed moment with Mr. Pearson one time—he was then Prime Minister and I was one of his Ministers so that must have been 1967 or 1968—I reminded him that I'd played Georges LeClair and he remembered LeClair. Mr. Pearson had a fantastic memory. Don't underestimate that. He said he could recall that. He was in his early forties and he was up against this hot-shot junior called LeClair, who was about eighteen, at the Rideau Tennis Club in Ottawa. And he looked at this guy and figured, God, he couldn't stand with him on the courts, so he'd try to lob him. And he lobbed him to death. He won in two straight sets. LeClair was so mad that he threw his racket over the fence into the Rideau River. I reminded Georges LeClair of that and Georges said that that was true. But he remembered Mr. Pearson with a great deal of affection.

In the summer of 1935 Lester Pearson was posted abroad for the first time, to Canada House in London. His appointment was approved by both Prime Minister Bennett and Prime Minister Mackenzie King because the Conservatives lost the election in October that year and the Liberals returned to power. As counsellor at the Canadian High Commission, Pearson reported to Ottawa on the rise of Hitler and the Nazis. After the German Anschluss *with Austria and the Munich agreement, followed by the invasion of Czechoslovakia, he came to the conclusion that war was more or less inevitable. All depended on Danzig and the Polish corridor. In the summer of 1939 Mike and Maryon Pearson and their children, Geoffrey and Patricia, returned to Canada on home leave and joined the Youngs for a family holiday at Lac du Bonnet, about an hour's drive from Winnipeg.*

CHRISTOPHER YOUNG

It was the last summer we were all together. My father was there. He subsequently went off to the war and was killed. The Pearsons were there for a good long time. So was another uncle, Herbert Moodie, who was my mother and Mrs. Pearson's brother. There must have been eight of us cousins and small friends. My grandparents came out from Winnipeg for their fiftieth wedding anniversary, which was in August. Would it be fiftieth? Whatever it was.

We had a big old farmhouse, and it was a great big happy time. There was a lake for swimming and a big field where we used to play a lot of baseball, which Pearson, of course, enjoyed enormously. Then one day, Pearson read in the paper about the

Danzig affair, and he concluded that war was about to begin. Anyway, he thought he should go back to his post; he took the train to Ottawa, went to see Mackenzie King at Kingsmere, and said he'd like to go back to his post. This was about the last week of August, a week or so before the war broke out. Mackenzie King told him he was silly and tried to talk him out of it, but he insisted, and [Mackenzie King] said, "Well, if you want to go, go; but it's not necessary." Furthermore, Mike said he thought he should fly because there mightn't be time to take a liner. That was considered rather eccentric at the time, but he did in fact take a flying boat, and he got back to London just before the war broke out.

Mrs. Pearson remained at Lac du Bonnet, but with the ominous news and Mike's departure, the joy had gone out of that summer holiday; in any case, there was little of it left. In January 1940 she rejoined her husband in London, leaving the children with her parents in Winnipeg; however, with the fall of France, she was persuaded to return to Canada.

It was not till 1941 that Pearson came back to Canada and, after a brief interlude in Ottawa, was sent to Washington as Minister-Counsellor; he became head of the Canadian mission there and when the mission was raised to ambassadorial rank, he was appointed the first Canadian Ambassador to the United States. He helped to set up UNRRA (United Nations Relief and Rehabilitation Administration) and was at the founding conference of the United Nations Organisation at San Francisco in the spring of 1945.

Although Pearson's relations with Prime Minister Mackenzie King were always correct, they tended to be much more formal than they had been with Prime Minister Bennett; furthermore, he did not agree with Mackenzie King's isolationist attitude, his distrust of international organisations and fear of foreign entanglements. He was delighted when Louis St. Laurent, the prominent Quebec lawyer whom Mackenzie King co-opted as his Quebec lieutenant during the war, was made External Affairs Minister because he saw eye to eye with him on foreign policy. At the end of 1946 Lester Pearson returned to Ottawa to become Deputy Minister of the Department of External Affairs. He could go no higher now without moving into politics—and both Paul Martin and Jack Pickersgill, who was at the time Prime Minister Mackenzie King's secretary, said that he discussed such a move with them.

J. W. PICKERSGILL

I think he would never have wanted to be a Member [as long as Mackenzie King was Prime Minister]. He told me this himself on one occasion, that he didn't feel that he would ever have been sufficiently in sympathy with Mackenzie King to take a share in the direction of the government—assuming, of course, that that share would have been primarily concerned with foreign policy. It was one thing to be a public servant, to do what he was told to do; but it would have been another thing to undertake to be Foreign Minister and then find that his initiatives were vetoed by the Prime Minister, as sometimes they would have been.

It's really quite a tribute to Mackenzie King's perception, and in some respects to his tolerance, that while he had grave suspicions about the direction in which Pearson wanted to move this country in the international sphere, he saw in Pearson a natural politician. Long before anybody else even thought, and, I'm sure, long before Pearson himself ever thought of being Prime Minister, Mackenzie King, as his diary shows, on several occasions said that he thought that Pearson should be his eventual successor.

PAUL MARTIN

Long before Mr. St. Laurent became Prime Minister [in 1948], I knew that [Pearson] had had some suggestions from Mackenzie King at various times, that he should go into politics. I'm sure — although I have no proof of this—that Mike took the initiative on occasion and let it be known in one way or another that he wasn't averse to going into politics. When Mr. St. Laurent became Prime Minister, Mike told me then that he was going to go in, that he had had some discussion with St. Laurent.

Before the decision was actually made that he should enter the Cabinet, St. Laurent told me, as he told Brooke Claxton [Defence Minister] that Mike was coming in, and he thought that he would like to discuss this with us because if Pearson came in, it would mean that neither one of us would become his successor as Secretary of State for External Affairs, that he would ask Pearson to become Secretary of State. He wanted us to know about this.

Now, I had no illusions that I would become Secretary of State for External Affairs after St. Laurent. I remember saying to him,

"Well, if Mike Pearson didn't come in, I would have thought that the next Secretary for External Affairs would have been Brooke Claxton." I had no hesitations. Brooke Claxton was a very great man and in the field of foreign affairs he had a very remarkable record. Not in public service, but in all kinds of activities in which I was also involved. But he was an older person, had been on the scene longer, and I think he had a strong claim because they weren't going to appoint a French Ontarian to External Affairs when you had a French Prime Minister.

Canada has grown away from that a good bit, but we're still, you know, politically elitist in our approach. It took a long time to bring a Jew into the Cabinet. It took a long time to appoint a Jew as Governor of the Bank of Canada. It should have been done a long time ago. But Canada, with all of its dedication to freedom and non-discrimination, is still very much an elitist society.

In any event, both Brooke and I knew perfectly well that Pearson was going to come in and that he would succeed St. Laurent in that particular portfolio, although we both appreciated the politeness of Mr. St. Laurent in going through the motions of consultation.

Although there was no doubt that Pearson had the highest regard for St. Laurent—J. R. Nicholson, a business executive who was to become one of Pearson's ministers, described him as a disciple of St. Laurent—some of his colleagues were surprised at his joining the Liberals. Perhaps, because of his close association with Prime Minister Bennett, they thought of him as a Conservative.

ROLAND MICHENER

I regarded him as a sympathetic Conservative, a Liberal Conservative. You remember the old Conservative Party was the Liberal Conservative after Borden's 1917 union of the two parties to carry on the war. So that left the party as the Liberal Conservative Party, and I used to describe myself as a liberal Conservative—a small "l" liberal and a capital "C" Conservative. And Pearson and I didn't differ enough on any of the issues to make one think that we had different political party inclinations. I noticed he called himself a small "l" liberal, and I thought he might just as well have been a Conservative as a Liberal if he ever took an active part, but he was a civil servant at this time.

WALTER GORDON

It was some time in 1948 Pearson called me up and said that he wanted to consult me about something, so we met in Toronto. He said that Mr. King had been suggesting, or implying, for some time that he should go into politics. I don't think Pearson wanted to do that under Mr. King, but he said that once Mr. St. Laurent was chosen to be the Leader of the party and was about to be Prime Minister, he felt differently. St. Laurent had asked him to be Secretary of State for External Affairs and he asked me what I thought he should do.

I said, "Well, I don't think that you should assume you can go on indefinitely advocating public policy"—he had been advocating the NATO business pretty strenuously—"as a civil servant. So if you feel strongly about NATO or any other issue of public policy, then I think you should be a politician." Nothing very strange about that, but that was what I said to him.

He wondered, and wanted my view as to whether he would be tough enough. I said to him, if I remember correctly, that I didn't think anybody could make that assessment. He would find it very different.

Up to that time in his life he had made hosts of friends because he was such a gregarious, entertaining man, and he didn't have any enemies, and I said, "How you will measure up in politics, where you are bound to make some enemies, I don't know." I did say that I thought his wit and his humour and so on would stand him in good stead in any occupation, but he would have to assess his own qualities in that respect.

Now, about money. He said that as far as he was concerned, the uncertainties of politics wouldn't worry him at all, that he could always go back to teaching if he wanted to, but that he had a family. Well, the net result was some of us subscribed a modest amount of money for an annuity for his wife. It wasn't a large amount, not nearly as large as some of the amounts that have been collected for people in public life subsequently. It would have been enough to provide a certain degree of assurance that they were going to be able to continue to eat. He never knew where the money came from, and it wasn't anything out of the way. But it did provide an annuity.

J. W. PICKERSGILL

I remember one particular occasion when C. D. Howe and Walter Harris* and Mike and I had lunch in the Rideau Club to discuss the question of what constituency he would represent. Mackenzie King disapproved of that because it gave rise to some rumour. He thought we were a lot of naïve people. He would have done it in some dark room somewhere, with nobody watching.

I persuaded Mr. St. Laurent to go up to his constituency when the by-election was on—we had to cut our visit short because Mackenzie King became ill and we had to go to London, where Mr. St. Laurent replaced him. When I first suggested he go up to Algoma East, Mr. St. Laurent said, "But Mr. King told me that Prime Ministers never take part in by-elections." I said, "But you're not Prime Minister. You're only Acting Prime Minister."

He really wanted to go. But I didn't have any doubt about the outcome of the by-election. I didn't think Pearson needed any help, particularly. What I was very anxious to do was to give Mr. St. Laurent some exposure to the electorate.

It was decided that Pearson was to run in Algoma East, a big rural riding in northern Ontario which was a safe Liberal seat—furthermore, the sitting Member, Tom Farquhar, was willing to vacate it for an appointment to the Senate. The constituency included Manitoulin Island, said to be the largest fresh-water island, and the uranium mines of Elliot Lake. Mary Macdonald, Mr. Pearson's assistant as Deputy Minister, was born in northern Ontario and had a special affinity for the people of Algoma East. However, it wasn't because of this—she doubts that her boss knew where she was born—that he made her the liaison officer with his constituency.

Mary Macdonald was attending a meeting of the United Nations General Assembly in Paris, as assistant secretary of the Canadian delegation, when L. B. Pearson won the October 25, 1948, by-election

---

*C. D. Howe was Minister of Trade and Commerce and, to all intents and purposes, Deputy Prime Minister in the St. Laurent government; Walter Harris was Finance Minister.

and became M.P. for Algoma East. But she worked on every subsequent election, all seven of them, and she recalled the miles of driving on gravel roads and an awful lot of flying in bush planes. There were adventures: on one occasion, during the 1949 election campaign, Mr. Pearson and Tom Farquhar were flying in a light plane in bad weather and disappeared. Radio contact was lost, and there were some anxious moments until they heard that the pilot had been able to make it to Sudbury.

MARY MACDONALD

I always had a very close liaison with the president of the Liberal Association in the riding. We'd talk about the issues or he'd phone if there was anything. So Mr. Pearson had a briefing about the local issues before he went, which was given through me through the association.

But the people mostly liked to hear him talk about the United Nations and his work as Minister. That was a new world for them, and they were really proud of him. I've heard him give the same speech out at the other end of Meldrum Bay in a very small town to nine people who'd come from Silver Bay—and it took them a long time, distances were great—as he'd given in a huge hall in Toronto.

As I said, he knew about the local issues and spoke about them if there were any. There was the time they wanted an eviscerating plant in Gore Bay. Yes, an eviscerating plant. Manitoulin used to be famous for its turkeys, and they didn't have any storage facilities or places to prepare them for shipment. They got one in Gore Bay not too long afterward, with Mr. Pearson's help. Some years later the turkey industry out there folded—the big food processors had taken over and it was too difficult to ship.

VIC MACKIE

I was in Algoma East several times, with Mary Macdonald very much in evidence. Mary was the one who organized Algoma East. She used to love to have newspapermen come up there and promote Mike. She was Mike's best promoter; She was always in the forefront, making sure that people came up and met him and shook his hand.

With all of his wonderful personality and easy-to-get-along-with nature, Mike was a little diffident and shy about campaigning. He was not a politician, never cut out to be a politician; he was a diplomat. This was all new to him, this business of forcing yourself forward and shoving your hand out and saying, "I am Mike Pearson, I am seeking your vote." It ran against his grain, but Mary egged him on and pushed him forward and would take him around and introduce him to people and say, "This is a man who wants to be your next Member of Parliament."

Mike with his boyish charm captivated them. He was a very good campaigner in his way, particularly when he was with a small group, talking to them on the floor of a hall or walking around a small town talking to people. His boyish charm was his greatest asset. People liked him very much, but when he got up on the platform and spoke, he lost that appeal and he knew it and he didn't like it. He didn't like campaigning for an election. That was not his nature. He didn't like pushing himself forward.

Politics had been made easy for Lester Pearson. He had been sworn in as External Affairs Minister on September 10, 1948, and the by-election in Algoma East was not till October 25. So he had run as a Cabinet Minister—and it was taken for granted that the electorate would prefer to vote for a man who was a Minister and already in the seats of the mighty than one who would only be a back bencher. This was the way that the Liberals brought in people whom they wanted in the government—they had done so with St. Laurent, who was to become Prime Minister, and they were to do so with Jack Pickersgill. However, such special treatment was resented by the ordinary backbench Member of Parliament. It could be argued that such a person as Pearson, who had an international reputation and was well known across the country, would improve the chances of all of them at the polls. Yet there was some grumbling, even by such a staunch Liberal as John Connolly, who was to become one of Pearson's Ministers.

JOHN CONNOLLY

I'll tell you something: Mr. St. Laurent brought him into the Cabinet; Mr. St. Laurent was the great man, so far as I was concerned; I thought he was a tremendous person. If he thought that Pearson was the right man, I thought that Pearson was the right man. But I had lost so much contact with Mike that I really couldn't come to that conclusion on my own.

The men that were in the Cabinet at that time, including Walter Harris and Doug Abbott [Finance Minister] and Brooke Claxton and these other fellows . . . I always felt that they were the fellows who had carried the burden of the day, and I rather thought Mike was a sort of a Johnny-come-lately. To tell you the truth, when I used to see him in the House of Commons performing—and he used to perform well, in those days before St. Laurent retired, before 1957, before there was any suggestion of a leadership convention to elect a new Liberal Leader, even though there was talk of St. Laurent resigning—in those days I rather resented Mike because it seemed to me that he was the one that was getting the kudos, he was becoming more prominent.

I didn't think that was completely fair to these other fellows like Harris, like Abbott, like Claxton, and like the others who were there at that time, Paul [Martin] included, who had been through the hard times, and the good times of course, but still they'd given up the important part of their working life for the public life of this country. Now Mike had too, but he had had the security of the civil service. These fellows had their hides on the fence all the while.

I can follow that up with another story. Mike's mother died about the middle of the summer one year when we were in Opposition. I don't know which year it was. She was very elderly, but they were very close. I don't think he was as close to her as he was to his father. He speaks more about his father than he does about his mother. But his mother had a pretty profound influence on him.

I went to Toronto for the funeral, and when the funeral was over Walter Gordon got me, and he took me up to his country place out of Toronto. It wasn't too far away from the Malton airport. I remember that Saturday afternoon Mike had had to go to South America that same day, so after the burial he went to the airplane and we went to Walter's place.

Walter said to me among a great many other things, "You know, we're both motivated by the same proposition, and that is to make Mike Pearson the Prime Minister of Canada." And I remember saying, "You know, I don't think that is my motivation. I think I feel that my motives arise out of the fact that I think the Liberal Party is the best party to govern this country, and it is the party that I am interested in more than the man."

Now Walter may have been saying this to me because if you're motivated because of an individual there's likely to be a more immediate kind of response, and a more continuing kind of response. But really I knew a lot about Laurier and a lot about King and a lot about St. Laurent and a lot about the people in the governments of those men; I think I was a dedicated Liberal long enough to say, "I am interested in party more than man."

I think that's been pretty true of my approach to politics. Of course, I should never have been in politics; I'm not cut out for it. I haven't got the touch—I haven't got the feel for it. But if I've done anything in politics, I think the motive would have been party rather than person.

Once he became a Member of Parliament, Mr. Pearson acted like any other politician. When his constituents came to Ottawa, he entertained them as if they were diplomats. Among them were Indians because there were many reserves in Algoma East, including the Wigwemekong Reserve.

MARY MACDONALD

There was a wonderful old chief in those days, his name was Joe Peter Pangouish, and he only died a few years ago. One day, he came with a delegation to see us. Joe Peter, when he introduced Mr. Pearson to the others in the delegation said they were proud that he was at the United Nations, and they were proud he was a Minister for External Affairs, but they also wanted him to always remember that when they, the band council, called on him, he, as their Member of Parliament, "has got to step up." Which meant: "You're my Member. If I need a new road, you produce it."

As Minister for External Affairs, Lester Pearson continued the work that he had been doing as Deputy Minister, only now he could take more initiative although he had to consult the Cabinet on major issues. There were international developments in which he played a part, including the creation of the state of Israel, and the formation of the NATO Alliance. He helped to bring about the Korean armistice agreement and was president of the seventh session of the United Nations General Assembly in 1952-53. He had an easy enough time in the House of Commons because there was little disagreement on foreign policy, which was felt to be a non-partisan matter, and Pearson kept to international affairs in Parliament. As a result he was a popular and well-liked Minister.

In 1956 there was the legislative explosion of the pipeline debate which, if not the cause, contributed to the destruction of the Liberal government. It affected the allegiance of intellectuals such as Pauline Jewett, professor of political science at Carleton University. The government introduced a bill to provide an 80-million-dollar loan to Trans-Canada Pipe Lines, and announced that closure would be applied, in order to get the money through in time for construction to begin that year. Pearson did come to the defence of the government in that debate but his performance was perfunctory.

J. W. PICKERSGILL

He showed very little interest in what one would call practical politics, and almost no interest in parliamentary tactics. But, after all, the spectrum of External Affairs is pretty broad. He was very actively interested in the whole question of trade policy. He was interested in immigration, and after I became Minister of Immigration there were some times when we didn't see eye to eye at all on some of these questions. He was interested in defence—very actively interested in defence.

But you could really say that, possibly excepting the expansion of social security on which he always expressed views, many of the other day-to-day concerns of government [were largely ignored by him]. I think he had a feel for his position, that as long as he was Secretary of State for External Affairs, he shouldn't be too partisan, or appear to be too partisan, because it was very desirable in the interests of the country to have as close to unanimity as possible about our foreign policy. And, as long as you can achieve it, it's a very praiseworthy objective of a Foreign Minister.

STANLEY KNOWLES

Now Mike Pearson wasn't in [the pipeline debate] very often, and when he was in it he indulged in a sort of a silly speech. I forget the similes or the figures of speech that he used, but it was obvious that he was just doing his duty to fill time. We laughed at his performace rather than being upset or offended by it. I mean, the villain of the piece, of course, was C. D. Howe, and the organiser of it was Walter Harris. The second was Jack Pickersgill. And then there was St. Laurent back in the corner, for whom we felt sorrow and pity as much as we felt anything else.

PAULINE JEWETT

I remember sitting all through the pipeline debate in 1956 in the Gallery. That was my first year teaching at Carleton—'55, '56. And I sat through the whole debate. Every Cabinet Minister had been pretty well called upon to defend the government at various stages of the closure. And if I recall correctly, thirteen or fourteen Cabinet Ministers spoke on that debate, which is most unusual.

There was a sort of rumour going around Ottawa that Mr. St. Laurent had said whoever made the best speech would be the next Leader of the party. Mike Pearson made by far the worst speech. He was not at all happy—that's the impression one had in the Gallery, listening—not at all happy to be defending this particular use or abuse of closure. And [he] really did a very bad job. Very bad indeed. So in spite of that he became the next Leader.

The pipeline debate, and the way that the government forced Parliament to do its will by means of closure, hurt the Liberals, but nobody expected an upset in the 1957 election. Nobody except Mary Macdonald, who accompanied Pearson during the campaign, not only in his constituency, but across the country. However, Mike's image remained bright among intellectuals.

MARY MACDONALD

Anybody that went through this country in that '57 election knew that there was going to be a change. Really, as I said, it was very sad. And even now I remember in British Columbia, a great long trek during the day and getting into New Westminster at night, and a sort of darkened hall and unethusiastic people. To me it was not a surprise. I think it was a surprise to everybody else, the way they started falling so fast in the east that night. To see C. D. Howe going down, people like that.

PAULINE JEWETT

To show how strong Mike's grasp on my kind of person was, I went to the polling booth in 1957 still very angered by the pipeline debate and by what the government had done, fully intending to vote CCF* because that would be my choice, my alternative, not Conservative. I even looked up the name of the CCF candidate in Ottawa West because there was very little campaigning. And I saw Mike's face just as I was about to put my "x" down. It was Mike's face, nobody else's, that came before me and said to me, "Tch." And I said to myself, "I cannot vote against the party that has Mike Pearson." It was then that I already made up my mind that he should be the next Leader if there was a change. So I put my "x" down beside the Liberal candidate, who was George McIlraith.

The results of the June 1957 election: Progressive Conservatives, 112; Liberals, 107; CCF, 25; Social Credit, 19; Independents, 2. No party had a majority and thus the Liberal government had the option of continuing and meeting Parliament (where it would be defeated) or resigning and letting the Conservatives form a government. St. Laurent chose the latter. And the new Diefenbaker government was sworn in on June 21.

PAUL MARTIN

I saw him [Pearson] shortly afterward because we met in Ottawa the next day or the day after the 1957 election to decide what we were going to do. The correct constitutional position for us to have taken at that time would *not* have been for us to resign forthwith, as we did, but to have gone to the House of Commons and let Parliament decide whether or not the government of the day had the confidence of Parliament. That is the correct constitutional practice. That is the course that I thought we should

---

*The Cooperative Commonwealth Federation was the Canadian socialist party, which later became the NDP (New Democratic Party).

have followed. There was only one other Member of the government, and that was Mr. [James G.] Gardiner, who felt the same way.

Mr. St. Laurent said that under no circumstances would he adopt that course. He felt that he had been repudiated, and the real fact was that he was tired and he wanted to get out. I appreciated that point, but I thought it was important to emphasise that the other course was open, even though he wasn't prepared to follow it. I never for a moment thought that he would follow the course which I thought constitutionally he should have pursued.

Pearson told me he agreed fully that my statement of the situation was correct, but that Mr. St. Laurent was in no way able to carry on and consequently it would be better to act forthwith; and it would appear, he thought, to be a more honourable course. I took him up on that. I said, "I don't think that is a more honourable course. The more honourable course is to do what has been and is constitutional practice."

J. W. PICKERSGILL

I don't think [Pearson] was depressed at all. He certainly was not one of those people who thought we ought to hang on.

Actually, that door was closed by Mr. St. Laurent the night of the election. The only reason we didn't resign right away was that I think he felt he had gone a little too far the night of the election without consulting the Cabinet—one or two of the Ministers certainly felt that he shouldn't have removed the options. He also knew that Diefenbaker wasn't ready to form a government at once. Therefore he hit on the expediency of saying that we should wait for the service vote [the armed forces vote was counted separately then]. He never thought the service vote was going to change the thing very materially. I think it did change one seat.

I am perhaps the best witness of all about this matter. When the results from Ontario were all in and the Manitoba results were just starting to come in, Mr. St. Laurent turned to me and said, "I hope they get at least one more seat than we do so we can get out of this thing respectably." So if there was ever any doubt—he saw clearly at once that to have been left in a position where he might have to meet Parliament would have been a false and indeed an impossible position. And he put this very strongly to his colleagues, and practically all of us agreed with him. Pearson certainly did.

As a result of that election, it was perfectly clear to people like Jack Pickersgill that Pearson was the only person left in the Liberal Party who had any chance of being Prime Minister within ten years. Walter Harris, the Finance Minister, who had been the heir apparent and was Pickersgill's original choice for the party leadership, had been among the half-dozen Cabinet Ministers who had been defeated.

In the late summer of 1957 Lester Pearson received a call from Renaud St. Laurent saying that his father, the former Prime Minister, was not well and would like to see him; Pearson, in his turn, rang Lionel Chevrier, the senior French Canadian Liberal Member, and asked that he accompany him to St. Patrick, Quebec, where the St. Laurents had a summer home.

LIONEL CHEVRIER

We took the train to Quebec City and there Renaud and Dr. Mathieu Samson, Louis St. Laurent's son-in-law, met us and drove us to St. Patrick. On the way down they told us about the physical condition of the father, Dr. Mathieu saying *qua* medical man that he didn't think Mr. St. Laurent was in a fit condition physically to carry on. While the actual question of resignation [as Leader] hadn't been discussed with him, they both felt that that's what he should do. And that's one of the reasons, I think, why Mike took me along with him—so that it wouldn't be thought that he was going down there to wrench out of Mr. St. Laurent a resignation.

We lodged in a *pension* at St. Patrick's not very far from the St. Laurent house, and we went over there for dinner that night. We both found Mr. St. Laurent in a pretty depressed state. He wasn't talking at all. Awfully nice to us, but he was not loquacious. This had happened during the pipeline debate, when he would sit there and say nothing. I didn't have evidence with my own eyes because I wasn't in the House at the time. But reading in the press and talking to former colleagues, that's what I gathered. Well, we had dinner, and after dinner we retired to the study.

There was just our group alone—myself, Renaud and Dr. Mathieu, and Mr. St. Laurent. It was then that he said he was tired, he was a man of years, he thought he should resign but he was worried lest they would say he was running away from the leadership and from the fight because he had been defeated. That was the last thing he wanted to do. During the course of the conversation he indicated that, notwithstanding that, he should retire, and of course Mathieu confirmed that from a physical standpoint it was silly to attempt to carry on. Then we asked if that was his wish and he said it was. And it was suggested that we might draft a letter of resignation.

So we went back to the *pension* and Mike drafted what we thought was the gist of what Mr. St. Laurent had in his mind. He showed it to me; I had very few corrections to make—I mean, in the phraseology.

The next morning, we returned for lunch and afterward showed [St. Laurent] the statement. He read it, put it down, read it again. It was in English. Finally he said, "Yes, I think this is fine. This is all right." But again he worried about having to do this, the impression it might create.

I felt, and I'm sure Mike did, that it was a relief to him to get that thing off his mind, and I know his family did too. Because, as you know, he lived many years after that. So it was understood that we would get back to Ottawa and give it to the press in the morning [September 6, 1957], but it would be issued from his office in Ottawa. I presume it was translated.

In due course the Liberal Party executive met and announced that a national leadership convention would be held in Ottawa's cow palace, the Coliseum, starting January 14, 1958.

At about this time a Montreal industrialist and staunch Liberal, Robert Fowler, who had just brought out a report on broadcasting, went to a small dinner party in Ottawa.

ROBERT FOWLER

It was at the home of Duncan McTavish [president of The National Liberal Federation], and as I recall it the others there were all friends—Walter Gordon, Maurice Lamontagne, Graham

Towers [former governor of the Bank of Canada], and myself. I think that was all. Others were involved in the activity a little later on. But we set up a little conspiracy to get Mike elected Leader of the Liberal Party. He wasn't terribly keen about it. He liked his role in international affairs. He, however, more or less accepted the inevitable. He could see, as anybody else could, that he was the obvious choice.

We talked it out with him and made it pretty clear to him that he was the man that had to do it. And he said, as I recall, "Well, I will accept if this comes along. I'm not going to scratch for it. And if you run into situations where you think I should not go forward, you're required to let me know and I won't feel too badly. But if it goes along, and if you want to go on with what your plans are, I'll go along with them too." Then we did a little, but not very much, in the way of preparation before the convention in January 1958.

After the Liberal government's defeat, Lester Pearson began writing a syndicated column, and Robert Fowler, who in his own words had become a persistent advisor, criticised it with the leadership in mind.

ROBERT FOWLER

I wrote him about his column and said that I liked it but that I wanted him to put more emphasis on domestic issues. He needed no build-up as an expert on international questions, but I wanted him to write on Canadian problems to show their impact on international affairs as well as on international problems to show their impact on Canadian affairs. As everybody says, foreign policy is merely an extension of domestic policy, but it was a question of emphasis. He accepted that piece of gratuitous advice, although he said he had a little difficulty because the people who were employing him to write the column wanted him mainly to talk about international affairs. But he tried to get as much emphasis as he could.

On October 14, 1957, Lester Pearson learned that he had been awarded the Nobel Peace Prize for his initiative in establishing the United Nations Emergency Force and resolving the 1956 Suez Crisis. Although the new Diefenbaker government had been sworn in on June 21, the opening of

Parliament had been delayed for several months because, for the first time in history, the monarch had agreed to read the Speech from the Throne and preside at the formal opening —and the day chosen was October 14.

As a result of the change in government Pearson had had to move from his ministerial suite in the East Block to a single room in the basement of the Centre Block, Room 101. Mary Macdonald had followed him over, but, as an Opposition Member, he was entitled to a stenographic secretary, and so she was, as she put it, a supernumerary paid for by the party. The news of the award lit up the cluttered gloom of Room 101.

MARY MACDONALD

That was very exciting. It was about noon. The radio first carried the news. Everything was quiet and peaceful, and all of a sudden somebody called me and said, "Did you know Mr. Pearson won the Nobel Peace Prize?" And I said, "No, I didn't know." A reporter from the Press Gallery had come into the office, and he said, "Oh, it's true, it's true!"

I said, "Well, for heaven's sake! Well, you must tell him." I said to Mr. Pearson, "Look, we have some good news for you." And he was stunned. Literally. I think he said "golly" or "gee" or something like that. Then we turned on the radio. In the meantime he wanted to talk to Mrs. Pearson, and we couldn't find her because she had gone to have her hair done someplace new, not where she normally went. We didn't know where she was. We couldn't find her till she got home, which was about an hour later.

This was October the 14th and this was the day of the opening of Parliament, and the place was full of press and full of media. Naturally. They were all outside on the lawns. The Queen was going to open Parliament at three o'clock with Mr. Diefenbaker. It was going to be the first formal opening. This was to have been the icing on the cake, it was to have been Mr. Diefenbaker's big day with the Queen opening Parliament—and Mr. Pearson was the news.

All the loudspeakers outside, they broadcast it on the hill . . . "Flash! First Canadian to win the Nobel Peace Prize, former Minister Lester B. Pearson." I think that really disappointed Mr. Diefenbaker. It seemed as if Mr. Pearson was always coming in between [him and the limelight].

I went with him, by the way, to Oslo for the ceremony, which was very nice. We stayed with the Drews [George Drew, newly appointed Canadian High Commissioner] in London on the way home. Mr. Pearson was awarded the prize on the 10th [December 1957] and he gave his lecture on the 11th. And Mrs. Pearson's birthday is the 13th. It was a big week.

The Nobel Peace Prize meant that Mike Pearson was assured of the Liberal leadership, as Paul Hellyer, who was appointed Associate Defense Minister in the last days of the St. Laurent government, observed. Although Paul Martin knew that he had no chance of winning, he nevertheless decided to be a candidate.

PAUL HELLYER

When Mr. Pearson got the Nobel Prize, that was it. I would say in a matter of forty-eight hours the situation changed from [Walter] Harris having been the front runner and the one with the most support from members of the parliamentary caucus and the party machine, that the situation reversed itself and Pearson became an odds-on favourite, an almost certain shoo-in. And Harris of course was smart enough to realise what he was up against, and procrastinated in his decision, but ultimately decided not to be a candidate.

PAUL MARTIN

Before Mike went to get the Nobel Prize in Sweden, he and I had lunch. We had talked about the leadership on many occasions. He used to always say to me—and I suspect that he meant this, but I think he could've meant it only up to a point—"You know, you are the logical man. You're the most experienced; you have other qualities. I don't deny that I have some," he said, "but you know, Paul, we have to look at the facts of life." And the facts of life as he revealed to me when we discussed this thing, particularly in the fall of 1957, were that Ontario in particular and the rest of Canada would not favour as successor to St. Laurent someone who was French or part French, and Catholic, and who came from Ontario.

I knew this; I knew it better than Pearson. But I had a deep resentment that this was the fact. I thought it was regrettable that there was such a thing as the principle of alternation that was recognised in the Liberal Party, and so did he. And so it was pretty well assumed, when he and I talked on that occasion, that not only would he be the candidate, but he would be the logical candidate.

However, before he went to get his Nobel Prize, we had a chat and I said to him: "Now, you're going away. By the time you get back there'll only be about a month or so before the convention. I may be a candidate, and I thought I'd better tell you. I don't want to be a candidate, but there are many people who feel that it's wrong that in the Liberal Party an English-speaking Protestant only can succeed to the leadership. You and I both share that view. This is not a strong enough reason in itself for me to do something which I know will not succeed, but there are a lot of people who feel strongly about this, and there are others who feel that I would be a better man than you. I don't agree with that necessarily, but I must . . ."

He and I were such good friends. When he was away, I did decide to go. I did it very reluctantly; I didn't want to; I knew that I wouldn't succeed. I'm not sorry that I did. I didn't want to put myself up simply to make a good convention. But if I hadn't done that, it would have been a very bad convention. It would have been a negative convention. But that isn't the reason I did it.

Once he decided to run, Paul Martin campaigned vigorously for the leadership. But Lester Pearson did little or nothing. In fact, Paul Hellyer considered him an on-again, off-again candidate, a reluctant candidate if he ever saw one. It was Walter Gordon, Hellyer said, who persuaded Pearson to be a serious contender and made all the financial and organisational arrangements. Gordon was assisted by Keith Davey, a young Liberal organiser from Toronto, among others.

WALTER GORDON

All I did was to call him up a few days before [the convention] and say, "What are you doing? Because while you'll probably win it, you aren't going to win it by all that much unless you do something." He said he wasn't doing anything, so I went down to Ottawa that night and said, "Where are your headquarters?" "Haven't got any." "Who's your manager?" "Haven't got one." "Where's your money?" "Haven't any money." So that was that.

There was Pearson, Mary Macdonald, and myself in this little room, or his office, I suppose, and none of us knew anything about politics. Mike had been in government for eight or nine years, but he didn't know much about the political side of it. We got a suite at the Chateau. That was our headquarters. Everybody was coming in from all over. They would rush in and say, "What do you want us to do?" and I would say to them, knowing nothing about it, "What do you think you can do best?" and they would say—and I would say, "Just what we want you to do," and away they would go and do it.

We didn't have any money, apart from only about 3,000 dollars. I think at the next convention the candidate spent about 300,000 dollars.

MAURICE LAMONTAGNE

There was no need to have a formal organisation. I remember, when the convention started, that Mr. Pearson didn't even have a hotel suite, so that Walter Gordon had to rent one for him. The organisation was quite limited.

Pearson did very little travelling at that time. I remember, for instance, I went with him to Quebec City. There was a special reception just after Christmas for Mr. St. Laurent at the Reform Club. I went down with him on the train in the morning, and when we got to the train, Paul Martin was there too. He was everywhere.

I had already started to prepare my first notes for Mr. Pearson in French at that time...I think it was his first interview on television in French, so I had to prepare the questions for the interviewer, and the answers, and then to rehearse with him and to avoid certain letters and certain words. So I had to learn my basic French again. Mr. Pearson could read French quite well, but he couldn't really speak it at all, except with a text, so it took a lot of rehearsal. He was very patient, much more patient than his wife because she always wondered why he had to speak French. Even when he was in Quebec City.

KEITH DAVEY

I phoned Mr. Gordon and told him who I was, and he said, "That's fine. Come on down to Ottawa, come down a day early to the convention, and we'll do something." When I got down to Ottawa I sort of unofficially, almost by osmosis, became the chairman of the Toronto Pearson delegation, and we delivered the overwhelming majority of delegates to Mr. Pearson. I think probably 95 percent of them. There was a guy called Bob Campbell, an advertising guy—he'd been a candidate in a by-election in York West—who was Paul Martin's chairman. He said to me on the train going to Ottawa, "Look, I'm going to help Martin simply because we can't have Toronto unanimously for Pearson." But it was overwhelming.

At the convention I was appalled by the lack of organisation and by the ezey-ozey way in which things were being operated. Walter Gordon said, "Well, just go out and do what you can, do whatever you want," sort of thing. It was really shockingly bad. So I just did the traditional thing. I just sort of made a book of the Toronto delegates and just worked them over and got them all.

WALTER GORDON

I was self-appointed [manager of his campaign] and I kept right out of the spotlight. Nobody knew I was even there. I didn't have much trouble doing that because I didn't know anything about it. But, in an amateur's way, we managed the campaign quite successfully. We did succeed, I thought, in swinging quite a few votes to Pearson that would have gone another way. So he won by a tremendous margin.

The vote (on January 16, 1958) was: L. B. Pearson, 1,084; Paul Martin, 305. Many voted for Martin, knowing that he would not win but feeling that he deserved their vote because he had made a contest of the leadership and assured the success of the convention, but an Ottawa Valley lawyer, "Joe" Greene, who described himself as a ward-heeler politician, did so on principle.

J. J. GREENE

I supported Paul Martin. I don't know that Mr. Pearson ever knew that, and being the kind of man he was he didn't worry much about it if he did, because obviously I didn't have much influence. For a naïve reason, possibly, I thought Paul Martin had chosen this lousy trade of politics, had practised it for some twenty-three years; whereas in the terms of the trite saying, "Some are born great, some achieve greatness, some have greatness thrust upon them," I really thought Mr. Pearson was having it thrust upon him. I thought if we're going to get good men in politics we've got to reward those who have worked in the field and not always bring in somebody from outside who take the big plums when they come, or there'll be nobody left in the field.

After all the triumph and applause of the leadership convention, Lester Pearson sank to the jeering depths of Parliament when he moved a non-confidence motion on Monday, January 20, 1958. Normally, the purpose of such a motion is to defeat the government and bring on an election, but that was the last thing the Liberals wanted, so Jack Pickersgill devised a motion which proposed that the Conservative government resign and let the Liberals return to power but without an election. He worded it in such a way that the minor parties, the CCF and the Social Credit Party, would vote against it. It might have worked if Pearson had been a better Parliamentarian, but all it did was make the new and inexperienced Leader look like a fool.

Pickersgill maintained that no preparations were made for the supply debate that was to begin on the Monday following the convention. However, Tom Kent, at that time the editor of the Winnipeg Free Press *and a friend of Pearson, said that the matter was discussed before the convention.*

TOM KENT

We met in order to discuss that problem, and we came unanimously to the view that the only possible thing for him to do was to *not* move a motion of censure at all, to make a speech on that supply motion saying:

"We've had our Liberal convention. We've laid down quite clearly the policies that we think are necessary in order to deal with this unemployment problem which this new government has so suddenly allowed to appear, etc., etc." And those were our policies. We offered them to the government at this point in the winter, early January, you remember. "The only thing to do is to apply those policies. We hope the government will. And let's see if that can minimize this terrible winter problem [of unemployment] that we're having, and we sincerely hope that they'll use these policies and that by the spring things will be better. But if they're not, we put them firmly on notice that we'll do everything possible to get them out and force them to face the Canadian people on this issue, but there would be no benefit in doing that at this moment." I actually drafted and I still have somewhere in my files the outline, just a one-page outline of a speech on those lines. That was what he was going to do.

On the morning of the day of the vote for the leadership at the convention, I was in Mr. Pearson's suite. Bob Fowler had prepared two alternative speeches for him to make, an acceptance speech if he won or nice things about Paul Martin if he lost. I'd read Bob's draft—I am not quite sure which of the two it was, but anyway, it was one or other of those speeches — and been asked to offer any comments.

Jack Pickersgill came in and said he must see him very urgently because he had to go up to the House which was sitting. So Mike said, "Okay, that's fine, I agree with you. Look, if you could make those changes and then we'll look at it again together when I've talked to Jack, because Jack has to hurry off."

It was not a very elaborate suite and there weren't very many rooms. I went and sat in one of the bathrooms and made these changes, and then I was due down at the cow palace for a meeting of the Resolutions Committee or something. So I was off. Jack was just leaving and Mike grabbed me by the arm and said, "Just a minute. Wait just a minute." He said, "Jack's just produced an idea about what we should do on Tuesday. I think it's too clever by half. We'll have to talk about it." That was his spontaneous reaction, "it's too clever by half." But he didn't tell me what it was. I was dashing off and that was the end of it. In fact, the whole thing got caught up in the business of the convention. You know how it is. I had no more private conversation with him and indeed

I caught 'flu after the convention, and I was in my bed in Winnipeg on the Tuesday when I got a phone call to tell me what he'd actually done. I mean it was unbelievable.

A day or so later I got a call from Mike, who had some speaking engagements in Western Canada, and the last of them was in Brandon. And he said, "I'll be on the flight out of Brandon into Winnipeg, gets into Winnipeg about eleven o'clock at night. There's a flight on to Ottawa"—there was a sort of connection around midnight—"but I very much want to talk to you. Could we meet if I wait until the two o'clock or three o'clock in the morning flight out of Winnipeg to Ottawa?" So I said, "Yes, fine."

I went out to the airport, met him, and took him to the house, gave him a sandwich and a scotch. I can still see him sitting, as he was rather inclined to do if he got a large armchair, with his legs up over the arms and saying. "Well, I don't know if I'll ever be any good as a political leader, but if there's one thing certain, no political leader ever began by making a bigger mistake." This was what was so charming about him. Of course, what he wanted to do, because he realised there was going to be an election, was ask me to draft a campaign statement in the course of the next few days.

Diefenbaker launched an attack that was described as devastatingly disastrous by George McIlraith, a veteran Liberal M.P. In the end the Prime Minister circumvented the device by going to the Governor-General and getting Parliament dissolved and an election called for March 31, 1958.

Pearson had had no time to set up an organisation but he had had the foresight during the leadership convention to propose that Senator John Connolly be the Liberals' campaign manager.

JOHN CONNOLLY

Paul Martin told me that when we were waiting for the vote [at the convention] he and Mike were chatting and Mike said, "You know, I think we're going to have an election very soon." And he added, "John Connolly has been very active here in the convention. He's done a great deal to try and keep it running smoothly and running well. I think I'm going to ask him if he will take charge, insofar as anybody can, of the campaign." Paul told me shortly after.

Well, this horrified me because I had no touch or feel for this kind of thing. Finally he [Pearson] went to the caucus and said, "This is what I think we should do," and the caucus said, "Let's do it."

[Senator] Chubby [Power] came to me that afternoon and he said, "You're pretty reluctant about this," I said, "Chubby, this is a terrible thing to have happen to the party, because I don't really know this party. I know a lot of people in it; but most of the people that I know outside of Ottawa are the Members. I guess they think I'm all right, but I don't know the party well enough in the constituencies."

Since the Liberals were not ready for an election, the 1958 campaign was an impossible struggle against an overwhelming opponent at the height of his popularity. But Mike persevered and was cheerful in adversity and never lost his sense of humour in defeat.

JOHN CONNOLLY

We both knew it was a hopeless, helpless proposition. You see, half of the Ministers had been defeated in '57, and the other half were to be defeated in '58. And there was very little that we could do. The reports that we would get by phone every day from every part of the country made it perfectly clear that not only were we not going to win, but we were having trouble getting candidates. The tendency was to rely on the old hands, and the old hands just weren't acceptable to people.

And John Diefenbaker had electrified the country to the point where it didn't matter what anybody said or did, he had it in his back pocket. And he put on an enormous campaign, a tremendous campaign, but he really didn't have to work very hard. We had no money, so that we had to use the scheduled airlines for Mike's appearances in different parts of the country. No charters of any kind. We had no research staff, and Mike was turning up in different parts of the West, different parts of the East, and wondering what he was going to say. You see, he hadn't been the Leader for more than a month.

TOM KENT

Mr. Pearson had very little help in that first and rather desperate campaign, and he asked me to give him some help, which I did. I did draft the policy statement in his name. It was a rather irrelevant activity because the state of the Liberal organisation was such that the campaign, such as it was, paid very little attention to the policy statement. After I drafted the statement, I went up to Saskatoon to meet him one snowy day so that we could go through it together before it was sent off for release. That was the one contact I had with him during the campaign. I was just somebody who was helping in a purely spare-time capacity.

MARY MACDONALD

I thought the most marvellous thing was how he went through that [campaign] knowing he wouldn't win. John Connolly and Chubby Power were the co-chairmen. I don't think that it's fair to say that the party abandoned him. I can't imagine how it could have. Chubby and John Connolly worked around the clock. They were just fantastic. The last day, going up the Ottawa Valley to Renfrew, that was wonderful. It was strange, the last week of that campaign there was a bit of a shift. You could feel Mr. Pearson was coming on. Not that it resulted in anything, but there was a difference in the attitude of people.

J. W. PICKERSGILL

I had a vote in Ottawa and I thought it might be needed, and my campaign was over [in Newfoundland], so I came home. On election day I was in Pearson's office in the House of Commons, with him alone, and I said to him, "Mike, you haven't any illusion that you're going to win this election?" He looked at me and he said "None whatever. I hope we might get about a hundred seats." That's as near to verbatim as it could possibly be. But even he didn't expect it would be forty-eight, and certainly neither did

I, though I knew we weren't going to do well. I knew that we didn't have a ghost of a chance of winning that election.

CHRISTOPHER YOUNG

He tells the classic story in his memoirs of Mrs. Pearson saying on the night of March 31, 1958, "We've lost everything. We've even won our own seat." If he had lost his seat, I think he would have quit and gone into academia or diplomacy. But having won his seat and, despite the initial reaction of depression and sense of failure, I think he felt that he had to stay on and couldn't quit in the face of adversity, but had to help pull the Liberal Party back to at least a respectable position, if not to power.

I don't know that he really expected to get into power at that point.

3 The Remaking of the Prime Minister

NEVER BEFORE HAD the Liberal Party suffered such a catastrophe as it did in the 1958 election, and so it was hardly surprising that, in the immediate aftermath of the debacle, the new Leader, Lester B. Pearson, would lie low and speak softly. There was a lot of reorganising and rethinking to be done. It was not the time to be an aggressive Opposition Leader. In his first speech when Parliament was recalled on May 12, Mr. Pearson said that the Liberals would try to be constructive in their criticism and would co-operate with the government in all those endeavours which they thought were in the national interest. However, he did sound a warning against the dangers of a one-party state. And it was the closest that Canada had come to a one-party state. the forty-eight Liberals, plus the one Liberal-Labor member and eight CCF—the Social Credit Party was wiped out—were faced by 208 Conservatives and seemed to be surrounded by them because the Tories overflowed across the aisle and occupied most of the Opposition benches. Of the forty-eight or forty-nine members, twenty-nine were French-speaking, although these included such persons as Lionel Chevrier and Paul Martin who were fluently bilingual. The Liberals had been reduced to a Central Canadian rump, having no representatives from the West or from six of the ten provinces; they had been wiped out in British Columbia, Alberta, Saskatchewan, Manitoba, Nova Scotia, and Prince Edward Island. Of the eight CCFers, three were from Ontario, one from Saskatchewan, and four from British Columbia.

One of the Liberal Leader's first tasks was to find a chairman for the Public Accounts Committee—Diefenbaker had promised that he would adopt the British custom of having an Opposition member head this watchdog committee. Alan Macnaughton, a Montreal lawyer, agreed to serve, and Pearson found that even this appointment had its political repercussions.

ALAN MACNAUGHTON

The committee started with an examination of the building of the Printing Bureau, [by the previous Liberal government] and the Tories latched onto this as a great opportunity. As I had suggested that we should go and visit what we were about to examine, we went to see that colossal building in Hull. And there were the comments in the press the next day—that fishing streams were running through the basement, that the lobby was the size of a football field. Incidentally, thirty minutes after we left the lobby, the ceiling fell down. That made the headlines. If you sat on the toilet, hot steam came out instead of water.

This went on for not less than four weeks, and in caucus I was attacked every week. I was told that I was ruining the party and that I should bloody well resign. Not less than three former Ministers, including Pearson, asked me to resign.

I said, in caucus, "I will not resign because the facts are true. And if the facts are true, how the hell can I resign? It's stupid. I'm there to do a job; I'll do it." Of course the headlines were ruinous—the Liberal Party this, that, and the other thing. "Furthermore," I said, "you know, my policy is very simple. If you kick a dog because he's bitten you, well, that's justifiable. And if he tears your flesh, well, you kick him twice. But you continue to kick that dog day after day, and people will tell you to stop."

I said, "You stick it out. Furthermore, the evidence is there and you can't deny it. And by God, as a Liberal I'm going to report the facts as they are—because in the long run it's going to help this party."

Anyway, after four weeks the press got fed up with this, and the tide begun to turn. So I put in this report, which the Tories accepted and the Liberals rejected, to the effect that there was waste and there was extravagance, but there was no fraud. And

that in my opinion was a plus. I feel that that maintained some of
the integrity of the party.

I don't think it's been realised that the first chairman of a
Tory-dominated Public Accounts Committee, if I may boast, had
the guts to tell the truth as he saw it, as the evidence was there. So
that the Liberal Party—stupid, beaten—nevertheless had its
integrity. There wasn't fraud. There was waste and there was
extravagance. After that I had no trouble at all with the next four
years' reports, and they were good reports.

*The most shattering blow for the Liberals in the 1958 election was not
that they had been wiped out of six of the ten provinces but that the
Progressive Conservatives had won fifty seats in Quebec, "our own
special preserve" as Pearson called it in his memoirs. There was no doubt
that this Tory triumph was due to Premier Maurice Duplessis and his
Union Nationale machine. Many of the newly elected Quebec
Conservative members were Union Nationale workers. It was an
extraordinary situation and presented a challenge to Maurice Lamontagne. He decided to meet it head on and thereby took the first step to regain
seats in Quebec.*

MAURICE LAMONTAGNE

I decided that the first priority was to strengthen the [Quebec]
provincial party, to try to get rid of Mr. Duplessis. At
that time the only man we thought could do the job was Jean
Lesage [Liberal Member and former St. Laurent Minister]. So I
remember, one week after the election of '58, a small group of us
met in Quebec City and we agreed that we should talk to him. I
knew that Jean would be interested. He was not very keen about
coming back to Ottawa [as a Private Member] without his wife
and his family. He knew that the Liberals were in Opposition in
Ottawa for at least four years, so he wasn't hard to convince.

It was a big sacrifice at the federal level because he would have
been most useful in the Opposition. But I felt personally, and I
convinced Mr. Pearson, that it would be a better investment to let
him run in Quebec.

JEAN LESAGE

I was in Florida after the election, and so was Mike. I didn't feel that I could take a decision without his advice, so I drove to see him north of Miami. I consulted him. He said he thought that in the state of affairs which prevailed at the time, the position of the Liberal Party provincially in Quebec was very important. There was not much hope in Ontario as Leslie Frost [Conservative premier of Ontario] was really deeply entrenched. Duplessis was still there but we both hoped that I could turn around the fortunes of the Provincial Liberal Party in Quebec, and so it was agreed between us that I would resign, and that I would run provincially.

Pearson didn't take the decision; he was much too delicate for that. He left me completely free. However, I could feel that, as much as he hated to see me go because our ranks were very thin in the House, in the order of priorities, the priority was given to trying to have a turnaround in Quebec.

It was hard for Lester Pearson to lose Jean Lesage so soon after the disaster of the 1958 election. Aside from the fact that he was one of the few former Ministers to be re-elected and would have been an addition to the Opposition front bench, he had been close to the Leader as his Parliamentary Assistant when he was Minister of External Affairs. Pearson was counting on Lesage for advice and support, which he had little of. Aside from Mary Macdonald, who moved up with him from the basement, and John Payne, who had acted as his press officer, he hadn't had time to organise a proper staff. Allan MacEachen, who had lost his Nova Scotia seat of Inverness Richmond by sixteen votes, was the first to come to work in the Opposition Leader's office after the election; Maurice Lamontagne soon followed. Later Dick O'Hagan and Tom Kent joined the small staff, although Kent spent only part of his time in the Parliament Buildings and most of it downtown in the Liberal Party's headquarters.

Meanwhile, Lester Pearson's friends and backers were trying to help. As a diplomat, Mr. Pearson had become used to working with committees and he was very much a collegial Leader; he needed advice because he was faced by a formidable Parliamentarian in Prime Minister Diefenbaker. An extra-Parliamentary group consisting of Walter Gordon, Robert Fowler, Maurice Lamontagne, Maurice Sauvé, and Tom Kent held meetings on

*Saturdays in Fowler's Montreal office; there they thrashed out policy
ideas, which were forwarded to the Leader's office. At the same time, the
old pros, such as Lionel Chevrier, Paul Martin, Jack Pickersgill, and
George McIlraith, had regular meetings with Mr. Pearson, and, as
McIlraith said, most of the day till ten o'clock at night seemed to be taken
up with meetings of one kind or another.*

ALLAN MacEACHEN

The first couple of years were pretty disappointing and difficult.
Who was around and had been in Opposition? None of our
members. I remember going to see [Senator] Chubby Power,
who was the only man I could find who had been a member of a
Liberal Opposition. I spent a couple of hours in his office over in
the Senate as he tried to pull out old files that he had about how the
Liberal Opposition operated. How would this new Opposition
operate and how would we organise ourselves?

I think maybe the strength of the operation was that there were a
number of key people in Parliament, there were five or six, who
kept in close touch. They always met and they strategised in the
morning. Maurice [Lamontagne] and I were providing whatever
back-up support was required so that the operation was well
co-ordinated, and could take advantage of difficulties that were
inevitable and would arise for any government. It was a small
group but very well organised.

Among the challenges that Pearson had to face were the old
supply motions. We had to move motions of non-confidence
regularly, and, of course, he used to move many of them, and, he
would have to swot up on questions like housing, regional
development, prairie agriculture, all of them. He'd go home, you
know, on weekends with a bag full of documents and memoranda
on these domestic issues, with which he had not been identified. I
think he knew a lot about Canada and what was involved, but he
certainly wasn't publicly identified with many of these issues.
Maurice used to turn out these long memoranda on various
subjects, and, Pearson would work his speeches out of these.

LIONEL CHEVRIER

How did he [Pearson] perform? Having regard to the
experience he had, I would say he performed very well. But he

was no match for the person [Diefenbaker] who had been a Member of Parliament since 1940 and who had great legal and court training in his own province of Saskatchewan. How do you feel when you have 205 or more Members across the way and you're all alone with a band of loyal followers on the other side? When you have the crowd with you, you're inclined to be much better than when you have the crowd against you. And mind you, there was a hell of a lot of booing and shouting and yelling across the floor of the House when we got up to speak.

So, having regard to all those circumstances, I think Mike did exceptionally well. And he learned as he went along. Because he took a lot of abuse, you know, from 1958 until 1962. He took an awful lot of abuse. And I know that at one stage he must have said to himself, "Is it worth the candle? What the hell am I doing here? Why don't I get out someplace where I can be of use, in the diplomatic field or elsewhere?"

I know that one day he came to me and said that he had had an offer—I can't remember how many months after the '58 election this was—"I've thought this over very carefully during the weekend," he went on, "and I've come to the conclusion that it's my duty to stick with this through thick and thin, take it on the chin if I have to, do the best I can under the circumstances and carry on. That's my duty, that's my responsibility, and that's what I'm going to do."

From that time on he seemed to have a different attitude. And there were times when he certainly put Mr. Diefenbaker in the corner.

It became evident to Paul Hellyer, when he entered the House after winning a by-election on December 15, 1958 (he had been defeated in the general election), that something should be done to bring the various advisory groups together.

PAUL HELLYER

A leader's advisory group was set up really at my suggestion to resolve a very difficult question. Mike didn't want to move without Walter Gordon. Walter Gordon was suspect by the "Old Guard." I suppose all of us, but especially Martin and Chevrier and Connolly and Pickersgill, were all less than enthusiastic or perhaps a bit suspicious of his role in things.

There was an impasse. Pearson wouldn't move and the others were not ready to accept Gordon as the chief guy from the outside, because he was outside then; he wasn't in the House. He had been approached to run in Trinity [a Toronto constituency] but he wasn't the least bit interested in taking that kind of a risk. So he was not there, not part of the show. Even such things as raising money, which the party badly needed, couldn't go ahead until this impasse was overcome. Some of us volunteered to raise money, but no, Mike said he didn't want us to, he wanted Walter to do that.

So, finally, I suggested an advisory group, which included the Parliamentary veterans and John Connolly and Tom Kent and Allan MacEachen and Maurice Lamontagne and Walter Gordon, and this was the vehicle by which the group was brought around the table in some sort of harmony, and it made it possible for Gordon and Kent to exercise the influence that they did during the coming months, sometimes with and sometimes without the approval of the others. But it had the advantage of holding everybody together, which was the initial problem that had to be overcome.

The Study Conference on National Problems, held at Queen's University in Kingston, Ontario, in September 1960 did much to revive the fortunes of the Liberal Party. The conference was Lester Pearson's idea, according to Walter Gordon, but it was undoubtedly discussed at the meetings of the Leader's advisory committee. It had its genesis in the fact that a national convention was being planned for the beginning of 1961, and it was felt that a thinkers' conference might produce new ideas and new people for the party meeting. Some members recalled a similar conference organised by Vincent Massey in the '30s when the Liberals were in Opposition, and Paul Hellyer was the one who hunted up a copy of the book on the conference and saw how successful it had been. Among the organisers of the Kingston conference were Walter Gordon, Robert Fowler, Maurice Lamontagne, Tom Kent, and Mitchell Sharp, then a big businessman whom Pearson persuaded to be chairman.

While the conference dealt with the questions of social welfare and such international issues as the atom bomb and the cold war, Pauline Jewett, who was a participant, noted that the "French Fact" and Quebec's role in Confederation were hardly discussed. John Turner, who was the president of the Junior Bar of Montreal and had no party allegiance then, presented a paper on legal aid. The speeches that aroused the most comment and controversy were those by Maurice Lamontagne and Tom Kent.

MAURICE LAMONTAGNE

At that time we were playing with the idea of having a special trade zone on the basis of the so-called North Atlantic triangle. Mr. Pearson had already made a few speeches along that line, and that was the kind of thing that I dealt with. It was also the first time that I talked about the creation of the Economic Council, when I said that inflation was not only a cyclical matter but a structural one as well. I spoke about cost-push inflation—and this was not discussed very much in those days—and I attributed this cost-push inflation to increasing monopolistic power both in terms of labour and enterprise and producers.

I suggested that we should have a special tribunal to pass judgement on price increases. And this raised quite a row. So much so that Mr. Pearson had some difficulty in keeping myself and Tom Kent from being thrown out of the party. Tom had suggested very strict succession duties to put a stop to inheritance and a tax on advertising.

TOM KENT

I think the first rather substantial disagreement that I had with Mr. Pearson was that the original concept of the conference had been that it would be a relatively small private meeting, not open to the public or the press, at which a relatively small number of people would spend three or four days talking about their views, arguing about their views on the future. Frankly, my paper was written in that spirit and was not exactly the paper that I would have written if it had been intended for publication. However, the conference attracted a lot of interest. There was a great deal of pressure from people wanting to attend. The attendance grew in size to the point at which, at the very last moment—not until after I had arrived there—the decision was made to open it to the press.

I was furious. Not so much from the point of view of whether it was the right thing to do, but I felt it was a great mistake to change gears on a thing like that at the last moment.

The part [of my paper] in which I was particularly provocative and would not have been if I had known that it was going to be a public occasion, was that, after discussing the various aspects of taxation and arguing that we couldn't stand a great deal more income tax, suggested that there were all sorts of sources of revenue that were untapped and specifically that there would be a great deal to be said for disallowing advertising expenditures above a certain level for tax purposes. Which is, I think, an idea for which a great deal can be said. But, of course, not a practical policy to advocate in relation to a party seeking office, for the basic reason, which we always have to recognise, that the Canadian tax structure can't depart very radically from the U. S. tax structure.

J. W. PICKERSGILL

Neither of those papers was ever taken up by the party. I think most of us were rather embarrassed by both of them; and we didn't think they had much to do with the mainstream of politics, and I don't to this day.

However, there's no doubt whatever that the conference brought a number of people into the mainstream of the Liberal Party who had not been there before, of whom perhaps the most important and notable of all was Jean Marchand. That's the first time I ever saw him. He impressed me more than anybody else who was at that conference. It also brought a lot of academics, some of whom had previously—like Frank Underhill, for example—been connected with the CCF. In that sense it created a broader spectrum.

But I was rather disappointed [in the conference] in one aspect, and I said so. I was the final speaker at the luncheon which closed it. And I said that I was really rather disappointed that there wasn't much originality, there weren't many new ideas. I said it wasn't like the '30s when I was young, when the place was in a constant ferment. But that's probably just as well. We weren't trying to create a radical party; we were trying to create a party that would appeal to the broadest possible spectrum of the Canadian people.

MITCHELL SHARP

Mr. Pearson phoned me after the conference. He seemed to be very happy about it and he said would I be chairman of one of the sessions of the forthcoming Liberal convention. I said I would. So I was chairman of the committee on economic policy. That was a political meeting. And this was the time that I became openly associated with the Liberal Party.

The National Rally of the Liberal Party was held in Ottawa between January 11 and 14, 1961. Walter Gordon played a prominent part at this political convention, but only after assuring himself that Mike Pearson agreed with his economic views. However, Tom Kent, who worked with Gordon in preparing the policy papers for the rally and was a close associate and ally, didn't believe that Mr. Pearson had ever made up his mind on the matter. It should be noted that the time frame of Kent's analysis was much later, when Pearson was Prime Minister, and therefore Gordon's assessment could have been right.

WALTER GORDON

Some time during 1960 I started to think out my views on a lot of subjects, including the Canadian independence issues, and I made three or four speeches. I think they were more in the form of essays than speeches. I went to a lot of trouble over them, and I remember saying to Pearson, "Now it would be fatal if I got involved and you and I then didn't agree. I want to know if you agree with these views." He said he did, and he convinced me that he did. In those days there wasn't any doubt about Pearson being a Canadian economic nationalist.

I said okay then, I'll really go to work on it, and he asked me if I would be the chairman of the Policy Committee at the Liberal Rally. So I certainly got involved. Tom Kent and Lamontagne and I wrote most of the papers. Hellyer was the over-all chairman but we handled the policy end.

TOM KENT

I think that what really happened was that the nationalist issue as such was simply never faced up to. It didn't feature in all the statements of policy that I drafted and were approved by Mr.

Pearson. We really just ignored that issue. I think that reflected essentially the fact that Mr. Pearson really never made up his mind about that. The traditions of the Liberal Party had been relatively continentalist. Mr. Pearson's personal view certainly tended, when he was in office, to be of the free trade and, if anything, continentalist kind, and while he was in one sense of the word a very firm Canadian nationalist, of course, he was uneasy about economic nationalism. I think really the issue was never joined; it was never officially the Liberal Party policy. It was Walter's view. It was an issue on which there would have been quite deep division within the Liberal Party and the government.

Shortly after the National Rally in Ottawa, there was a staff crisis at Liberal headquarters, and Walter Gordon, who had kept a watching brief on the party for the Leader, had to look for a new director. He talked about his problem with Keith Davey and the other bright young men who had taken over the Liberal Party in Toronto; he had been going to their Wednesday night dinner meetings and, according to Davey, seemed to enjoy the informal attitude and being called Walter. There was a good deal of brainstorming and a lot of names were mentioned.

KEITH DAVEY

After the meeting I was driving [Royce] Frith home and he said, "You know, the guy who should really do this is you." At that point I had never thought of leaving Toronto, never thought of leaving broadcasting,* never thought of being a professional politician. So he phoned Walter the next day, Walter phoned me, and I found myself in his office talking about it, and the next thing I knew I was despatched to Ottawa on a Saturday to see Mr. Pearson. The appointment, in effect, was made by Walter. I went to Ottawa and Mr. Pearson more or less gave my appointment his imprimatur. I remember at the end of the meeting saying, "Oh, by the way, I want to talk about money." And he said, "Look, Keith, you don't talk to me about money, you talk to Walter Gordon about money." Which, of course, I did.

This would be March 1961. I started on the 15th of May, 1961. I

---

*Keith Davey was Sales Manager for Foster Hewitt Broadcasting in Toronto.

deliberately waited until the Maple Leafs were out of the play-offs to tell Foster Hewitt because that was a very important time to him and I didn't want to distress him. I don't know how the Leafs did that year; I can't recall. But in any event as soon as they were out, I went in and told him I was leaving, which was a great shock because I'd been there for eleven years, and we had a good association.

The next thing I remember was some kind of a policy conference which I sat in on for a little while. Boy, I was so naïve. Then Mr. Pearson said, "Look, you'd better go down and meet the president of the party," who was John Connolly. I phoned Senator Connolly and said, "Keith Davey from Toronto." I didn't know him. He has since become an extremely close friend of mine. I said, "Mr. Pearson has suggested that I come down and meet you. I'm the new national director of the Liberal Party."

Imagine, in retrospect. If I were the president of the party and some guy phoned me and said, "I'm the new national director." This is just incredible. So down I went to John Connolly's house on a Saturday night. And he was terribly curious and terribly generous and very friendly. I guess it must have been a bit of a shock to him, the way that happened. To the best of my knowledge the first he knew of me as the national director was when I phoned him and said Mr. Pearson had appointed me and I was coming down to see him.

There were several dichotomies in the party. There clearly was a left wing, which was Tom Kent and Walter Gordon; there clearly was a right wing, which was Bruce Matthews and John Connolly, and so on. There clearly was an Old Guard, which was Martin and Pickersgill; there clearly was a New Guard, which was Sharp and Gordon. And so we had all kinds of combinations. We had Old Guard right wing, we had Old Guard left wing, New Guard right wing, New Guard left wing, and so on. And I realised early on that my effectiveness would be enhanced if I could be on a side with all of these various groups, and so I tried to be, and I think to some extent I was.

While Keith Davey tried to be a conciliator of the various Liberal factions, his advent at party headquarters began the remaking of the Leader. The Liberals had always had an affinity for the Democratic Party in the United States and when John F. Kennedy became president and ended the business-as-usual normalcy of Eisenhower's Republican regime, the bright young men who had resurrected the Liberal Party in the Toronto area were cock-a-hoop. Besides Davey, they were Royce Frith and Dan Lang, both of whom were to be summoned to the Senate, and David Anderson, and they were all of Kennedy's age or younger; they saw in his election the beginning of an era of youthful politics. Theodore H. White's The Making of the President: 1960 *became their bible, and Keith Davey admitted that his copy was heavily underlined and that he read it half a dozen times.*

All of them believed in the modern approach to politics, with its reliance on telecommunications, on polling and market surveys for issues and image-making. In fact, one of the first things the new national director did was to form a Communications Committee. Davey said that when Walter Gordon, made up his mind to run — he had told Pearson earlier that there was no point in being a candidate if there was no chance of being elected — he had surveys conducted in the Toronto ridings of York Centre, Eglington, Rosedale, Davenport, and two others before deciding on Davenport as the place where he could win.

On his arrival in Ottawa, Davey found that he had inherited a polling organisation that neither he nor Walter Gordon regarded as satisfactory. Both of them had independently arrived at the view that they should hire Lou Harris, who had been Kennedy's pollster, and Davey was delighted when Bob Winters, then a big businessman in Toronto, talked about this most marvellous book, The Making of the President, *and this fellow Lou Harris. They were having lunch, and Winters said that he would be glad to arrange a meeting with Lou Harris because he was a friend of a friend. That was how Lou Harris was taken on and his polls showed that the Leader was consistently running behind the party in popularity.*

KEITH DAVEY

We'd go out to Stornoway [Opposition Leader's official residence]. Harris would arrive from New York. I'd meet him at the airport, and then Walter Gordon and Harris and I would meet Mr. Pearson. There'd just be the four of us, usually. As soon as Mr. Pearson saw Harris at the door, he'd always say, "Okay, how bad am I this month?" He was just great.

WALTER GORDON

All these surveys, naturally, tell you how the public feel, and a lot of people didn't like Mike's bow tie. I never asked why. Our surveys showed how people reacted—you don't ask them why they react this way. They just didn't like it. They thought it was effeminate or they thought it reminded them he had been a diplomat or some damn thing. People don't like diplomats in public life. They don't like people who are too sophisticated.

KEITH DAVEY

As far as the bow tie was concerned, we had great arguments at our Communications Committee meetings about whether or not we should use the bow tie in the 1962 campaign. The fact was most Canadians, because we tested this, were more appealed to by Mr. Pearson when he wasn't wearing his bow tie. As a matter of fact, from the 1958 convention through until 1961 in the fall, I wore absolutely nothing ever but a blue and white polka dot bow tie. That's all I wore, literally. Now the Communications Committee was meeting one day, and we were going to be looking at the Pearson pictures, and so I came in in a straight tie, the first one I'd worn in four or five years. Everybody said to me, "Gee, you look great today," and nobody knew why.

Of course this impacted itself upon me. That certainly persuaded me, and I was also persuaded by the fact that our survey showed people liked him in a straight tie. And Mr. Pearson did not wear bow ties exclusively; even prior to this he would wear the four-in-hand frequently. I didn't. I wore a bow tie to bed. But he didn't. For the '62 campaign we went for the picture of Mr. Pearson with the straight tie . . . it's very important.

I don't mind you saying that we changed his image. I don't think the terminology is accurate, and I guess I sort of resist it a little bit. If that's what you want to say, that's fine.

RICHARD O'HAGAN

I think there was no question that for large sections of the Canadian population the bow tie reinforced an unfortunate and quite unwarranted picture of Mr. Pearson as a diplomat-cum-academic, remote from the aspirations and needs of the common man. You remember the complaints against Mr. Pearson's capacity to be an effective politician. People would say he was a wonderful diplomat but no domestic politician. And so there was a feeling, and it may have been entirely self-conscious on the part of some of his political advisors and others active in the Liberal Party, "Gee, he's a wonderful man, but God, he shouldn't be wearing bow ties and all those things. They only reinforce, you know, the negative impression that so many people have of him."

It was ironic, having won this quite universal acclaim as a diplomat and problem-solver in the field of international relations, to have that then seen as a liability in domestic political terms.

J. W. PICKERSGILL

I was on this publicity committee or whatever we called it. It used to meet regularly at the Liberal Federation. And the amount of time that was spent discussing whether he should wear a bow tie or the kind of tie I've got on today was, I thought, silly. But my son, who is a cartoonist, regards me as a visual illiterate anyway, so I was a little hesitant about saying how silly I thought these things were. I have never believed that anybody should try to be anything except what he can do naturally and without apparent effort. Unfortunately, Pearson tended to listen to some of these things if they were constantly being pointed out to him.

The only thing that I ever pointed out—and I didn't do it very often because I knew that this did come naturally to him — was that I did not think that the Leader of a party, whether he's the Prime Minister or in Opposition, should conduct seminars. I think that the average voter, no matter whether he's conservatively or liberally inclined, or even radically inclined, likes to feel that people know what they're doing and why. I think I am about as sceptical intellectually as anybody you'd meet in the day's march. I really don't think that the wisdom of the ages has been distilled and put into my brain. But I do know—and I'm sure of this—that when a public man speaks, people want him to be clear and they want him to be comprehensible, and they want him to say the same thing the next day. Pearson, because he had doubts, could not help but put the other side of the case, or part of it, at the same time. It made people think he didn't know where he was going. Bob Stanfield is exactly the same way. I have a feeling that this is a real handicap. But if it's your nature, it's pretty hard not to do it. And if you try to do it by appearing to be cocksure when you really aren't, people will see it's a fraud. And this was the thing that bothered me most about Pearson's leadership.

It was fine in the House, it didn't do us any harm in the House at all, because there you're supposed to be debating things. But on television it was not good, not effective. And I suspect that if he could have overcome this, if he could have overcome it naturally, he wouldn't have had any trouble getting a majority in 1962 or 1963 or 1965, regardless of how badly the campaign might have been conducted,

KEITH DAVEY

We tried to make him more effective on television. Our TV guy in those days was Bob Chrone, who had a company called Film House, and he and Mr. Pearson got along extremely well. I think to say we schooled him would overstate the case. I think we worked with him. I remember one "Nation's Business," and I don't know when in the Pearson years this was; I can't actually recall. But I remember we went out to the CBC studios and we said to Mr. Pearson, "Here it is. Why don't you just run through it, and we won't film it. We'll film it after you go through it once. We won't take any pictures. Relax and just go through it for timing and so on." He did, and we did film it. And we said, "Okay, now go ahead and do it. You're on camera." We turned on the camera, and of course he was just dreadful. But he was pretty good on the one that he didn't know was going to be [filmed], and so we used that one.

Television was beginning to become extremely important. Mr. Pearson had a number of mannerisms which were very difficult. For example, we knew from the polls that people thought he was a smart-aleck. Now, Mr. Pearson was probably the least smart-aleck I've ever known in my life. He just wasn't. That wasn't his style to be a smart-aleck. And I think one of the reasons was he had a mannerism—he would be on television and he would say, "The unemployment statistics are really bad this month," and then he would smile. Which was a mannerism, you see, but that was bad.

There were all kinds of little things. When he closed his fist he'd keep his thumb outside his fist. We used to try to get him to put his thumb in—"You don't want your thumb sticking out; put it in there." Those are little things. I doubt that's changing his image. I think those are ways to make him a more formidable kind of a political figure.

We used to say in those days that if Mr. Pearson could meet every person in Canada informally, he'd score a landslide, which was true. But unhappily, that wasn't possible. The closest we could come was on television, and the trick with Mr. Pearson on television was to get him to relax. And we did that in various ways and used various techniques. I mentioned one. Another one was the interview—we used the interview technique frequently.

RICHARD O'HAGAN

We practiced him in front of television. We tried to get him working with teleprompters. We tried to make him more at ease in the mechanical environment of television. He had a tremendous self-consciousness in the midst of television apparatus. Unlike many public men, he found it difficult to elevate himself, to motivate himself to give a spirited statement or deliver a speech with vigour sitting isolated in front of a television camera. He found it all terribly impersonal. So it took some doing to put him at some sort of ease in this environment.

There was a constant comparison, even an unconscious comparison, with Mr. Diefenbaker, who was a powerful orator and had a very arresting presentational style—and this heightened Mr. Pearson's own self-consciousness. It made it difficult for us to believe that he could meet this challenge by going his own way. He didn't have a very strong voice, and a slight lisp which bothered many people and tended to make his presentations less forceful. And there was a period when his formal statements were looked at from the standpoint of trying to eliminate too many vowels so that the lisp wasn't too pronounced.

It was no wonder that at times he felt that he was the subject of almost endless experiment. But he was enormously patient, but then occasionally he would just say: "I don't want to hear any more of this. I'm just going to make my own speech in the way I want."

J. J. GREENE

One of Mr. Pearson's *bêtes noires* was that people were trying to make him into a Kennedy when that wasn't his bag. He had a *modus operandi* of his own which might have worked—consensus. It worked in international affairs, and I think had he been left to his own devices to try and evolve this technique in a parliamentary sense, it might have worked. It would have been difficult with Mr. Diefenbaker there in the House because he was not one to compromise. But they did try to make a Kennedy out of Mr. Pearson, and I think that was a great tragedy. That's one thing you can't do is change. If they don't like you the way you are, well, then, you'd better become a plumber or something more respectable. I can remember poor John Wintermeyer, who was a coeval in provincial affairs; they even tried to teach him to talk like Kennedy. Gave him a Boston accent. And he was no orator on his own, but he'd have done much better without the Boston accent.

The reorganisation of the party was completed with the holding of the 1960 Kingston Conference, followed by the National Rally in January, 1961, and the appointment of a new director who took over the headquarters on May 15, 1961. The Liberals were ready to challenge the government. By now Judy LaMarsh had been elected as the Member for Niagara Falls, but the Liberals were short of good debaters and most of the parliamentary skirmishing was done by a corporal's guard, which included the veterans—Pearson, Chevrier, Martin, and Pickersgill, who came to be known as the Four Horsemen. Every day, when the House met, the Four Horsemen were up, hammering away at unemployment, unemployment, unemployment, until the Conservatives protested with catcalls. It was a demonstration of how effective a few disciplined and determined Members could be. They were helped by the fact that Prime Minister Diefenbaker kept attacking the Liberals as if he were still in the Opposition.

GEORGE McILRAITH

As Prime Minister, Mr. Diefenbaker tended to want to criticise and destroy the Liberals, whom he had thoroughly defeated at the last election, a past event; and he was spending his time presenting legislation on quite an important subject, maybe timely legislation, trying to defeat further the Liberals. This began to emerge in the public mind. You could see this developing, this negativism. And the success Mr. Diefenbaker had in demolishing Mr. Pearson politically in the January '58 speech he seemed to follow as a pattern, because it had worked that once. There's no use wasting your effort destroying something that had been destroyed. And he and the government tended to do this to a very great extent.

He was whipping a dead horse, which is putting it rather harshly, and the public began to catch on to this, and eventually the media caught on to it. The media in that instance were behind the public. It was quite interesting to watch.

MAURICE LAMONTAGNE

We were quite sure the moment we would make a proposal in the House that Mr. Diefenbaker would reject it immediately, so that gave us a great freedom to work. We knew that by being positive, this was probably the best way to attract new blood to the party as candidates. So this is how we proceeded, both in the House and elsewhere. I knew and Mr. Pearson knew that he would never be a great Leader of the Opposition. He was not partisan enough to do that. It was not in his own personality and character. So we started to develop this kind of strategy. That didn't mean that we didn't criticise. Of course, we did. But we always took care to be as positive as we could.

J. W. PICKERSGILL

He [Pearson] was a superb Leader of the Opposition. Of all the various careers he had, that was the one in which he was most successful. To take fifty people—because when Paul Hellyer won that by-election we got up to fifty—to take fifty people with no hope of winning for ten years, keep them together, organise them as a team, get them to consult every day before they went into the

House instead of working at sixes and sevens, to get people stimulated all over the country to support the party, was a simply tremendous achievement. It was something that very few people could have done. I would never say that Pearson was a great Parliamentarian because no one would believe me. He occasionally was good at Parliament but as a day-to-day Parliamentarian he was not much above mediocre, but he was a superb captain of a team.

As a result of varied and detailed surveys that Lou Harris had conducted, Walter Gordon, who had been named campaign chairman, and Keith Davey were able to devise a strategy for the election, which was called for June 18, 1962. The polls showed that despite their efforts to remake the Leader—and they had made changes—he was no match for Diefenbaker. So they decided to play up the team rather than the man. The Pearson Team. It was a fairly obvious response, and the Four Horsemen could have told them that the main issue was unemployment. But Davey was pleased that the scientific technique that they were using had turned this up. Seven of ten Canadians, he said, disagreed with Mr. Diefenbaker on unemployment, no matter what he would say about it. The Harris surveys showed that this was the first issue of concern in Canada, and Davey thought that this was fortunate because Kennedy had had to go to the sixth issue, which was America's image abroad, before finding one on which the Republicans had a negative rating. That was the strategic side of the Liberal campaign.

The organisational side, according to Keith Davey, was a school of practical politics which he and Charles Templeton, a former evangelist, ran. There were half a dozen of these campaign colleges where papers were presented on such matters as fund-raising, door-to-door canvassing, and advertising. Tom Kent joined the Leader as speech writer and travelled with him throughout the campaign.

Of course, The Pearson team included the veterans, Lionel Chevrier, Paul Martin, Jack Pickersgill, Paul Hellyer, and George McIlraith, but tended to feature the newcomers such as Walter Gordon, Mitchell Sharp, Maurice Sauvé, John Nicholson of Vancouver, and C. M. Bud Drury of Montreal, all of whom had some experience in the Ottawa bureaucracy. There was also Hazen Argue, the CCF Leader, who had crossed the floor of the House and joined the Liberals after his failure to win the leadership of the new party, to be called the New Democratic Party; Jack

Davis, the economist engineer from British Columbia, and Harry Hays,
the mayor of Calgary. Keith Davey put some of the younger members of
the team, Rick Cashin from Newfoundland, Pauline Jewett, and Larry
Pennell, on a bus and used a film of them alighting as one of the party's
television commercials. Red Kelly, the Toronto Maple Leafs' star, was
the most celebrated member of the team, and Davey told how he got him to
join.

KEITH DAVEY

I knew Red [Kelly] a little bit, and Red is a very superior person,
a very fine person. He's a great Canadian. And I persuaded Red to
run in York West, which we'd never won. But he had great
misgivings about it, so a meeting was duly set up at the Park Plaza
[Hotel] in Toronto with Red Kelly, Mike Pearson, and me. We
had lunch. Of course, Mr. Pearson was a great, great sports fan.
Indeed, I remember many meetings with Gordon and Pearson
when Pearson and I would start out with a hockey or baseball
discussion. And Walter would say, "Look, I didn't come here all
the way from Toronto to hear you guys talk about hockey. Let's
get on with it."

In any event, Mr. Pearson was almost in awe of Red Kelly. He
walked into the room and here was Red Kelly—he couldn't
believe it. Red's a very sincere guy and he said, "Look, Mr.
Pearson, Keith is trying to persuade me that I should do this, but I
just wonder how on earth can I play hockey and be a Member of
Parliament at the same time. I think it's just about impossible."

Well, my heart sank to my boots when I heard Mr. Pearson say,
"I agree with you, Red. I don't see how you can do both. It's just
not sensible." I hustled Mr. Pearson back out to the airport, put
him on the airplane, with visions of how Dief would have handled
the situation, knowing Dief, and I started all over again with Red,
and never let Mr. Pearson near him until he got the nomination.

Just to show how much Mr. Pearson changed by the '63
campaign, I was in the Chateau Laurier with Red. There was some
kind of a Liberal convention on, and he said, "Look, Keith, I really
don't think I want to run this time." And I said, "Look, Red, what
you've really got to do is talk to Pearson." At which point, as if on
cue although it certainly wasn't arranged, Mr. Pearson walked

into the room. I described what had been happening and Red told him about wanting to quit, but now Mr. Pearson said, "Look, Red, I need you, I want you to run for me." Kelly did and won again. That's a measure, I think, of how Mr. Pearson had developed politically in that period of time.

MAURICE LAMONTAGNE

We were well prepared for the 1962 election in terms of our platform; and we had decided that we would go to the people with that platform and with Mike as our Leader. It would be the Pearson team as opposed to the Diefenbaker party. I think that these two approaches fitted very well the characters of the two leaders—Mr. Pearson as the leader of a team and Mr. Diefenbaker standing more or less alone by himself.

From '61 to '62, Mr. Gordon was very active in recruiting new people in Ontario. I was active in trying to recruit new people in Quebec. At that time I had tried to persuade Jean Marchand to run in '62. He felt that the time had not come yet to go into politics. I found a riding for Maurice Sauvé in Îles de la Madeleine because I was more or less in charge of the organisation for the whole Quebec [City] district, and Mr. Chevrier was in Montreal. I ran again in Quebec East in '62 and was again defeated, because this was the Social Credit phenomenon. [Social Credit won twenty six seats in Quebec.] We elected only five Members from the whole Quebec [City] district in the 1962 election.

LIONEL CHEVRIER

I think that the Créditistes were using, to the nth degree, this slogan of Caouette's—"You had the Liberals; you know what they're like, and not so long ago. You had the Conservatives; you see what they do when they get in office. You can't do worse by voting for us." And a lot of people did, particularly in the country ridings.

WALTER GORDON

Keith Davey was in Ottawa full time and he was on the telephone to me two or three times a day. I was trying to get elected in [Toronto] Davenport. I was travelling around Ontario helping other people get elected, and I also travelled around in the West and in the Maritimes—not so much, but a bit. But Davey and I had a very good working arrangement.

TOM KENT

It's always hard for anybody who is closely involved to be quite sure that he is being objective, but trying to be objective, I would have thought there was no doubt that the '62 election was a well-run election. After all, a party that had been so utterly defeated in '58 came very close to regaining equality with the government party after only four years. It was a well-run election by any technical standards. But I don't think one would say the same about any of Mr. Pearson's other elections.

KEITH DAVEY

We had a great momentum in '62. That campaign peaked at its opening. I've been in campaigns which have never peaked at all. I believe we opened in Charlottetown. We got out almost two weeks ahead of Dief, if I recall correctly. It has to be remembered that we were coming from fifty seats, and we turned around in that election, I think 116 seats or 106, whichever it was. I forget. [Liberals won ninety-nine seats; Liberal Labor, one.] It was more than a hundred. But in any event, the point is that Dief suffered a landslide defeat.

We ran out of steam toward the end of the campaign. That's really what I'm saying, but that was inevitable because we'd gone so hard so fast.

Election night, 1962, Mr. Pearson came to the Liberal Federation [headquarters in Ottawa]. I remember very very well I said, "Oh gosh," I was all excited and I said, "Gee, we just got word in Spadina that John Bassett [Toronto newspaper publisher] had lost," and he said, "Oh, that's marvellous." And the two people he asked about . . . he said, "Did Red Kelly win in York West?" I said, "Yes, he did." Then the other one he asked about was Dave Walker [former Diefenbaker Minister] and I said, "No, Don Macdonald won." And he said, "Oh boy, that's terrific." That was the other one he was extremely interested in.

About midnight he came into where I was in the campaign headquarters and he said, "Look, Keith, I planned if I lost this election that I was going to quit, and I know that it was your intention to go back to Toronto after the campaign to resume your private life, but you and I are football fans, and it turns out it's half-time, and I'm staying on for the second half, and I'm just automatically assuming that you're with me." And so the decision was made that I would stay.

One of the hundred Liberals elected in 1962 was Ralph Cowan, who had known Lester Pearson as a boy in Peterborough and had been one of his students when he was professor of history at the University of Toronto. Cowan was so close to the Pearson family that Lester's younger brother, Vaughan, appeared with him at two or three Liberal gatherings, and Lester's aged mother attended a garden party on Cowan's behalf on the Saturday before election day. The Leader had agreed to his mother's going to this affair, if she was well enough, and, according to Cowan, she spent a couple of hours in the garden of the old people's home, known as Beech Hall Apartments, in Toronto. A couple of months later the elderly Mrs. Pearson died; she was ninety-four years old.

There was a meeting of the Liberal M.P.s in Ottawa shortly after the election, and Cowan recalled that they had a buffet dinner in the parliamentary restaurant, which had been opened especially for them since the House of Commons was not sitting. He said that Lester Pearson made a point of coming and sitting beside him at his table. However, the friendship was not to last.

RALPH COWAN

I never knew until I got to Ottawa in 1962 that the Liberal Party is simply run by the Quebec Bloc, lock, stock, and barrel. I had thought the Liberal Party was a party of conviction from coast to coast, but when you have a solid block of votes like Quebec delivers and five or six similar seats out of northern New Brunswick and one you can usually count on out of Manitoba, it's not a national party at all, it's one block securing its will.

Beside the bilingual pledge with its appeal to French Canada, Pearson took another initiative before the 1963 election that would have an impact on the voters. The Diefenbaker Government was being torn apart over the question of nuclear warheads for the Bomarc missiles and other armaments, and there were charges that Canada was not living up to its commitments with its allies. The Liberals had gone on record as being opposed to nuclear weapons, and it was assumed that this was the only position that a Nobel Peace Prize winner could take. But there were public and political pressures: a contemporary Gallup Poll showed a majority of Canadians in favour of accepting the warheads. At the end of 1962 Paul Hellyer returned from a NATO Parliamentary Association meeting in Paris and told his Leader that the Canadian troops in Europe whom he had visited were fed up with the situation, and so were the NATO allies. Mr. Pearson began to waver.

On January 12, 1963, he spoke in Scarborough, a suburb of Toronto, and said that a Liberal government would discharge the commitments regarding nuclear weapons under NATO and NORAD agreements, thus reversing Liberal policy. His speech came as a surprise to his colleagues because he had not consulted them. It had two immediate consequences: it hastened the collapse of the Diefenbaker Government and it led to the loss of Quebec labour leader Jean Marchand as a candidate and to Pierre Trudeau's bitter denunciations.

PAUL HELLYER

When I had been over in the first NATO trip in '55, when the NATO Parliamentary Association was just beginning, the morale of the Canadian armed forces had been very very high. They'd just gotten a souped-up Sabre and it was superior to the American, and they were just gung ho, tails-up, and very proud to be Canadians and very proud of their contribution to the Alliance.

Then, when I went over the next time, the attitude was just the opposite. They were tails-down, and they were dispirited and they were disheartened. They felt that Canada had defaulted on its commitments, they told me, almost ashamed to go in the mess at night for fear they would have to talk to officers of other countries and explain to them why Canada was defaulting on its obligations. It was this contrast which affected me so much. When I came back I reported this to Mr. Pearson privately, and I reported to a senior group of the party at a dinner meeting in the New Zealand Room off the parliamentary dining room.

Subsequently, I made a speech at Walkerton [Ont.] at a political meeting, where I personally took the stand that we should reverse our policy. I deliberately didn't advise Mr. Pearson in advance that I was going to do this. It was in effect flying a kite, but it was a decision I made, not one that he made. I took my speech to Walkerton and put a copy in the mail to him so he would have it simultaneously with the speech but wouldn't have the chance to be able to find me and say, "Don't do it," because I had decided that in the interests of the country it had to be done.

My speech really started a wider national discussion of the issues, which went on for some weeks, and during that time Mr. Pearson had a number of inputs.

Then, someone else told him almost exactly the same thing that I did, and I'm not sure who this was. I know that Dick Malone, the publisher of the *Globe and Mail,* claims to be that person. But I don't know. I never was told by Mr. Pearson, nor have I seen on any paper or document who it was. But he did say that someone else had told him practically the same thing.

Just at the turn of the year, John Gelner [military analyst] wrote me a letter in which he said, although he was very reluctant to do so, for reasons which I well understood, that he had come to the conclusion that there was really no alternative to the policy that I had set out. He felt that Canada had to live up to its commitments, even if in fact they were not the right commitments and that others should have been made. We had an obligation to fulfill them until we could negotiate new ones. I took advantage of Mr. Pearson in the sense that I knew that probably Gelner's opinion rated higher in his mind than mine and I sent him a copy of that letter. I know it was during the holiday period because my secretary had to stay late to type it and was not too pleased about it, and I sent it by hand to Mr. Pearson.

It was over that weekend that he made up his mind because he phoned Jack Pickersgill the day after the holiday, and said, "I finally decided." During the next ten days he wrote the Scarborough speech, which, to a large extent, was paraphrased from what I had said at Walkerton.

GEORGE McILRAITH

I certainly encouraged him in that Scarborough speech to make the change [in nuclear policy], and went over it with him twice. I had two distinct discussions with him alone, and I think the last one was on the morning he delivered the speech. He had his text right there and went over what he proposed to say in precise terms, and there was little change made in the phraseology.

Lubor Zink, a columnist for the Toronto Telegram, *had also attempted to act as an intermediary between the Opposition Leader and Prime Minister Diefenbaker—Zink had got to know Pearson well, largely because of the latter's interest in the fate of Jan Masaryk, the Foreign Minister of Czechoslovakia for whom Lubor had worked before fleeing the Communists.*

LUBOR ZINK

I tried very hard to persuade Pearson to change his attitude on the nuclear warheads situation and I think he started really listening after the Cuban Crisis. As we all know, Paul Hellyer was working on him in exactly the same way, which I didn't know at that time, and maybe it was Paul who persuaded him. Maybe it was the combination of circumstances and what Paul was doing and what I was trying to tell him—all these things put together. Anyway, he was far more receptive after the Cuban Crisis, and after [General Lauris] Norstad came to say good-bye as Commander-in-Chief of NATO; he told a press conference at Uplands Airport that Canada was not fulfilling her role and could not fulfill the role unless she accepted nuclear warheads.

At my next meeting with Pearson we discussed this whole situation all over again and Pearson started saying, "If only Diefenbaker were willing to change his attitude, I would be glad to support him wholeheartedly and this whole thing could be taken out of the political arena and the country could have a sane defence policy again, and I wish somebody would tell him," and I offered to do it. I think that Pearson opened this line of arguing for me to make the offer, that he didn't want to ask, but was wishing I would volunteer.

Although I was not on very good terms with Diefenbaker at that time, on account of his defence policy and chiefly on account of his support of what I regarded as a completely disastrous foreign policy, I said I would try to convey this message to him, which I did. It took me a few days to catch Dief alone and I wasn't even able to finish outlining what Pearson was offering—but I'm sure Dief got the message all right—before he said he was not interested in what Mr. Pearson is doing or thinking or what he intends to do.

Pearson told me at that time that unless Diefenbaker changed his position, he had already made up his mind and he was going to make a major speech during which he would announce a switch in the Liberal Party's stand on nuclear warheads.

PAUL MARTIN

A political leader, in Government or in Opposition, has to take a lone position sometime. The nature of consultation can be stifling and arresting. I suppose [Pearson] felt that there had to be a change in this thing and it had to be done as he did it. I see that he did discuss it with Paul Hellyer. That I didn't know really until I read it in the third inadequate volume [of Pearson's memoirs]. I think he was right.

I didn't think so at the time, and I told him so in no uncertain manner. When I heard his speech in Toronto I was flabbergasted because I thought that the role we had taken on nuclear weapons was a very sensible role, one that was in keeping with our whole nuclear policy, the position that Mr. King had taken when he and Atlee met with Truman in 1947. We were a nuclear power but we were going to use our nuclear knowledge and capacity only for peaceful purposes.

But the fact is that the Diefenbaker Government did commit Canada, at NATO and to the President of the United States. And that I was able to ascertain when I became Foreign Minister. While I didn't have the positive proofs after Pearson's speech that that was the case, Pearson did convince me that it was the case. And it did take some time for some of us to acknowledge that if there had been a commitment made, there was a national obligation to honour that commitment.

MAURICE LAMONTAGNE

I think that the speech, irrespective of its content, provoked the immediate downfall of the Diefenbaker Government. The Diefenbaker Government would have gone anyway; it was a matter of weeks. We were living week by week or even day by day in the House of Commons in those days. But it was the immediate cause of the downfall, so that was the positive side.

On the negative side, I was working in the province of Quebec trying to get Jean Marchand to run, and when that speech appeared in the press I was in discussion with Mr. Pelletier and Mr. Trudeau and Jean Marchand at that very time. Jean Marchand was not particularly worried—he was too practical for this—by the speech, but Mr. Trudeau and Mr. Pelletier were very worried. They were intellectuals, so they could not reconcile themselves with that kind of policy. Mr. Trudeau was very much against nuclear weapons. He was less against it later on because he accepted the same policy when he joined the Liberal Party two years later. But again, that's politics. So as a result of this, Jean Marchand didn't get the advice and support he expected from Mr. Pelletier and Mr. Trudeau, and decided not to run in that election.

I think that that decision cost us in Quebec perhaps four, five, or six ridings. So that the net result of the speech was to destroy the Diefenbaker Government, but at the same time the negative aspect was that without the speech we might have formed a majority government in 1963, and this might have changed the whole behaviour and the whole spirit of the first Pearson Government.

JEAN MARCHAND

The first time I met [Mr. Pearson] he said there would be no nuclear weapons: "This is against our program." But when he came back from a trip to England, he had changed his mind.

After we read the statement on the warheads made in Scarborough, we met—I don't know if we had a formal meeting or we just got in touch together—we said, "Well, we surely cannot run into those circumstances." Except Guy Favreau,* who

---

*Besides Trudeau and Pelletier, Marchand's friends included Favreau, who was a Liberal candidate in 1963.

said, "I have not this kind of opposition to running, even if we're going to accept Bomarcs in Canada."

I met Mr. Pearson in Quebec City to tell him why I was in opposition to running, because nobody would forgive me in Quebec if, after taking such a strong stand against nuclear weapons, the following day or the following week or month or two later I joined the Liberal Party that had just accepted the American nuclear weapons here in Canada. I said, "I cannot, because I cannot defend myself, so it's impossible. Maybe you have good reasons to do it."

"Well," he said, "you know, I'm sure that we will be in power at the next election. I'll be the Prime Minister of Canada, and I have to assume full responsibility for that," and so forth. Well, I said, "I recognise this role, that probably you're right. But I cannot share your responsibility."

WALTER GORDON

He did not consult me before the speech reversing nuclear policy. What was my attitude?. I was very surprised. I didn't agree with his arguments. I didn't think he should have reversed that policy, which had been approved by the Rally, without consulting at least the caucus, and in some ways you can say that that reversal cost Mike Pearson a majority in the '63 election. If Trudeau and, more importantly, Marchand had been with him in that election, I think he would have got enough votes to win, because the nuclear-arms issue was not all that important to the public.

His reversal of the policy did stir up more controversy in the Conservative ranks and it did lead to Harkness' resignation, I guess. So you can argue that it brought down the Diefenbaker Government sooner than otherwise would have occurred. But it was going to happen within a few weeks anyway.

Many people thought that this would be the issue on which he'd win the election. And he talked a lot about it until we went to him and said, "Look, this isn't the issue that people are most concerned about. If you want to win the election, you've got to go back to talking about the grubby bread-and-butter issues. How are you going to put people back to work?" So eventually he eased off on the nuclear issue.

But it was very upsetting to me that he would make such a change in policy without consulting some of his close advisors. You know, everybody has been guessing as to who did advise him. I am sure Hellyer advised him. It didn't seem to me that Hellyer was the man that you should necessarily look to for wisdom on a lot of things. I don't know who else there was. I think he probably made up his own mind. He had just come from New York, and he may have seen some of his friends there who talked about it. I don't know. He never told me.

TOM KENT

I certainly had considerable doubts about the wisdom of it [the reversal of the nuclear policy]. Although I know Mr. Pearson always felt that it was a great political success and helped to bring down the Diefenbaker Government, I think my analysis would be that the Diefenbaker Government at that point was destroyed anyway. While it may have slightly accelerated the final event, it didn't really have any causative influence. I think that if that issue had not been fought in that way, Mr. Pearson would probably have had a majority in 1963 instead of a minority. Remember the campaign. Diefenbaker was far more successful in defending himself on that issue than Mike was in putting it across.

It was a very difficult dilemma. I had a great deal of sympathy with the Pearson position in the form of saying—we've built our defence policy on this, we've made commitments which are pointless unless we do have nuclear weapons. Therefore, to contract out, to withdraw from having them, is unforgivable. I think one must recognise the force of that case. On the other hand, if it was a great mistake ever to have nuclear weapons at all, which had been Mr. Pearson's own previous position, you really don't make it right by suddenly coming out and saying that we should have them. I think politically it was an issue on which he lost more than he gained.

CHRISTOPHER YOUNG

I was at that point the editor of a newspaper [Ottawa *Citizen*] which had been taking a very strong position against taking nuclear weapons, and we were also supporting the Liberal Party, so that we got caught in a situation where they reversed themselves and of course we weren't going to reverse ourselves. We continued to argue that they shouldn't accept nuclear weapons, and I think that was right.

Pearson's argument, even privately, was that although he had been opposed to nuclear weapons, a commitment had been made by the government and it had got so far then that it had to be carried through. I didn't find that very persuasive, personally, but he would argue that. On the other hand, he would sometimes give a wry grin and admit that the Gallup Poll figures on the subject, which showed that the Canadian people thought that Canada should discharge its commitment, was also part of his calculations. As it was with Dief, but in the other direction. He got scared off by the peace movement and thousands of signatures against the bomb, and that was very much a political swing in his case. Pearson was as capable as any other political leader of taking a pretty practical vote-counting decision on the matter.

As Lester Pearson recognised, the 1963 election was the second half of the 1962 election, just as the 1958 election had been the second half of the 1957 election. It had taken two elections to turn the Liberals out of office and achieve the great Conservative majority, and two elections to reduce that and restore the Liberals but in a minority role. The Scarborough speech on January 12 had shaken the Diefenbaker Government, and some three weeks later it was defeated in the House of Commons; Parliament was dissolved and an election was called for April 8, 1963.

Walter Gordon and Keith Davey were ready and so was the Pearson team, which was being dubbed "the team of all the talents" by a friendly press, but the Liberal campaign never seemed to get going. There were complaints that Keith Davey and the others in charge were obsessed with The Making of The President *and the Kennedy election and relied too much on gimmicks. There had been gimmicks in the 1962 campaign, but the "Diefenbuck" lampooning the devalued Canadian dollar was effective in deflating the Conservative colossus, whereas the Truth Squad and the other gimmicks of the 1963 campaign backfired. Then, John Diefenbaker, who had done little or nothing to save himself and his Government, was like a giant revived on the hustings.*

KEITH DAVEY

The Truth Squad was an idea which . . . gosh, I'm the guy that should know. There are all kinds of suggestions about where it came from. The Truth Squad, in fact, came from Winnipeg, and it came through the Winnipeg *Free Press*. Someone at the *Free Press* phoned a Liberal in Manitoba — and I won't say who the Liberal was in Manitoba because I can't be sure. But he phoned me and put the idea to me, and I thought it was a pretty good idea, and, in retrospect it was very sound, but we made a couple of mistakes.

"Squad" had a Gestapo-like connotation which was a terrible title for it, and indeed "Truth Squad" was just the wrong name, and we did it the wrong way. The way we should have done it was to have had a press conference in Ottawa and announce that we've had someone travelling with Mr. Diefenbaker for the last week and a half, and Mr. Diefenbaker said these things and we don't think they're right. We think these are the facts. And if we had done it that way, I think it would have been a very successful venture. But instead we did it right up front with this terrible name, which really called Dief a liar—which I think in retrospect he probably was, but you just didn't say it. Then, the person picked to head the Truth Squad was Judy [LaMarsh].

Diefenbaker was such a remarkable campaigner—I have enormous respect for him as a campaigner, and I like him as a person, as a matter of fact—he just turned that thing to his advantage. As soon as it was apparent what was happening, when the thing really did so disastrously, I came to Toronto and offered to resign. I saw Mr. Pearson at the Park Plaza Hotel and I said, "Look, I'll resign." He, of course, wouldn't hear of that.

GEORGE McILRAITH

I remember expressing myself to my wife and whatever children were around the house when the Truth Squad thing came out and was reported in the paper, and I'm afraid my expressions were not moderate or temperate. They were disastrous and quite improper techniques to use in any national election by any party, and as far as I'm concerned not to be countenanced. Those are rather strong views on the subject, but they're my views.

Walter Gordon and Keith Davey were in command of the party at that time and one of their failures was they didn't co-operate with local candidates throughout the country—we were considered local candidates. They rather regarded themselves as being the great national proponents of party doctrine and overevaluated the advertising media, quite overevaluated it, as if they were selling a product, a physical product in the biggest centres of population. And, of course, it did work, if I remember correctly, in the Toronto area where you have a great density of population and that kind of advertising reaches them. It worked very poorly in the areas where that kind of advertising never reaches them. If you look at our Ontario results in that election, you'll find that a very disproportionate number of our Members came from the Toronto city area, and we did badly in equally or more Liberal areas throughout southwestern Ontario. That was due to a wrong assessment of the value of certain of the advertising media, an overuse of it and an underevaluation of the method of reaching people in all the other local constituencies.

PAUL MARTIN

Mike made courageous and strong speeches in answer to Diefenbaker, and I used to tell him, "But you're not hitting him hard; you're giving him a jab here, and a jab on the shoulder and so on, but you're not going after him like he's going after you. This is a courtroom battle. He's going at the jugular, and you're going at his hair." "Well," he said, "how would you do it?"

Actually, one time, we were in a room together and we did actually go through the experiment of how to do it, and he said, "Well, I can't do that. I just can't do that."

KEITH DAVEY

It was on or about St. Patrick's Day, and our campaign hit rock bottom. We had purchased network time on television in Quebec on a Sunday afternoon—Mr. Pearson was to be on the network from five o'clock for half an hour to make a speech. By the time they got through the introduction of the county chairman and the aldermen and every local person in the room, and Mr. Pearson finally got to make his speech, it was past five-thirty and the purchased television time had elapsed. We were pretty scared. Our numbers were down, we were doing very badly, and something had to be done. And I was the one who came up with the hundred days of decision. And everybody agreed that was a great idea. Because I said, "It's going to be a hundred days of decision, and we'll just announce every day what we're going to do."

WALTER GORDON

I flew down to Halifax where [Pearson] was, to see him, to try and sell him on this [hundred days of decision]. He and his wife looked depressed and exhausted. They were fed up with campaigning. I talked to them long enough to get them changed around and then I came out with Davey's suggestion. "Oh, I couldn't do that. Everybody would realise that was the hundred days before the Battle of Waterloo."

I said, "Mike, 99 percent of the people in Canada have never heard of the Battle of Waterloo, and if they had, they couldn't care less. There are a few, but it would be a small percentage who would know about the hundred days of decision after Roosevelt got in, and that might be a good thing."

"No," he said, "as an old history professor I couldn't do that. You are quite wrong; everybody knows about the hundred days leading up to the Battle of Waterloo."

We argued about that for a while and he finally said he'd go for the idea, but he wouldn't stick to the hundred days; it had to be some other period. The hard thing was to get him off external affairs and nuclear weapons and onto domestic issues, and he finally agreed to do this. We listed them — one a day — what he'd have to speak about, and we agreed that we'd get some stuff together, and I left.

He said he'd call me within a day or two as to the number of days he was going to put on this tag, and he did; he said, "Sixty." I said, "Oh, God, that's shortening it down too much." Or I think I did; I can't remember. "No," he said. He'd settled it in his mind that's what he was going to do. We'd got the rest of what we wanted, and we couldn't change it anyway, you know. After all, he was the Leader. So that was that.

LUBOR ZINK

Once I caught [Pearson] in a very, very depressed mood and he was also exhausted and altogether downcast. It was in Montreal in his room in the Queen Elizabeth Hotel. We were there alone and he was lying on his bed and we were talking about the outcome of the election. During the conversation I tried to explore the various possibilities and one of them was what he would do if the two parties came out neck and neck, pretty close. His answer, and I used it as a quote in a column I wrote, and I think I should read the quote—it was reprinted about a week or two weeks later in *Time* magazine. Now here is the quote:

"Unless we have a workable majority I'll resign and hope that Mr. Diefenbaker will do the same. There are no unbridgeable differences between the two parties and new younger men on both sides, and I mean new men, not the old guard, might be able to join forces and give the country the strong stable government it needs so badly."

VIC MACKIE

I remember his saying if we don't get a majority, Mr. Diefenbaker and I should resign. But I don't remember his going so far as to say we need a coalition government. It was in Montreal he said this; we were up having a drink with him in his hotel room.

That was one of the problems with Mike. He liked to talk off the record to a group of press people about maybe what the future was going to bring and he would do this freely with those whom he knew, and then when he went on campaign and he had a lot of strange reporters with him whom he didn't know too well, sometimes he'd lapse into doing this with them. Naturally the fellows would want to know what they could do, and there'd be a great discussion in the press bureau: was this supposed to be off the record or on the record? Some people would write it and others wouldn't. They were awkward situations which caused his press secretary headaches. But typical of the man—he used to like to talk freely to people, with the idea that they weren't making notes and quoting everything he said. But that changed gradually as the microphones appeared and everything he said was taken down word for word. It had to stop.

RICHARD O'HAGAN

Mr. Pearson made these observations at a sort of small reception for reporters in Montreal, if I remember. It was one of those hypotheses that he had a tendency to respond to, and it gave rise to the notion that he might be seriously entertaining this [the idea of a national government], which in turn was seen as a reflection of lack of confidence on his part that he would attain a majority. That was controversial. It caused some very real difficulty, all right. Subsequently we put out a statement in Vancouver in which we denied that Mr. Pearson was thinking in those terms.

LUBOR ZINK

I know that Dick [O'Hagan] was fuming. Dick was terribly mad when this column appeared.

Let me quote what *Time* magazine said: "So little did Zink consider the value of the Pearson quotes that he waited a week before casually bringing them into a column." The magazine quoted me—"I only used it to illustrate that Pearson is a sensible man. I had no idea of upsetting anything or betraying any confidence." *Time* went on:

"As Diefenbaker hopped on the story as evidence that the Liberals had given up hope of winning a majority, Pearson characteristically seemed more concerned with the strain of his friendship with Zink than the damage to the Liberal campaign, but he issued a flat denial."

Many people, including Bruce Hutchison, the West Coast writer and editor who was a good friend of Mike Pearson, and some Ontario Tories, believed that the Conservatives would be wiped out, that they would be lucky to retain thirty-nine seats, which was the number that R. B. Bennett held after the 1935 election. How was it then that Mr. Pearson failed to get a majority in the April 8 election? Certain Liberals, including the prime movers at the time, Walter Gordon and Maurice Lamontagne, felt that Mr. Pearson's reversal of the nuclear policy was a fatal blow in that it lost them the important Quebec candidates; Tom Kent furthermore felt that it put Pearson on the defensive. There is no doubt that the Liberal campaign was badly run, whereas Mr. Diefenbaker,alone and unencumbered, put on a superb campaign.

MITCHELL SHARP

My guess is that what prevented him [from getting a majority] was the problem that has dogged our footsteps ever since, and that is the difficulty of winning seats in Western Canada, particularly on the prairies. There is something about Western opinion about the Liberal Party that persists, that it is the party of the Eastern Establishment. It was what gained Mr. Diefenbaker power indeed, when he rose so rapidly to power, and that enabled him to hold ninety-five seats in the election of 1963. It was his appearance as the man who stood up for Western interests against the Eastern Establishment.

KEITH DAVEY

Our majority wasn't lost on the prairies; it was lost on the Atlantic. I was extremely optimistic in Nova Scotia. We had won six seats in '62, and I thought we could win eight or nine in '63. We had the biggest rally which has ever been held in Nova Scotia in the Halifax Forum in the 1963 campaign. I did not understand in those days the tremendous leverage of [Premier] Bob Stanfield in Nova Scotia. But Bob Stanfield stayed out of the campaign until the last week or ten days, and then he came in with all of his provincial forces, and he literally did us in. Dief got his majority in Nova Scotia, and we got shut out in Prince Edward Island; we'd expected to win a couple of seats there.

J. W. PICKERSGILL

Everybody knows exactly why he didn't get a majority: because nobody paid any attention to the fact that there was a grass-roots movement of the really poor in French Canada which elected enough Members to put us four short of a majority. It had nothing to do with the contest between the Liberals and Conservatives. It perhaps is a certain reflection on our capacity to hold French Canada, in spite of what we'd done, but I don't think it was because of the loss of the few people that were concerned about nuclear weapons, because I'm practically sure most of those people who voted Social Credit didn't know what a nuclear weapon was and cared less.

There may have been many reasons why Mr. Pearson didn't get a majority, but there was only one reason why he got enough seats to form a government. That was a thick-set French Canadian MP named Yvon Dupuis who was an orator of the old school. And Mr. Pearson was to acknowledge his indebtedness to him both privately and in caucus. It was Maurice Lamontagne who realised that the main problem for the Liberals in French Canada was not the Conservatives or the Union Nationale but the Social Credit Party, which had won twenty-six Quebec seats in the 1962 election, and he picked Dupuis to carry the fight to Réal Caouette, the Créditiste leader who was no mean orator himself. Reporters covering the campaign, including myself, remarked on the way that Yvon Dupuis could bring an ugly and riotous crowd under control at a rally for Lester Pearson in Montreal.

MAURICE LAMONTAGNE

We had to organise that fight; we had to find somebody to carry the fight on as popular a basis as Réal Caouette did. That's why we selected Yvon Dupuis. He was a great speaker, a great popular speaker, and we developed a television series of thirteen programs for him. They were quite well prepared although the intellectual content was not very high.

I think that Dupuis did a very good job. I remember it was a subject of contention between myself and Mr. Chevrier, who thought that, when we found the money to put on these thirteen programs, Mr. Chevrier should be there and be speaking on all of them. I was quite sure that Mr. Chevrier or myself or anybody else couldn't do the kind of job which had to be done. And which Yvon Dupuis did.

YVON DUPUIS

They needed a man who was popular in the province, a debater, let's put it that way. It was not that I was happy to fight Caouette because personally I have lots of admiration for him as a man. But

Caouette was dangerous to the Liberal Party. He had elected twenty-six Members in '62. So the Quebec caucus chose me to be the answer to Réal Caouette. They had to find a fiery speaker. Supposedly I was.

I remember that meeting in Montreal. There was a group of antagonists in the hall who were trying to break it up—they were what you call hustlers in English. At any rate, I started to speak. I told them that this was a free country, that we had the right to speak, and if they didn't like it, they could get out. In a few moments the hustlers were quiet. Mr. Pearson thanked me for the intervention. I made a lot of speeches with him across the province. We toured Quebec together.

On several occasions after the election, he said that if it hadn't been for me, he wouldn't have taken power in Canada. He said, "Gee whiz, it was a good thing to have you, Yvon, in Quebec because we wouldn't be in power today, eh?" That's what he told me several times and he said so publicly in the caucus too. So he was aware of the importance of my participation in that specific year.

As a result of the strategy of pitting Yvon Dupuis against Réal Caouette, the Créditistes lost six seats and were down to twenty; the Liberals won forty-seven seats in Quebec but only three in the three prairie provinces. The results of the 1963 election: Liberals, one hundred and twenty-nine; Progressive Conservatives, ninety-five; New Democratic Party (NDP), seventeen; Social Credit, twenty-four.

4 Search for Security

THE LIBERALS WON the election but failed to get a majority, and for a few days after April 8, there was some uncertainty as to whether Lester B. Pearson would be able to form a government. It was a brief moment for plotting and planning combinations and coalitions, and attempts at improbable alliances. John Diefenbaker had the precedent that W. L. Mackenzie King had set in 1925: King had headed a minority government, just as Diefenbaker had done, and been soundly beaten by the Conservatives, who had won 116 seats, just a few short of a majority, to the Liberals' 101, and yet King had carried on with the help of the Progressives. The least that Prime Minister Diefenbaker was expected to do under the circumstances was to continue in office and leave the fate of his government to Parliament. Then, suddenly, over the radio on April 12, came the startling announcement that six Social Credit M.P.s had signed a declaration saying that they would support a Liberal government.

This was to become known as L'Affaire des Six and was to give rise to charges of bribery and corruption. It was to shake the Social Credit Party to its foundations and lead to a split between the followers of the leader, Robert Thompson, and the followers of the deputy leader, Réal Caouette, and the final break-up of the federal party. In the background of this affair was the shadowy figure of John Doyle, an American wheeler-dealer who was a protegé of Premier Joey Smallwood of Newfoundland and the Liberals; Doyle had also contributed to the election campaign funds of the

Tory Cabinet Minister, Pierre Sévigny. It was the latter who first heard of the affair and made it his business to find out what really happened.

Despite the fact that he had resigned from the Diefenbaker Cabinet, Pierre Sévigny ran as a Conservative in the 1963 election and was defeated.

PIERRE SÉVIGNY

On the night of April 8-9, I got a call from the Windsor Hotel [in Montreal] and it was a chap by the name of Hubert Ducharme, a lawyer, who had been a friend of mine for years, and one of my organisers. He was working with John Doyle. He said, "Look, we feel sorry you have lost but we are having a party at the hotel and on the way home why don't you stop. John would like to see you." On the way in, I said to my wife, "Why don't we stop and say thank you and that will end this. After all, I mean, he did what he could for us and he is probably sorry that I lost. Let's stop for a minute."

My wife agreed, so we went to a suite at the Windsor Hotel and there we met John Doyle, Hubert Ducharme, and four or five others. No sooner had I been told that they were sorry I had lost than Doyle cornered me and said, "Do you know of any Conservatives who would shift to the Liberals?"

I said, "I certainly don't."

"Well," he said, "that's very important for me because the results are final and Pearson doesn't have an absolute majority and he needs this absolute majority because we have consulted and we know for a fact that Diefenbaker will never give up if he feels that he has a chance to ally himself with the Social Crediters or others. And Pearson needs an absolute majority."

I said, "Look, my good man, I have just been defeated. This part of my life has ended and I certainly am not going to approach any Conservative to shift to Pearson and his Liberals. He can bloody well go and attend to his own business. I mean, that's his problem. I have got mine. I am sorry. I am leaving."

He said, "If you don't know of any Conservatives, what about Social Credit?"

"Oh, come on," I said. "I don't know these Social Credit

fellows. I have met them in Ottawa. I know Réal Caouette. You can't approach people like that. In any event, it is two in the morning." That was about the time by then and I said, "Let's all go to bed." My wife was pretty fed up with all this nonsense because we felt pretty sad—after all, we had been defeated.

The next morning when we got up, I said to my wife, "Let's pack up the family and the dog and go away." She said, "Where shall we go?" and I said, "I have always wanted to go to New York and spend a week there." And that's what we did. We didn't make any phone calls, we just packed up, left a forwarding address, took the three children, the dog, and off to New York we went.

One day in Times Square I picked up the Montreal *Gazette* and I read that six Social Credit members had defected to the Liberal Party. I put two and two together and I said, "My God, it is impossible that these guys were talking about getting to the Social Credit and that so quickly should happen," but I paid no attention to it.

In due course I called up Doyle because I had some business arrangements with him and spoke to him and Ducharme and they were laughing like hell. They told me that they were leaving for Nassau, that everything was fine. They were very pleased that Pearson would form the next government—that would be very helpful to them.

Before the six Socreds signed the declaration to support the Liberals, there were moves afoot in the other direction. The day after the election Dr. Guy Marcoux, the Social Credit member for Quebec-Montmorency, had received a telephone call from a Social Credit organiser in the Gaspé and a Quebec Tory, Dr. Albert Guilbeault; both wanted him to consider the possibility of a three-party coalition to keep the Liberals out of power. When Dr. Marcoux argued that such a coalition was impossible, Dr. Guilbeault said that he had put the proposition to Gérard Picard, a member of the New Democratic Party, who thought that something could be done; Picard had spoken to Michael Oliver, the then party president, who said that he would contact the leader, Tommy Douglas. At Dr. Guilbeault's suggestion, Dr. Marcoux got a long-distance telephone call through to Robert Thompson, who was in Alberta: Thompson pointed out the Conservatives were the Socreds' main enemies in the West but agreed that if this was what the Quebec Members wanted, he would have to go along. They would discuss the matter further at a special Social Credit caucus meeting, which was to be held in Ottawa on April 11.

ROBERT THOMPSON

We did not have a complete turnout at this caucus. Of the twenty-four Members who were elected, there were probably not more than sixteen or eighteen present. At the meeting, which took place in the Parliament Buildings' Centre Block on the Senate side in the afternoon, we confirmed what had been our decision prior to the meeting. That was that there should be no statement from our group, that we should go back to our own constituencies and let the initiative be in the hands of Mr. Diefenbaker or, from the other side, Mr. Pearson. This was clearly accepted. It was passed unanimously by everybody who was there. Mr. Caouette arrived, having come from Toronto, at the close of the meeting, and while he was not in on the actual vote, he gave agreement to what had transpired in caucus.

Now, the interesting aspect of this caucus as it relates to the Affair of the Six, is that at least three of the Members who were present left that meeting room at about four o'clock in the afternoon and proceeded by a very direct conveyance to Montreal. Apparently a meeting was held in Montreal that evening. They moved on to a motel in Quebec City and were in session by ten o'clock that night.

With them at that session was the man who was actually the organiser of what turned out to be the Affair of the Six, a man who was later convicted of arson, served time, a man who had been an organiser for the Liberal Party. I speak of Moise Darabaner. This was the French version of his name. Actually, he was not French Canadian at all. He was Moses Derabonner. He was the man who brought the six together. He was the man that arranged the deal, he was the man that set it up.

It was about three o'clock in the morning—this again is the night following the caucus meeting—that a document was drafted in the office of a Quebec attorney. The identity of this man was never revealed to us so that we could not be sure of his name. The six who agreed to go along with the plan signed that document. As far as we could determine in our own caucus hearings that took place afterward, the document, which committed these six Members to supporting Mr. Pearson's leadership and forcing Mr. Diefenbaker to resign as Prime Minister was drawn up in legal terms, duly signed and witnessed. Copies were also signed of this document.

Then between four and five o'clock in the morning, when the meeting broke up, this document was transported back to Montreal and then to Ottawa, and was delivered before nine o'clock in the morning to Rideau Hall, to the Governor-General. Who delivered it? This is the big question.

He was supposed to have been a priest. Apparently, there was a priest involved, a man who was the brother of one of the Members of Parliament. Who the second man was or how they travelled, I don't know. But obviously, they didn't travel by train; they could hardly have travelled by car. They must have travelled by airplane. It had to be a private airplane because there were no commercial air flights available. They might have caught an early flight from Montreal and driven to Montreal from Quebec City. But even then, they would have been hard pressed to get to the Montreal airport from Quebec City. Our own conclusion was that they were flown from Quebec City to Montreal and they took a commercial flight up from Montreal.

An interesting sidelight of this thing, as we in caucus attempted to trace down actually what happened, was that Mr. Pearson was quite aware of everything that was taking place. In fact, the tracks lead right up to his door. A copy of the document was delivered to Mr. Pearson at the same time or very close to the same time that it was delivered to the Governor-General. So Mr. Pearson knew all about what was going on. This was the one proof that we did have, or the one evidence that we did have, that he was being kept informed of what was happening.

As far as I know, there was money involved, but it didn't reach all six of the men. It only reached two of them.

One of the men, of course, whose name was circulated very much in the hearings that we had in caucus, was a friend of Joey Smallwood. I speak of John Doyle. It was reported to us that it was his airplane that provided transportation to Montreal, and probably from Montreal to Quebec City, because these men didn't have time, leaving caucus as they did and driving to Montreal as they did, to get to Quebec City except to travel by plane. The rumours—and I have no way of verifying them; I've never made any public statement about this—the rumours that came to us in our own hearings in caucus was that the former Premier of Newfoundland, Mr. Smallwood, was himself involved somehow in getting this thing going.

This man, John Doyle, was not in Newfoundland at the time. He had a suite in Ottawa. Another man who was associated with Doyle and who was involved with Darabaner at that end was Noël Dorion [former Conservative Cabinet Minister]. And again, we were not carrying out a judicial enquiry, and we could only try to come to the root of it as best we could in caucus. These are things that came up in caucus.

The statement the six signed—which was only read to me; I was never able to get my hands on a copy—was a well-worded legal document in the sense that it was drawn up by someone who had far more ability and knowledge of legal terminology in drawing up documents than any one of the six Members of Parliament, or for that matter Moise Darabaner. So there was some other person who did this.

If there was one event in politics that has been frustrating in the extreme and caused me to be disappointed and disgusted with men as such, it was this case. Because if the truth were really known on this case, it's one of the dirtiest political games that I have ever been confronted with or have ever personally, in any way, known about.

The people around Pearson said that they were unaware of the affair. Tom Kent heard of the charges of bribery and corruption but since no one seemed worried, he concluded that there was no scandal. Dick O'Hagan did speak to Mr. Pearson about the turn of events, and he remembered that the Liberal Leader seemed to be pleased that the declaration meant that he had a majority and would be forming a government.

RICHARD O'HAGAN

As I recall, I came in on a Sunday to work on the press side of that [affair of the six Social Crediters]. But it was not something that I knew a great deal about, quite frankly, and still don't. You know, it flared up and I had to get myself briefed, as I recall, and deal with the many press calls that came in as a result of that. But I was not really very close to that matter and not very well informed either.

One of the six Social Crediters whose defection helped Pearson to power was Raymond Langlois; he was born in Wolseley, Saskatchewan, in 1936 but worked in Quebec as a teacher before being elected the Member for Megantic in 1962. Langlois was attending a supper at Black Lake near Thetford Mines in his Megantic constituency when he received a telephone call from a fellow Social Crediter, Gérard Perron, the Member for Beauce.

RAYMOND LANGLOIS

He asked me if I could go up to Quebec City immediately. I said, "Is it anything special?" He said, "It is something of very great importance. We would like you to attend a meeting." I said, "I won't be there much before midnight anyway because it is already close to ten o'clock." He said, "That's fine."

So I excused myself and drove up to Quebec City. He had given me the motel; it was the great big motel, the Motel du Boulevard just near the Quebec bridge. I went to the room where he said that he was going to be, and there were Lucien Plourde, Member for Quebec West [R.] Beaulé of Quebec East [P. A.] Boutin from Dorchester, and myself, Perron, and Mr. [A.] Bertrand, vice-president for the Ralliement des Créditistes in Quebec at that time. [Gilbert] Rondeau came after. From what I gathered, Mr. Perron and Mr. Rondeau had driven down that day to Quebec City from Ottawa, following something they had heard.

I said, "What is this all about?"

Mr. Perron gave me, in fairly brief terms, the reason why I was called there. I had been aware, prior to the election, of goings-on but nothing that you could put your finger on in any way or form. But the idea that some of our people were going to support the Conservative Government came as quite a shock to me. Apparently Perron and Rondeau got wind of it when they went to Ottawa after the election. They were pretty mad about it and they said, "It doesn't make much sense that we got rid of John Diefenbaker when he had 116 seats, and we are going to start supporting him with ninety-five. We are the people who actually threw him over, and now we are going to form a coalition or get some sort of a deal with the Conservatives."

Perron said, "There have been negotiations going on. To what extent, I have no idea. But I am certainly not going to wait till the thing has crystallised. We will look damned stupid if we are going to support the Conservatives again." I said, "I am not going in that type of a boat. First of all, it won't work."

There was no proof that any Social Credit Members were negotiating with the Tories, and Raymond Langlois admitted this. It was intuition on his part. He had probably heard about Dr. Guilbeault's proposal for a Conservative coalition and suspected that Dr. Marcoux and Robert Thompson were trying to make a deal. So did Réal Caouette.

RÉAL CAOUETTE

Gérard Perron, Member for La Beauce, came to me and said, "I've just heard in the corridor that Marcoux and Thompson are trying to reimpose Diefenbaker as the Prime Minister of Canada." He said, "What do you think of that?" I said, "I don't want any one of our Members of Parliament to compromise himself. But if you can stop Thompson and Marcoux, go ahead and stop them." Because they were working behind my back. Marcoux was just like a snake, with Thompson.

Perron did organise the whole thing, and I said, "This is wrong. It will never be admitted by me that you have signed those papers." They were told by Perron that Perron had my okay for the signatures of those people, and it was not true. I had said, "Don't have anyone sign anything."

Raymond Langlois knew about the allegations of bribery and he denied that there had been payment to anyone. Certainly he had received none. His account of the midnight meeting in the Quebec City motel room could be summarised as follows:

After a drink, they listened to Perron's argument that they should sign a statement supporting the Liberals, and agreed to do so. Apparently Perron and Rondeau had a prepared statement. There were a couple of clauses that the others wanted to add. Rondeau went with Bertrand to the

Ralliement office to have them typed. Then they signed with Bertrand witnessing their signatures. The document was notarised by Moise Darabaner. At first, Raymond Langlois denied ever seeing the Liberal organiser, but then he recalled the stranger who entered the motel room with the Socred Party official, Alexandre Bertrand.

RAYMOND LANGLOIS

I saw a gentleman—I did not know him, and he was with Alexandre Bertrand. I remember him because of the cigar that he was smoking. That gentleman went out with Bertrand, and Bertrand came back in after, and that was it. I was going to say that was the time that I saw Darabaner but I did not know who he was. I have never seen him since and I never saw him more than that.

I hadn't heard anything or seen anything that would have made me suspicious in any way or form that night. When I met Darabaner, had I known who he was, I would have been a little more hesitant about his presence because of the value of the document. I would have preferred having another notary and waiting until morning and getting it notarised then. Because I wouldn't have wanted his name on the document.

I have hever seen or heard or never was aware that anybody received anything. From what I gathered that night, aside from Rondeau and Perron, who had come up here and were going back and had come out with that idea, the other four definitely did not know anything about it prior to that.

It was not till past four o'clock in the morning, according to Robert Beaulé, that the meeting broke up. He had left earlier, saying that when the corrections were made and the clauses added, they could bring the document around to his house for him to sign, which was the reason why his signature was the last of the six. Langlois spent the rest of the night in the motel room where the meeting was held; he got hardly any sleep because of a toothache and had only a hazy memory of what happened to the statement after they had signed it and how it reached the Governor-General. Langlois did recall that there was such a strong public reaction that Beaulé and Boutin repudiated their signatures the next day.

Robert Beaulé, the Member for Quebec East, wrote a confidential letter to Robert Thompson saying that he had no evil intent and that he had been deceived. He asserted that it was Moise Darabaner who had put the proposition to them and insisted that the declaration be in the hands of Governor-General Vanier before nine o'clock in the morning. But how did it get to Ottawa in such a short time? No one seemed to know. Beaulé claimed that he had no knowledge of money changing hands and that he himself had received nothing.

Some weeks after Pierre Sévigny returned from the post-election holiday in New York City, he met John Doyle and his right-hand man, Hubert Ducharme.

PIERRE SÉVIGNY

They were openly boasting, these two fellows, that they were the ones who had managed to get six Social Credit Members to join the Liberal Party, and they were saying how they had done it. They had promised them up to a half a million dollars; it had cost them 50,000 dollars in cash to do it. They had found the proper men to do the job and get the Social Credit Members to defect, which had been done through a statement sworn to in front of a commissioner of the Superior Court. They felt very proud of their achievements and were talking openly about it.

Fifteen thousand dollars was disbursed to one of them, 15,000 to another, 15,000 to the third, and 5,000 dollars to a fourth party.

That commissioner of the Superior Court in the province of Quebec [Moise Darabaner] actually had engineered this thing because he was a friend of Ducharme, and he is the one who had been contacted by Ducharme and Doyle to get these Social Credit Members. The reason they contacted this fellow is because they knew he was in the finance business and was financing one of the Social Credit Members. So they said: "You know these people, you finance them, you can get to them. Now here's a chance for them to make money so as to pay you, a chance for you to make a few dollars, and a chance for you to ingratiate yourself with the Liberal Party."

This guy had agreed on the spur of the moment, very foolishly as he has admitted since then, to do this. It was he who rounded up the six Social Credit Members. They met in Quebec and were told: "Look, you are going to get so much, each of you is going to get up to 100,000 dollars, in some instances, and to prove my good faith, money will be disbursed now and all your election expenses will be paid and you are going to be members of the Liberal Party, you are going to get all kinds of favours. It is going to be marvellous for you." These six dumb bunnies, lured by money, had agreed. Now this could not be done that easily.

It was decided that there had to be a statement, sworn to and signed, so that Diefenbaker would know that this was serious that these guys were giving the absolute majority to Pearson. This statement had to be drafted and the good services of Jack Pickersgill were engaged—he prepared in his own handwriting in English the statement which was translated into French, signed by these fellows, and attested to in the presence of Moise Darabaner, that finance person in Quebec, a commissioner of the Superior Court, who put his seal on this document.

After it was signed, they all got together in Doyle's plane. Doyle, Joey Smallwood, and a few others stopped off at the Windsor Hotel in Montreal. The plane carried on to Ottawa and Hubert Ducharme, that lawyer, went right to the door of Rideau Hall, rang the bell, and gave that statement to be delivered in person to Mr. Vanier, who released the news to the press that six Social Credit Members had defected. That's the way it was done.

At some point I did mention to Ducharme and Doyle that what they had done was highly illegal. I said, "My God, if it is a crime to impersonate a voter at the polls, how much more criminal is it to go and bribe the elected Members of Parliament. That's equivalent to actually falsifying the votes of at least 100,000 people."

"Oh well," they said, "we are in power now. We are protected and we are saved. Everything is fine. Everything is great."

It was Dr. Guy Marcoux who found out that the man responsible for drafting the statement the six signed was Guy Paget, a lawyer and later legal counsel for the city of Montreal; at the time he was an associate of Hubert Ducharme. Dr. Marcoux's claim would seem to contradict Sévigny's assertion that it was Pickersgill who wrote out the agreement, a translation of which the six signed.

GUY MARCOUX

This man [Paget] knew nothing about the situation. The only thing he knew was that Ducharme asked him to write something, saying so and so and so and so. I met Guy Paget. He said, "Sure, I remember that. I even remember some of the paragraphs." And he repeated the paragraphs, and they were from the statement. I said, "Do you know something more than that?"

He said, "I know that Doyle was connected with that. I know that Darabaner was connected with that. I know that J. Pickersgill was connected with that." I said, "How do you know?" He said, "I met them." "Where did you meet them?" He said, "I met them on the plane because they wanted this statement to be brought direct to Quebec, and they had a Canadian Javelin plane. So that's why I met those guys."

Some two years were to pass, and Moise Darabaner was charged with fraud and arson and sentenced to prison. Pierre Sévigny, who for personal reasons wanted to expose The Affair of the Six, *visited him in St. Vincent de Paul Penitentiary near Montreal and obtained an affidavit from him. In this sworn statement Darabaner said that sums of 15,000 dollars were paid to two of the Social Credit M.P.s in his presence in the Chateau Frontenac Hotel, Quebec City, and that a similar sum of 15,000 dollars was paid to a Social Credit Party official. He declared that promises of sums up to 500,000 dollars were made to the two M.P.s, said sums to be paid by John Doyle or his nominees at a later date.*

Darabaner claimed that during the negotiations that led up to the defection of the six Social Crediters to the Liberals, John Doyle and his assistant, Hubert Ducharme, were in constant touch with Joey Smallwood and J. W. Pickersgill by telephone. After each conversation Ducharme would mention that Pickersgill was referring all matters to his boss, Mr. Pearson. Darabaner swore that, after the defection of the six, he accompanied John Doyle, Hubert Ducharme, and Joey Smallwood to Nassau in the Bahamas where the matter was constantly discussed. After his arrest on August 13, 1965, Darabaner swore that he was repeatedly questioned about L'Affaire des Six, *although that had nothing to do with the charges that led to his arrest. In the deposition Darabaner declared that he did receive the sum of 5,000 dollars from John Doyle for his help in getting the six Créditistes to defect to the Liberal Party, with promises of future benefits.*

When Jack Pickersgill was asked whether he knew of the affidavits asserting that Social Credit members had been bribed to support the Liberals, he denied any knowledge of it. Joey Smallwood said that he was

*in St. John's at the time that he was supposed to have been with his friend,
John Doyle, in Montreal and in the Bahamas celebrating Pearson's
becoming Prime Minister and the Liberals' return to power.*

J. W. PICKERSGILL

I can assure you that this whole question was aired during the
1965 election campaign and I made a public statement about that. I
stand by that statement as I made it. I can't repeat it word for word
at this moment but to my knowledge, so far as I know anything
about this matter, there was no bribery or corruption or anything
of that sort at all, and, as to what really happened, so far as I was
concerned I have no intention of making any statements
whatsoever except to say that I had nothing to do with any bribery
or any corruption or anything that could possibly be in any way
improper. But I feel that beyond that I am talking about things that
affect other people who are still active in public life and I might
conceivably be imputing motives to them that would be unfair,
and though I have nothing whatever to hide myself I have no
intention of saying anything more about it than that.

J. R. SMALLWOOD

I wouldn't be surprised to discover that he [John Doyle] had
something to do with it. He was a Montrealer, he had a great many
friends and acquaintances and a great many connections, and he
had no reason to love Mr. Diefenbaker. He didn't have any
particular reason to love Mr. Pearson, but he didn't dislike him.
And as between the two, I would imagine he would prefer Mr.
Pearson. There's no doubt at all about that. If those Social
Crediters came to him, or if one of them came to him, or if a friend
of theirs came to him, it wouldn't surprise me if he had said to
them, "Well, you fellows have it in your own hands. It's such a
tight fit in Parliament today that why wait until the House opens?
Why not take the action now that you intend to take when the
House opens? Why not do it now? Why not notify them of what
you intend to do?" I can imagine his giving that advice, and I can
imagine their following it.

At any rate, that's what they did. Whether it was because he
gave the advice and they followed his advice, or someone else gave

it, or they just thought of it themselves, I wouldn't know. I wasn't in their confidence.

L'Affaire des Six was a self-destructive political bombshell: it expedited the formation of the Pearson Government—Diefenbaker resigned the following Monday—but it also led to the destruction of the Social Credit Party as a national force. There was an immediate investigation by the Social Credit caucus and on May 9, 1963, it took disciplinary action against the six Members. The caucus "emphatically reprimanded" Messrs. Perron and Rondeau, the organisers of the defection, and Langlois, the willing accomplice, and withdrew their rights and privileges during the coming session; it issued a warning against Messrs. Plourde, Beaulé, and Boutin, who had apologised and claimed they were dupes. This action did nothing to resolve the affair and only increased resentments. Raymond Langlois was indignant at "this inquisition," as he called it, and blamed it all on Robert Thompson who, he said, took orders from Ernest Manning, the Social Credit premier of Alberta. Dr. Guy Marcoux felt that the caucus had not gone far enough and that it was impossible to get the truth; he resigned from the party and crossed the floor of the House to sit as an independent.

The Social Credit Party that emerged from the 1963 election was an unhappy amalgam of the country's two solitudes: although there were only four Western M.P.s, they came from the Social Credit power bases of British Columbia and Alberta, they were English-speaking Protestants, the cultural opposites of the twenty Quebec M.P.s who were practising Catholics—Réal Caouette, when he was first a Member, between 1945 and 1949, proposed that a cross should be placed above the Speaker's throne. The leader spoke no French and had difficulty communicating with the majority of his followers; although a newcomer who had only recently returned to Canada, Bob Thompson had the backing of the Alberta Social Credit Party, which had always been interested in federal politics. He had been imposed on the 1961 National Convention called to revive the movement after its annihilation in the Diefenbaker landslide of 1958. No one expected Quebec to play the dominant role in the party, and Caouette was to recall Manning telling him that the West would never accept a Catholic French Canadian as Leader. There was bitterness and resentment among the Francophone delegates and it only required an incident such as L'Affaire des Six to bring the racial tensions in the party to the breaking point.

ROBERT THOMPSON

The caucus action infuriated a man who was not involved [in the affair] but, in my opinion, was one of the key figures behind what happened. That was Gilles Gregoire. Apparently he knew nothing about this declaration by the six. Gregoire was too clever in the eyes of his own fellow Members of Parliament from Quebec to be brought in on the scheme. He would have taken it over. But blood runs thicker than water, and he immediately came to the defence of these men. He had a great influence on Mr. Caouette. It was my opinion that Mr. Caouette knew nothing about this [affair] too. But they rallied to the defence of the six, particularly to the defence of Rondeau and Perron. They could not very well come out and attack me on the situation, so they went after Marcoux.

I believe that Gilles Gregoire more than anyone else was responsible for the split in the Social Credit Party. I don't think Mr. Caouette wanted to split. He certainly had never given any evidence that he was a separatist of any kind. But he was persuaded by Gregoire that this was the only thing they could do.

I had insisted that they form their own provincial party, so that all the pressures that came out of Quebec could go to Quebec City, where they belonged, instead of coming here, where many of them had no place in the federal scene in Ottawa. Gregoire took great offence at that because obviously he couldn't control both of them.

As I said, Gilles Gregoire was the man who engineered the split. It was he who got the men involved in the Affair of the Six to withdraw. I had made up my mind that they would not be expelled. They would have to withdraw. I would never be put in a position of forcing them out. It would have destroyed my credibility in Quebec.

It was at the annual meeting of the Ralliement des Créditistes, which was held in the Monsignor Prince School, Granby, Quebec, between August 31 and September 2, 1963, that the final break came; the party divided between the Thompsonites and the followers of Réal Caouette. The Social Credit Party of Canada was left with ten Members, the four

Westerners and six Quebec loyalists—the latter included Marcel Lessard, who was later to join the Liberals and become a Cabinet Minister, and Dr. Guy Marcoux, who returned from his lonely independence to become Thompson's deputy. The Créditistes counted fourteen, the rest of the Quebec Members: Réal Caouette was leader and Gilles Gregoire his number-two man as House leader. However, Gregoire was soon to split with the Créditistes and sit as a separatist before departing the Ottawa scene.

The majority that the six Social Crediters provided Pearson didn't last long; three of them backed off almost immediately because of the furious public reaction, which included threats of violence, and the others withdrew after the Liberal Government was formed. But there was no need for alarm because the New Democrats were not going to vote the government out of office and bring on another election, not when they had had two elections in less than a year. Yet Lester Pearson worried about the lack of a majority; he felt insecure because he was not a good enough Parliamentarian to steer a minority government through the shoals of the House of Commons. And he was faced by a formidable opponent in John Diefenbaker. His sense of insecurity rubbed off on some of the new Liberal M.P.s like Jean-Luc Pepin.

JEAN-LUC PEPIN

He was erratic on the floor of the House. In those years, '63 - '64, when Mr. Pearson was out of the country or out of Ottawa, the acting Leader in the House would be M. Chevrier. If you had talked to the younger Members of the House of Commons at that time, they would have told you how much more secure they were when they were in the hands of M. Chevrier than when they had Mr. Pearson. That's a fact. M. Chevrier was a superlative athlete on the floor of the House of Commons; Mr. Pearson was not. This was not his normal habitat for some reason. There was also this Freudian relationship between him and Diefenbaker which contributed to his erratic character.

Later on, in the fall of 1963, the Liberals made another attempt to assure Pearson of a majority, this time with the New Democratic Party. It was Keith Davey's initiative: he approached Douglas Fisher of the NDP whom he knew very well as they had been friends and classmates at the

University of Toronto. They talked it over and arranged for the top party leaders to get together in Walter Gordon's suite in the old Roxborough apartment block opposite the Lord Elgin Hotel in Ottawa; it was to be a very private meeting. The NDP were represented by Tommy Douglas, David Lewis, and Fisher; the Liberals by Gordon and Davey—Prime Minister Pearson was supposed to have been at the meeting but could not attend and Gordon, who was inclined to dismiss the whole affair, said that Allan MacEachen was invited but did not show. Douglas Fisher wanted the meeting because he believed that a minority government posed a danger for a third party such as the NDP; furthermore, he was disappointed in the fact that the New Democratic Party, which had been founded at a well-publicised convention in 1961, had made so little progress in two elections. David Lewis felt that the meeting was merely a continuation of Liberal efforts to seduce the NDP.

DOUGLAS FISHER

We had not got to the stage [of discussing a coalition] although Keith was prepared to talk romantically about it, of a couple of New Democrats entering the Cabinet. That was certainly not in my mind. I just wanted to get a discussion going. There was an enormous amount of uncertainty around Parliament then. No one could read what the Social Credit were doing, they were tending to split in all directions. It was an odd time and everybody scrambled.

We were there with seventeen Members and I thought we should be facing the reality that the party had lost two federal elections in a row and wham! we'd even lost [Walter] Pitman, the first New Democratic M.P., and David Lewis, the real strong man—one brief Parliament and out he'd gone.* I just thought we should be realistic, and I also had a theoretical view that we might be in for a minority Parliament for some time and that maybe we'd better learn how to exploit it as a minority group. But we were sitting there number four, you see. Here is this grand new party that had been launched with the most tremendous convention in '61 and suddenly not one election but two elections had translated us into the fourth party. Now, that's the background.

*Pitman was elected at the by-election for Peterborough October 31, 1960, and defeated in the 1962 election; Lewis was elected for York South in 1962 and defeated in 1963.

The assumption had been that somehow the New Democratic Party in its first run would leap over the 20 percent of the total vote across the country, but that didn't happen. We were sitting there with the Gallup Poll showing us somewhere between 10, 11, and 12 percent in that range, and we're the fourth party with seventeen seats.* Well, what do you do?

DAVID LEWIS

The Liberal Party was seeking all the time to win labour and to get the NDP people to join with them or in some way compromise ourselves as part of the Liberal machine, the Liberal umbrella. I've had a great deal of use for a good many Liberals, but I never have had any use for the consistency or principles of the Liberal Party. I think it's the nearest to political prostitution that any country has had, the Liberal Party as a party. And that's what they tried to do in Walter Gordon's [apartment].

There were some minutes of feinting. There were some minutes when you were being nice to each other and feeling each other out. But it became so very clear that nothing was going to happen, that if they had any specific suggestions to make, they wouldn't make them. I don't know what Walter had in his mind, if there had been a readiness on our part to listen . . . But as far as I was concerned—and I speak for myself partly because I remember it better and partly because I think I did take a pretty active part in the conversation—I made it clear, and all of us made it clear, that there was no deal on anything possible so early in the conversation that there would obviously be no sense in making any [specific] suggestion.

T. C. DOUGLAS

When we went there, Walter said, "Mike wants to talk to you." I said, "I thought he was going to be here." And he said, "There's something he wants to talk to you about."

So he called Mike and put him on the phone and he said, "Look, I'm terribly sorry but I'm in bed with a cold"—and he sounded as

---

*Social Credit won twenty-four seats in the 1963 election, and the NDP placed fourth but the Social Credit split-up came before the meeting in Gordon's apartment, so the NDP was back in third place.

though he had a cold—"I want to assure you this is not a diplomatic cold." Mike went on, "This is a genuine cold and I'm
really in bad shape and I just can't come out. I wanted to let you
know that the meeting has my full approval and that whatever you
suggest or whatever comes out of it will be transmitted to me by
Walter Gordon and Keith Davey and will be given very careful
consideration." My reply was, "Personally, I don't expect much
to come out of it but I'm prepared to listen."

We sat down and nothing did come out of it. It started out with
the points I wanted to raise and a number of things we
wanted—we wanted improvements in the Old Age Pension, we
wanted Canada Pension Plan, we wanted Canada Development
Corporation, we wanted some redistribution of income through
changes in the budget so as to raise the income deductions for
lower-income groups, and tightening up on some of the corporate
loopholes and so on. They listened and knew there was nothing
new in that. We had said that in the House of Commons hundreds
of times. They talked about the take-over tax, and of course that
was something we could support.

Then Keith Davey started to get the conversation round into
—he and Doug began a theoretical discussion on what is a merger.
I said, "Now look. We stop right here. We're not talking about
mergers. We're talking about parliamentary business and how we
can get the most we can out of this session in terms of what we
think is good for the people of this country and what you're
prepared to concede is good for the people of the country. But any
type of merger or even any type of continuing organisational
structure—of course, that's completely out of the question."
Walter Gordon immediately came in at that point and said,
"That's absolutely the same [with us]. We have no authority to
even discuss this and all we've come to discuss is parliamentary
business." That ended the discussion, and I don't suppose it lasted
more than an hour and a half or two hours.

WALTER GORDON

It goes too far to say merger talks. The purpose was to see if
there was any possibility of a working arrangement, and I think
Lewis and Tommy Douglas and Fisher were there. And my

recollection is that Davey and I, and we were to be joined by MacEachen and Pearson, and MacEachen and Pearson couldn't come, so they never got anywhere. An hour's conversation, and that's about all.

DOUGLAS FISHER

He [Tommy Douglas] was bargaining. He wanted to know very clearly from Gordon what was in his mind and where he thought the government was going in policy terms. He put it pretty bluntly, as I remember, to Gordon that it didn't look to him like a radical reforming party; it looked like a business party that was more interested in power and administration and so on.

David [Lewis] spoke—David always speaks wherever he is—but Douglas did most of the talking, as did Gordon. When we left, my understanding of it was that we were to think it over and then get back together and the real question was getting Douglas to sit down with Pearson.

There was to be no further meeting because reporter Mark Gayn got wind of the get-together in Walter Gordon's apartment and broke the story in the Toronto Star. *Douglas Fisher blamed David Lewis for the leak and said that, in leaking it, Lewis had added an air of mystery and possible subversion to the affair. On his part, David Lewis assumed that Walter Gordon, who was very close to the Toronto* Star *"gang," was the one responsible for tipping off Mark Gayn. At any rate, the revelations caused an uproar across the country; NDPers such as Bert Herridge, M.P. for Kootenay West, were outraged that there should have been these secret negotiations, and so the second attempt to find security came to naught.*

KEITH DAVEY

I remember it was agreed that if there was any kind of a press leak we would all say "no comment," just "no comment" period. The thing did inevitably leak, and I don't know how it did or who or where or why or what; I've always believed that maybe David Lewis leaked the thing because he didn't want it to happen, but I don't know that.

When it did leak and they called me I said, "No comment"; they called Walter Gordon, he said, "No comment"; I can't recall what

David Lewis said but probably, "No comment"; they called Fisher, he said, "No comment"; they called Tommy Douglas, and he said there was no such meeting, that the meeting never took place. He issued the most categorical denial. If he was going to say anything, he could have said, "Yes, there was an exploratory meeting but it wasn't serious," or "Yes, they wanted to see us so we went," or any number of things. But instead he issued the kind of a denial which sort of indicated that the meeting hadn't even taken place. I remember being really pretty dismayed by that because I hadn't thought that Douglas would be that devious.

Despite every effort and all the considerable skill the Liberals had in subverting opponents and especially third-party adherents—a skill that prompted David Lewis to say they were the closest approximation to a bawdy house that any political party could be—the majority seemed out of their reach. Yet they never gave up this search for security: the majority, or the need of a majority, became an obsession with the likes of Walter Gordon and Keith Davey, and the lack of it the reason for all their failures and frustrations. It was comparable to original sin; it was the universal excuse for everything that went wrong; the lack of a majority was blamed for the fact that the Pearson Government was so accident-prone and seemed to stumble from crisis to crisis; it was the reason why the Prime Minister himself seemed to show such poor judgement on occasion, and got into so much trouble. There was never any suggestion that it might be responsible for the productivity of the period, the amount of social welfare legislation which was adopted—at least not from those Liberal stalwarts. There was no redeeming feature as far as they were concerned.

5 Sixty Days of Decision

THERE WERE MANY people whom Mike Pearson could have consulted in making up his first Cabinet. Robert Fowler, who was not involved in the 1963 election campaign, had been asked to do some planning, and he submitted what he called a blueprint for a future Liberal Government in which he suggested the names of persons who might be suitable for various ministries. Pearson had talked to Walter Gordon about the appointments and asked for his comments, and Gordon remembered saying that he thought that Bud Drury, not Paul Hellyer, should be Minister of National Defence, but his advice was not taken. Quite clearly, the Leader felt that he had an obligation to the few Liberal stalwarts who had kept the party's hopes alive during the dark days of the great Diefenbaker majority, and he had told Jack Pickersgill that he could have any job except Finance and Trade and Commerce, which Pickersgill didn't want in any case. There was no mention of External Affairs, which was reserved for Paul Martin, but everyone had taken that for granted. Lionel Chevrier was given Justice, which was the traditional post for the Quebec lieutenant.

Maurice Lamontagne was the third or fourth person to be called to Stornoway, which the Pearsons still occupied—it was to be some weeks before they moved to 24 Sussex Drive and exchanged residences with the Diefenbakers. Lamontagne was offered Health and Welfare and Pearson was surprised when he turned down this big-spending department and *asked to be President of the Privy Council, which was hardly a full portfolio then. However, Lamontagne said that he wanted this sinecure so that he could be of more help to the Prime Minister. He was of immediate assistance to him in forming the government, and it could be said that Lamontagne was the only one whom Pearson consulted in making up his first Cabinet.*

Judy LaMarsh got Health and Welfare. In retrospect, she said that hers was a token appointment, that Mike Pearson was enough of a traditionalist not to name the first woman to the Cabinet — that had been done by Diefenbaker when he made Ellen Fairclough a Minister. Yet Judy was, in her own words, wildly enthusiastic when she was told that she would be responsible for starting the Canada Pension Plan and Medicare.

There is evidence that Pearson was uneasy about making Walter Gordon Minister of Finance and, according to Christopher Young, asked him if he could consider Trade and Commerce instead. But Gordon insisted that he had been promised Finance and would have nothing else. So Trade and Commerce went to Mitchell Sharp. Pearson had not much choice as far as Minister of Agriculture was concerned because Harry Hays was the only Liberal elected between Winnipeg and the Rockies and Agriculture was traditionally a prairie portfolio; however, the new Prime Minister had some idea about dividing the department and having separate Ministers for East and West.

HARRY HAYS

Mr. Pearson during the '63 campaign and the '62 campaign, was committed to two Ministers of Agriculture. That had functioned in Britain. There was a Minister of Agriculture in Scotland and there was one in England. He thought that that might work. He appointed René Tremblay and myself, and Tremblay was going to be the Minister of Agriculture for Eastern Canada and I was to be the Minister of Agriculture for Western Canada. I told Mr. Pearson I didn't think it would work. And at that time he said to me, "Well, you're going to be the Minister of Agriculture, and you do it the way you want, and if I'm unhappy about it, I'll call you in and you'll no longer be the Minister of Agriculture." And that was a very happy agreement.

They would have to make some changes to have two Ministers of Agriculture, so that Tremblay was appointed a Minister

Without Portfolio. Anyway, we had offices together, and of
course it didn't work.

*Of all the Liberal Members from Quebec, Maurice Sauvé had as great a
claim as any to be among the first selected for the Cabinet. He had been one
of the prime movers of the provincial party and an architect of the Quiet
Revolution; even after he had been elected to Parliament in 1962, for Îles
de la Madeleine, his services were requested by Jean Lesage and Sauvé
helped the premier in that year's provincial election campaign. He had
been one of Pearson's proponents and had played a small part in getting
him elected Leader. It was therefore not surprising that the press in
Ontario as well as Quebec should expect him to be appointed a Minister.
When he was offered only a Parliamentary Secretary's job, Maurice
Sauvé turned it down angrily and argued with Pearson that he should not
be by-passed by someone like René Tremblay, who was a recent Liberal
and only elected in 1963.*

MAURICE SAUVÉ

I saw Mr. Pearson again on the Sunday before the appointment
of the Cabinet. I had a long talk with him, and I said to him, "I
don't want to be Parliamentary Secretary. I don't understand you,
why you're doing that. If I was not representing the Magdalen
Islands, a riding which needs federal intervention, where I
committed myself to do a lot of things, I would resign *hic* and *nunc*
because I don't want to be a Member of Parliament and be a back
bencher when I feel that I should be a Minister."

I couldn't figure out what was happening. I mentioned the Old
Guard before—I think that Azellus Denis and Lionel Chevrier and
Jean-Paul Deschatelets opposed my appointment to the Cabinet
on the grounds that I was a reformist and they didn't like me and
probably I would make trouble. I don't know how these people
could have had [so much] influence on Mr. Pearson, except that
Chevrier was then the Quebec [lieutenant]. And I don't really
know what was the attitude of Maurice Lamontagne. Maurice
was very friendly with Tremblay, and eventually Tremblay was
appointed to the Cabinet. We had only one Minister from the
Quebec district, and Tremblay got the job. I think that those
three, and probably Maurice, had some reservations. I know that

my English friends, Walter Gordon and the others, put a lot of pressure on Pearson to get me in the Cabinet, because they told me so.

But what happened? It's a question which I've never been able to answer in detail. And after Mr. Pearson left the government I met him once and he said to me, "Maurice, you phone me in Ottawa; I have notes of those days and I'll tell you what happened." He died before I could go back to him and speak to him. Because he told me, he said, "I have notes, I know who was opposed to what."

"Anyway, at the end of '63 in December, both Chevrier and Azellus Denis went out of the Cabinet, and I was asked to go into the Cabinet. I must confess that I was not very excited then, because I considered that my Leader, Pearson, whom I had liked, had really killed me politically by not appointing me to the Cabinet on the first occasion he had in April '63, and that my political career had ended that day. I was very much aware of this.

The only way for me to have survived politically would have been for the Leader to recognise my merits and not to succumb to the pressure of the Old Guard or the reactionaries in the party from Quebec, who then took courage by the fact that I had not been appointed, and were in a position to destroy me politically. If I had been appointed immediately, that would have been stopped—I would have been clearly designated by Mr. Pearson as one of his. Then my future would have been different. But this killed me forever.

There were seven former civil servants in Lester Pearson's Cabinet: Mitchell Sharp had been Deputy Minister of Trade and Commerce, the department he was now heading as Minister; Bud Drury was another former Deputy Minister (National Defence) and Guy Favreau a former Associate Deputy Minister (Justice); Maurice Lamontagne had been Assistant Deputy Minister of Northern Affairs and Natural Resources; Jack Nicholson had been a dollar-a-year man in Ottawa during the war, and so had Walter Gordon, who had actually worked for the Department of Finance in the '40s and helped in the preparation of a couple of budgets; René Tremblay was a former Quebec government official, and Pearson himself had been the bureaucrat of bureaucrats as Deputy Minister for External Affairs.

One of the Prime Minister's first acts was to call a meeting of all the top civil servants; it was like a family reunion and a group photograph was taken. George McIlraith, who could be critical of officials, felt that Pearson had had to do this in order to boost the bureaucrats' morale. Alvin Hamilton, the former Conservative Agriculture Minister, was appalled.

GEORGE McILRAITH

With the Diefenbaker Government in a state of total disintegration as it was in the last year it held office, deputy ministers had been handled exceptionally badly, and it was very clear that the then Prime Minister had no confidence whatever in any deputy, no matter how good his record was. I don't know why he took that attitude, but he did. And very unfairly, because a great many of them were Conservatives, as he apparently didn't know, but I knew well, being a local Member here. He was equally harsh on them as he was on the Liberals. He seemed to distrust them all politically. And in point of fact there was a very high calibre in the deputy ministership of the day, and they were men who could be trusted by any party.

In any event, they were so demoralised that Mr. Pearson decided, correctly, that he had to do something to show them that he was not going to get rid of them or treat them the way Mr. Diefenbaker had, and that they were free to go on and do their job as deputy. He got them all together, and I remember the occasion very well, and the discussion with all of them. In my view it was the correct and proper action, and it brought the morale of the civil service right back to the point where it went on doing its work and performing its duties and carrying on.

ALVIN HAMILTON

I don't think any country with a British Parliamentary system of government ever witnessed what we witnessed here in Canada in '63. That was when the Liberal Government came in as a minority government, and all the deputy ministers gathered in one spot to welcome Pearson. They were now out of the aberration, as they called it, of the Conservative period of five and a half years.

Now, this was a disgraceful demonstration of partiality on the part of the senior mandarins of the civil service, and the Canadian people should be reminded of that. The deputy ministers don't gather around each new Prime Minister and say, "Hurrah, we're glad you won. And we've got rid of those s.o.b.s that were here before," and all the rest of it. Their job is to serve the political masters of the country who are elected by the people. But they consider themselves the masters, so they welcomed back Pearson as one of their own. We've had eight or ten civil servants who just don't hide their feelings—they want to move right into the political field, join the Liberal Party and come in as Cabinet Ministers.

It is not only in Canada that we have the civil service issue but in many countries of the world. One of the great challenges of the next thirty years is: How can the elected representatives and so-called democratic governments regain control of the decision-making?

Although some politicians might demur, the number of former deputy ministers in the Pearson Government did not diminish the Liberals' claim that they would provide a competent administration that would clean up the mess left by the inefficient Tories. They might be bureaucratic or technocratic but they had the managerial capacity to rule well, which, Tommy Douglas said, was due to the fact that they had been in power so long that the mandarins, as the top civil servants are called, were part of the Liberal establishment in Ottawa. At any rate, the new Ministers were supremely confident as they took over their offices and brushed aside any advice or aid which their Conservative predecessors might have proffered. Walter Gordon expressed the government's attitude when he said in an extraordinarily partisan budget speech on the night of June 13 that "Canada is beginning to recover from the loss of confidence resulting from the financial and economic mismanagement of the previous administration."

However, there was the campaign promise of "sixty days of decision" hanging like a Damocletian sword over the collective heads of the Cabinet. Lamontagne pointed out that it would be impossible to fulfill such a promise under a federal system of government because so many of their proposals required provincial consultation, which was usually a lengthy process.

To make matters worse, the Canadian news media began counting from the day that the Pearson Government was sworn in: April 22, 1963. Thus May 16th, the day on which the Twenty-sixth Parliament opened, was counted as the twenty-fifth day of decision. Many Liberals felt it was unfair not to start the counting with the opening of Parliament. However, the new Prime Minister said nothing, which could have been a sign of Lester Pearson's political inexperience or a shrewd move on his part to get rid of an embarrassing pledge as quickly as possible; it would soon be forgotten because the public memory is short. In any case, there was an easy way out: they could say they had kept their word by filling the House of Commons' order paper with legislative proposals before the sixty days were up, which they did do.

There was a commitment for a budget within the period, and on June 13, the fifty-third day of decision, Walter Gordon brought down his budget. By the sixtieth day it had been torn to pieces and its author on the point of resigning. Most if not all the members of the Cabinet, according to Jack Nicholson, regretted that the promise was made, and political observers at the time assumed that the pressure to get things done in a hurry led to the disaster of the first budget. Certainly, a number of Ministers thought so. George McIlraith was opposed to an early budget, but Walter Gordon said that the time limit set by the sixty days of decision did not have any effect on him.

GEORGE McILRAITH

I quite firmly opposed the presenting of a budget so quickly and tried to get the Minister of Finance, Mr. Gordon, to simply present an accounting statement and to say that he would be giving that part of the budget that involved any tax changes later in the fall of the year, six months later, but to make no legislative changes at all in the budget—just say that we were continuing with the present law without change for the time being and give the statement of the accounts. I was not listened to at all. I got what I've always thought was less than a fair hearing by either the Prime Minister or Mr. Gordon.

Mr. Gordon pooh-poohed the idea of not being able to prepare a budget in two weeks . . . well, I'd known all the earlier Ministers of Finance like Mr. Ralston and Mr. Ilsley and Doug Abbott pretty well, and I had known how budgets were prepared, and I didn't think it could be done in that short time. And I still think that. In any event, Mr. Gordon said oh no, he could do it in two weeks or whatever the time was, and he could have it ready. Mr. Pearson simply [nodded]. Mr. Gordon's word and it didn't matter what anyone else said. That was it. I've always been cross with myself for not making a more vigorous and possibly even a little bit more violent protest.

MAURICE LAMONTAGNE

I remember at one stage asking Mr. Pearson—because I didn't want to ask Walter—"What about the forthcoming budget?" Mr. Pearson told me—I remember this very well—"Oh, this will be the most original budget. I cannot tell you more, but this will be formidable." And in all that time Walter Gordon was urging Mike to get permission to consult a few of us, including me, on this budget. But he didn't get the permission. So Walter Gordon never talked to me about his budget.

WALTER GORDON

It wasn't prepared too hastily. I had been thinking for about eight months—it was perfectly clear that Diefenbaker was about to be defeated—I assumed I was going to be Minister of Finance, and I naturally started to think about the kind of things we'd put forward in a budget. I was quite clear about them. So I wasn't starting from scratch.

Where the problem came was that I discovered that the Department of Finance was completely demoralised and unorganised. Poor old Ken Taylor [Deputy Minister]—I didn't know what the problem was but he had advanced senility. So the three or four assistant deputies went their own way. There was no co-ordination at all. It had been agreed that [Robert] Bryce would come in as Deputy Minister, and I told Ken Taylor that when I first met him, so his nose was naturally out of joint. Then Mike Pearson said, "You can't have Bryce for two months." So I'd made it awkward.

Gordon's controversial budget included not only the withdrawal of the exemption of the sales tax on building materials and a proposed 30 percent take-over tax (a levy on the sale of Canadian firms to foreigners) but also a proposal to increase the withholding tax on dividends of companies with less than 25 percent Canadian ownership and the lowering of that tax on companies with 25 percent or more Canadian ownership. However, the take-over tax was withdrawn and the withholding tax was modified.

It was not the budget itself that got Gordon into almost immediate trouble but the fact that he had taken on outside consultants to assist him, with all that meant as far as secrecy was concerned—and, under the British Parliamentary system, the preparation of the budget is a closely guarded secret.

WALTER GORDON

I did bring some people in to pull things together, which I didn't think was anything very special. I had done the same thing myself on two budgets for Ilsley. I'd been in on budget preparation; I'd written parts of the speeches; I produced some of the ideas, and I am sure other people have before and since. It's true that the officials in the department and in the Bank [of Canada] were very much opposed to anything that might conceivably upset the Americans. From this distance, it would look as if they still are. Except for the odd American like Walton Butterworth, who never should have been allowed out of the United States, I found most of the Americans quite sensible and quite understanding that we would like to have a little more control over our own affairs. They didn't like any measures that were proposed, but they could understand them.

Anyway, with the help of the men I brought in and with the help of the officials, especially Wyn Plumptre, who I'd gone to school with—I knew him very well—we prepared the budget. I went over it several times with Pearson. At one stage I told him that [Louis] Rasminsky [the governor of the Bank of Canada] was very upset about anything that would upset the Americans. I thought he should hear this from Rasminsky himself rather than through me.

So we went down to the Bank and had lunch with Rasminsky, and on the way back I remember Mike saying, "You've got a first-class budget. Don't pay any attention to this criticism. You'll be all right." And I remember saying, "Well, how about talking to

Kent and Lamontagne and Sharp or anybody else you'd like?" No, he didn't want me to do that. So the Cabinet really didn't know what was in the budget until either that morning or the night before, so they never had a chance to think about it much.

The outsiders Walter Gordon brought in were David Stanley and Martin O'Connell, both of whom were with financial houses in Toronto, and Geoff Conway, who was then at Harvard University. All three of them were closely associated with the Liberal Party and O'Connell was to become the Liberal Member for the Toronto riding of Scarborough East and briefly a Cabinet Minister. Their names were given to the House of Commons by the Finance Minister as a result of the questions of Douglas Fisher of the NDP, who had found out about their activities. They were variously called the three tinkers, the whiz kids, the bright boys of Bay Street, Toronto's financial district, by a gleeful Opposition.

DOUGLAS FISHER

This was an odd thing [how I found out about the three outsiders]. You see, an old classmate of mine, Ernie Steele was the number-two or number-three guy in the Treasury Board. Brian Land, who is a librarian like myself, was Walter Gordon's Executive Assistant and I'm always a nosy guy, I'm always looking for strange people.

One day, the day before the budget, I guess, I'm in the House of Commons dining room and I had had a phone-call chat with Ernie Steele just before. Ernie is an excellent civil servant; even though he knew me well, he was never going to give me anything. But he said one thing indirectly; I had sort of been teasing him about the new mandate and the new broom sweeping clean, and he was going to be swept away and so on, and he said, "Oh, I think I'm fine, but I'll tell you there are some very hurt feelings around, at least in one of the departments."

I thought to myself, what department could it be, and the only conclusion I could reach was Finance, eh? So I had that in my mind. And I went in the dining room and I spotted Brian with two guys having lunch and one of them looked vaguely familiar. When I'm going out, Brian is going out and is paying, and I said to Brian, "Who are those guys you are having lunch with?" and Brian was a very natural guy, very lovely guy, and he said, "Well, you know one of them, he was a classmate of ours at Toronto." This is Martin O'Connell. And he said, "I think you may have met the other one back at University." I said, "What are they doing here?" and a sort of mask fell over Brian's face: "Well, they're doing some work for the Minister."

So I went away and thought, "This is bloody odd." I knew Brian was right in there with Gordon. These guys were having lunch with him, chatting intimately. They just had to have something to do with the budget, and so I put that together with what Steele had told me and thought to myself, "Well, there's something here."

Then I phoned another chap I knew in the Treasury Board, at a lower level than Steele and a great gossip, and I said to him, I forget my question, but it was something like, "Are there a lot of noses out of joint over in Finance these days?" And he said, "Are there ever. They're not really sure they like Gordon. He isn't really paying that much attention to them."

Well, there I had it. That was the basis for my question. That's what I had to go on. I put it together from a number of things. And it really rolled from there. I knew I had something that could cause a squall. I'd been in the House long enough to know what gets press attention and what doesn't. I had become very good at what you might call that kind of managing. But I also knew that in order, given the timing and everything, in order to get the thing picked up and moving, it had to broaden out that very day or else it would be forgotten because so much was happening, particularly in relation to reaction to the budget.

As soon as I asked that question [in the House] Gordon got a funny look on his face; he was looking around, and Pickersgill went like that, and he made some kind of a signal—I still remember the scene, I was keyed up enough to be watching. Diefenbaker spotted it and Diefenbaker knew from Pickersgill's reaction that there was something here, and he came piling in on it, following it up. And then Douglas came in on it, and Gordon gave an unbelievably bad answer. If he had been precise and candid right off the top, it would have defused.

But that incident, if you go back and analyse it, had a double-barreled effect. The thing that opened it up was the outside advisors, which is really a nonsense thing, but there was that tradition. But the real sleeper was the business community's reaction to some of the taxation innovations.

WALTER GORDON

As for the business advisors, which Doug Fisher brought up, that was just politics. Their names had been in the press; everybody knew they were there; the whole story had been written up three weeks before, but [the Opposition] had made it into a beautiful scare. The suggestion was these guys would come in and their firms were benefitting and all that kind of thing. Which was nonsense. But it certainly did us a lot of harm.

The outsiders coming in, that was a phony issue—it had been done many times. I was brought in twice myself on two different budgets. This was under Ilsley. Then, when Walter Harris was Minister of Finance, I'd suggested this idea of a Royal Commission on Canada's Economic Prospects in a draft article. He called me up and said, "Instead of writing the article, can I use your ideas in my budget speech? I've cleared it with the Prime Minister; he thinks it's a great idea." Well, that was the guts of his budget speech, which I, as an outsider, had given him. I didn't go running around saying to people that the Minister of Finance is going to use my idea, and he knew I wouldn't. Those were three occasions when I was involved myself. These fellows had all taken the oath of secrecy, so I thought it was a phony issue, but it was a damaging one.

Mitchell Sharp did not consider the employment of outsiders as great an error as the way that Walter Gordon had ignored the advice of the permanent officials.

MITCHELL SHARP

He brought in three quite bright young fellows; but he was not listening to the advice of the permanent officials, and that was a serious mistake because they had had quite a lot of experience. I don't think they would be so concerned that they hadn't proposed ideas as that the Minister was not listening when they pointed out the pitfalls that lay across the path if the Minister was determined to move in this direction. And that was very serious.

I heard about this, and it did concern me. They were never disloyal. However, I knew them well enough to know that they had not been consulted. They didn't criticise the ideas to me directly. They simply said that they were not in on [the discussions]. It wasn't until after that I heard from some of them that they had actually advised against some of these policies. That gave me pause for thought because they were experienced civil servants whose only interest was in having policies that would work. They were not partisan in any sense.

However, it is very difficult for a Minister to criticise his colleagues, and particularly to the Prime Minister. You're all part of a team, and you feel that if you have responsibility you want a minimum of interference. You take that same view about your colleagues. After all, they are the ones who have to defend the policy. They are responsible for it. And so relations between Ministers, except under the gravest of emergencies, are usually very careful. However, perhaps if we had been a bit more outspoken it might have made a difference.

On budget night E. J. Benson, a chartered accountant and M.P. for Kingston who had been personally selected by Walter Gordon as his Parliamentary Secretary, had the job of phoning the presidents of the Toronto and Montreal stock exchanges and telling them about the changes proposed, especially the 30 percent take-over tax and the introduction of the sales tax on building materials. Benson recalled that they weren't very happy but they hadn't thought through the full implementation of these measures. He said that Gordon had been advised that the take-over tax was workable, but the Parliamentary Secretary admitted that it would have been difficult to find out who owned the shares and might bring the stock markets to a halt. Mitchell Sharp said that the take-over tax did a lot of damage to the government, and to the Finance Minister in particular, because businessmen could not understand how a proposal could be included in the budget which was so obviously unworkable. One who was incensed was Eric Kierans, then president of the Montreal Stock Exchange, who took immediate action.

ERIC KIERANS

The focus of my attack, of course, was what he called a 30 percent tax on the sale of Canadian firms to foreigners. Well, in the first place, although this is just a semantic thing, it wasn't a tax. A tax is really between two different points in time. A tax is on an income flow or on changes in capital values between year one and year two, and so on. This was a straight levy of 30 percent, and he had absolutely no comprehension whatsoever of the impact that this would have on stock exchange values, which as a president I was bound to and, in fact, pleased to protect on this particular occasion. Then, there were a number of other objections to the budget, his definition of what would be a satisfactory percentage of Canadian ownership and so on. So I wrote him a very strong letter and asked for an appointment, which I got for the following Tuesday.

A number of the governors of the exchange went to Ottawa with me. I may say, for the record, that no member of the Board of Governors of the Montreal Stock Exchange had seen my submission until they were on their way, the reason being that I was afraid that they might want to water it down, in which case it would have lost a good deal of its impact. I know that one of the governors later told me that when they got around to opening the envelopes—they went by limousine and I went up by train with the vice-president of the Stock Exchange—when they got to Ste Anne de Bellevue they began to look at the submission and then they started to roll down the windows to get some air. But by this time it was too late.

Since it was an all-out battle, I had arranged to have a number of copies of the presentation xeroxed or mimeographed, and available for release to the press, within minutes of seeing the Minister of Finance. As he rather bitterly said—and he was quite right—the opposition seemed to have been well orchestrated.

We went through the various points that we had against the budget. Among other things I said—part of which might have been misconstrued by Mr. Gordon—that as president of the Stock Exchange, if effect were given to his measures in the budget, I could only suggest that it would be very advisable for Canadians at large to sell stock short, because I said certainly all the more sophisticated people were going to do it, and I would hate to see ordinary Canadians caught buying stocks in a situation what was obviously going to lead to a falling market.

He later said that I had suggested or recommended that Canadians short the market in order to put pressure on the government, but this was not true.

Mr. Gordon, at the meeting, was certainly very gentlemanly, but I think he was rather astonished at the violence of the attack, which I suppose he had every right to be because I was quite upset by the measures in the budget and thought that they were very ill conceived and had taken no account whatsoever—however well motivated they may have been—of their impact on the economy. But I think he became very much more bitter when the meeting was over in half an hour, and he came to the door with me and with my colleagues, the governors, who had said nothing at all during the meeting, and saw that the press was gathered outside in force. I think this was a shock to him.

WALTER GORDON

There was a lot of criticism [of the take-over tax], and Kierans was one of the most vocal. He eventually turned up in my office with eight or nine brokers, and he practically told them that they should sell the markets short. Well, what do you do? He had written a letter to me, but he had given it to the press before he came. It was pretty exaggerated and intemperate, but Eric was out to accomplish something, and he did.

I said to Pearson the next morning—I'd thought it over in the night—that perhaps the only solution was to withdraw these provisions, because, otherwise, there'd be a flight of capital from Canada, and we ran the risk of a second devaluation within fourteen months of one that occurred under Diefenbaker and Fleming. So rightly or wrongly, that's what we did.

Shortly after the House of Commons met on Wednesday, June 19, Walter Gordon rose to say that the take-over tax would be withdrawn because of administrative difficulties. He made this announcement before the stock markets had closed in Canada.

ERIC KIERANS

I was in my office at the Stock Exchange. Gordon must have announced it sometime around two-fifteen because a group of floor traders came in and told me it was on the Dow-Jones and they were all whooping it up because the market promptly reversed itself. I don't think really that it was that costly to people, the manner in which he did it. I guess his reasoning would have been, "Well, if we have to take it off, take it off!" He could have waited, but then he would have had to wait till six o'clock. But I think that was a detail. It may have been a sign of panic.

After this retreat Walter Gordon spoke to Prime Minister Pearson about resigning. It was not a formal offer and he was easily dissuaded from doing so.

WALTER GORDON

I don't know if Pearson dissuaded me [from resigning]. I wasn't all that keen to do it anyway. I may have said, "If it would help you, I could always resign." And I think he said, "You feel you can carry on all right?" And I said, "Sure." It wasn't all that serious.

Then later, he told somebody I hadn't [resigned]. So I said, "Well, now, you know, what happens if I am asked?" "Well," he said, "You didn't in writing; it was just in conversation. I don't call that offering your resignation seriously." So I said I hadn't.

MITCHELL SHARP

Walter Gordon offered his resignation, and Mr. Pearson called me in and said that if he accepted it he would like me to take over as Minister of Finance. I said, well, I hadn't sought the job but if he wanted me to take it I would take it. Then he consulted various other people, and some of them spoke to me. I heard nothing further after that one interview with the Prime Minister until Cabinet, when the Prime Minister said that he had received an offer of resignation from Mr. Gordon, but he had said to him he would accept it only if Mr. Gordon felt he couldn't carry on. Mr. Gordon said that he was able to carry on, so he asked him to withdraw it, and Mr. Gordon remained as Finance Minister.

MAURICE LAMONTAGNE

I remember very well, one afternoon during the budget debate, Mr. Pearson, who had just been out of the hospital after a small operation—he had been afraid before that it might have been cancer; it was not, fortunately, on that occasion—called me with Allan MacEachen to 24 Sussex and told me, "Are you ready to become the Minister of Trade and Commerce?" I didn't want that.

He said, "Well, I'm thinking about making a few changes, and of course this will involve a new Minister of Finance." I said, "What? After what you told me about the budget, after what Walter Gordon has done for you, you're ready to let him go [*snaps fingers*] like this?" I said, "Well, make your own changes if you want, but I certainly will not become the Minister of Trade and Commerce."

J. W. PICKERSGILL

I don't think I was consulted about it [Gordon's resignation] in any formal sense, but Pearson did speak to me about it, and I said, "You never do this kind of thing under fire. We're all committed to this. It was something that the Cabinet accepted, whether most of us understood what was in it, it doesn't matter. We accepted it and we can't let him go unless he insists on going." And he didn't insist. I don't think he should have, and I would have been very sorry if he had. I think the government would have suffered far more if he had quit. I don't know that every one of my colleagues agreed with that view, but it was certainly mine.

PAUL MARTIN

When Walter resigned, Mr. Pearson didn't want him to, I can assure you of that. He felt so obligated to Walter, and he liked him personally so much. There were few things in Pearson's life that gave him more anguish than his disagreements with Walter Gordon. He had every reason to be very grateful to Walter, both politically and otherwise. And the fact that they differed to the point that they did was a matter of great disappointment and concern to him throughout the whole of his life, right up until the end. I know that. But Walter shouldn't have resigned the first time and Pearson dissuaded him doing that, and I think rightly. Because that would have been a very serious thing, not only for Walter but for the government.

Tommy Douglas felt that he should have resigned, that it would have been better for him if he had done so, while Lionel Chevrier recalled the difficulties that the government had in the House of Commons with the constant demands for his resignation.

T. C. DOUGLAS

I think Gordon would have been wise to resign in the first place when the question of the financial experts came up. As a matter of fact, I understand he did offer his resignation to Mr. Pearson and Pearson didn't want to accept it. But this was not an indication of his incompetence. It was an indication of his political inexperience. If he'd been in the House before, if he'd ever been a parliamentary assistant, if he'd ever been in the Opposition, if he'd ever held any post or had been a financial critic for the Opposition, he would have known you never make announcements—even pretty bland announcements about some change in the oil regulations—you don't make them till eight o'clock at night because there might be just a possibility that somebody on the West Coast gets it over the radio and can jump on the Stock Exchange and make a killing out of it.   But why did this Deputy Minister and staff not advise him? They would be familiar with the usual procedures. I don't know whether he didn't listen to them or whether he didn't consult them or whether they were so annoyed about the financial experts from Bay Street being brought in that they were saying to Walter, "Well, you wanted to have these fellows tell you what to do, so ask them what to do, we're not going to give you any advice."

LIONEL CHEVRIER

We ran into trouble with Walter Gordon not because of the contents of the budget but because he got those three or four people in from Toronto. Should he have done it? Perhaps he shouldn't have, but he *certainly* shouldn't have without consulting

the Deputy Minister of Finance and others who were responsible
for the preparation of the budget. And that's what [the
Opposition] centred on during the whole discussion on the
budget—the manner in which it was done, bringing in these
fellows from the outside. What happened in Britain? The fellow
resigned when he was in a similar position. Resign! And of course
that kept on and on and on. And then we withdrew, we
abandoned some of the things in the budget. And the more we
withdrew, the more they attacked.

*As Walter Gordon put it, there was not much rallying around, although
he did say that Mitchell Sharp made what he described as a good speech
and so did Maurice Lamontagne, while Jack Pickersgill had done a lot of
interjecting on his behalf.*

*It certainly looked to us observers of the Parliamentary scene at that
time that the Finance Minister had been abandoned by his Cabinet
colleagues and left alone amidst the uproar of the House to face the taunts
and jeers of the Opposition. Certainly, there were not many Ministers
who came to his defence during the budget debate. The veteran
Parliamentarians, the experienced members of the government—and
these included Lester Pearson—were notable by their silence or by their
absence from the Chamber. Douglas Fisher said that it was almost
shameful the way that Pearson had not backed up his Finance Minister.*

WALTER GORDON

For some reason or other, once the storm began, Pearson didn't
do anything about it. He not only didn't say anything in the
House, but he didn't support me in Cabinet. Again, he'd had a
cyst removed from his neck, and maybe he wasn't up to it, but he
didn't support the budget in Cabinet, and that was what really led
to the trouble, because I had to make [concessions] in the face of
little support in the Cabinet. I know Harry Hays must have
supported me because he would, and Lamontagne and Judy
[LaMarsh] and maybe one or two others, but the rest were all in
favour of retreats. And when the Prime Minister didn't support
me, I had to retreat or quit. So that's what led to most of the
trouble.

PAUL HELLYER

The Cabinet didn't know about the budget until the morning it was brought down. By which time it was absolutely useless to say anything because it had already been printed and distributed across the country and was in the hands of the Bank of Canada for distribution later in the day. So that it was a *fait accompli* and consequently there was no sense, really, in trying to do anything. We were accused later of not having come to Gordon's rescue in the shambles, but I think a lot of us felt that if we had any direct responsibility for what happened, we would have been more than pleased to. But having been faced, as we were, with something that we didn't necessarily agree with and which we knew instinctively in advance was going to cause a lot of trouble, it was pretty hard to go out and beat the drums and say what a great thing it was.

TOM KENT

Walter was a confident, proud person. I would say that Walter Gordon without any question was one of the most charming, delightful, honest in every way, best people that I have ever known in my life. I have the greatest regard and fondness for Walter, and I'd stay with him whatever mistakes he made or anything else. I've great personal regard for Walter. That's not saying, however, that I didn't disagree with him on lots of issues, but that's not the point. As a person, he was a little impatient, a little haughty. He was the man who filled the vacuum primarily. And naturally old politicians resent that. They were prepared to go along with it if it was winning, but when Walter slipped, they weren't going to come to his help.

I think there was a period of a couple of weeks or so when Walter was so dispirited that he didn't want to go anywhere or do anything. I know there was a whole series of days when I went and had a sandwich with him in his office for lunch because I knew otherwise he'd be sitting there alone having a sandwich.

But, that is the nature of the political process. It was the tribute to the enormous central importance of the role that Walter had played up to that point, but when he slipped, the more traditional members of the party, the veterans, they weren't going to get in there to help him.

Then there was the business of Dick O'Hagan polling the members of the Parliamentary Press Gallery on the question of whether or not Walter Gordon should resign. Had the Prime Minister asked his press officer to do this?

RICHARD O'HAGAN

I do know that Mr. Gordon felt that I had somehow been, not so much undermining his position, but more seriously than that, that I might be acting on behalf of the Prime Minister in seeking views as to how people felt about him. And given the pressures that were on Mr. Gordon as Minister of Finance, I think that it was understandably not well received by him to think that some person on behalf of the Prime Minister was informally and semi-publicly taking soundings on whether or not he should continue in office. As I say, this impression may have been formed in the minds of certain people, but it was certainly an erroneous one.

I couldn't do my job at that time and not talk to some degree or entertain conversation on the subject of Mr. Gordon. And the press was filled with speculation about his future and whether he could stay on in the circumstances and so on.

Mr. Pearson kept in touch personally and through people like myself, with what was being said in the media about questions of this kind. He followed this sort of thing very, very closely indeed, and there was nothing uncommon or exceptional in these circumstances or in any other about his wanting to know what were people saying, what was the media saying, and so on. It was just part of his normal information-seeking process.

Further changes in the budget had to be made. In the end there was little left of the original one. The construction industry protested the 11 percent sales tax on building materials and, while this was not withdrawn, it was modified so that it went into effect in easy stages. Walter Gordon recalled that this was one suggestion that officials of the Finance Department had made. When he asked them how he could raise more money, they said to withdraw the sales tax exemptions. They didn't tell him that there was an old memorandum warning a previous Finance Minister of the troubles that he would get into if he lifted the exemptions—Gordon said they probably forgot. During the frantic days when the budget was being torn apart, Ben Benson, the Parliamentary Secretary, actually attended a Cabinet meeting.

E. J. BENSON

I did go to a Cabinet meeting. I think it was the first time a Parliamentary Secretary had gone to one. The Cabinet was very nervous; they had just taken over power and they were unsure of themselves, and here there was this big fuss all of a sudden over the budget. I think they were very nervous about it. Also, they weren't familiar with what was involved in the steps that were being taken in the budget. This sometimes happens. It isn't a matter of not supporting one [the Minister], it's a matter of not having knowledge of the particular subject. None of them got up and contended the budget or resigned or anything.

MAURICE LAMONTAGNE

We had to start to repair the damage and, unfortunately, Mr. Pearson didn't help very much. But he appointed a small committee of the Cabinet, Mitchell Sharp, and the Minister of National Revenue at that time [J. R.] Garland, and me. Walter didn't want to make too many changes, and he had to give way in certain places. We were discussing this, and I think that secretly—and I don't want to be too bad about him—but I think that secretly Mitchell at that time had the call to become the Minister of Finance, and was not too helpful in trying to reform the budget. We were working, Garland and I, and that's where we worked this escalation for the application of the tax on building materials.

Then we had this tremendous Cabinet meeting at Harrington Lake one morning, everybody going for the kill again. Walter survived this very well. I was one of his last supporters in the Cabinet. I remember saying at the coffee break that morning,

"Well, we don't have many friends around here," although he had been one of the great architects of the Liberal victory.

Just a few weeks later we had a meeting of the national federation. Mike was joking about the budget and saying that Walter had made mistakes. Walter was very humiliated inside. Mike's remarks were made with good intentions, in a joking way, but it certainly didn't help. That was the beginning of their mutual distrust—not mutual, but I think that's when Walter began to have questions about our leadership.

TOM KENT

What was actually done was not only to withdraw the take-over tax but to beat a retreat from all sorts of other provisions of the budget. The withholding tax was reduced. The rate of sales tax, the form in which it was extended to other things, was toned down, and so on and so forth. Really the whole budget was rewritten. And that was a major political mistake. That is what I think created such a bad feeling of government incompetence and indecisiveness and so on which really continued like a cloud around the Pearson Government for the rest of its life. But that wasn't Walter. That was forced on Walter in his time of weakness by the rest of the Cabinet. It was a very, very serious setback for the government.

PAUL HELLYER

To start off this way wasn't exactly proof positive that we were the absolute ultimate managers that we had suggested we might be. It was quite a black eye. There's always the question under those circumstances as to whether retrenchment will take place or whether it won't, and if it does who will resign, and if it doesn't who won't and who will, and all this sort of thing. So it was a tense time in the government.

GEORGE McILRAITH

It destroyed the confidence of the Prime Minister in the man who had done so much for him, and to whom he felt so grateful, and to whom he'd given so much confidence. The Prime Minister

really had given, if you like, all his confidence to this one Minister.
And it destroyed his confidence in himself rather badly, to realise
that maybe he'd made a bit of an error.

Perhaps it's fair to say it showed up the Pearson Government.
But it tended to be local in its damage, as distinct from being
damaging to the government. Perhaps it was locally damaging to
Mr. Gordon personally, very damaging, and to Mr. Pearson quite
a bit—more so than to the government collectively.

*Just before the sixty days were up, the government loaded the order paper
with resolutions proposing the establishment of an Economic Council, a
separate Department of Industry with an area development agency, and
on June 21, the last day, a technical and vocational training act, the
Canada Pension Plan, amendments to the National Housing Act to allow
for urban renewal programs, and a special committee to consider the
hazards of food contamination from insecticides and pesticides. So that
when Maurice Lamontagne entered the budget debate on June 25, he could
say that "in the sixty days just passed, the decisions that were promised
have been made."*

*However, Lamontagne devoted most of what was his maiden speech in
the House of Commons to the dangers facing the country with all the talk
of separatism in Quebec and of the convening of the states general. He
warned of the disastrous economic consequences of independence for French
Canada. Then he declared that the government was proposing a new
alliance, a confederation that would be developed in accordance with the
principle of equality between the two founding nations. Canadians would
soon have the opportunity to state their views on this objective before the
Royal Commission on Bilingualism and Biculturalism, which, in the new
Minister's words, would be conducting "a referendum on the future of our
country."*

*This commission, "charged to study, thoroughly but urgently, how the
fundamentally bicultural character of Canada may best be assured and the
contribution of other cultures recognized," was the first proposal in the
Speech from the Throne opening the Twenty-sixth Parliament, and
Lamontagne had been working on its make-up ever since the Pearson
Government was sworn in on April 22. It was a slow business, partly
because this was one matter where there had to be consultations with the
provincial governments and partly because it was difficult to get the people*

they wanted. Prime Minister Pearson found Frank Scott, the McGill law professor and poet, hesitant about joining the commission and asked Robert Fowler, a fellow Montrealer and friend, to persuade him to accept, which Fowler did.

MAURICE LAMONTAGNE

As a Minister, I had to prepare the terms of reference of the commission. I gave this three days of very intense thought. George Davidson was my so-called Deputy Minister and he had prepared the terms of reference, and they were just terrible. I liked George, but he was not in it, really. So I had to work on this, both in French and in English, very carefully. I had mentioned in the terms of references *les deux peuples fondateurs,* the two founding peoples.

When I came to the Cabinet there was only one thing changed in the English version, which gave us quite a bit of trouble afterwards. Pickersgill suggested "the two founding races" [instead of the two founding peoples]. The Jews felt they were excluded but we wouldn't change the terms of reference for just that one word ["race"]. I remember Pearson pleading with a big Jewish delegation. He said, "We didn't mean this." I was very glad that I had not made that error; because Pickersgill was older than I was and in those years they were speaking of races as ethnic groups, really—not black and yellow. That was the only change which was made in the English version.

Then we had to set up the commission, so I said to Pearson, "This will be worse than a Cabinet meeting," I wanted to have [André] Laurendeau by all means. My idea was to have a very balanced commission with four English-speaking of English stock, Irish, Scottish, and four French Canadians, and then two from the new groups because they were included in the terms of reference. I had three interviews with Laurendeau. This was the first time that, having made a proposal, he was faced with the responsibility. We have an old saying in French: *Vouloir, c'est vouloir aussi les conséquences de ce qu'on veut.* He was faced for the first time with that kind of responsibility and challenge. I had to see him three times to convince him to become chairman.

My co-chairman on the English-speaking side was to have been [Roland] Michener, but it proved to be impossible because he was engaged as the chairman of a Royal Commission on Local Government Organisation in Manitoba. Then Mike thought about it and he said, "Well, Davie Dunton," I had known Davie Dunton, and I was a little bit reluctant because he was too much on the French Canadian side, and would unbalance the commission. He came from Montreal and all that. All these people had to be bilingual—speak French and speak English. After a while Laurendeau accepted, and then we had to balance everything.

Marchand was on the list, and he was not too much in favour of Jean-Louis Gagnon but Gagnon was the only Liberal that we wanted to appoint because we knew he was a strong federalist. I have always had a great admiration for Jean-Louis, not as an administrator but as a good writer, a good thinker, and a real liberal with a small "*l*." So I said to Jean, "This is a take-it-or-leave-it proposal." Then I had to interview my old friend Frank Scott, who had been identified with the CCF. At one stage when I came to Cabinet with just five people, they said, "Where are the Liberals?" On the English-speaking side, Pickersgill provided the name of that great woman from Alberta, Mrs. Gertrude Laing. Then we had Father [Clément] Cormier who was a student of mine at Laval University, and as the rector of the University of Moncton, represented the Acadians. We had trouble with the last two. I had met a great Ukrainian in Montreal, but he didn't fit. We had to have a Ukrainain from the West because the Ukrainian from Montreal was too assimilated. We appointed J. B. Rudnyckyj who came from Winnipeg and had to be fluent in English and French as well. And we got a Pole, Paul Wyczynski, a professor at the University of Ottawa.

We had consultations with all the provinces and it was a very exceptional step that we took at that time, to have a federal royal commission with consultation on the terms of reference and the membership with all the premiers. They all accepted this because we wanted also to include in the terms of reference the teaching of languages in schools. I think it was a unique event. When the whole Cabinet approved this, the premiers accepted this, we were going.

DOUGLAS FISHER

What was emerging was a whole new interpretation of the Constitution, that is, new to English Canada. And the irony of this is Frank Scott. I had had a lot of fun in the House of Commons over the years with the Tremblay Report. This was the commission that Duplessis had set up to report on the Constitution. And the Tremblay Report came out I think in 1958, with these recommendations built upon the two-nations theory. And one of the constitutionalists who shot that down—Trudeau was another—was Frank Scott, the great McGill lawyer, constitutionalist, civil liberties man. Read that analysis where he kicked hell out of the Tremblay Report's two-nations theory, this whole idea that we were two nations and that the Confederation was based upon a compact — he just ruined it.

They made him one of the B and B commissioners and all of a sudden that became legitimate. Frank Scott wound up being a booster, because of the crisis that was developing, for the compact theory of Confederation and the two founding nations. Well, this is the old thing that anybody who has read much history knows—Toynbee made much of this. Each generation rewrites history to suit its own situation. So what the B and B did, they went back and bastardised and plagiarised and distorted the Confederation and the intent of the Fathers and decided that we'd been two founding people who'd come together in a compact. When you translated this into 1960 terms, it meant all these things, and one of them was bilingualism.

The Royal Commission on Bilingualism and Biculturalism, or the B and B Commission as it was called, was like no other commission in Canadian history. It broke with the tradition that a commission should be representative of the country at large, of its regions: there was no member from British Columbia and none from Saskatchewan, and the Atlantic Provinces were represented by Father Cormier, who belonged to a distinct minority in New Brunswick, the French-speaking Acadians. No previous commission had two chairmen, and, since André Laurendeau and Davidson Dunton, the co-chairmen, were bilingual, they must have been chosen to represent French and English Canada. And, as Maurice Lamontagne said, bilingualism was a qualification for membership on this extraordinary commission. So four members whose mother tongue was French—Laurendeau, Jean Marchand, Jean-Louis Gagnon, and Father Clément Cormier—represented French Canada, while four members whose mother tongue was English—Davie Dunton, Royce Frith, Frank Scott, and the lone Westerner, Mrs. Gertrude Laing—represented English Canada. The other two members J. B. Rudnyckyj and Paul Wyczynski were representative of Canadians of neither British nor French descent. Thus the B and B Commission was a binational commission and was set up as such.

It was a most expensive commission , and the millions that it spent were a harbinger of the amount that bilingualism would cost.

STANLEY KNOWLES

I think it was a break with tradition, and I think it was something that [Pearson] had to do. We can't cope with or resolve the problems of the English and French languages in this country unless, in consideration of them, we give them equal status. We can't do it as a nine-versus-one proposition. We can't have a commission made up of nine times as many from English Canada as from French Canada.

MITCHELL SHARP

There was some dissent in Cabinet about confronting the problem frontally, as this [commission] appeared to do. However, I don't recall that it led to any Ministers seriously threatening to withdraw from the government or anything like that. For most of us—and I must confess that I was one of them—it was a new and rather strange problem. We understood a bit about bilingualism. We hadn't really examined the problem, nor had we examined the aspirations of those who were trying to change the relationship between Francophones and Anglophones in the country.

There were some questions, as I recall it, raised right at the beginning as to whether it was bicultural, but at that time those objections weren't raised in a sufficiently forceful way to change the name of the commission. There were quite a number of people who pointed to the fact that there were other communities in the country that would resent being categorized as *Anglais,* including myself, who considers himself a Scottish Canadian rather than an English Canadian. But this was true of many people who had a greater reason to resent it.

This was to me the beginning of the development of the bilingual approach, and there have been so many developments since that time it's difficult to put oneself back in the frame of mind we were in at that time. We understood that there were serious problems of separatism. We did have in the government some excellent representation from the province of Quebec, very vigorous people. However, we were not as much aware then as we are now of the basis of their legitimate complaints against the situation as it then existed.

So the B and B Commission was accepted, more I think as an experiment. I didn't believe that they would come forward with recommendations that were going to revolutionise the country. I didn't foresee the way things would develop in this sphere. I don't know whether the Prime Minister did or not. And as the reports began coming out and the vast amounts of money that were spent began to emerge, there were some who doubted whether it had been a wise decision. I have no doubt that it was an excellent idea. I really don't think that the country would have stayed together as it did if there has not been an opportunity for the Francophones in particular to express in this tangible form their grievances.

JOHN CONNOLLY

Mike [Pearson] was a very fair fellow, he was fair in everything that I ever knew him to do. I never knew him to take an arbitrary stand, even for political purposes. When it came to the question of the French Canadian and his opportunities, certainly even in the public service, it was obvious they were limited; and it was I think more the desire for fairness, to do the right thing, to bring them into the mainstream of national life, to let them know that their opportunities here were just as good as anybody else's. This was the thing that seemed to dominate the thinking that went into the establishment of the B and B Commission. We didn't talk about the power base in Quebec. Nobody can say that it wasn't in the back of our minds.

JEAN MARCHAND

This is what I learned in the commission when we went around meeting the people. We visited a small place in the Lake St. John area [in Quebec]. I'd say: "What's wrong?" And the people would say: "The manager of the mill or whatever it was has been here for ten years—and he has never learned to say either 'yes' or 'no' in French. We all had to learn English." The population in that area is 99.9 percent French.

So, for me, this was much more the cause of the trouble in Quebec than the fact that there was no bilingualism, say, at the Vancouver airport. Actually, at that time, nobody was travelling by airplane, or just a few people. I think that the main source of dispute or conflict or tension or friction—call it whatever you want—was Quebec itself and the federal institutions where there was surely no equality for all practical purposes.

GEORGE McILRAITH

I know [the co-chairmen] were both bilingual, but neither one of them would have got a fair hearing in all parts of the country. In dealing with the subject of bilingualism, no matter how careful you are, you always have a danger down the line of somebody trying to interpret it as a biracial or binational thing. But I think on balance that that commission could not have been heard across the country with one chairman, no mater how bilingual he was. That was the regrettable fact at the time [the commission] was created.

DOUGLAS FISHER

They had such marvellous incidents. My favourite one is about the guy who was the first head of Information Canada, that Liberal hack, Jean-Louis Gagnon; Jean Marchand, who was also on the commission was given the job of raising hell with Jean-Louis Gagnon about his expense accounts. I heard this from one of the permanent people, and he said it was just a classic because Gagnon had terribly expensive tastes. He's been living in the public trough for many years through his connection with the Liberal Party, and wherever he goes it's filet mignons and royal suites and this kind of thing. That was a big expense-account operation because naturally the commissioners had to visit almost any place in the world that spoke more than one language. Well, Jean-Louis Gagnon was running up the expense accounts and Marchand, who is a simple man and tough, was given the job of trying to bring Jean-Louis into line, without any bloody success at all. And I'm very pleased that Jean-Louis, when he became an embarrassment to Information Canada, his Liberal friends were able to give him those fine years in Paris with the best cuisine in the world [as Ambassador to UNESCO].

JEAN-LUC PEPIN

I made a very impassioned speech on bilingualism in Montreal, I think it was in '64. I got carried away as some of us do, and I said, "This is an objective that has got to be implemented, and very rapidly. We've been waiting for 96 years. This is something that's got to be done in the next five years, otherwise all of us will resign, and I will." And this is when Pearson gave me a scolding—not personally but by letter. I received a little note one day to tell me that this was very, very, very bad and would I kindly not do it again.

Not everybody was in favour of the B and B Commission when it was set up: there were those in the Liberal Government who had their doubts, but they didn't vote against it, as Agriculture Minister Harry Hays said. According to Lawrence T. Pennell, who was to become Solicitor General, it made little impression on Liberal M.P.s at the time.

HARRY HAYS

I think [Mr. Pearson] thought they were going too far. He didn't want to hold them back. He became annoyed about these things—he was really a middle-of-the-roader—particularly when the bills started coming in. It was a costly thing. But bilingualism? Other than think that it was out of hand, we agreed with it at the time. Everybody agreed with it. Everybody agrees with something new, and then when it doesn't work there are always those doubting Thomases who will have forgotten how they voted.

LAWRENCE PENNELL

As I recollect it, it [the B and B Commission] didn't seem to make a great impact on the caucus, though I had had the benefit of a talk with Mr. Pearson before this and I think the present advances have proved his pre-vision. He said to me then, "Use all your spare time to study constitutional law. I know you're a lawyer, but perhaps you haven't been doing constitutional law." But he said, "The French Fact in Canada is really going to be at the forefront of Canadian politics."

J. J. GREENE

Mackenzie King was my model as to how to run Canada. On this pervasive issue, which will always be there as long as we attempt this impossible dream of running East and West instead of North and South, you don't rattle the crockery, as the mandarins of the civil service put it. It's a Mackenzie King deal, it's two steps forward and one step back. It's not some great solution. I didn't really think anything as blatant as the B and B Commission would work—it has led to all this being too much a national issue, and the expectation of some overt and complete solution. There is none.

Lester Pearson was surprised that Maurice Sauvé should be so outspoken in his opposition to the whole bilingual policy. Sauvé, who was not a Minister at the time, asserted that the commission would only do damage to Confederation. That was also the view of Gordon Churchill, a former Conservative Cabinet Minister and Diefenbaker's right-hand man.

MAURICE SAUVÉ

I was totally opposed to the concept [of bilingualism] and totally opposed to the royal commission. I said it would only clearly establish in a more scientific way the situation of the French Canadians in Canada, it would only give more ammunition to all the people who are opposed to Canada, and it would only help the strong separatist and nationalist element in Quebec with arguments to fight against Canada in favour of isolation in Quebec.

I said: "We have enough trouble now and I don't want any more trouble stirred up. The commission will not help. The problem of language is an emotional one and, in any case, it's not the real issue. The real issue is the economic domination of the Francophone by the Anglophone. And as long as we have not resolved that, we're going to have trouble."

When the royal commission was announced, I was not very pleased. I was not in the Cabinet at the time, and Mr. Pearson never asked my advice on the subject.

GORDON CHURCHILL

I suppose it was a delaying tactic. I was opposed to it [the commission] from the start. I thought it would do nothing but create disunity. At one of the meetings that we had on it in our caucus I raised the question about other people in Canada who are neither English or French. Coming from Western Canada, I was thoroughly familiar with the activities of other groups within our country who don't trace their origins to the British Isles or to France. But I was brushed aside on that. I think it offended a great many of what we call the ethnic groups in Canada; it made them feel as if they were second-class citizens. I think the pressure came from Mr. Lesage and this was Mr. Pearson's typical response to that.

Instead of creating unity, it has created more disunity than I have known in my lifetime, except in 1917 over the conscription crisis.

DOUGLAS FISHER

When you look back on the commission, it was very much a joke. They spent many millions on some of the most ill-conceived and fantastically optimistic research projects. They didn't get that much published, but they got a library shelf published, and I suppose it's gathering dust in libraries all across the country. Awful crap! It was a sociologist thing. They imported sociologists from the United States and they had them doing the damnedest things in terms of surveys and exercises. I think the most beautiful one was the one that's never been published—the survey they did of the members of the Parliamentary Press Gallery.

Bruce Hutchison, the West Coast editor, felt the commission was a sign of how well Pearson understood the problem of French Canada.

BRUCE HUTCHISON

My belief is that Mr. Pearson was the first English-speaking Prime Minister who really had grasped what we now call the Quebec fact: that we were in great trouble, that in some fashion, which he wasn't very clear about—nobody was—in some fashion the aspirations and the rights of the French Canadian people must be respected and codified and understood by the English-speaking majority in this country. He was groping—as he did so often in international affairs—for some form of compromise, of agreement, of conciliation between the two communities of Canada.

To that end, and partly I think to buy time, but still to develop the situation, to explore it, and to above all educate the English-speaking community and the French too, he established the Bicultural and Bilingual Commission whose report made little impression at the time but has proved to be profoundly right. It said, "Look, we are facing a great crisis. It will grow increasingly great," as it has until we've reached the critical stage. Mr. Pearson obviously did not foresee, nor did any man foresee, exactly how or when the crisis would develop, but it seems to me that he did grasp the fact that we must deal with this problem.

It was on July 22, 1963, less than a month after Maurice Lamontagne made his maiden speech during the budget debate, that Prime Minister Pearson announced the formation of the Royal Commission on Bilingualism and Biculturalism. Some eighteen months later, in February, 1965, the commission published a preliminary report which said that "Canada, without being fully conscious of the fact, is passing through the greatest crisis in its history." The commission went on to say that this was a time when decisions had to be taken and developments must occur leading either to the break-up of Canada or a new set of conditions for its future existence. At the time there were doubts expressed about the assessment, which was considered to be somewhat exaggerated; however, the crisis was more deep-seated than was understood then, according to Mitchell Sharp. Douglas Fisher was of the view that the crisis was the creature of the commission, and that if there were bad political leadership, there would always be a crisis since the two peoples, the French- and the English-speaking Canadians, had no love for each other.

When he made his maiden speech, which was a summing up of the sixty days of decision, Maurice Lamontagne said that the government would not wait for the B and B Commission's recommendations before taking action. As far as Ottawa or the federal administration was concerned, he said, "We want to achieve as soon as possible perfect equality for the two official languages, not only with regard to verbal or written communications with the public, but within every department."

RALPH COWAN

The funny thing about that B and B Commission: do you know that the House of Commons was never asked to vote on the acceptance of the report of that commission? Never! The commission just wrote and wrote and wrote and wrote; it was the most expensive commission ever appointed by the House of Commons since Confederation. And it never had a report adopted by the House of Commons.

6 A Flag for All

AT THE END of December 1963 Lionel Chevrier and Azellus Denis announced their forthcoming resignations as Justice Minister and Postmaster General, which allowed Prime Minister Pearson to restructure his government. Both Ministers were veterans of the Liberal years in Opposition, and some astonishment was expressed in the papers that they should have quit so soon after enjoying the fruits of office. There was talk that Chevrier as a Franco-Ontarian — he had represented the Ontario riding of Stormont for twenty years before switching to the Montreal constituency of Laurier — had never been fully accepted as leader by the Quebec caucus, but Chevrier denied this; he said that he had found the work as Justice Minister and Quebec lieutenant just too much and was glad to accept the post of Canadian High Commissioner in London. Azellus Denis was made a Senator as his reward for stepping down.

Now that these two members of the Old Guard were gone, there would be no serious opposition to making Maurice Sauvé a Minister, which Pearson did on February 3, 1964. He replaced Senator Ross Macdonald with Senator John Connolly as the Senate Member in the Cabinet, and appointed Yvon Dupuis, the rousing young popular orator whom he had credited with winning the 1963 election, Minister Without Portfolio. He told Dupuis that he wasn't giving him a department because he wanted him to be free to act as his substitute in receiving delegations and making speeches and representing Canada abroad. There were half a dozen changes in portfolios on February 3, 1964, when Lester Pearson made his

152

first Cabinet shuffle, the most important of which was that of Guy Favreau, who was moved from Citizenship and Immigration, where he had been praised as a great humanitarian, to replace Lionel Chevrier as Justice Minister and Quebec lieutenant; he was also made government House leader.

The uproar in Parliament over Walter Gordon's budget had died down but the House of Commons was not a quiet or peaceful place; there was the continuing clash between Prime Minister Pearson and Opposition Leader John Diefenbaker, which was developing into a classical political feud. The Ministers were busy with their new departments and Judy LaMarsh was hard at work developing a pay-as-you-go Canada Pension Plan, which was the greatest project envisaged by the sixty days of decision. Then a federal-provincial conference was held in Quebec City at Eastertime of 1964 (see Chapter 7) and the government was in desperate straits again. What was needed, in Tom Kent's view, was a period of consolidation so that people could catch their breath and get the government sorted out. However, there was to be no relaxation because Pearson was off proposing a flag for Canada based on a maple leaf design.

There had been no demand for a Canadian flag at the time of Confederation; none of the founding fathers had given it a thought. "A British subject I was born," said Sir John A. Macdonald, the first Canadian Prime Minister, "a British subject I will die." The Dominion of Canada was part of the British Empire, on which the sun never set, and the Union Jack was the flag for everybody and represented a nice contrast to the Stars and Stripes on the other side of the border.

The red ensign, which has the Union Jack in the upper corner next to the staff, was the traditional flag of the British Merchant Marine, and in 1892 the British admiralty authorised Canadian ships to fly the red ensign with the Canadian coat of arms in the fly. This became known as the Canadian Red Ensign and was looked on as the Canadian flag by the country at large, except for Quebec. In 1924 Prime Minister Mackenzie King ordered it to be flown from Canadian buildings abroad and thus gained it external recognition as the national flag. The Canadian Red Ensign was carried into battle by Canadian forces in the Second World War and was recognised as the symbol of Canada by the United Nations. In 1925 Mackenzie King appointed a committee of public servants, including the heads of the three services, to consider and report upon the design for a Canadian flag. When it turned out that the three service chiefs were all Roman Catholics, the Protestant Orange Order raised so much hell, according to John Matheson, that the committee was hastily dissolved and Mackenzie King gave a commitment that the Liberal Party would never bring in a flag without Parliamentary approval—a commitment that was honoured by Lester Pearson.

If it had not been for the opposition of the French Canadians the Canadian Red Ensign would have become the country's flag —just as the "differenced" blue ensigns had become the Australian and New Zealand national flags. Before Quebec got its own fleur-de-lis flag, it was common to see the tricolor of France being carried in parades or flown from buildings in the province. In 1945 Mackenzie King made a further attempt to gain approval for a national flag, and this time his efforts were frustrated by a group of newly elected Quebec M.P.s, among them Jean Lesage.

JEAN LESAGE

When Mr. King brought up the question of a national flag — he wanted the red ensign, the people wanted the red ensign — but I was forcefully against it. I was one of a group of Quebec M.P.s. There were twelve of us, and we were all mighty young — they called us "the little Chicago." I still see myself with my French-speaking colleagues, newly arrived in the House in '45, in Mr. King's little office behind the Commons Chamber, and he was trying to convince us to be in favour of the red ensign.

We said, No. Our spokesman was Edouard Rinfret, who is now Justice of the Court of Appeal in Quebec, and he said, "No, we are all decided. We will vote against it," which would have meant the defeat of the party because the over-all majority was only three. So it never came up.

Although Tom Kent was all in favour of a distinctive Canadian flag he felt that this initiative, in terms of political tactics, was almost Pearson's worst mistake. Yet Victor Mackie suggested that Pearson seemed to enjoy crises.

VICTOR MACKIE

A problem with Mike was that even when he wasn't in trouble, when things were going smoothly, he'd go out of his way to start stirring up trouble. For example, the flag was typical of him. Things were proceeding quite smoothly, I remember, and for the first time, his Cabinet were relaxing and enjoying life, relatively speaking, and suddenly out of the blue he boosted the flag idea. He invited myself and some others over to his house. As a matter of fact, I think he had two or three groups over a period of a week, a week and a half, and unveiled this flag and said, this is going to be the new Canadian flag.

I remember being absolutely astounded because things were going very quietly and work was getting done in the House, and making progress, and out of the blue he suddenly says, "I'm going to push through a flag. Got to do this to make Quebec happy." I never was—and neither were a lot of other people — sold on the idea that producing a flag was going to make Quebec happy, and I don't think it made much difference to Quebec.

Mike Pearson chose the Royal Canadian Legion's annual convention in Winnipeg as the place to officially announce the maple leaf flag—and in doing so he knew that he was entering the lion's den, for the Legion was the upholder of the Canadian Red Ensign, recognised abroad as the country's flag but not accepted at home. The Legion knew of Mr. Pearson's intentions in advance, and Canadian Red Ensigns were to be seen everywhere in the hotel where the convention was being held. On Sunday May 17, 1964, the Prime Minister addressed the veterans of two world wars: he said that there was a crying need for patriotism in Canada, and he advocated a national symbol that would encourage national unity as well as reflect Canada's status as a independent sovereign nation. Then, he declared, "I believe that today a flag designed around a maple leaf will symbolise—will be a true reflection of—the new Canada." There were shouts of No, No, No, and a storm of booing, and, according to a news report, one veteran leaped to his feet and bellowed "You're selling Canada to the pea-soupers."

John Matheson, M.P. for the Ontario riding of Leeds, a disabled war veteran who became the Prime Minister's spokesman and chief aid on the flag, and Dick O'Hagan accompanied Pearson to the Legion meeting.

JOHN MATHESON

First of all he didn't want to take his medals. I insisted. I went and got his medals; he had seven medals in a row. He put them up.

I remember getting off the aircraft [in Winnipeg] and shaking hands with these old fellows, and do you know, in spite of the danger and the harassment and the fear, he loved it. He felt at home with those guys. It was like walking into Christie Street Hospital, in Toronto, with the fellows being blind or legs off. He identified. And I think he would have been ashamed of himself if he hadn't put that issue in that forum, the forum of honour as he saw it, the best and highest forum in Canada. He didn't expect to be supported. He knew perhaps we'd have a bad time of it. But that didn't matter. This man was more veteran that night than he was a politician.

RICHARD O'HAGAN

The audience was overwhelmingly opposed and hostile to the idea that he was proposing. It was quite an unruly scene. There were moments when one might have thought that it would really break up and that Mr. Pearson wouldn't be able to proceed. He was halted a couple of times by the racket, but he took that well. As I say, it was worse than he expected, but he knew it would be bad, and I think he knew the mood of certain constituencies in the country who would be deeply offended and emotionally engaged by this. Mr. Pearson was never troubled by people who gave expression to their emotions in a unbridled way. He understood that this was the way people in communities acted when things were being taken away from them with which they closely identified, as soldiers who had fought under a flag, this kind of relationship. But he didn't resent it or he didn't go away saying, "These people were unspeakably rude to me", and so on. Nothing, no recrimination, nothing.

Robert Stanfield, who was to become Conservative Leader but was premier of Nova Scotia at the time, was embarrassed by the way Pearson involved him in the maple leaf flag issue.

ROBERT STANFIELD

This is just a footnote, but I made a speech at the Canadian Club in Montreal a couple of months before Mr. Pearson made his speech before the Canadian Legion in Winnipeg at which he announced what he was going to do with the flag. Among other

Prime Minister John Diefenbaker and Liberal Leader Lester Pearson, January 30, 1958. *(Public Archives Canada PA-117093)*

Lester Pearson with Judy LaMarsh (above) and Pauline Jewett.
(Public Archives Canada PA-117097 and PA-117094)

Prime Minister Pearson at Government House, April 17, 1963.
(Public Archives Canada PA-117126)

Mike Pearson with Azellus Denis and Yvon Dupuis,
April 1963. *(Public Archives Canada PA-117096)*

Social Credit Leader Robert Thompson and Deputy Leader Réal
Caouette, May 1963. *(Public Archives Canada PA-117102)*

Finance Minister Walter Gordon with Pearson before presentation of the budget, June 1963. *(Public Archives Canada PA-117104)*

External Affairs Minister Paul Martin, June 1963. *(Public Archives Canada PA-117127)*

John Matheson during
the flag debate *(above)*
and Alvin Hamilton.
*(Public Archives Canada
PA-117122 and
PA-117124)*

Douglas Fisher, June
1960 *(above)*, and
Gordon Churchill,
December 1964. *(Public
Archives Canada
PA-117106 and
PA-117095)*

Allan MacEachen *(left)* and Maurice Sauvé. *(Public Archives Canada PA-117121 and PA-117123)*

Lester Pearson with Quebec Premier Jean Lesage at the federal–provincial conference in Ottawa, November 1963. *(Public Archives Canada PA-117101)*

things I said in this speech in Montreal that it's not necessarily patriotic of me to insist that a Canadian symbol that I admire must be preserved, if in fact that symbol is divisive. I picked up the paper, the [Halifax] *Chronicle Herald* one Monday morning—it was the morning following Mr. Pearson's speech in Winnipeg—and he wound up quoting me, as the premier of Nova Scotia. This didn't put me in a particularly pleasant position as far as my federal colleagues were concerned. That's a small point but I felt perhaps he was using me a bit for his own purposes in that connection.

Aside from Prime Minister Pearson, John Matheson was the only Liberal Member who had any concern about a national flag. Most of the others regarded it as a perennial pledge that had been on the party's platform since Mackenzie King's days, but Matheson took it seriously. He was worried by the fact that the Liberals had promised during the the 1962 and 1963 election campaigns that they would bring in a distinctive Canadian flag "two years after assuming office." Matheson, who had been severely wounded at the Battle of Ortona in Italy, returned from the war in a wheelchair but with a tremendous feeling for Canada—he called it a love affair. He took up heraldry as a hobby, which was to prove useful in helping to design a new flag. When he was elected to Parliament at a by-election on May 29, 1961, he found that Mr. Pearson was looking for a symbol to bring about national unity. He talked to him about the flag on many occasions and wrote him a lot of letters. During his time in Opposition Matheson was doing research on the flag.

JOHN MATHESON

I put a whole series of questions on the order paper, asking the government what was Canada's emblem, what was Canada's colours, what was this, what was that. They were usually innocuous questions; they were put in such a fashion that they weren't signalling what I had in mind. As a matter of fact the questions ended up with public servants in some cases phoning me up and saying "Well, we don't know how to answer that." And I said, "Well, how about looking at this, this, and this." And they said, "Oh, that's very helpful," and they did in due course give exactly the answer that I thought they must give.

What were Canada's colours? The colours are red and white.

This was established in 1921 when George the Fifth gave Canada a patent of arms by proclamation. So they gave exactly the answer that I wanted. Then I asked, "What is Canada's emblem?" and they said, "Three red leaves conjoined on one stem." Those are the answers I wanted, and I got those answers, those specific answers on the last day of the Twenty-fifth Parliament. I'd been waiting for them for a long time.

Another thing that tended to confirm this view was the fact that after he assumed power, Mr. Diefenbaker, through the Honourable Ellen Fairclough, made, simply by order-in-council as I recall, or some administrative order, the correction to Canadian arms which had been in error for a long while with three green leaves on white. She corrected them to three red leaves on white, something that some of our functionaries had been hoping for a long time, to actually reform the arms that had been granted back in 1921.

Two experts in heraldry, Commander Alan Beddoe, a retired naval officer who had illustrated the Book of Remembrance *for Canada's* War Dead, *and Colonel A. Fortescue Duguid, a retired army historian, were enlisted to help John Matheson in designing the flag. Matheson thought that his instructions were simple enough —to put three red maple leaves on a white field — but he was astonished at what Commander Beddoe produced when they visited 24 Sussex Drive to show Mr. Pearson a few examples.*

JOHN MATHESON

While we were there Alan Beddoe pulled out of his briefcase another design, that he had done up himself the night before, with blue bars. I was shocked that he should produce this when he was, I thought, working under my direction and guidance, and in accordance with principles that had been so firmly established by his former boss, Colonel Scotty Duguid, who was skilled in heraldry. But Mr. Pearson, who was a very impulsive person, said, "What are the blue bars?" Allan said, "Why, that's from sea to sea." That was all that was necessary. When Mike Pearson heard "sea to sea," that, by gosh, was his idea.

All the argument in the world then, saying, "Look, Mr.

Pearson, Canada's colours are not red, white, and blue, they are by Royal Proclamation red and white," couldn't change his view. So I then became locked in as one of his principal debaters for a design that was very amateurishly drawn initially—Mike wasn't a great student of aesthetics or art. He had the Queen's Printer go to work and the next day or within a very short while these things were on everybody's desk. And they looked dreadful. They were poor-looking leaves. Alan Beddoe has always acknowledged that drawing a leaf was an extraordinarly difficult thing technically to do well. It wasn't well balanced; the blue was a terrible colour—it would have faded right into the sky—it would have frayed; it had all kinds of technical faults. But fortuitously the result ultimately was that we got back to the principles of the answers given by the Conservative Government, namely Canada's colours are red and white, which is absolutely indisputable.

The design with three red maple leaves on a white field and blue bars at either end became known as the Pearson pennant. The Prime Minister liked it so much that he had a full-sized flag made up and showed it to friends at Harrington Lake, his official residence on the Quebec side of the Ottawa River. When Mr. Diefenbaker found out about this, Mr. Pearson had it displayed on a temporary mast in front of the Peace Tower on Parliament Hill. It was not a beautiful banner and this Beddoe design or Pearson pennant only served to complicate matters still further, as John Matheson feared. The Cabinet Ministers were divided over the necessity of adopting a flag at that time, but Mike Pearson was determined to have his way.

BRUCE HUTCHISON

I think we needed a flag, and I think history will give Mr. Pearson marks for his courage in insisting on having such a flag. Of course, the Cabinet itself was divided on the thing. Not that they didn't want a flag. Really everbody wanted a flag—that is, in the Liberal Party—but they thought the timing was wrong. It was too soon and it was too divisive and too difficult. And Mike, who was sometimes regarded as a meek man, showed such tremendous strength. He just drove that thing through. He was determined to do it, very tough and very stubborn, and he finally got it. Now, whether it divided or unified the country, I don't know whether anybody knows that. I'm not sure.

MITCHELL SHARP

The flag was a great accomplishment because it gave us a national symbol we had never had before, and this was Mr. Pearson's own project. His enthusiasm was not shared very widely by his colleagues, although we all liked the flag and all fought very hard for it. Indeed, I think I am the only English-speaking Minister that participated in the debate on the flag. I felt very strongly about it. But it was Mr. Pearson's own initiative. This would never have got the centre of the stage if he hadn't insisted upon it.

Then there were the Newfoundlanders, who were champions of the Union Jack and wanted no other flag, and their representative in the federal government, Jack Pickersgill found himself in a dilemma.

BRYCE MACKASEY

I remember the day that Pearson announced the maple leaf flag in the caucus—and the reaction. He used caucus very astutely to reinforce his own position or a point of view that he wanted endorsed. On this occasion he said that "since this is what you want"—nobody remembered ever asking for it. One fellow, a Newfoundland Member, got up in tears and recited sixteen stanzas of a poem on the glories of the Union Jack. He was Bert Tucker [J. R. Tucker, M.P. for Trinity-Conception]; he was a dedicated Member. He used to sit in the corner and work on his mail during the caucus meetings.

J. W. PICKERSGILL

I nearly resigned from the government over the flag—not because of any quarrel with Pearson, but because Joe Smallwood at one stage had misunderstood something that happened during the debate. I was in Montreal that day. He got Charlie Granger [M.P. for Grand Falls-White Bay-Labrador] and sent messages through him to Pearson that unless certain things were done, he was going to introduce a resolution in the [Newfoundland] Legislature and it would be seconded by the Leader of the Opposition condemning the government for going ahead with the flag.

I called him when I got home, and he said there were some things that were more sacred than friendship and everything else, and he talked about this business. Finally I said, "Well, of course, if you do this I will resign from the government. I won't resign from the House, but I'm not going to stay in the government if I can't be an effective Minister representing Newfoundland, and I can't be an effective Minister representing Newfoundland if the Legislature is going to censure the government of which I'm a Member."

J. R. SMALLWOOD

I said, "Jack, I would hate like hell to see that happen. But I would rather see you resign and go out of politics than change. I'm not going to change. I'm a Union Jack man and that's that." And I went on, "I'm going to put this thing above the Liberal Party. In Newfoundland we stand for the Union Jack."

So he [Pickersgill] read out the clause of the bill. I said, "No, it's not good enough. There's got to be a clause in the bill denoting the Union Jack. Not ordering and not commanding but authorising the flying of the Union Jack as the flag denoting Canada's membership in the Commonwealth."

J. W. PICKERSGILL

He [Smallwood] said, "If we only had some assurance." When he said that, I said, "You give me some five minutes and I'll call you back." I scribbled out something that Pearson could send him as a telegram, and I called him back and I said, "Would something like this meet your needs?" He agreed that it would, and then I had the unpleasant task of calling Pearson and saying, "Well, here's what's happened. Here's what you have to do if you're going to avoid this censure and if you're going to avoid my resignation, because I really mean it." I said, "In resigning, of course, I'll announce my support of you and of your policies."

He altered a couple of words in it, and he sent the telegram, which Joe read in the House of Assembly the next day.

In a way, this showed two things about Pearson: how determined he was to get the flag; and how far he would go, even almost in humiliating himself before a provincial premier, in order to get it. Another thing about Pearson was—and I learned slowly—that you could often persuade him to delay something, but if he had made up his mind there was something he really wanted to do, he got his own way in the end. This whole flag business showed how tough he really could be. I mean, having undertaken this he was going to see it through. And he never showed any sign of giving up, ever. I think there were times when there would have been a majority in our caucus which would have said, "To hell with it; let's get on with something else."

As a result of the compromise reached with Joey Smallwood, the Union Jack was retained as a flag to denote Canada's membership in the Commonwealth and Canada's allegiance to the throne; it was to be flown twice a year in Ottawa, although not from the top flagstaff. While Pickersgill maintained that all of this was in the legislation and the Newfoundland premier had just misunderstood it, the so-called Two Flag Policy was credited to Joey Smallwood. It gave Opposition Leader John Diefenbaker some of his better quips; he called Pickersgill "two-flag Jack" and jeered at the two flags, describing them as "one for show and one for Joe."

The flag debate began on June 15, 1964, and, although there were lengthy interruptions, was not to end till six months later on December 17. Most Conservatives were bitterly opposed to the imposition of the maple leaf flag and clung, as the Legion did, to the Canadian Red Ensign. Gordon Churchill, Alvin Hamilton, former Diefenbaker Agriculture Minister, and other Western Tories were furious. Even Robert Stanfield was critical of the way that the Prime Minister had handled the issue; he said that Pearson had deliberately provoked the bitter, hostile, and prolonged reaction from Mr. Diefenbaker and most of the Progressive Conservative Members of Parliament. The New Democratic Party accepted the flag as necessary for national unity, but some of the NDP members from British Columbia voted against it.

T. C. DOUGLAS

In the speech I made for our party, I said that, with my antecedents born in Scotland, the Union Jack had a great appeal for me. I'd like to see the red ensign. My father fought in two wars in the interests of the security and safety of Great Britain and so if I were picking a flag, I'd pick a flag with the Union Jack in one corner and the fleur-de-lis in the other, in whatever colours you want to designate because I think it ought to express the two basic language groups.

But I said I recognise that we're not picking a flag for my generation or for my liking. The fact is that my children couldn't care less whether the Union Jack is on it or the fleur-de-lis is on it. They're Canadians and their children are Canadians and this flag is not for today and tomorrow. This flag is for a hundred years, we hope five hundred years from now. So you want to pick a flag that is a distinctly Canadian flag. And so I backed the government, but I didn't like this particular choice. I would have liked one maple leaf on a white background in the centre with blue stripes on either side—from sea to sea. But everybody had their own pet design and you couldn't expect to get what you wanted.

GORDON CHURCHILL

During the lead-off speech which Mr. Pearson made on June 15, he used the following words, and I quote: "The red ensign was not in use during World War I in any way, shape, or form by the Canadian forces." During the course of the debate those of us who were veterans of the First World War drew Mr. Pearson's attention to the fact that we had seen the Canadian Red Ensign in France and Flanders. George Nowlan, who was an artilleryman, mentioned this. I was a machine-gunner, I mentioned it. Others mentioned it. We had photographs to prove that the Canadian flag had been flown in France. General Crerar stated, I believe, that it had always been flown at corps headquarters. And there was Mr. Pearson making this bald statement which was quite untrue.

Late in the debate, on December 11, after all this evidence had been presented to show that this earlier statement had been incorrect, Mr. Pearson went beyond that statement of June and he said, and I quote: "None of us saw a Canadian Red Ensign in those years [World War I]." I interrupted him and I said, "That is not right and you know it." He replied, "None of us saw a Canadian Red Ensign in those years." I answered, "You didn't serve in France either." To which he replied, "No."

Well, a good many years have gone by, and normally you mellow a bit as the years pass, and I have always regretted that Mr. Pearson, who was himself a veteran, had made that statement. It so happens that he didn't serve in the trenches. He wasn't in France or in Flanders, but that was the luck of the draw. He became incapacitated in England when he was training for the air force. But those of us who had served there and had served with the Canadian Corps, we had a legitimate pride in having served with that great fighting organisation and we were offended by his statement. I don't know to this day why he insisted on making that, and persisted after he was shown to be at fault. And that has rankled with me since.

I've often wondered why did he do it? I suppose, in order to win his case, he may have thought that it was essential to refuse to accept the statements made by former soldiers and the campaign against the new flag that was being waged by the Royal Canadian Legion. The flag wasn't flying at all times of course, but it certainly was flown on special occasions. There was a great sports day held on Dominion Day, the first of July, 1918, at Tanques, and there were scores of Canadian flags and Union Jacks flying. I marched with the army of occupation into Germany at the end of the war, and when you crossed the bridge at Cologne there was a reviewing stand there, and the general was taking a salute. At one end was the Canadian Red Ensign and at the other end the Union Jack.

ALVIN HAMILTON

This was a beautiful political device to make us stand up and fight on an emotional issue that we felt very deeply. We knew we were going to lose—there was no question about that. That alliance between the NDP and the Liberals to get rid of the Canadian Red Ensign—that was their main objective, just satisfy the few extremists in Quebec, that's all. Now the French people today have no more use for that leaf than they had for the Canadian Red Ensign. So the great posture failed in uniting Canada. You left these deep hurts among the one-third of the people of Anglo-Saxon origin, and you didn't appease the blackmail of these few extremists from Quebec. And this is one of the most divisive factors.

No one says anything about it because we all know we have to honour the flag of our country, regardless of what it is. That's our flag, we'll honour it. But it's hard, hard to follow a leaf when your people for a thousand years have followed a cross. And where the battle went we followed that cross. And now suddenly you look at that leaf and say, "God, that's the flag of my country and I've got to be proud of it," but there isn't that gut feeling that you have when you see those strong colours of the red and the blue and white. Our flag, when you compare it to the colours of the Union Jack and the American flag, it looks so anaemic.

So this flag debate was used as a device by Pearson to deliberately provoke the Conservatives into a hopeless last-ditch fight for their principles, knowing he could with the support of the NDP roll our faces in the dirt.

It was a hot and frustrating summer for Parliament, that summer of '64, as the flag debate droned on. The Progressive Conservatives kept the House going or, as Gordon Churchill said, they sacrificed their summer vacation in the interests of the country, and were able to maintain the necessary quorum to prevent adjournment. For those of us who reported on Parliament then, it was the dreariest debate; after the first few days there was nothing new to say and it went on for a total of thiry-seven sitting days. Robert Coates, M.P. for Cumberland-Colchester North in Nova Scotia, spoke seven times; Gordon Churchill, the Tory House leader, spoke five times; he denied that Mr. Diefenbaker was the one who prolonged the debate and said that this was a joint effort by the English-speaking Conservatives—the French-speaking Conservatives were just as much opposed to the retention of the Union Jack as their compatriots in other parties. Tommy Douglas, the NDP leader, found himself acting as a go-between in the negotiations with the party leaders.

GORDON CHURCHILL

We had eight Conservative Members, French-speaking from the province of Quebec in our party, at that time. We had a whole series of meetings with them with regard to the flag, to get their point of view and see if they would go along with us. One of the eight was sympathetic toward the loss of what we considered to be our heritage, another one disliked the proposed flag and had a different design, but none of the eight wanted the Union Jack. The Union Jack to them was a symbol of dominance, Mr. Pearson must have known all of that. He may have honestly thought that in the interests of national unity we should get rid of the heritage of the past. I don't know. Or maybe he did it because of pressure from his followers in Quebec.

Dupuis, who subsequently was fired by Mr. Pearson, was the leader of the Quebec group on the government side. Our good friend Réal [Caouette], who was a very staunch and good Canadian and very outspoken, he didn't care what was on the Canadian flag so long as the Union Jack was removed. I questioned him in the House, and he said that he didn't care what was on the Canadian flag, it could be a sheaf of wheat or a beaver or anything. Douglas Fisher, who was deputy leader of the NDP at the time, he didn't care what was on the flag. I interrupted him during the course of the debate and I said, "Are you prepared to accept any flag that is brought in by the Liberal Government?" And his his answer was, "I am prepared to accept any flag that is brought in by the Liberal Government." So that's what we were up against.

JOHN MATHESON

My impression of the French Canadian input—and I studied it very, very carefully—was I would say neutrality and standing aside. It's a most interesting thing that there was actually no participation on the part of French Canadian Members in the creation of what is our flag. They were there, trusting. They were trusting that Mr. Pearson, and, in a modest way if I can say so, they were trusting that I, had enunciated the concept that Canada was too big for its parts and that there could not be any element in this country that was excluded for any reason by the symbol that flew in the name of the nation.

T. C. DOUGLAS

That was my closest experience working with Pearson, because he would call meetings of the Leaders and Caouette and Thompson and Diefenbaker and myself would go down and sit in his office and Diefenbaker would just shake his head and say, "No, no, no, no." We kept trying to find some sort of compromise. Then we would break up and meet again and break up, and finally Pearson would phone me and say, "Look, what do you think about so and so?" I'd say, "Well, it might be possible." "Would you talk to Diefenbaker?"

"No reason why I should talk to Diefenbaker. You can phone him. You're the Prime Minister."

"Oh, he won't even talk to me," he said, "You talk to him."

So, I'd go and talk to Diefenbaker and say, "Mike is worried about so and so and he wonders if we couldn't do this about this flag question. Would you give him a ring?"

"I won't talk to him. Why don't you tell him so and so?" "Why should I tell him? You're the Leader of the Opposition." "No, you can talk to him."

Then I'd go and talk to Mike. I learned what one of his friends said to me: "If you're giving advice to Mike, it's always wise to be at the end of the line." He would say, "All right, we'll do that," and he'd phone back two hours later and say, "I've been talking to some of the boys here and they don't think that's a good idea." After he'd got you to talk to Diefenbaker and Caouette and they'd agreed, then somebody'd come and get him to change his mind.

I made one very nasty speech in the House one day in which I went after both of them and said they were like two old bulls out on the prairie, batting their heads against each other and wasting six weeks of precious time. They ought to be dealing with this thing in a sensible way, and the only sensible way, since we wouldn't get anywhere in the House, was to set up an all-party committee and let them wrestle with these designs, because none of us were going to be completely satisfied with any design. Everybody will have his own design and we'd better try to get a consensus.

Reluctantly Pearson jumped on the proposal and Diefenbaker agreed and it went to the committee and finally we got the design we have now, which I like. It wouldn't have been my first choice, but certainly my second choice.

On September 10, 1964, the flag debate was suspended and the issue referred to a fifteen-member committee with instructions to report in six weeks time; Léo Cadieux, the Member for Terrebonne who was to become Associate Defence Minister, was the only Quebec Liberal on the committee.

LÉO CADIEUX

The people who, in my estimation, were more attached to the Union Jack were the new Canadians because in the case of at least one representative who came from Central Europe after the first war, it represented liberty. So this is a very honourable sentiment. There was an effort made by the Conservatives to suggest a design in which there was no precedence. If you leave the Union Jack in the corner next to the pole, which is the place of honour, you're giving it precedence even if you have the fleur-de-lis included. So they designed a flag in which you had two roundels, and therefore no precedence, and in the roundels you have the Union Jack, stylised a little bit but very easily identifiable, and the fleur-de-lis.

I remember saying to a Member who was not of my party, I said, "Look, we want to have this thing settled, and we want unanimity. Maybe that's the way. But personally I think we should have something that is definitely, entirely, exclusively Canadian. No fleur-de-lis, no Union Jack—but let's go home over the weekend and ask our constituents."

In my case I talked to certainly fifty people, and asked them, "What do you think if we came out with a thing like that?" Everyone: "Why the hell do you want to put the Union Jack and the fleur-de-lis? Why can't we have . . ." So we came back convinced that it had to be simply a Canadian emblem.

We discarded the real symbol, that is by Royal Proclamation, designated as the Canadian emblem, the three red maple leaves on one stem, because we claimed it was politicised. So the next one is the red maple leaf on top of the coat-of-arms in the lion's paw. It is one single red maple leaf and, according to the heraldic explanation we have, it represents the sacrifice of soldiers who died in the wars or in the 1914 War. It's a secondary emblem, but it is still a maple leaf, and it's very dignified.

Then there was the question of whether it was advisable to be 100 percent orthodox and say, "This is strictly a white field and the red maple leaf." That would have been heraldically more correct. We decided that a plain white field would easily get dirty, that there wouldn't be any contrast on the sides, and if we go back to the definition of it being a telegram saying "here is Canada," that it would be difficult to identify. Therefore we settled for red borders because the colours of Canada in the Royal Proclamation are white and red.

On October 29, 1964, the flag committee brought in its report recommending a single maple leaf flag. But the debate was not over, and Mr. Diefenbaker said, in a interview on television, that the design was almost a replica of the Peruvian flag, with the Peruvian coat-of-arms replaced by a red maple leaf, and if this flag were ever adopted, "we'd have the Peruvians saluting it anyway." Léon Balcer, the Quebec leader of the Conservatives, called for the adoption of the new flag that the committee proposed, and, finally, on December 9 broke with his party and asked Prime Minister Pearson to end the debate by invoking closure. A couple of days later this was done. There were wild scenes in Parliament on the night of December 14-15 which threatened to get out of control. Prime Minister Pearson pleaded for adoption without a recorded vote, but the division bells rang and at two o'clock in the morning the new Canadian flag was passed by 163 votes to seventy-eight. The Members sang "O Canada" led by Yvon Dupuis and "God Save the Queen."

JOHN MATHESON

Remember Léon Balcer coming over and changing sides? And Mr. Pearson gave me the honour of sitting beside him. Léon Balcer had been a deck officer in the Royal Canadian Navy in World War II in the convoys. He was at sea with a cousin of mine, and I always liked Léon very much. I knew his wife, who was a Quebec City girl and lived not far from where we lived. And I thought that when Léon moved over and urged closure, that this was wisdom speaking. I think you must feel that, all things considered, on a number of things Mike Pearson showed audacity and great daring. Whether they were wise moves or not, history will tell.

GEORGE McILRAITH

I'm the one who moved closure on that debate. I had just been made Government House Leader, and there were no estimates through, and this debate had dragged on four or five weeks, and I used to sit there day after day. I remember one of your colleagues from the Press Gallery sending a note down to me saying, "Do you realise you already read that *Citizen* newspaper fifteen times?" I wrote on the bottom of it, "No, you are wrong. I have read it sixteen times," and sent it back up to him.

But I listened to every word of the debate from the point at which I was appointed Government House Leader, and I carried that motion of closure in my pocket and never got up until I had a proper opportunity, and I thought the atmosphere was right, and then moved it, bang! I didn't even have a chance to get Mr. Pearson down to the House to tell him. It had been done. I read it before anybody was told or anything. The Cabinet, except Mitchell Sharp and maybe Mr. Pickersgill, didn't know.

I never got a word of criticism for that motion of closure, never, from anybody, in or out of Parliament.

STANLEY KNOWLES

Let me make a comparison [of the closure of the flag debate with the closure of the pipeline debate] in this vein. We in our party were bitterly opposed to the pipeline deal, and we were bitterly opposed to closure being applied to it. When it came to the flag, to the final decision, we were in favour of the flag. We voted for it. But we were opposed strongly to closure being used on the issue. We voted against the closure motion, and then when it passed and the vote had to be taken on the main motion, we voted for it. Now there was quite a contrast there, but it at least demonstrates our feeling about closure.

KEITH DAVEY

My recollection of the flag debate is particularly about the night of the final vote. When it ended, Mr. Pearson came out of the House and up those stairs to his office, and I just happened to come down, and I walked up with him. It was one of those unusual situations. You would think that he'd go up surrounded by people. Instead, he went up all by himself, with me. And I wasn't there as a counsellor or an advisor. I was there as a friend and supporter. And I've never forgotten this. He turned and he said,

"Keith, imagine, John Matheson down there blubbering," because John was so emotional, okay. And I've only twice in my life been visibly moved in a political sense, and that was one of them.* I couldn't even talk. And here he was, he said this to me, and here I was just sort of choked.

Canada had at last acquired a national flag, and, on February 15, 1965, a crowd of several thousand braved Ottawa's wintry weather to attend the official flag-raising ceremony on Parliament Hill. As a twenty-one-gun salute sounded, a cold wind caught the bright red maple leaf banner and blew it out so all could see it. Prime Minister Pearson declared that this day would always be remembered as a milestone in Canada's national progress. There were other flag-raising ceremonies that day across the land and abroad, and the new Canadian High Commissioner in Britain, Lionel Chevrier, presided at the one in London.

LIONEL CHEVRIER

I was given the responsibility when the flag was passed to show the design to Her Majesty, and then in due course I was asked to raise the flag at Canada House, as all other embassies did all over the world. I was to read the proclamation about the flag, which wasn't very long. I worried whether I shouldn't read it also in French. And there was quite a mob of people. We had given some publicity to this, and we gave a reception at Canada House afterward. I worried if I were to read it in French lest I might be interrrupted, and I wanted to do what was the right thing. I knew down deep I should read it in both languages, because I knew that in Paris it was going to be read in both languages, so why shouldn't I read it in London? Finally I decided to do so, and the thing went beautifully. Not the slightest objection. The Commonwealth Secretary who was there, Arthur Bottomley, said, "Well, that's great. I'm glad you read it in French." Then we had a reception to toast the flag.

Looking back over the years since the flag debate, James Walker, a Toronto Liberal Member, said that it had given Canadians a sense of national pride that they didn't have before.

*The other was Pearson's farewell at the 1968 Convention.

JAMES WALKER

I don't think the public generally realise that this [flag] was the beginning of them feeling pretty dog-gone proud travelling abroad now. I've heard it so often and I've experienced it myself. They had that little lapel pin with the Canadian flag, and all over the world people would say, "Ah, Canadian." I offered a taxi driver a rather large tip in Malaysia once—I was over on a tour—and he said, "Mr. Walker, I don't want the tip but can I have the little maple leaf lapel . . ." I met one American businessman in the Far East and he came up and introduced himself, and we were chatting for a while, and he said, "This is a terrible thing for me to ask, but would it be possible that you have another of those little flags?" And I said, "Sure. What do you want it for?" And he said, "I can't get any appointments that I've come over here for, and I think it, would help if I had a maple leaf pin."

This is what I think was Mr. Pearson's legislative achievement, the Canadian flag, again having to do with Canadians suddenly beginning to find out who they are.

Although the Canadian Red Ensign lost out to the maple leaf flag, it was not entirely rejected. Ontario, the most populous province where a third of all Canadians live, adopted a modified version, the red ensign with the provincial coat of arms instead of the Canadian coat of arms in the fly. So did Manitoba. Somehow the flag debate that had gripped Parliament for so long and the adoption of the maple leaf flag as the national flag released pent-up emotions, and there was a storm of flag-waving and flag-raising. Every province had to have its own official flag. Newfoundland had always had the Union Jack and continued to wear it proudly. Nova Scotia's flag, the blue cross of St. Andrew with the arms of Scotland, was granted by Royal Charter in 1625. Quebec got its fleur-de-lis flag shortly after the Second World War. Since 1960 British Columbia had had a flag which was a copy of its shield, with a yellow half-sun on blue wavy bars and above a flattened Union Jack, the whole having at its centre a crown. However, the Pacific province where the tall Douglas fir trees grow was not content with one flag; outside the legislative buildings and other provincial buildings are four standards, the Canadian maple leaf flag, the provincial flag, the Union Jack, and the old Canadian Red Ensign.

Just before Lester Pearson proposed the new maple leaf flag, he asked Stanley Knowles of the NDP if he would be Speaker of the House of Commons. Knowles remembers the date: May 12, 1964. It was a singular honour for the New Democratic Party's expert on parliamentary procedure since he had been offered the Speakership by Prime Minister Diefenbaker in the summer of 1957: that had been made in writing and both Mr. Diefenbaker's letter and Stanley Knowles's reply declining the proposed nomination were tabled in the House of Commons.

Prime Minister Pearson had not been satisfied with the performance of Mr. Speaker Alan Macnaughton, nor had the Liberals generally. They felt that he favoured the Opposition and they resented the way he seemed to lean over backward to please the Conservative Leader. Mr. Speaker Macnaughton acknowledged that he had done this deliberately and said that he needed Mr. Diefenbaker's co-operation in the difficult situation that existed in Parliament with a minority government and a multiplicity of parties. He had told the House that he took the attitude that when a man had been Prime Minister he was entitled to a little more consideration than the average back bencher. When he had said that to Tory applause and Liberal jeers, Pearson had shot back, "Well, I wish you'd treat me in that way."

The date that he made the offer to Stanley Knowles was five days before he spoke to the Canadian Legion meeting in Winnipeg and about the time he was seeing reporters like Vic Mackie and telling them that he was going to push for a maple leaf flag. Obviously, Pearson expected that the Conservatives would be up in arms over this proposal and that John Diefenbaker would raise a storm, and he wondered whether Alan Macnaughton could handle the uproar and whether he shouldn't have someone else in the Speaker's chair.

STANLEY KNOWLES

When Mike asked me whether I would consider it [being Speaker] he did so in a way that had a jocular tone about it. But it was in his office in the midst of a difficult [Parliamentary] situation. He told me that he had discussed the matter with some of his Quebec Members and that there was no problem. That sort of takes away from the jocular nature [of his offer], that even though I was not a Quebecker that they accepted me as a fair person and so on. I just laughed and I remember saying to him, "I turned Diefenbaker down. Your main troubles are with Diefenbaker now. If I had to take the Speakership at your invitation and judiciate between you and Diefenbaker, it would be an impossible situation." My reason for treating [the offer] carefully and not speaking about it is that Mike isn't here now—had this come out when he was alive he could've said, "Oh, I was just joking." But I think that was a serious proposal.

Any Parliament where the government has not got a majority is an awkward and trying situation for the Speaker and the Twenty-sixth Parliament was no exception. Mr. Speaker Macnaughton spoke of the unequalled strain of the flag debate and the angry confrontations over the scandals that occurred at almost the same time (see Chapter 8). There was the way that Pearson and Diefenbaker were carrying on a vendetta which no one enjoyed, least of all the Speaker. The Chair was an uncomfortable place during those tumultuous sessions. But Alan Macnaughton kept the Chamber operating, and he felt that if he had not been Speaker, the first Pearson Government might not have lasted as long as it did. There was the occasion when the relations that he had developed with Diefenbaker paid off—that was at the beginning of the flag debate. It had to do with the increase in the Members' indemnity from 10,000 to 18,000 dollars a year, and it was the Speaker's worst moment.

ALAN MACNAUGHTON

Over the weekend Diefenbaker, at some public meeting, said, "The only reason Members want to be elected is to go to Ottawa and collect 18,000 dollars." Well, this was a bloody insult, not only to me but to every Member in the House, and I knew perfectly well there'd be violence on the following Monday. Every day in the morning I'd get an agenda which didn't mean a thing. You could just tear it up because you never knew what was happening at two o'clock. And if you didn't have some excitement it was a very dull day. You get inured to this sort of stuff.

But anyway, Monday, two o'clock, and immediately some Liberal got up a privilege motion, attacking Diefenbaker for saying this about Members of Parliament. I was very sympathetic. After all, I wasn't going through this pain and suffering for 18,000 dollars either. I was 100 percent with the motion. But that wasn't my job. There was point and counterpoint, and I had to decide very quickly whether this was a matter of privilege, so I called on Dief to withdraw. He got up and he said, "No, Mr. Speaker, I won't."

What do you do? Suddenly a blanket of silence came down on that Chamber. This was the moment people were waiting for. They said, "The guy is afraid of Diefenbaker," and this was the crucial test period. I interspersed with something or other, and then I said, "I'm now going to ask the Right Honourable Leader of the Opposition to withdraw." This was the second time. And he got up and said, "Well, Mr. Speaker, I have great respect for you, but I won't."

So I was faced with the decision of naming him and putting him out—the former Prime Minister and Leader of the Opposition. You have to be in my position—the Clerk was silent. All the advice I could get was out in the prairies. I had the glorious moment of being alone. What do you do, crumble? I didn't know what the hell I was going to do. Then a little bird lighted on my shoulder, and I got up and I said, "This is a most embarrassing situation," or words to this effect, "for a Speaker of the House of Commons." And I said, "I am going to make a personal appeal to the Right Honourable Leader of the Opposition to help the Speaker out of a most difficult situation." Otherwise, I would have named him.

He got up, and he said, "Well, Mr. Speaker, while I have respect for you, nevertheless I have the greatest respect for the Chair." So in the circumstances he waffled, and the incident was over like a clap of thunder. He didn't really withdraw, but it was sufficient.

Then I went out and checked the law—and Diefenbaker was right and I would have been wrong. He was entitled to say anything he wanted outside of the Chamber, and in the circumstances he was doing that. I didn't know my law on the subject. If I had thrown him out I would have been wrong, and he could have appealed and the government would have been defeated. There would have been scandal all over the place, and I would have been wrong.

There was another incident that taxed Mr. Speaker Macnaughton. That was when Alvin Hamilton had the dubious distinction of becoming the first Privy Councillor to be named by the Speaker and expelled from the House of Commons. On June 18, just after the flag debate began, Gordon Fairweather, the Conservative Member for Fundy Royal, New Brunswick, asked Prime Minister Pearson whether a CBC camera crew had recorded part of the proceedings of a Cabinet meeting. He was referring to the film called "Mr. Pearson," which had evidently proved to be a political embarrassment, because it was not being shown. When Pearson replied with a sharp "No, never," Alvin Hamilton asked if he could follow up and Fairweather agreed. The former Tory Agriculture Minister got an angry denial from Pearson and Mr. Speaker Macnaughton said that there had been enough questions on the subject and the matter was closed. However, Hamilton reserved his rights to bring it up again as he said that the Prime Minister's answer raised serious questions and he wanted to check his information. The next day, June 19, he decided to put the question to the Minister who had complained, outside the House, about the CBC crew's invasion of a Cabinet committee meeting and said that he had thrown them out.

ALVIN HAMILTON

I asked not Pearson but his President of the Privy Council [George] McIlraith. McIlraith is a Presbyterian and believes if you tell lies you go to hell after death. So I asked him a very simple question: was he present in the Cabinet Room when political matters were being discussed and the CBC crew were taking sound on film? As he was thinking this over, and slowly getting to his feet, a message ripples down the front bench of the government and he's pushed back in his seat. Pearson said that he had answered that question twice. There had been no filming of a Cabinet meeting—and surely his answer should stand.

This caused a great uproar in the House. I said, "Well, that's the third time that you've misinformed the House."

Then after some minutes, probably half an hour of this uproar, Pickersgill went over and whispered to Pearson that I had accused the Prime Minister of deliberately misleading the House three times, and I should withdraw. The Prime Minister got up and asked me to withdraw, and my answer was very simple: "Yes, I'll be glad to withdraw, on a very simple condition," namely that he allow his President of the Privy Council to answer without being interfered with, and I turned to the Speaker who nodded approval. I asked McIlraith the question again: was he present in the Privy Council chambers when this CBC crew was taking film on sound when political matters were being discussed, yes or no? This time he didn't get the chance to think or even get up. Somebody behind him reached out and just pushed him right down in his seat.

I said, "There you have it, Mr. Speaker. I've said I'd withdraw on a very simple condition. It hasn't been met. I now put myself in your hands." And his answer's on the record: "I know the Member from Qu'appelle, and I'll make a reservation on this decision and will announce it on Monday." This was Friday. I walked out of the House. You don't feel happy when you've said the Prime Minister is a liar and everyone believes you and doesn't believe him. I was going to go home and mow the lawn.

During the uproar in the House over Alvin Hamilton's charge, Douglas Fisher of the NDP said that he had seen the film in question and that it showed the Prime Minister and other Ministers discussing affairs of state—were they play-acting? If not, then they must have been at a Cabinet committee meeting. This was an awkward situation for Lester Pearson, who had to tread a fine line, and it may have been because of this that the Speaker decided to make known his position before the weekend. At any rate, Hamilton never got to mow his lawn that hot afternoon because he was recalled to the House. When he refused to withdraw his accusation that the Prime Minister had misled Parliament, he was named by the Speaker and left the Chamber. However, he had to return because Diefenbaker had pointed out that, according to the rules, the Prime Minister had to move a motion to have him expelled. There was some argument about this and by the time the proper procedure had been followed and the Honourable Member was "suspended from the service of the House for the remainder of today's sitting," it was five o'clock. So Alvin Hamilton was out of Parliament for an hour.

ALVIN HAMILTON

It demonstrated to me, and I've seen it happen over and over again, that Pearson was unable to accept blame for things. He always blamed his Cabinet Minister or fired somebody else but never could take blame himself and say, "Okay, I made a mistake." If he had only stood up and said "I made a mistake or misinformed the House," that would have ended it all. Or if he'd simply said, "Well, they were in there and there was a film crew taking pictures when we were talking and I shouldn't have allowed it, and Mr. McIlraith stopped it," and that sort of thing. That would have been the correct answer.

The "Mr. Pearson" film which was shot in the latest cinema-vérité style of making a documentary, was the idea of the bright young men in the Prime Minister's Office. Dick O'Hagan felt that a greater effort should be made to bring the public into the decision-making process and to demystify the office, as he put it. He persuaded Mike Pearson to let the camera crew follow him around and invade his privacy; it was a bold venture but he was sure that the Prime Minister could carry it off beautifully and would benefit from it politically. O'Hagan didn't see any unmanageable problems when the project was completed but admitted that others did and they became rather anxious about it before it was to be put on the air. However, the press officer said that it was the CBC itself that decided not to show the film.

"Mr. Pearson" was an embarrassment for the Prime Minister's appointments secretary, James Coutts, who had such a big part that he was the star of the picture, or "anti-hero" as he called himself. Young Coutts was in his early twenties then but looked like a schoolboy; he said that the reason he was in the film so much was because the camera crew could not get into the Prime Minister's office as much as they expected.

JAMES COUTTS

As the film was about a day in the life of the Prime Minister and his time and his schedule, they kept shooting the clock in my office to show that it was nine o'clock now or ten-thirty now or noon now. There were a lot of clock shots. Then they would move from the clock back to me answering the phone or doing some other thing.

I guess the most embarrassing episode was a shot in the car. We were driving to the airport, and they were hoping to film the Prime Minister on the plane going somewhere—this went on for several weeks so I became oblivious to the camera—and I was talking to Dick [O'Hagan] or someone in the back seat about something that had been said about the Prime Minister, and I said, "Well, he's not such a bad guy, and he's basically honest." There were a few other terribly inappropriate and condescending remarks, and they showed up halfway through the film in blazing black and white.

Mr. Pearson had two comments. He was appalled by it, by the extent to which I was in it. He didn't say anything. We watched it together in the East Block on one occasion. I was so embarrassed I could hardly stay in the room. At the end of it the Prime Minister said. "My God, it looks like my grandson is running the country." It was his remark. I was not involved in the negotiation of the editing process and all those things that later became issues. I was just dreadfully embarrassed by the exposure. And it came about simply because they parked in my office.

TOM KENT

There were, I remember, solemn screenings of the film and all sorts of people saw it—I certainly remember Allan MacEachen and Jack Pickersgill and myself and various other people watching it. My main comment on it, as I recall, was that it showed that the world of entertainment had lost a great personality when it didn't have Jim Coutts. Jim Coutts was the star of the film.

It emphasised the pleasant, charming, but always rather harassed and fumbling style of Mr. Pearson. And if you knew Mr. Pearson and you knew both his strengths and his weaknesses, it was fine. But I am sure it did not give a true picture to anybody who didn't know him and made him seem a much less effective person than in fact most of the time he was. Therefore, in that sense, it was something that had been actively dumb, so to speak. I think it was a mistake. I don't think there was anything terribly wrong with it and it wouldn't have done any great harm, but it certainly wasn't a film that was worth having had made, given all the trouble it caused.

On June 26, 1964, Prime Minister Pearson told the House of Commons that the federal government was making a study of the economic, social, and political effects of the separation of Quebec on the rest of Canada. He was replying to a question from Reid Scott, a Toronto NDP Member. His announcement astonished John Diefenbaker, who said that it was the most surprising thing that he had ever heard that the government had civil servants giving consideration to the effects of separatism; the Prime Minister's statement was a shock to his officials because no such investigation was being carried out. It was an example of Lester Pearson's somewhat erratic behaviour, which Tom Kent blamed on his being worn ragged, as he put it, by the appalling flag situation.

TOM KENT

I and a couple of officials struggled with preparing a short statement which would correct the situation in the sense of saying that perhaps he had been misunderstood and he hadn't intended to say that there was a study of separatism. But there was a continuing study of the Canadian economy, its interrelationships, the importance of its unity and so on, and how this would certainly be used to show how bad separatism would be in its economic effects.

Mike at that stage was in a state of considerable exhaustion. I knew he was sufficiently distressed by the whole thing that when I was talking to him over the phone about how we'd put out this statement, this correction, I remember he quite literally almost broke down into tears in expressing his relief and his gratitude that we had helped him to cope with a situation he felt so foolish about.

7 Changing Confederation

JUDY LAMARSH HAD been ecstatic when Lester Pearson told her that, as Minister of National Health and Welfare, she would be responsible for putting into effect the Canada Pension Plan. She recalled that, after the new government's first Cabinet meeting, she telephoned the Deputy Minister of Welfare, Dr. Joseph Willard, whom she had not yet met. Tom Kent, the author of the Liberal Party's election plank on the pension plan, was with her when she made the call. Dr. Willard was on the point of leaving Ottawa to chair a conference at the United Nations; he asked if he could go and said that he would be away for several weeks. Judy replied that it was all right with her but Tom interrupted and when he found out what Dr. Willard wanted, he said, "Oh, tell him no, he'll have to cancel that trip. You've got to start tomorrow." And the next day they did begin working on the Canada Pension Plan.

An interdepartmental committee was set up to assist the Minister; it included senior officials from the departments of Health and Welfare, Finance, National Revenue, Justice, as well as the Unemployment Insurance Commission. Dr. Willard had done some preliminary work because Judy said that the Diefenbaker Government had thought about having a contributory pension plan, and the Deputy Minister came armed with a big black book of material. The planning group also included Jack Garland, the Minister of National Revenue, Ben Benson, the parliamentary secretary to the Minister of Finance, and Tom Kent. It was to have been a pay-as-you-go pension plan, which meant that the pensions

181

would match the payments received and that the pensions would be
adjusted to be in line with the amount received, and that was what the
White Paper of July 18, 1963, proposed. However, it had to be reworked
and redrafted to meet Opposition and provincial objections that, by the
time the third version was brought down on March 17, 1964, just before
the confrontation with Quebec, it had become a partially funded plan.
Meanwhile, Judy LaMarsh got embroiled in a slanging match with John
Robarts, the premier of Ontario, over the Canada Pension Plan.

JUDY LaMARSH

Originally, it was to be an instant pension plan, and was to be
phased in over a short period of time. Robarts wanted it not to be
applicable in full for twenty years, and we finally made the
compromise of ten years, which I found very hard to do. It was a
pay-as-you go plan, and pay-as-you-go survives or any pension
plan survives because there are far more people coming into it than
going out of it.

When we had done an awful lot of work in the pension plan, Dr.
Willard said, "You'll have to go to Europe." I couldn't understand
exactly what for. It sounded like a lot of swanning around to me.
But I had to go to Scandinavia and Britain to talk to people, and I
found that enormously useful in being able to discuss the kinds of
plans they had and the kind of decisions that had been made to
shape them. It was a very tough crash course.

TOM KENT

It was a pay-as-you-go plan, and the civil servants had flushed it
out and taken some rough edges off it, improved it here and there,
but essentially it was as had been proposed.

My own suspicion is that if there had never been the budget
problem, that plan would probably have gone through without
too much trouble. I don't mean quite how it was, but I think
something quite like it would have done. We drafted the sort of
outline of the plan very quickly. Some of the Ministers from
Quebec showed the outline to Mr. Lesage and he raised no
objection to it at that stage. He did a little later. I suspect that the
firm way in which he did, the way that really destroyed it at birth
so to speak, in its original form, I suspect that he would not have

handled it that way if the government had looked strong. It was because the government already looked weak that he dealt with it so cavalierly. We're really going back to an earlier point. From the federal government's point of view we were going to introduce the pension plan. It was sound economics that it be a pay-as-you-go plan.

PAUL HELLYER

The pension plan—I don't think Pearson could have devised a worse plan if he'd stayed up late nights worrying about it. Just horrendous. Most of this legislation originated on the back of a matchbox. The man in the street thinks that it's all carefully thought out and that they can trust their governments and that their governments know what they're doing. And they have no fear. But if they knew how these things were done, they would be very concerned. You get someone close to the Leader writing down little bits and scraps on a matchbox, and this finds its way into a speech, and it becomes party policy, and then the government's elected and it's got to implement it. Often the hard, hard look at the options of how you achieve certain goals is never taken. And that is certainly true of the Canada Pension Plan, which was ill conceived—it was an abortion if there ever was one—and which still isn't solving the problem of an inadequate pension for a lot of Canadians. Sure, it's helping in many cases, but as you know, some Canadians now have four pensions and some only one.

The law and its application is very unjust because some people have too much, some too little. The Canada Pension Plan just does not fill the void that I think its promoters advertised that it would.

TOM KENT

The pension plan resolution had been introduced in June, the legislation was being prepared during the summer, but there was an Ontario provincial election called for September 25, 1963. The truth is, I suppose, that the Liberal Opposition in Ontario didn't have many issues of its own. The Robarts government was pretty strong and they decided to make the pension plan their issue.

[John] Wintermeyer, who was the Ontario Liberal leader, campaigned in support of the Canada Pension Plan. That was the issue on which he was going to defeat Robarts.

Meanwhile I was advocating an immediate shift over to a funded plan—I mean arguing that it was unavoidable, that it was going to happen. But, in that political situation, Mr. Pearson and Judy LaMarsh couldn't possibly make that shift. They had to wait until after Mr. Robarts had won the election. Then, of course, Mr. Robarts was in a very strong position. We now had not only Quebec saying it must be a funded plan, and anyway they had their own, but we also had Mr. Robarts saying, "Well, you know, your plan was defeated in Ontario. You fought the election on it." And Judy campaigned in support of Wintermeyer.

So the government was in a very, very weak position. And we rewrote the pension plan a bit to try to make it more acceptable to Ontario.

JUDY LaMARSH

There was a federal-provincial conference in early September [1963]. Robarts came and we had a kind of a clash and I think that was the time he said, "I'm never going to talk to that woman again. I'll just talk to the Prime Minister." This always struck me as being funny because Ministers don't do much talking to premiers anyway. But he used it with great enthusiasm and it was very helpful to him in his election. But I always liked Robarts, and I must say he used me as a whipping boy very cleverly, and without really raising any resentment amongst women over the fact that he was beating a woman over the head. He got away with it.

We had a kind of a running battle for a long time. I had a listed telephone number, and reporters used to call me at seven in the morning and waken me and say, "You know what John Robarts said last night?" and he'd say something. So I'd say something really snarky back again, and God it was all over the news. Then they'd phone him and say something. And Mike said, "What are you doing!" And I said, "I'm not doing anything." So I unlisted my phone, and a lot of that trouble disappeared.

But because of that, the pension plan became an issue at once in the provincial election, and because it was my job and because I had been a supporter of Wintermeyer, I went into the provincial election campaign—a not unusual posture, but Robarts made it sound like the first time in history that a federal Minister had ever done that. There was lots of argle-bargle back and forth on that. In the development of the [pension] plan, it was Robarts first who was not keen about the form, long before Lesage had said anything.

It was as a result of an invitation from Premier Jean Lesage that the federal-provincial conference was held in Quebec City from March 31 to April 2, 1964. Lesage had said at the last meeting in September that these first ministers' conferences were very important for Confederation and that they shouldn't always be held in Ottawa, and why not have the next one in Quebec City? Everyone accepted with pleasure. Prime Minister Pearson and the federal Ministers approached the conference with confidence, if not complacency, because Lesage had seemed co-operative enough at the last federal-provincial conference; it wasn't the Quebec premier who had raised all the row about the Canada Pension Plan but Premier John Robarts of Ontario. Robarts had won an overwhelming victory at the provincial election and the pension plan had been redrafted to take into account Ontario objections. Neither the Ottawa delegation nor the other provincial delegations from English Canada realised that Jean Lesage had invited them to Quebec City in order to present what amounted to a bill of particulars for staying in Confederation. The bill included such sweeping demands as 25 percent of the income tax which the federal government collected, 100 percent of the succession duties, and millions more money from Ottawa. Lesage let it be known that Quebec was going to insist on its own pension plan, which he said was better than Ottawa's.

The atmosphere in Quebec City was tense. At the end of January terrorists who were linked with separatist organisations had raided the armoury of the Fusiliers Mont Royal in Montreal and stolen 100 weapons and 20,000 rounds of ammunition. In February more weapons were stolen from another armoury at Shawinigan, near Quebec City. There was fear of violence and assassination.

JEAN LESAGE

My opposition to the [Canada Pension] Plan was not only because I didn't think it was Ottawa's business and that Quebec should do it, but for another reason. In 1950 I had been the chairman of the Old Age Security Committee in the House of Commons and Senate, a joint committee. We had studied all the pension plans in the world. We had studied especially the contributory pension plan of the United States, which was on a pay-as-you-go basis, and we would come out condemning the system. In our report we recommended the system of old age pensions that we have now, saying that maybe later we could build on this basic thing the contributory system. But we condemned the U.S. system because there was no funding, so I knew what I was talking about.

When the Ottawa pension plan came to me, I said, "No, to heck with it." I wouldn't adopt it as my plan, because it was a pay-as-you-go system, which means that with the years the contributions would increase and there was no interest being built in the reserve. I asked Claude Castonguay, who was an actuary—he later became the Minister of Health and Social Affairs in Quebec—to prepare a plan for me which would be as much funded as possible. He prepared the plan, and when we had the federal-provincial meeting in Quebec, and Miss LaMarsh explained to the provincial representatives what the federal plan was, a pay-as-you-go system, the contributions being very low at the start, I came out and explained my plan. When I finished, the first reaction of Mr. Pearson was, "Jean, can we join your plan?" Miss LaMarsh has never said "hello" to me since. She never forgave me for that.

TOM KENT

Jean Lesage came out with a much more attractive plan, wider in the scope of its benefits, on balances good, but funded; therefore capable of producing savings available to provincial governments for social capital. The response in the conference was electric. Lesage handled it very, very cleverly, there was no question that at that moment the Canada Pension Plan was dead. In my view it had been dead for some time before that in reality, but then it was completely dead. Robarts had throughout taken the position that he'd go along if it was truly national, but obviously it wasn't going to be national on the basis of anything that the federal government had proposed. And the federal government position was destroyed.

The most extraordinary thing about the whole situation was that the federal government had been so completely unprepared for it, for the whole aggressive, powerful stance of the provinces in relation to the federal government. I don't think that Mike was personally really unprepared or surprised, but his Ministers who were with him were, I think, just completely unprepared.

JUDY LaMARSH

Maurice Lamontagne, Walter Gordon, and I, and Tom Kent and the Prime Minister were the main people in the delegation. There had been a bomb threat so that we were put up all on one floor of the Chateau Frontenac. We had to have guards with us when we went out to eat or when we went in the cabs, and there were guards on the floor. Quebec City was like an armed camp.

The meeting was in the Quebec Legislature. Mike sat at the head of the table and I was to his right and Lesage to his left, and in the seat behind Lesage was [René] Lévesque, who kept muttering to him all the time. The Lesage advisors had worked very quickly and had put together an alternative plan. We had heard some rumours about this but we didn't know anything more than that. He presented this plan at the meeting and it was a real bombshell. Originally the contributions were to be 1 percent of wages from the employees and 1 percent from employers—this would have doubled them. Anyway, what it did was to provide very large sums of money that the provinces would have access to, and it was obvious that Lesage was not looking at it so much as a pension plan as he was looking at it as a means of funding. Things were becoming more difficult with Lesage, who had plenty of problems in his own province, and the biggest problem was finding money.

I was pretty shocked that Mike didn't say no at once. But in effect what Lesage was saying that if we didn't accede to some of the things that he was asking for, there would be double taxation.

He would tax and we would tax and we'd have to take the responsibility. And it was thought by many people that that would be a real blow to Confederation.

I remember sitting in one of the hotel rooms with Lamontagne and Gordon Robertson [Secretary of the Cabinet] and Tom Kent, all trying to persuade the Prime Minister to give way on this, and Walter Gordon and I a mass of fury about it on the other side. And certain concessions were made.

J. R. SMALLWOOD

I remember [that meeting in Quebec City]—it was sickening. Lesage sat there, and sitting behind him was this grey eminence, Claude Morin, and Lesage did nothing without getting instructions from him—he'd hardly speak. Then, something would come up, and then again he'd lean back for advice or instruction. He just sat there absolutely mulish. No, no, he wouldn't budge an inch. No. It was terrible. The non-Quebec delegates there were furious, and all they could do was just remain polite. It was all they could do to restrain themselves from turning on Lesage, "You son of a bitch, what are you trying to do?" No one did, but you could cut it with a knife.

WALTER GORDON

It was a complete and utter disaster. The Quebec government of Jean Lesage were very nervous that there would be riots, that the separatists would come and disrupt things; there were police everywhere; we were told we couldn't go from the Parliament Buildings to the hotel without police escort. At the end of the conference Lesage rather ostentatiously separated himself from Pearson and gave his own press conference. We went back to Ottawa thinking really that Confederation might easily break up.

JUDY LaMARSH

I remember when we were leaving Quebec City Pearson said to me, "There's been a bomb threat on the government plane." So when we were going up to it he said, "I want you to precede me." And I said, "But you said there'd been a bomb threat," and he said,

"That's why you're preceding me." He had kind of a wry sense of humour and very often there was an edge of truth in it. You never quite knew whether he was saying a nasty thing in a nice way or whether he was just being humourous about something. I had kind of a feeling that maybe he would just as soon if anyone was going to blow up it would be me.

Prime Minister Pearson and the rest of the federal delegation flew back to Ottawa in complete disarray, as Tom Kent described it. The Liberal Government was involved in another crisis and, if anything, this one was worse than its predecessors. There were so many crises that Jean-Luc Pepin wondered if Lester Pearson subscribed to the theory of government by crisis, that you could only move great objectives in an atmosphere of crisis. This was the same as brinkmanship, but Pearson seemed to be the victim rather than the practitioner and, from what he himself said, would have preferred a calmer and better-ordered regime.

In the end the pension plan crisis was resolved largely because neither Ottawa nor Quebec City wanted an open break. The only question was, who took the initiative. At the time there was a report that Claude Morin, the Quebec official who became a leading separatist, had telephoned Maurice Sauvé, the newly appointed Forestry Minister, but Sauvé made no mention of this and said that he had asked the Prime Minister's permission to approach Quebec City on the matter. Sauvé had been worried by the news that Premier Lesage had held his own press conference and threatened to bring in a budget in a couple of weeks' time which would provide for double taxation. At any rate, it was the team of Maurice Sauvé and Tom Kent who conducted the successful rescue operation for the Pearson government.

MAURICE SAUVÉ

When Mr. Pearson came back from the federal-provincial conference I went to see him, and I said, "Mr. Pearson, we're in deep trouble. Lesage is a Liberal, an ex-federal Cabinet Minister. He likes the Liberal Party, but the way he's doing things there, it's going to be terrible. There must be a way of accommodating not only Quebec but other provinces. And besides," I said, "the Canada Pension Plan is essential. It's a good proposal. It has to be accepted by all provinces, and if Quebec rejects it then we won't have it."

"Oh," he said, "Maurice, I'm too tired; come and see me Monday." I remember this very well, "Come and see me Monday about it."

TOM KENT

That weekend I wrote a memorandum—it wasn't really in thought new to Mike but it was setting it out in a formal way—that we had to try to reach a settlement, that my assessment, based on the private talks I'd had with Lesage and others in Quebec City, was that they would be prepared to find a compromise on the pension plan provided they got the savings, the funds, the social capital for provincial use, which, in my view, was entirely how it ought to be anyway, and provided that we did what, again in my view and I think equally in Mike's private view, was right and proper, which was to increase the pace at which more tax resources and more equalisation [payments] was provided to the provinces. I think that Mike accepted that memorandum but wasn't quite sure how to handle it.

It was a desperate situation, sufficiently desperate that Maurice Sauvé, who had not been trusted to be part of the delegation going to Quebec—I may say it was a peculiar delegation since it included Guy Rouleau, who was at that time Mike's Parliamentary Secretary and who was supposed to be a contact with Quebec. I remember Sauvé came to my office in the Centre Block [of the Parliament Buildings] in a state of considerable concern. He was the one federal Minister at that point who had good contacts in Quebec City. He came to talk about [his concern]. As I had some of the same contacts, I took the plunge of telling him what sort of solution I thought was possible and what I'd said in the memorandum to Mike. Sauvé seized on that at once as being correct, but whereas I had been planning a more gentle rapprochement, Maurice persuaded me that we should go to Mike at once and insist that the only solution was that Sauvé and I should go to Quebec City right away and go into immediate negotiations with Lesage.

There was a reason for urgency in the sense that Lesage was due to bring down a budget very shortly, and that budget would, if things remained as they were, include a large increase in provincial taxes and an attack on the federal government for making that necessary.

MAURICE SAUVÉ

On Monday morning I went to see Tom Kent and I said to Tom, "You were at this federal-provincial conference. What happened?" He told me of the circumstances, and I said, "Something must be done." And he said to me, "Well, I've just written a memo to Mr. Pearson on this," and then he showed me a memo that Robertson had written on the same subject, saying "We must do something to avoid a conflict between Quebec and the federal government."

Having read those two memos, we went to see Mr. Pearson and I said to Mr. Pearson, "Something must be done. I don't know what, but something must be done. Do you give me permission to speak with my friend Claude Morin?" who at that time was Deputy Minister of Intergovernmental Relations and who was pretty disturbed by what was happening. He said, "Yes, but do it in great secrecy." I phoned Morin and I said, "Claude, there must be something that we can do about this conference, which failed so badly. Would you be ready to see me with Tom Kent?" He had to talk to Lesage first and then he said, "Fine, I'm ready to see you. I don't know what we can do but . . . " So Tom Kent and I went in great secrecy to Quebec City.

TOM KENT

It was an uncharacteristically aggressive way of doing things and Mike, I think in some desperation, agreed to it. Sauvé and I went to Quebec City that evening [April 7, 1964]. I was due to have dinner with several Ministers the following evening. We put that off. Mike called a small meeting of Ministers at 24 Sussex for eight o'clock on the following evening, on the basis that I'd get back by then. Sauvé and I spent an intensive morning and afternoon discussing with Claude Morin first, and then with Lesage, Morin, Lévesque, and [Paul] Gérin-Lajoie. And came back confirmed in the view that the sort of formula that had been suggested in the memo could in fact be the basis of a settlement with Quebec. Nobody was making any commitments at that point, but it was clear that in fact it could be done. Lesage had agreed on the basis of this preliminary exploratory negotiation to put off his budget, give it time.

MAURICE SAUVÉ

The agreement was on two different counts—on some fiscal arrangements pertaining to the opting-out formula and on the Canada Pension Plan. On the opting-out formula, I don't remember all the details but essentially it was an agreement that the federal government would give any province the right to administer its own social security or education program, and transfer to those provinces a number of percentage tax points. This was acceptable to Quebec, and we felt that it could be acceptable to Ottawa. On the Canada Pension Plan, it was a reconciliation of the proposal that Quebec and the federal government had made on the Canada Pension Plan, and we found ways of reconciling both which would give the province of Quebec and the rest of Canada a good pension plan with some possibilities for the provinces, if they so choose, to administer their own. It was in a way an opting-out formula applied to the Canada Pension Plan. We came to a full agreement on this.

Tom Kent and I came back to Ottawa that evening on a Quebec government plane, and we went directly to Mr. Pearson's residence.

There were some Ministers at his home, Walter Gordon, Maurice Lamontagne, Bud Drury, I don't know about Jack Pickersgill, and he [Pearson] had not told them about our mission to Quebec City. When they saw Tom Kent and me come in—and I had agreed that Tom Kent should make the report on the negotiations—some of the Ministers were pretty much surprised and some of them were pretty mad. They were angry because they were senior to me and felt that they should have been involved or at least informed. I guess that this didn't help me with them but I thought that the country was over and above my own personal relations.

An agreement was reached on Saturday April 11, 1964, when Claude Morin and Claude Castonguay repaid Maurice Sauvé and Tom Kent's visit to Quebec City by coming to Ottawa. Dr. Joe Willard, the Deputy Minister of Welfare, was among those who participated in the negotiations but Judy LaMarsh did not. Although Premier Lesage talked about the compromise that was reached, and Premier Robarts said how he agonised over keeping Ontario in the Canada Pension Plan and not opting out as Quebec had done, the fact was that the provinces had won most of their demands, especially that it should be a funded program, which would provide them with the money they needed.

MAURICE SAUVÉ

Walter Gordon said, "I'm only ready to accept the proposals that Tom Kent and Sauvé negotiated with Quebec if they can settle the details of the Canada Pension Plan." I phoned Morin and said, "The Minister of Finance is ready to accept the fiscal arrangements if we can settle the details of the Canada Pension Plan. Can you come to Ottawa this weekend and we'll arrange a meeting between the interested parties and your group to settle the details?" He phoned me back and said, "Yes, we can be there Saturday."

Then I went to see the Prime Minister and I said that Morin was going to come, and would he inform the Minister, Miss LaMarsh, and the others that the meeting would take place, and that they should determine the place and the hour. And he said, "Well, Maurice, I want you to be there because you have been involved." I said, "Fine." And I always assumed that when he said, "I want you to be there," that I would be there with Judy LaMarsh and some officials of the Department and Tom Kent. When we had the meeting in the morning there was a Deputy Minister there and Tom Kent, and maybe somebody else. I said to the Deputy Minister, "How is it that Miss LaMarsh is not here?" He said, "She was not asked to come to the meeting." The meeting had been organised by the Prime Minister's office. I know that Judy hates my guts for that because she thinks that I plotted against her. I had nothing to do with that, and I've never been able to speak to her to tell that I had nothing to do with it. It's just that the Prime Minister, probably because of the failure of the negotiations in Quebec City, didn't want her to be there. I don't know what the reasons were. I was the most surprised to see that she wasn't there.

We negotiated in the morning and things were not going very well, and we went to lunch in the Eastview Hotel because we didn't want to be seen in Ottawa. After lunch there was no more progress. At four o'clock somebody—I think it was Jim Coutts—came in and said the Department of Transport plane would be ready at such-and-such a time to take the Quebec delegates back to Quebec City. At that time I went to the washroom with Tom Kent and Claude Morin, and there was some discussion. We said, "We must accept this and you must accept that, and we came back, and in about forty-five minutes we settled all the problems. At five o'clock we were through, and we had resolved all the major difficulties.

JUDY LaMARSH

I was in my constituency [Niagara Falls] for a weekend and when I got back to Ottawa I heard something on the radio about some agreement having been made with Lesage.

Tom Kent came into my office and told me that Mike had sent him down there, and that they had made an agreement with Lesage. I said, "Why didn't you tell me that you were going; and why didn't Willard go; why didn't I know about it; why wasn't I sent?" He said, "Well, those are the Prime Minister's decisions." And I remember picking up a framed photograph I had of Mike and slamming it down on the desk and broke its face. You know, I really felt humiliated. Pearson never explained that to me and never did, in fact, discuss it with me. He very often gave Tom Kent dirty jobs to do, and I think probably what I should have done was resign, but I didn't know whether anybody else would pick this up and do it or just what would happen. Anyway, in short, I didn't resign, nor did I discuss it with him.

TOM KENT

I don't think I've ever worked harder in my life or probably never has Claude Morin. We negotiated a very complicated settlement in hours and hours of drafting of documents over the telephone and so on. We did it within a few days. But, you know, that was the purely mechanical stuff.

There is no question it was a superb political achievement of Mike Pearson to get that settlement accepted, not by Quebec, but by English Canada. I think it was the right settlement, but I think it required a good deal of wisdom and detachment to see that it was what was necessary to the country as it had become by 1964. It was, without any question, one of Mr. Pearson's great achievements. I do emphasise that while the mechanics were other people's the essential political act was his. And it was the kind of thing at which he was superbly good.

WALTER GORDON

The federal government agreed to change its Canada Pension Plan to the Quebec style. And more money was given to Quebec, which was really the key to the thing in those days. It was agreed that we'd introduce legislation which would give any province the right to opt out of certain shared-cost programs, and Quebec opted out of all of them.

Now, those arrangements—and they were expensive and they were messy because every province was on a different basis from then on—were intended to buy time. But while we bought the time, clearly we didn't put it to the best possible use, because now we're back not only to where we were then but worse off. I remember in those days two of the people involved were Réné Lévesque, who was a [Quebec] Minister and who was extremely critical and contemptuous of anybody coming from Ottawa, and Claude Morin, who was a civil servant but was obviously a separatist.

JEAN LESAGE

Our proposal was for a twenty-year initial period, before anybody could profit by it, so, of course, the funding was much more important than what was finally agreed to, which was ten years. That was the compromise that was reached. It was less funded, but it was funded—to the extent that we have over four billion dollars in the kitty in Quebec. Which was very important for the financing of government and hydro and municipalities, and it is the same for the other provinces too. They draw on the federal government, which holds it as a bank for the borrowing by the provinces.

JOHN ROBARTS

I could have opted Ontario out just the way Quebec opted out, but it seemed to me that there wouldn't be any national pension plan; if Quebec opted out and Ontario opted out, what would happen to the Western provinces and the Maritimes? They wouldn't be big enough. So I made that very agonising decision that we would stay with them, but I asked for certain concessions, which Mr. Pearson gave to Ontario, the greatest one being that the money collected in Ontario was returned to Ontario for investment by the provincial government.

Later on I think that the government in Ontario indicated it would like to opt out, and I have always wondered whether I should have opted out. Because when Mr. Pearson offered the option of opting out to Quebec, of course it was also open to any other province, and we could have at that time. I thought that it would be very divisive for the country as a whole, so I didn't do it. I wondered after, one always does, whether it was the right decision or not. In any event, that's the decision I made.

ALVIN HAMILTON

The pension plan? I don't think governments should be party to wholesale theft from kids, because you're stealing from one generation to provide the pensions for your own generation, and that's why I didn't vote for it. There were several of us who didn't vote for it in the House, even though the Gallup Poll showed everybody in support of it. Somebody's got to speak up for the future generations. And this is what we're doing increasingly that's causing us our inflationary cost-push. We're transferring from one generation to pay for the next generation. Eventually that load gets so heavy on the working population—the load of less and less people working to support more and more people. And this was essentially the cause that broke down the Roman Empire.

STANLEY KNOWLES

I was pretty close, for an Opposition Private Member, remarkably close to and kept informed of what was going on over the Canada Pension Plan. I felt it was one of the best examples of co-operation between Canada and Quebec, between English and French Canada, or English Ottawa and French Quebec. The Canada Pension Plan without that separate right for Quebec wouldn't have succeeded. This would have been bad for the Liberals, but it would have been bad for Canada. Negotiating that kind of an arrangement so that face was saved on both sides and nobody lost anything [was a great achievement]—the provision in the Canada Pension Plan for any province—it wasn't just Quebec but any province—to opt out and have its own. And these were on terms that were obviously acceptable to Quebec. For a while we wondered whether Ontario might do the same. It was the only province financially strong enough that it could have.

I think Confederation was saved at that point. I think there was a risk of Confederation coming apart at the seams over that whole social security package, and that was avoided, and avoided successfully.

On April 20, 1964, there were simultaneous announcements on the terms of the pension plan settlement by Prime Minister Pearson in Ottawa and Premier Lesage in Quebec City. These included the Quebec government's agreement to seek an amendment to the Constitution that would allow the Canada Pension Plan to have survivors' benefits — as Judy LaMarsh said, the federal government had to have such an agreement since survivors' benefits came under provincial jurisdiction.

Jean Lesage told the Quebec Legislature that he had been under terrible strain during the course of the negotiations: "I used all means that Providence has given me so that Quebec, in the end, would be recognised as a province with special status in Confederation. And I have succeeded." This could be dismissed as special pleading but David Lewis of the NDP and others felt that the government did grant a special status to Quebec without saying so, and they pointed to a speech that Lester Pearson made on January 5, 1964, in which he said that Quebec was not a province like others but the homeland of a people. Lubor Zink recalled the Prime Minister's interest in the make-up of the old Austro-Hungarian Empire.

DAVID LEWIS

I think that the Pearson Government treated Quebec in a special way. I remember those of us in the NDP who were making speeches, including myself and Tommy [Douglas] gave these [Canada Pension Plan and opting out generally] as examples of special status. In fact, Quebec was always treated differently from the rest of Canada. Since it was done subterraneously, it was done hypocritically if you like—whether consciously hypocritically or not is irrelevant—it was resented by the rest of Canada.

All through my political life I've heard Western Canada and the provinces east of Quebec, but particularly Western Canada and some in northern Ontario saying, "Look, everything is going to Quebec!" You know, when you listen to the PQ say that Quebec hasn't done so well by Confederation, you say to yourself, "What country am I living in? Because all my political life everyone else in Canada was sore at the fact that Quebec was getting too much."

LUBOR ZINK

I remember very vividly one long talk we had because Pearson wanted to know anything I could tell him about the Austria-Hungarian model of political dualism in one state. I knew quite a bit and I told him all I remembered. And he found it interesting but not entirely applicable to the Canadian situation. But he was interested in any historical precedent where two nations speaking different languages found some kind of political arrangement which enabled them to manage their own internal affairs and at the same time have a joint foreign policy and joint defence and joint over-all economy and joint political framework. So Austria-Hungary was always an obvious one and we discussed it at length. The purpose of his talk with me was to find out whether there was enough similarity to let a group of people go into it in great detail. And he didn't.

TOM KENT

It was Mr. Pearson's opinion that all provinces by the nature of things were going to have more authority than they had had in the abnormal period of the '40s and '50s. And that a move toward some degree of decentralisation of power from Ottawa was necessary and desirable, quite apart from the particular pressure from Quebec. I think that his view was that this was increasingly the right way to govern the country, and certainly it was a way which was pressed equally vigorously by other provinces, as well as by Quebec. And so I think it would be accurate first of all to say that if Mr. Pearson appeased at all, he wasn't appeasing Quebec, he was appeasing the provinces. But his motive for appeasing the provinces was that he believed that there should be a shift back of power toward the provinces and away from its centralisation in Ottawa. That's a view that I would share.

That federal-provincial conference of March 31 - April 2, 1964, led to the opting-out or contracting-out formula becoming an established provincial right. Actually, the idea that provinces could opt out of joint federal-provincial programs such as the pension plan and hospitalisation and receive the equivalent amount that the federal government would have spent in tax points was envisaged by Maurice Lamontagne in the 1950s when Louis St. Laurent was Prime Minister; it was used by the Diefenbaker Government to get around Quebec's objections to the university grants, but that was considered exceptional then. It was not till the Quebec City conference that opting out became an accepted practice — that conference which had seemed such a disastrous failure at the time probably did more to change Confederation than any other federal-provincial meeting.

It could be said that the Quebec City conference gave rise to the whole policy of co-operative federalism. While there was argument about what co-operative federalism meant, with some politicians deriding it and others going to great lengths to define it — Maurice Lamontagne wrote a book about it and Jean-Luc Pepin an article — the basis of the policy would seem to have been the federal government's equalisation payments — these payments were made to equalise standards and opportunities across Canada. On July 7, 1964, Walter Gordon increased the equalisation payments to bring the poor provinces up to the average of the two richer provinces. Co-operative federalism also meant more consultation and, therefore, more federal-provincial conferences.

TOM KENT

The agreement we reached in 1964, which was implemented in the 1965 legislation, was that the opting-out option would be provided, but would be on the basis of a gentlemen's agreement and that was to the effect that Quebec, having got the right, the theoretical right, to change the programs, would not in fact do so for the next few years. There would be no real change for some time. There wouldn't be a break. There wouldn't be a creation of great differences between one part of the country and another. Quebec was the only one that was going to take advantage of it [the opting out formula] to take tax points instead of shared-cost arrangements, but having done that, they would in fact use the tax points to continue the program virtually without change.

R. L. STANFIELD

It was a technique developed on the theory that other provinces had no particular motivation to opt out—and most of them were too small to consider opting out. Ontario was the only other province that could have opted out of the Canada Pension Plan and written its own plan. Nova Scotia couldn't consider anything like that. This technique didn't bother me as long as it was available to all. I thought that was a small price to pay for maintaining some type of cordial relations with the province of Quebec.

MAURICE LAMONTAGNE

Of course, at that time, Quebec was the only province to avail itself of this new formula. In a way it was a face-saving device, because they had to comply with the federal conditions anyway, but at least they could say that they weren't receiving a grant from the federal government, they were more or less raising the money themselves. And it satisfied the Lesage government. There was no opposition at all from the other provinces, but they hadn't the same problems—the same pride, if you want. So I think it was a very useful formula at that time because we applied it systematically; and if we had not applied it that systematically, Quebec would not have gone for these strong [social welfare] programs; and if Quebec had not gone for these programs it would have been very difficult politically to advance them for the rest of the country and remain politically fair.

WALTER GORDON

Opting out gave any province that wished the right to assume full control of certain programs, which up until then were joint, and under the agreement they'd be continued, I think, for two years, but after a period they could be changed around or abandoned, and in exchange the province would receive more room in the tax fields. Now, while this was made for any province, the only one to take advantage of it was Quebec. And I think we all knew that would probably be the case. We weren't sure. I rather hoped Ontario would take over one or two things, but in the end Quebec was the only one to do it.

What was meant by co-operative federalism? It was one of those phrases that mean that the federal government and the provincial governments have to work together to make our system effective. And it led to a whole series of federal-provincial conferences.

MAURICE LAMONTAGNE

I have written a book on federalism. I had developed the formula which provided for equalisation payments on the basis of the top two richest provinces in 1954, and it was embodied into legislation in early 1957.* It became effective on April 1, 1957. This provided for equal opportunities for the provinces.

One thing which had worried me was the very unequal yield of taxation, especially direct taxation, as between provinces. The little agricultural province of Prince Edward Island, for instance, could have 100 percent tax on corporation profits, but there are no corporations there. So this was one of the reasons why our federalism really failed during the depression. The responsibilities were provincial and there was no financial capacity to support

*Changed by the Diefenbaker Government to the national average.

those responsibilities. I came to Mr. St. Laurent's office—it was my second assignment in the federal civil service—to develop that new formula. And I had great, great difficulties. I had to fight the whole Finance Department at that time, including the Assistant Deputy Minister in charge of taxation, and the then Minister of Finance.

I had in my book said that it was impossible in a federal system, given the complex problems of modern societies, to assign completely different responsibilities and clear compartments to different levels or spheres of governments. For instance, during the depression the provinces were supposed to be responsible for unemployment but they were not able to cope with that problem [and the federal government had to take over]. Of course, there was defence policy, this had to be a clear federal responsibility— that was one extreme. At the other extreme, the control over education in terms of programs and curricula and all this had to be an exclusive provincial responsibility. But in between, as modern society became more complicated, there were more and more grey areas.

Classical federalism rested on the basic concept that we had two independent and autonomous levels of government, and there was no need to co-operate. The spheres [of jurisdiction] were there. This was a very abstract view which was espoused for many years by the Privy Council in London. But it failed to cope with real life.

So, realising that there were more and more of those grey areas where joint action was required, I started to develop this idea of co-operative federalism that was ridiculed at one stage because people were saying, "Well, federalism involves co-operation." But in the classical concept, which had been accepted more or less by Quebeckers, we had spheres and there was no need for consultation. When we organised, back in 1955 under Mr. St. Laurent, the program of equalisation payments, I didn't realise that we had developed an instrument which could be applied to the concept of co-operative federalism.

JEAN-LUC PEPIN

In my article on co-operative federalism, I have a philosophical introduction, which is on the concept of nations and the concept of nationalities. And I say that these concepts are relative and they're only worthwhile inasmuch as they serve the objective. Then I talk about the techniques of co-operative federalism.

The first point I make is economic decentralisation and binationalism. This is one of the shocking things: I come out in favour of the two-nation concept. Then my second point is, to each level of government according to its attitudes. This is very, very anti-legal. I say there's no way to divide the jurisdiction between the central government and the provincial governments. I state it very emphatically: stop talking about division of power. In contemporary life the two areas are so intimately related that the idea of dividing it should be abandoned.

In other words—and that's the third point—unavoidable overlapping of jurisdiction. So, you see, from a French Canadian in those years this was very, very strong wording. Unavoidable overlapping, and then provincial priorities. I state here that at that time—and there's still a lot of that now—the provincial jurisdiction had acquired priorities that should be very much respected. I talk about the division of income to each according to its needs. I talk about tax decentralisation and so on. Then I talk about co-operation and co-ordination. In other words, the purpose of the essay was to de-emphasise all that business about division of jurisdiction and emphasise that in today's society, in a federal state, you've got to operate in co-operation and co-ordination.

TOM KENT

I don't want to put views retrospectively into Mr. Pearson's mouth on this because I am not sure that I can recall his ever formulating it this precisely, but I think on balance his judgement on special status was that if one established a situation with any considerable degree of special status, then the role of Quebec M.P.s and Quebec Ministers in Ottawa became so compromised, so different from that of others, that on balance it was not a workable solution. Therefore, we stuck to our approach of "co-operative federalism."

Now, that in itself is not a very meaningful phrase, I recognise, but essentially I think what we meant was that first and foremost we accepted the attitude that the relative role of the provinces by the whole nature of things in the 1960s, 1970s was greater. Secondly, we did, as you will recall, move a very long way to making that a reality for the poorer, as well as the richer, provinces by the equalisation program in federal-provincial fiscal relations. Then, the whole shift toward making many decisions through— at least as a result of—federal-provincial conferences, federal-provincial contacts of all kinds, rather than by isolated federal action. There was over the early years of the Pearson Government, an enormous shift in the whole style of Canadian government in that respect.

That was what co-operative federalism was and the hope was that that, combined with what at that early stage was a very gentle approach to bilingualism in Ottawa, would solve the [Quebec] problem or at least ease it.

ALLAN MacEACHEN

Co-operative federalism basically was probably an expression like "just society." What is it? Obviously, it is attempting to co-operate with the provinces in joint activities in the federal system. It was never intended to mean, at least in my opinion, that the federal government would be powerless to act unless they had unanimity from the provinces or consent from the provinces.

J. R. SMALLWOOD

I'm not sure that I ever did understand it, or that I understand it now. Certainly the word "co-operative" is a healthy word. That's a mother-love word. And Canada is a federal state. So co-operative federalism to me meant very little more—not that this is anything against it—than a friendly and co-operative working together of the provinces to make federalism work. I didn't understand any more than that about it.

JOHN ROBARTS

I'm not much for catch phrases. I don't really know what co-operative federalism was. I didn't see any particular thing that I could label, but these things are really hard to put labels on.

I think what Mr. Pearson really wanted was a degree of co-operation between the federal government and the provinces and the people who make up the federation, and he did strive mightily for it. And Mike Pearson basically was an international diplomat, and his idea of the right solution was that everybody went away more or less happy, instead of sort of figuring out whether you had in fact arrived at the right result. There is a difference in the approach. If success is getting some form of agreement at any cost, then you get a certain result. And he was very good at that. He was a great compromiser. But he was what he was, a highly skilled international diplomat, a negotiator, and a bargainer and conciliator. I don't know whether it really worked for Canada or not, but history will tell.

DOUGLAS FISHER

So we went all through that terrible crap and mugwumpery, I call it, of co-operative federalism. Then Pearson and the Liberals just had to win and they had to revivify themselves for '65 so they went out and picked up Marchand, Pelletier, and Trudeau and they were in that order of merit, as it was seen then. Once those three got in, of course, they couldn't buy co-operative federalism. So here you had the Pearson Government between '63 and '65, and '65 and '68, doing a complete switch from co-operative federalism to the Trudeau brand, which was much harder and firmer.

Co-operative federalism suggests that you can have an immense number of very flexible arrangements between the provinces and the federal government. In other words, everything is loose in the goose; the main thing is let's sit around the table and work things out. Well, Trudeau in particular along with Pelletier brought in a much stronger construction of the Constitution—get the federal government out of university education, end shared-cost programs, and all that.

I used to tease Jean-Luc Pepin about this. Jean-Luc was one of the great enthusiasts, I suppose, as a political scientist, for co-operative federalism. He had a whole series of speeches written and I once debated with him on a platform about it, an enormous enthusiast for co-operative federalism. Even today, I'll say,

"Jean-Luc, where's your stuff on co-operative federalism?" He told me shortly after '65, he said, "You know, you put those things away when you see where things are swinging" because co-operative federalism in the Maurice Lamontagne line was out. It no longer stood up.

There was no satisfying Quebec, as Lester Pearson found out, and the way that the Lesage government exploited co-operative federalism to its political advantage made the Pearson Government feel that it would have to harden its position toward the provinces. The latest demand of René Lévesque that family allowances should come under provincial jurisdiction came as a shock to Ottawa. Then, to have Jean Lesage not only backing his minister but saying that Quebec intended to take over the whole fabric of social legislation including the old-age pensions—the premier had made this statement in the Throne Speech opening the 1966 legislature—where was it all going to end? However, Lesage was defeated in the June 1966 election and the Union Nationale leader, Daniel Johnson, became premier; Prime Minister Pearson was no longer inhibited by having to deal with fellow Liberals in Quebec City. Furthermore, the advent of Marchand, Pelletier, and Trudeau meant strong support for a tougher line toward the provinces. There were to be no more fuzzy grey areas of jurisdiction but a return to clear-cut divisions between federal and provincial responsibilities. By the end of 1966 co-operative federalism had ended.

In retrospect, René Lévesque seemed to be a separatist or extreme nationalist to many of the federal participants at the 1964 Quebec City conference, including Prime Minister Pearson. However, Jean Lesage maintained that he was not an indépendantiste *or* séparatiste *while he was a minister in his government, and gave as proof of this the fact that Lévesque had publicly defended the so-called Fulton-Favreau formula.** *At first, there had been general agreement among the provinces on this formula, which was a complex instrument but in a sentence meant that Quebec and Ontario would have the veto in amending the British North America Act. If the formula had been adopted, it would have meant that the BNA Act, which serves as Canada's Constitution, could have been*

---

*First devised by Davie Fulton, Conservative Justice Minister, and adopted by Guy Favreau, Liberal Justice Minister.

brought to Ottawa.* However, Quebec reneged at the September 1964 Charlottetown Conference, which marked the hundredth anniversary of the first conference on Confederation. Lesage said that the tide of popular opinion in French Canada turned against the Fulton-Favreau formula, despite Lévesque's best efforts on behalf of unity. Yet, a couple of months later, Jean Chrétien claimed that René Lévesque let it out that he was a separatist while trying to recruit the young M.P. as a provincial candidate.

JEAN LESAGE

I myself agreed [to the Fulton-Favreau formula] and I had the full power to do so from my cabinet, including René Lévesque. That's why I am saying that his independent faith didn't show, because not only was he in favour of the Fulton-Favreau formula, but he defended it publicly at my request afterward. As a matter of fact, he clashed with Jacques Yvan Morin, who became his minister of education and who was the leader of the movement against the Fulton-Favreau formula, on that question. I could not be led to believe that Lévesque was for independence at the time.

Then, the public reaction—it was clear that, with the months that elapsed, this wouldn't be accepted by the people. You know, there has always been in Quebec a deep feeling that the protection against what a number of people call the Anglos, in Montreal especially and in the other provinces, lay in London. It had the protection of London but very often it's subconscious. Either they want to keep London as a protector or they want to be free and independent because what they are afraid of—and again for most people it's subconscious—are the Anglos and the Anglos are not the British.

JOHN ROBARTS

All the provinces agreed to the Fulton-Favreau formula at Banff but when we got to Charlottetown, Quebec backed off. There's no doubt that, for Mr. Pearson, the term for Quebec in those days

*The BNA Act, which established self-government and Confederation for Canada, was an act of the British Parliament and could not be patriated without an agreement by all the provinces on a method of making amendments.

would probably be "exasperating," because whatever he did it wasn't enough. He was always seeking what seemed to be an unattainable solution, and I'm sure he found it extremely exasperating.

JEAN CHRÉTIEN

The Quebec Liberal Party was weak in my area because it was the kingdom of Duplessis, the north shore between Montreal and Quebec. There were very few Liberals there, and René Hamel [MLA Iberville] was leaving to become a judge. They needed a guy who could keep the party alive and improve its fortunes there. René Lévesque had asked Lesage to give him the responsibility for organising the by-election. He came to the riding, and they said, "The best man we have in the area is Chrétien." In those days, to be a federal M.P. did not mean much because locally all the *patronage* and activity were provincial. There was nothing federal. The people at home felt that they would be more useful in Quebec [City].

Lévesque approached me. For all the intellectual honesty that everyone gave him, I have the proof that he has not that much, because he was already a separatist. I was bargaining with him. I said, "What will Lesage be offering to me? I'm doing well in Ottawa, really." I think I was chairman of the Justice Committee, or I was to be the chairman of the Justice Committee. And I said, "I will become a Parliamentary Secretary; I've not done badly in one year and a half." I wanted them to offer me a cabinet job.

He said to me, "Oh, Jean, don't be worried about your career in Ottawa. In five years' time there will be no such thing for us as the federal government."

"Come on, Lévesque, are you a separatist?" I said, "I'm not a separatist; I'm a Canadian."

"Oh," he said, "forget about it."

When he said "forget about it," I knew that he'd gone too far. And I said that [he was a separatist] for years, and nobody ever printed it. Because to attack Lévesque with the press, English and French, is like attacking God.

I saw Lesage. I will always remember, it was the first week after Advent. Because Lesage recited to me *l'Évangile* of that

Sunday—when the bark of the tree is tender enough, that's a sign that the time has come. And I said, "What does that mean?"

Mr. Pearson learned about it because Lévesque said, I think to Maurice Sauvé, that "we're drawing one of your good young men from Ottawa," and Sauvé reported that to Pearson, who called me into his office. He explained to me his problems, and he said, "If you go, Jean, they will say, 'There's a young man of the New Guard who's fed up with the Old Guard and is quitting.'" And he just asked me one question. He was a great psychologist. He said, "Jean, do you believe in Canada?" And already the week before I had said to Lévesque that I was a Canadian. So I said, "I believe in Canada and I will stay."

He said, "Oh no, don't make that type of decision here." It's very impressive for a young man to be talked to in this way by the Prime Minister of his country. So he sent me home for a week, despite the fact that we were in a minority position. And I consulted all of my organisations, and eighteen told me to go to Quebec; two told me to stay, plus my wife. I stayed.

8 *Toil and Trouble*

AT THE END of November 1964 when the dark days of winter were descending on the Ottawa landscape, Canada's Parliament became involved in a succession of so-called scandals. There were charges of bribery and corruption in connection with attempts to prevent the deportation of a Quebec underworld figure, Lucien Rivard, to the United States, where he was accused of trafficking in heroin; as the newspapers said, the tentacles of the Mafia reached into the highest places including the Prime Minister's office. Before the disclosure of the Rivard affair and other scandals, Hal Banks, a labour gangster, had fled the country that summer after being convicted of conspiracy to do bodily harm, the Opposition Members asserted that the government was doing nothing about finding him or bringing him to justice because Banks had made campaign contributions to Montreal area Liberal M.P.s. Rumours of fraudulent bankruptcies were rife in the capital but these never surfaced in the House of Commons. However, investigations did turn up a furniture deal, which was a picayune affair but led to the downfall of two Ministers. Finally, Yvon Dupuis, the rousing campaigner and debater, was fired from the Cabinet because of allegations that he had tried to fix a race-track application in Quebec. All of these scandals, both large and small, brought Parliament to its lowest ebb, as Prime Minister Pearson observed, and Canadian politics into general disrepute.

It was not so much that the scandals were so damaging as the way they *were handled or mishandled in the House, the contortions the Cabinet went through, and its indecisions. Tom Kent blamed the flag debate for Pearson's being under so much pressure at the time and being so exhausted, and said that if the issue of the flag had not been joined, most of this trouble could have been avoided. Lester Pearson claimed that parliamentary procedure during the flag debate prevented him from making a statement in the House confessing that he had been told about the Rivard affair well before it came up. Perhaps the worst feature of this whole sordid business was the fact that, aside from Hal Banks, who was a relatively minor figure, all those implicated in the scandals—Guy Favreau, Maurice Lamontagne, René Tremblay, Yvon Dupuis, Guy Rouleau, and Raymond Denis—were French Canadians. There were too many English Canadians who were ready to believe that their French compatriots were a corrupt and untrustworthy crowd, and these malfeasances seemed to lend credence to their views. It was an ironic situation for Lester Pearson because he had worked so hard to find a solution to the problem of national unity, only to have it compromised in this manner.*

Guy Favreau was a particularly tragic figure. So much had been expected of him, and Christopher Young remembered Mike Pearson's telling him that this was the man who was going to be not only his Quebec lieutenant but, he hoped, his successor as Prime Minister. Too much was given him, but this was not entirely Pearson's fault. The story begins with the resignation of Lionel Chevrier. Maurice Lamontagne didn't want to see him go since he didn't think he could be replaced as Quebec lieutenant; he said that if he had stayed, there would have been none of this trouble because Chevrier was a superb Parliamentarian. However, when Prime Minister Pearson told him that he wanted to appoint George McIlraith as Justice Minister to succeed Chevrier and Guy Favreau as Secretary of State, Lamontagne protested on behalf of Quebec and said that Favreau should be made Justice Minister. He, Lamontagne, would agree to being Secretary of State if all the cultural agencies were put under that department. Meanwhile there was a power struggle in the Quebec caucus.

MAURICE LAMONTAGNE

Some of what was called at that time the old gang started to work on Guy Favreau. As my family was here, I went home every evening when the House adjourned and Guy was having talks with these guys. I think that they were afraid that I might become the Quebec leader—however, I'm sure I would have resisted that temptation. In any case, there was a push at a certain stage to make Guy Favreau the leader, and I resisted that movement at the time. I didn't want the job; I was not ready for it; and I thought that even if he wanted it, he was not ready for it. Then there was Maurice Sauvé pushing. At some stage Sauvé wanted to have a kind of triumvirate in Quebec with Guy and myself and Sauvé. I said to hell with it. I was not interested in this, especially with that kind of organisation.

So that's how Guy Favreau became the Quebec leader [Quebec lieutenant] and he really destroyed himself, unfortunately. He was a very nice guy, very generous, very naïve in a way. And he could not refuse any assignment. I had fought for him to become Minister of Justice, and then he became Quebec leader and then on top of that—and probably because of Pickersgill's advice; Pickersgill wanted to leave that job—House Leader. And he didn't know anything about the rules of House.

Erik Nielsen, Progressive Conservative Member for the Yukon, was the one who opened the Pandora's box of scandals in Parliament. There had been rumours around Ottawa of wrong-doing but it took the painstaking investigations of Nielsen, a lawyer and one-time prosecuting attorney, and Paul Akehurst, a radio reporter in the Parliamentary Press Gallery, who worked with him, to come up with all the facts on the Rivard affair. Briefly stated, they were: in the summer of 1964 Lucien Rivard was being held in Bordeau jail near Montreal awaiting the result of extradition proceedings: he was wanted in the United States on serious narcotics charges. Through the connections he had with the Liberal Party, Rivard was able to get Raymond Denis, executive assistant to the Minister of Citizenship and Immigration, René Tremblay, to offer a bribe of 20,000 dollars to Pierre Lamontagne, a Canadian lawyer acting for the American government, to withdraw his opposition to bail. Guy Rouleau, the Prime Minster's Parliamentary Secretary, also made representations on behalf of Rivard. Lamontagne refused but telephone calls he received indicated that the underworld believed that he had accepted the bribe and he was worried.

As a flyer who had won the DFC in the war, Nielsen had taken risks but he was meticulous in this probing and would not move until he had proof. Once he had that, however, he made sure that his disclosure would have the greatest impact.

ERIK NIELSEN

I knew by the time that I had come back from Montreal with my colleague from the Press Gallery who was collaborating with me [Paul Akehurst] that I had something that was really wrong and was politically an atomic bomb. On our return, I went to see the old Chief [Diefenbaker] at Stornoway. He was in bed. I told him what I had. He didn't say so, but I got the feeling that he wanted to use it. He wanted to go deeper into the background, because he is a very skilled forensic person. He wanted all the data so that he wouldn't be caught hanging out in left field. I was not prepared to tell him where I got my information. Despite his urgings, I did not tell him. Under those circumstances he said. "All right you raise it, and arrange it with Churchill, the House Leader."

I went to see Gordon Churchill, and displayed to him essentially what I had revealed to the old Chief. We decided that the best vehicle for the exposure was the estimates [expenditures] for the Department of Justice, which fortuitously were coming up that following Monday, November 23, 1964.

Mr. Diefenbaker left it pretty well to me. I know that he would have liked to have done it himself as senior counsel, so to speak, in a court of law. But because of my undertakings to people from whom I had gained my information, I was not prepared to give that kind of solid base upon which to act as senior counsel. I was the only one that could have done it, and if it was going to be done at all, it was going to be done by me because I was not going to betray those that had confidence in me to give me the information. Once he knew that, as a lawyer and as a Parliamentarian, he appreciated that undertaking of a colleague.

MAURICE SAUVÉ

In those days the Opposition wouldn't pass the estimates of the various departments—and you've got to remember Pearson was always in a minority position—they were using delaying tactics. And the estimates had to be passed. One day the Conservative House Leader [Churchill] came to our own House Leader [McIlraith]* and said that they would pass all the estimates as long as they could study in detail the Department of Justice estimates.

This proposal came to the Cabinet and there was a lot of discussion—should we accept this or not? There were many Ministers who were glad that their own estimates wouldn't be discussed and said that it was a good scheme, a good proposal. I remember very well that four Ministers, including myself, said, "You know, Mr. Pearson, we don't know what there is there but we're not in favour of it. We believe that we're falling into a trap." We opposed this arrangement but everybody else was in favour and it was accepted.

DOUGLAS FISHER

I always remember how the word came to me about Nielsen. Alistair Fraser, who is now the Clerk of the House, came into the coffee shop in the middle of the afternoon. I was there, and he had a funny look on his face, and I said, "What's the matter, Alistair?" He said, "Nielsen is delivering a speech down there that I think is going to blow this place wide open." I said, "What's it about?" He said, "Well, it's about a Quebec scandal, a jail, and so on."

And I thought to myself, gee, that has a familiar ring. He said, "There have been rumours floating around here for a while but Nielsen seems to have got it cold, and he's really taking his time about presenting it. He's not sort of blurting it out and saying did you or didn't you. He's developing this in there." So I galloped down to the House and caught the tail end of Erik's thing and it began to move.

MAURICE SAUVÉ

After the Minister of Justice had made his presentation, I left the House of Commons because Guy Favreau had told us at lunchtime that there was no problem. We had all had lunch together in the parliamentary restaurant, Lamontagne, Tremblay,

*George McIlraith was appointed Government House Leader in place of Guy Favreau on October 30, 1964.

myself, and Favreau, and we asked Favreau about his estimates. He said, "I've heard a story that somebody wants to talk about a certain Rivard affair. But that's not serious. There's no problem there." And he repeated that there was nothing. So we were confident. And I left the Chamber for my office, which was nearby.

I came back in the House an hour later, and a Member of Parliament who is a very wise man said to me, "Do you see [Guy] Rouleau behind the curtain?" I said, "Yes." He said, "He stayed there all afternoon. You know he's not always present for a debate of the House," and he added, "I don't understand, but there must be something. He's there and he's following the discussion."

ERIK NIELSEN

It was a very exciting time. I knew the volatility of what I was dealing with. It was like zeroing your sights in on an ME-109 travelling at 400 miles an hour, and knowing that this is going to be your last shot. So you have to be accurate.

At that time I had the information not only about Denis, who I was satisfied had committed an offence under the criminal code—after two appeals he was convicted and sentenced to serve his time—but I knew about Guy Rouleau and I knew about Guy Lord [special assistant to the Justice Minister].

In the estimates discussion, I described Guy Lord's participation as that of an innocent dupe but I didn't even mention Rouleau. But I knew of his role at that time and I was ready the next day, if something didn't happen, to reveal that. In other words the whole bolt wasn't shot at once.

But Rouleau resigned the next day and Guy Lord made his confession of purity and which I believed. Tremblay, I had never accused of impropriety, although I did come so close as to say that the negotiations with Pierre Lamontagne went on in the Minister's office, which was true, but the Liberals accused me then of asserting by inference that the Minister was involved. I had at no time ever said that the Minister, Tremblay, was involved, nor indeed was Favreau.

Although Guy Favreau had been warned well before the disclosure in November that Erik Nielsen was investigating the Rivard affair, the

Justice Minister seemed totally unprepared for the Yukon Member's onslaught. Actually, Nielsen had made no attempt to hide what he was doing; he had seen Pierre Lamontagne quite openly in the law offices of Geoffrion and Prud'homme, and he had taken it for granted that the senior partner, A. Geoffrion, who was a prominent Liberal, would inform the government, which he did do. Furthermore, Nielsen had suggested to Lamontagne that he tell the Justice Minister that he, Nielsen, was going to raise the matter in the House. Yet Favreau appeared confused, and, instead of taking the Members into his confidence and admitting there had been bribery and wrong-doing, he tried to deny everything.

The next day Prime Minister Pearson fired Guy Rouleau before Nielsen could charge that he was involved. When the sitting began on November 24, 1964, the Justice Minister agreed that there should be an enquiry into the whole affair. The Prime Minister, in replying to an Opposition question, said that the first he had heard of the Rivard case was on the day before the Justice Department's estimates were brought before the House of Commons—that was November 22, 1964. Then Mr. Pearson left for a tour of Western Canada.

ERIK NIELSEN

There is a certain sadness about the way Favreau reacted on this matter because he was a man of honour, I am convinced, and a very fine Canadian, but he just didn't know how to handle it politically in the House of Commons. The way to have handled it was honestly and forthrightly and to say that these people have been caught with their trousers at half-mast and they are going to be disciplined or fired or charged or whatever. He tried to cover it up, which was fatal.

JUDY LaMARSH

I just loved Guy Favreau. I think he was a marvellous, great-hearted human being. He came to Cabinet, and the first thing I said, "Guy, why in hell didn't you tell the Prime Minister?" He said, "But I did'" I said, "Well, you couldn't have. Didn't you hear what he's just said in the House?"

Guy had not heard the question and the answer in the House, and Mike had gone out West.

We then discussed it, and Favreau told us the circumstances

under which he told the Prime Minister. Paul Martin was there and Martin tried to get the P.M. but he'd left. He tried for some time. We'd leave the House after question period and go into nonstop Cabinet meetings about this damned mess. Finally Martin got him on the phone, and said, "Favreau says that he told you before." And Mike said, "Oh yes, I remember."

It had been on September 2, 1964, while flying back from the federal-provincial constitutional conference held in Charlottetown, Prince Edward Island, that Guy Favreau had mentioned the Rivard affair to Lester Pearson. He had had very little time with the Prime Minister and, from all accounts, had not impressed him with the importance of the matter.

JOHN CONNOLLY

I was with Favreau on the plane. We were sitting facing each other. It was a very small plane. Mrs. Pearson was sitting with her husband, and she left her seat for a moment [to go to the washroom]. Favreau excused himself and went over and sat with Mike. When he came back he said, "I had to tell him about a problem that I have."

Guy might have picked the wrong time to talk to Mike about this; probably did. Mike was working on papers but he listened and I guess he said, "You'll have to handle it." And that was how he learned. If he forgot about it, I could understand it, because I forgot about it. I forgot about it completely.

MAURICE LAMONTAGNE

Favreau spoke to him on the plane coming back from P.E.I. Mike hated to be on a plane. He was always almost sick in a plane. He did a lot of travelling in a plane. I don't know why he didn't adjust to this. I remember going to Murray Bay with him to make a speech shortly after he became Prime Minister in August '63, and he was sick on the plane—just vomiting and all that. Of course, it was raining, the weather was not too good.

It was not the proper place to start this kind of discussion, and Guy admitted that he spoke to him for only about one minute. And knowing Mike as I do, Mike forgot, I'm sure.

While Prime Minister Pearson toured the prairie provinces, attending Liberal fund-raising dinners, his government struggled with the Rivard scandal. Paul Martin, who was Acting Prime Minister, kept in touch by telephone but there were demands that Mr. Pearson should return to his seat in Parliament. At a series of Cabinet meetings, it was decided to appoint Mr. Justice Frédéric Dorion to head a commission of enquiry into the whole affair — Mr. Dorion was known as a bleu, *a true-blue Quebec Conservative, but sat as an independent Member of Parliament for Charlevoi from 1942 to 1949.*

PAUL MARTIN

I phoned Mr. Pearson, who was in Brandon, to tell him about the situation. He had just learned about the demand for an enquiry. I said, "We'll have to discuss this is the Cabinet. What are your directions? What are your views?" I called him a second time, after we had met, and Mr. Favreau thought there should be a royal commission, and thought that the royal commissioner should be Mr. Justice Dorion. It seemed to some of us that we were rushing into this thing without a great deal of thought. When you look back on the whole thing, as far as the Favreau end of it was concerned, there was really no justification for a royal commission. You don't have a royal commission over a Minister who commits an error of judgement, and that is all that he had ever done. If he had really gone that far.

But it was largely as a result of Mr. Favreau's own initiative, his insistence on a royal commission and his insistence that the royal commissioner should be Mr. Justice Dorion. He wanted someone who he thought would be objective. He and Dorion had been classmates apparently. I was criticised for picking Dorion, but the responsibility for that resided with Guy.

J. W. PICKERSGILL

Pearson wanted to come back, and twice he started cancelling his engagaments to come back. But the consensus in the Cabinet, which I shared and which Paul Martin also shared, was that this would just magnify the thing, that intrinsically there was nothing to it, as there wasn't. It was too bad he'd gone away, but this was a program that had been laid on long before. But to interrupt it and come rushing back would look as though we were on the edge of a war or something. Now, this may or may not have been an error in judgement. But it wasn't Pearson's error, except to the extent that he accepted the advice of the Cabinet. And he was consulted about everything, including the choice of the commissioner.

MITCHELL SHARP

My strongest impression from that period was what a grave mistake was made in appointing the royal commission. That was a mistake, and most of us who were around at the time said, "We will never make that mistake again," because that was to throw into doubt the word of a Minister. It was a sort of public admission there was something to be enquired into. Favreau was extremely well liked in the Cabinet; we had confidence in him. We thought the Prime Minister had made a mistake in appointing him as House Leader; that was our general view. But while he was there we did our best to support him. But he was a victim of a whole series of circumstances. It was a great tragedy.

JOHN CONNOLLY

When Favreau came along with the idea that Dorion should be appointed, I was rather flabbergasted because Dorion had been in the House of Commons during the war, and Dorion was a bitter partisan as I remembered him. I hope I'm not doing him an injustice. A bitter partisan. And I couldn't believe that [Favreau] would recommend him to be the chairman of such a sensitive commission, when politics were bound to play such an important part in the deliberations. I remember afterward speaking to Chubby [Power] under his oath as Privy Councillor and saying, "This is what is proposed," and Chubby couldn't believe this, he just couldn't believe it.

When Prime Minister Pearson returned to Ottawa from his sojourn in the West, it was fully expected that he would immediately go to the House of Commons and tell the Members that he had been informed of the Rivard affair by Guy Favreau on that plane coming back from the Charlottetown conference—and that was long before he had said that he had heard about it first. But he did not, and this caused a great deal of anguish. Why didn't he simply admit that he had forgotten? Instead he wrote a letter to Mr. Justice Dorion, telling him that he had made a mistake and that he now remembered being told about it on September 2, 1964. There were all kinds of excuses why he shouldn't make a statement in the House —the procedures being followed in the flag debate did not allow any intervention, and there was the enquiry itself, which made the matter sub-judice, but none of them should have prevented him from telling the House that he had been in error if he had wanted to.

However, not everyone blamed Mike Pearson for this lapse and for not supporting his Justice Minister.

J. W. PICKERSGILL

I've always believed that Mr. Pearson completely forgot that conversation. I was also very troubled by the fact that when he was reminded of it, he didn't deal with it promptly. Now, there are a lot of arguments on both sides on the state of the situation in the House, the fact that we had no question period during that period because of some quirk in the rules. But it could all have been got over. It was one of those times when I felt very unhappy. Not so much, in my case, that I felt it was an injustice to Favreau as I felt it was going to be terribly damaging to Pearson himself.

I've always taken the view that if something very unpleasant has to be done and there's no way you're going to escape it, you should do it at once. And that every hour of delay makes it that much harder, makes it that much more inexplicable. And I felt it was going permanently to weaken his credibility. I was just as much attached to Guy Favreau as Judy LaMarsh. We were very intimate friends indeed. And I've never been able to escape the feeling that if he had only told me three or four days before his estimates came up about this Rivard business, there never would have been a scandal.

TOM KENT

Jack Pickersgill and I fought about a lot of things and agreed about some things, and we both strongly agreed about this one. I forget how long it was but it felt like several weeks after that incident, I think both Jack and I, together and separately, almost wore out our welcome with Mr. Pearson, urging on him day after day that the only thing to do was to make a statement [that he had been told about the Rivard affair on September 2] today, tomorrow. I remember I drafted statement after statement. You know, get up in the House and say it today, and then the next day, get up in the House and say it today, and I'd change the statements a little and kept on preparing revised statements and talking closely to Jack Pickersgill about them at the time.

The obvious thing to do was as quickly as possible to say, "I am sorry. I made an error." And if he'd done it immediately, there would have been no harm at all. If he'd done it after a day or two or a week or two, there wouldn't have been very much harm. But for some reason, while he never said no, Mr. Pearson did not say yes and do it until the very last moment, when he wrote a letter to Dorion.

JUDY LaMARSH

It was just a holding operation till he [Pearson] got back to Ottawa, and we assumed he was going to go right in the House and say that Favreau had told him on September 2. But I have never known the answer to this particular question. I suspect it's Mike's complete inability to face confrontation, and also his feeling that, given the ugly mood in the House, he would be charged with being a Prime Minister who had lied to the House deliberately. He couldn't stand being called a liar and he couldn't stand historically what might then have happened. What with a minority government, he could have been called before the Bar of the House or before a Committee on Elections and Privileges. He simply couldn't stomach it. So he never did do anything.

J. W. PICKERSGILL

Don't you think that it does seem to indicate that Mr. Pearson was not a very good Parliamentarian? I once said that here was a man who played professional hockey and professional baseball, and maybe football too for all I know, and I am quite sure that when he played those games he learned the rules, and yet I said, here he is in the biggest game of all and I do wish he would learn the rules. So often in Parliament the invocation of the rules and the use of the rules in the right kind of way would have saved us endless grief. That is still the only serious criticism I have of Pearson as a politician.

TOM KENT

I would have to say that, at that point, Mr. Pearson was suffering from exhaustion and the enormous emotional problem that he had in the House of Commons, given the sort of attack the government was under, and particularly the emotional problem he had in dealing with Mr. Diefenbaker. I don't want to be misunderstood in this. I am not in any way suggesting that the analogies I am going to use are correct as to the characters of either party, but in the specific relationship in the House of Commons, Mr. Diefenbaker seemed to interact with Mr. Pearson in a way that produced what I think is the conventional reaction of the rabbit to the snake. Mr. Pearson really was sort of frozen by Mr. Diefenbaker. He couldn't cope with him. They were entirely different people. And his mind just didn't work, faced with the kind of attack which Mr. Diefenbaker made. There was no communication. There was no capability of understanding. And, as I say, Mr. Pearson just sort of emotionally and mentally froze, as some animals freeze when faced with a snake. It really was that effect.

Now, I emphasise I am not for one moment trying to press this analogy, to say that either was a rabbit or a snake. But in that particular forum of the House of Commons, it had something of that effect on Mr. Pearson. And, you know, I think this was almost his greatest problem, his greatest tragedy, and it was what made the whole process so exhausting for him.

DOUGLAS FISHER

The Favreau thing was something that really should have been settled very quickly if Pearson had been more honest and candid. He could have gone to the people very quickly. I don't mean in electoral terms, but I mean gone to the people and explained his oversight and admitted his mistake. But instead, in his desire I suppose to protect himself and the government, he left Favreau out, as the Nixon saying goes, "to twist in the wind."

T. C. DOUGLAS

My impression was, from the very beginning, that [Pearson] was going to play the role which many Prime Ministers have played throughout British and Canadian history, and that is if there's a scandal, you don't rush in to defend the government. You let the Minister defend it, and if he can't defend it then you throw him to the wolves. You don't throw the whole government to the wolves. And in some ways I suppose that makes sense. There's nothing worse than to dash in and say, "There's no evidence of this, it's completely innocent, and I'm convinced nothing wrong has been done," and then subsequently some type of judicial investigation or parliamentary enquiry proves that there was something. Where are you? So I can understand that.

One had the feeling throughout that whole thing that Pearson was just not going to commit all his troops to one pitched battle, that he was going to hold something in reserve so that if the scandal turned out to be as bad as it appeared on the surface, he could sacrifice a few people and still save his army—and that was the impression I got throughout the entire thing. There's no doubt that Guy Favreau was really the sacrificial lamb in this whole thing.

MITCHELL SHARP

Pearson never talked in the Cabinet about what had happened, other than to explain what he explained publicly. My impression is that he didn't accept the judgement of Judy LaMarsh that he had let Favreau down. I think to him it was probably one of the great tragedies of his career, that he should have been accused of it.

There are some people who think Pearson could be fairly ruthless. I doubt whether that was justified. He was Prime Minister and he had to do things that may have appeared to other people to be fairly ruthless; however, my impression was one of patience rather than anything else, that there were times when he could have been more ruthless to the benefit of the government. And I feel that it was the one incident that cost him more heart-burnings than anything else that happened to him—the idea that a good man like Favreau should have been destroyed, and in some people's judgement because the Prime Minister had not supported him adequately. And that was obviously what Judy LaMarsh felt.

JUDY LaMARSH

Then Mike wrote that extraordinary letter to Dorion, which Dorion read at the opening of the commission. I've never heard of such a circumstance. Who advised him on that I don't know, because we didn't know about it in Cabinet. He was incensed when the judge put it on the record. But you don't write judges or commissioners that kind of thing, tell him in the back door something you won't tell him in the front.

It completely disaffected me from Mike, that he would let that sort of thing happen to Guy—and after, when he was ill, pass him at least twice a day and never go in to see him in the hospital—that because of his own conscience.

I was hoping that Pearson would live long enough to finish his book on that particular era. I know Favreau was an honourable man, and yet it was his name that kept coming up again and again and again. You know, for a man of such tremendous talent, it was awful, devastating. It was just a disaster, a personal disaster.

There were those who felt that Guy Favreau had asked for trouble in his foolhardy attacks on John Diefenbaker during the debate.

JEAN-LUC PEPIN

Guy Favreau was good, unselfish, patriotic, generous, everything—but he simply was not a good politician. He couldn't defend himself. And he attacked. There are people in politics who can defend themselves, but they're usually cowards; they don't attack; or they attack, as I used to, in an oblique way. They don't go straight to the jugular. Well, history will tell you, and if you look at Guy Favreau's speeches, that he went at Diefenbaker in a straight line. He really challenged Diefenbaker! He really provoked Diefenbaker.

I'm talking with knowledge now because I was there on the floor, and I was suffering because I knew in my blood, in my instincts, that Guy Favreau was no match for Diefenbaker ... that if Diefenbaker decided to crush Guy Favreau, Diefenbaker would win, and with the support of Nielsen and Fulton and a few others. This is what happened. But when people say to me, "Diefenbaker was unfair going after Guy Favreau," I say tut, tut, tut, no, no. Favreau, like the Don Quixote that he was, really went after Diefenbaker. So Diefenbaker did the only thing he knows how to do. He defended himself, and reciprocated in kind, plus. So, in some ways, being very fair about these things and being one of the admirers of Guy Favreau, he asked for it, and he got what he asked for.

Mr. Pearson's mistake in Guy Favreau's life was not to understand that, was not to realise how fundamentally fragile Guy was, and to pile the jobs on him—Minister of Justice, House Leader, head of the Quebec Wing; and anything that Pearson piled on him at the suggestion of Pickersgill, Guy was willing to accept. They could have appointed him Ambassador to Washington and he would have accepted at the same time. That was the extent of his dedication, and his naïveté in some ways, too, because had he been able to defend himself he would have realised that any one of those jobs was good enough for a normal human being.

On November 30, 1964, the day after returning from the Western tour, Prime Minister Pearson addressed a lengthy letter on political morality to his Cabinet colleagues. It had been drafted and redrafted by his aides while he had been away and made the point that in no case must a public servant seek to gain treatment for a particular person that would not be accorded any citizen. The letter also said: "In order that honesty and impartiality may be beyond doubt, members of Ministers' staffs, equally with Ministers, must not place themselves in a position where they are under obligation to any person who might profit from special consideration or favour on their part, or seek in any way to gain special treatment from them. Equally, a staff member, like a Minister, must not have a pecuniary interest that could even remotely conflict with the discharge of his public duty."

In the middle of December 1964, the Dorion Commission began its hearings in Ottawa in the old railway station building. On March 2, 1965, which happened to be the day on which Mr. Justice Dorion was ending his sessions in the capital, Lucien Rivard escaped from Bordeaux jail. That evening, he and another prisoner received permission to water the jail's rink even though the outside temperature was 40 degrees Fahrenheit and the rink was full of water. They used the hose to clamber over the prison wall, hitched a ride from a passing motorist, and disappeared. Erik Nielsen was in the House of Commons when the news of the escape was received.

ERIK NIELSEN

It was electrifying. I can remember the news coming down from the Press Gallery, and I knew that it was coming down to Guy Favreau. If he could have literally torn hair from his head, he would have done so. He, in fact, made the gesture; he put his hand on his head and pulled both sides out, a "what else could happen" sort of thing. The utter despondency of the Liberal benches when this came out—politically one had to be completely insensitive not to revel in it.

Rivard was recaptured on July 16, 1965. The Dorion enquiry was a matter of concern to the government, and the worst fears of some Ministers were found to be justified when Mr. Justice Dorion's report was tabled in the House of Commons on June 29, 1965.

MAURICE SAUVÉ

Senator Connolly, a Cabinet Minister, was appointed to follow this enquiry. And from time to time, at Cabinet meetings, he would report on how the enquiry was going. It was always, "Oh, everything is okay; there's no problem. Everything's going fine."

I had very able executive assistants working with me who were very friendly with the lawyers working on this commission. And they were saying to me every time, "Mr. Sauvé, we're going to be in trouble, we're going to be in trouble." And every time Senator Connolly was reporting that everything was fine, I was reporting, "I cannot judge, but the information I have is that we're in trouble." And the Prime Minister would say, "Oh well, there's no problem; Senator Connolly says so."

Then one day I was in Quebec City before the report was published, and a friend of mine comes out of the courthouse—I was walking toward the Chateau Frontenac—and he says, "Oh, Maurice, I think you should tell your Prime Minister that the report of Dorion will not be very favourable to Favreau." I asked him a few questions, how he knew and whether he was sure that the information he was giving me was good.

When I arrived back in Ottawa I went to see the Prime Minister and I said, "Prime Minister, I am told by so-and-so"—and I identified the person to the Prime Minister and he knew who he was—"I am told that the Dorion Report will not be very favourable to Guy, and I think we should prepare for that." "Oh," he said, "Maurice, the reports we have from Connolly are that there's no problem." "Fine," I said, "I told you what I had to tell you, Mr. Pearson, and I'm a junior Minister, so that's all."

Then the famous report came out, and it was given to us in the evening prior to a Cabinet meeting. All of us, I suppose, read it. We came to a Cabinet meeting at ten o'clock the next morning. The Prime Minister made a few comments, and then he said, "I have decided to accept the resignation of the Minister of Justice." The Quebec Ministers were flabbergasted by this. And he said, "I'm going to tell this to the House when it meets this afternoon."

We said to the Prime Minister, "We would like to see you before you make this announcement, because it's very serious. We don't feel that there is very much in that report, and we should fight for Guy and we should fight for the Minister of Justice. He's an honest fellow, he's done nothing wrong," and so on. There was a lot of discussion in the Cabinet, and it was evident that things had been precooked. My own feeling about this is that Pickersgill had been talking to Favreau and had convinced Favreau that he should resign. Because during the discussion Favreau said, "No, no, no, I want to resign." He was very much a part of it. He wanted to resign. And we told him that we didn't want him to resign, that we should fight.

There was a clear distinction between the attitude of the English-speaking Ministers in the Cabinet and the French-speaking Ministers. The French-speaking Ministers really wanted to fight, and the English-speaking Ministers seemed to be resigned to total acceptance that Favreau should resign.

So we met Mr. Pearson that afternoon around four-thirty in his office. Maurice Lamontagne and I said to the Prime Minister, "We feel that Favreau should not resign, that if he resigns it's an acceptance that he's guilty. We feel that the report doesn't show that he's guilty, that he might not have been careful enough but there was nothing wrong in his own attitude, and that we have to fight for him, and that he has to remain Minister of Justice, and if you appoint him President of the Privy Council you will just destroy him physically because he will not be able to survive this." I don't think that Favreau was there when we had that meeting in the afternoon.

Anyway, for the first time in my life, the Prime Minister, Mr. Pearson, was a little rude with us. He said, "I don't want to hear any more about this. I have decided to accept Favreau's resignation, and I will make him President of the Privy Council. And that's the end to it."

Following the Rivard revelation, there was a reassessment made of Erik Nielsen's taxes. Not once but twice. As a result, the Yukon Member had to pay 25,000 dollars in back taxes, which was the reason he gave for being absent so much of the time from the House of Commons. Was this the Pearson Government's revenge?

ERIK NIELSEN

One can't make that direct accusation but the coincidence is too startling to be denied some sort of connection. Within two months of the parliamentary upheaval that was caused by the Rivard disclosures, the National Revenue officials swooped down upon my office—they were given free rein to do as they pleased—and that resulted in a reassessment of tax payable over the previous five years, in connection with items which were claimed as deductions from income, and which National Revenue officials wanted included in income. All of the items which National Revenue questioned in the reassessment had been discussed thoroughly with the director of the district taxation office in the Yukon, and each of these items had been implemented as a matter of internal management, with the blessing and sanction of the then district director of taxation. On the strength of that, I appealed. This appeal was heard by the income tax appeal board. The rationale of the decision resulted in a saw-off roughly speaking; I won half of the appeal and the government won half of the appeal—the government won their half on the basis of regardless of whatever permission was given by one of their officials with respect to the implementation of internal management policies resulting in deductions from income, this did not change the law of the land, and therefore the reassessment applied. So that reassessment was disposed of.

The attempt at a second reassessment of the Yukon member's taxes was made a year and a half later, at the time of the Munsinger affair. Nielsen wrote to the Department of National Revenue trying, as he said, to reason with them. But he got nowhere, so he wrote to the Minister, Jean Pierre Côté, protesting what he described as a completely unjustified attempt at reassessment.

ERIK NIELSEN

I said to Côté, "After you have looked at the department's side and after you have looked at my submissions in reply, you can't escape the conclusion that there is a deliberate attempt at harassing me in order to keep me out of the mainstream of my activities in the House of Commons," which I had to diminish somewhat in order to meet the first reassessment by spending more time in my practice.

The Minister agreed with me because the whole reassessment was dropped; it never got to the stage of being considered. It was simply withdrawn—and so it should have been.

It could be said that the case of Hal Banks started the whole series of scandals in Parliament. The boss of the Seafarers' International Union SIU had fled to the United States in July 1964 after having been sentenced to five years in prison for ordering the beating up of a rival trade unionist. The small amount of the bail—it was only 25,000 dollars and he forfeited this in skipping across the border—and the failure of the RCMP to track him down aroused suspicions among Opposition M.P.s that he was being protected. Many trade union leaders knew that he had escaped to Brooklyn and were not surprised when, on October 1, 1964, Robert Reguly, a reporter from the Toronto Star, found him sitting on his luxury yacht in Brooklyn harbour. There were angry protests in the House of Commons. Some time later Lester Pearson admitted in a television interview that Banks's SIU had provided electoral funds for some of the Montreal Liberal Members of Parliament.

Hal Banks, an American labour hoodlum with a criminal record, was brought to Canada by the St. Laurent Government in 1949 to break the Communist hold on the Canadian Seamen's Union, which was paralysing Marshall Plan shipments. After some bloody skirmishes Banks took over the waterfront. He was protected by a succession of Liberal Ministers and, although he had been convicted and served three and a half years in San Quentin, was granted landed-immigrant status; in return, he sent his goon squads to support Liberal candidates in election campaigns. It was a horrifying example of how anti-communism could lead to gangsterism, according to Maurice Wright, Q.C., who was the counsel for the Canadian Labour Congress at the hearings of the commission of enquiry under Mr. Justice T. G. Norris of Vancouver; the commission was appointed by the Diefenbaker Government to look into violence on the waterfront.

MAURICE WRIGHT

If anyone asked what was going on, well, the answer was a rhetorical question: "Are you or are you not in favour of getting rid of the Communists?" The Canada Labour Relations Board and the courts held that the waterfront was riddled with Communists. "What I'm trying to do," said Mr. Banks, inferentially, "is to get rid of them, and sometimes one has to use extreme measures." It gave him a marvellous justification; it clothed his exercise with a lot of political respectability.

One of those who worked with Maurice Wright in preparing the CLC case against Hal Banks was Harry Crowe, who was later to become Dean of History at York University, Toronto, but at the time was research director for the Canadian Brotherhood of Railway, Transport and General Workers, the union that was largely responsible for the Norris enquiry. Crowe met thirty to forty men who had had their kneecaps broken by Banks's paid thugs, and said that they were by no means all of those who, as Crowe put it, had had the boots put to them. This was the vicious and brutal manner by which Banks enforced his rule. Not only did he drive out union rivals but his demands were such that he succeeded in driving out most of the shipping companies as well. Wright believed that, in some fifteen years of depredations, Banks had cost Canada millions of dollars.

MAURICE WRIGHT

I'm personally of the opinion, just as an observer, one who reads papers and who hears things, that, thanks to the intervention of Hal Banks, Canada's coastal shipping on the East Coast was thoroughly destroyed. I think Canadian National Steamship Lines were about the last ones, and they finally folded.

My own theory is—but I couldn't possibly substantiate it—that it was part of a scheme of destroying the Canadian coastal shipping in order to deliver it to American interests. It's the only way that I can assess this thing intelligently. There must have been a reason for it. They deliver a certain amount of shipping, a total package of shipping, and if it isn't going to be done by ships of Canadian registry, maybe it will be done by ships of American registry. It was the same union. The Canadian ships went to foreign registry. Panamanian, things of that kind. Liberian registry. And the Canadian coastal shipping on the East Coast was effectively destroyed.

As might be expected, the Pearson Government was embarrassed when Hal Banks was found lolling on his yacht in Brooklyn harbour, and the claim that he could not be brought back to Canada to face justice because conspiracy was not an extraditable offense did not satisfy the Opposition. However, the Hal Banks affair did not cause as much trouble as Douglas Fisher expected.

It was Erik Nielsen's investigations into the Rivard affair that turned up other scandals, including the furniture deals, which may have been of little importance compared to the rest but probably had the greatest impact on the public. The bankruptcy of the Sefkind enterprises in Montreal revealed that Maurice Lamontagne had received two lots of furniture worth 6,800 dollars, on which he had made no payment until the Bank of Montreal, which was the Sefkinds' main creditor, sent him a bill. On December 8, 1964, the day on which the news of the Lamontagne deal was broadcast, René Tremblay gave a press conference in which he said that he had received 3,935 dollars worth of furniture from the Sefkinds and claimed that he had paid for it in full although some of it, including a love seat, had not been delivered. Then he went on to protest that there was no connection between his furniture purchase and the fact that as a Quebec provincial government official he had approved a loan of 1,200,000 dollars to the Sefkinds.

MAURICE SAUVÉ

Now I'll tell you what I know about this story. I remember that there was an executive committee meeting of the Liberal Party at the Club de Réforme in Montreal one Saturday afternoon [some years before]. Many of us had been invited to visit the showroom of a furniture dealer who was an associate of a Member of Parliament by the name of Prosper Boulanger [Montreal Mercier]. As the meeting ended early, we decided to accept the invitation. While we were there, Prosper Boulanger said that there was a showroom across the street which had much better quality furniture. So we went there, maybe half a dozen of us, including Maurice Lamontagne and Mrs. Lamontagne. And Mrs. Lamontagne got into conversation with the owner and said, "Oh, this is such beautiful furniture, and, gosh, we just had a fire in our house." They had had a fire which had destroyed their living room and dining room, and, for some reason, their insurance had lapsed.

Then, a few months later, Maurice Lamontagne's daughter, who was very beautiful and very young, decided to get married, and Mrs. Lamontagne said, "We have not bought furniture yet for our living room and dining room ... and the reception is going to be here." And Maurice said, "Well, maybe if we phone this man we visited two or three months ago—I don't remember his name but we can find it—maybe we can buy the furniture wholesale."

Evidently they bought the furniture. Then, when it came time to pay, Maurice's brother, who was a priest, said he would like back the money that he had loaned him as a student; it amounted to 3,000 dollars and he needed it for his health. And so Maurice paid him the 3,000 dollars he had set aside for the furniture. And he said to the furniture people, "I cannot pay you now, I'll pay you later on." And then the people went bankrupt. And that's the story.

I remember one day during all the scandal two newsmen from the Ottawa radio station who were chasing everything came into my office at nine o'clock and they said to me, "Mr. Sauvé, we have the proof that you bought furniture from this gentleman."

"Oh, well, if you have the proof and you publish that, I'm going to have you arrested. I'm telling you, you're going to be arrested for false declaration. Because I never bought furniture there. The furniture we have in our house in Montreal is Scandinavian, and old French Canadian, and they don't sell that kind of furniture there."

"It's in your house in Ottawa," they said. I was sharing at that time a flat with four other Members. We were renting it from an old lady in Cobourg Street. I said, "If you think that I bought it for my own flat, I'll give you the keys; you'll go and see it. Because it's old Victorian furniture and it has nothing to do with that." And it stopped. But was I ever furious!

I guess if Maurice had done the same thing, it would have stopped too. But I felt very sorry for him. And in the case of Tremblay, it was furniture for which he had paid which had not been delivered! How can this be a scandal?

MAURICE LAMONTAGNE

The situation at that time was really terrible. You remember all the rumours which were circulating in the corridors involving all kinds of people. But only our names came up. And I really resent especially what was done to René Tremblay. Nobody in the press can prove what they wrote about him. And he did exactly *nothing* even indiscreet. He was crucified. I was crucified too, but he was crucified for having done exactly nothing. And that's a sin that some members of the press have to bear still, I think. Tremblay began to be sick after that. He died in January '67.

As far as I was concerned, mine was a completely private thing. There was no public side effect to this at all. And yet I was crucified in the press. Not in Parliament really, but in the press. And there was no defence. And no support. Partly, it was Mr.

Pearson's fault, but I think that we have to feel a certain collective guilt complex on this.

I have met a number of reporters since, and I remember one telling me, "Well, we had to report everything on this, and we had to have blood up to here because otherwise we would be fired by the owner of the paper." And so it was a competition for blood. I really resent the role that the press has played on that occasion.

On December 7, 1964, the day before the news of the furniture deals, Prime Minister Pearson got another shock when he was told by Premier Lesage that another of his Quebec Cabinet Ministers was in trouble: there were charges of corruption against Yvon Dupuis, the recently appointed Minister Without Portfolio. Dupuis was accused of accepting a bribe of 10,000 dollars for helping to arrange a race-track charter in St. Luc, which was a part of his federal constitutency of St. Jean-Iberville-Napierville. After some hesitation Pearson ordered the RCMP to investigate, and on January 17, 1965, called Dupuis to his office and asked for his resignation. However, Dupuis refused to resign, thereby causing a constitutional dilemma which took a few days to resolve. In the end he was ousted and charged on three counts of influence peddling; he was found guilty and sentenced to a fine of 5,000 dollars or a year in jail. But when the appeal was heard some years later, he was acquitted.

As Minister Without Portfolio, Yvon Dupuis had substituted for Lester Pearson at various functions. It was when he was returning from representing Canada at the celebrations marking the independence of Northern Rhodesia as the new nation of Zambia that he heard rumours about his being implicated in the scandals.

YVON DUPUIS

When I came back, the newspapermen around the House thought that I was in the furniture deal too with Lamontagne and Tremblay. And finally it turned out to be the alleged scandal of the race-track where I was supposed to have accepted a gift of 10,000 dollars to get a race-track charter. I had to fight for three years, and I was cleared from that accusation. And you should read the judgement of the Appeal Court, which was very strongly in my favour. It was all a frame-up against me, as it was frame-ups against Favreau, against Lamontagne, against Tremblay, against Rouleau ...

It was a very, very difficult period. And in that period Pearson showed his weakness. He was definitely a very, very weak leader. Instead of saying, "You have to produce the evidence that our friends are guilty and after that we'll see what we'll do," he was asking everyone to resign. That was a very, very, very great weakness because if he hadn't asked me to resign, I would have been cleared, I'm sure. When you ask a Minister to resign, there's all the publicity and the conclusion that "if he hadn't been guilty, the Prime Minister would never have asked him to resign."

When Mr. Pearson asked me to resign he said, "I know, Yvon, that you're not guilty. I know you, you're sincere, you're honest, but you have to make your own fight." I don't think it was fair. Because the moment that you are asked to resign, you're finished. Your image in the public is tarnished. So that was Mr. Pearson's weakness. When he asked me to resign he was crying. I said, "Mr. Pearson, I am not crying myself. I'm accused of something I didn't do. I'm an honest man, you know that." He said, "I know you're honest, but you have to fight your own ... what can I do? I have enough of all those scandals."

JUDY LaMARSH

I don't know the right of Dupuis' mix-up, but I do know that he refused to resign, which left us in a terrible constitutional dilemma because to resign, a letter must go to the Governor-General. That's the only way you do it. There appears to be no way in which a Prime Minister can go to the Governor-General and say, "Fire him!" You must write your letter of resignation, which is then accepted. And they couldn't find Dupuis. I think it was Maurice Lamontagne and somebody else went out looking for him. It was two or three days before they found him, holed up someplace, and they worked on him for several days until they got a letter out of him. In the meantime the government was paralysed.

J. W. PICKERSGILL

I would not agree with that view. I know that it has been frequently expressed. But it is my opinion, and it's not my opinion alone, that the composition of a Ministry is determined by the Prime Minister, and that if he chooses to advise the Crown that he doesn't want one Minister any longer, that the Crown or the Governor-General would have no option but to dismiss that Minister—or to dismiss the Prime Minister, if the Prime Minister insisted. In other words, if we have responsible government, we have it. And the fact that this has, in Canada, never been done does not mean that it can't be done. All it means is that we tend to try to preserve certain decencies. And when Ministers leave, however much pressure may be put on them, it's nicer and politer to resign.

MAURICE LAMONTAGNE

I had organised a conference on cultural affairs and the arts at Ste Adèle in the Laurentians, north of Montreal. I spent the whole week there. It was the end of January 1965. I didn't know anything about the Dupuis affair except that I had received a call from Guy Favreau at my hotel telling me that they had problems and all that in Ottawa. I was having lunch with a group of people when my executive assistant came and told me, "Dupuis is in your room."

So I went up, and I had to convince him that the only dignified way as far as he was concerned was to write a letter of resignation. The only other way was for Mike to go to the Governor-General and ask for the complete resignation of the Cabinet and form another Cabinet without Dupuis. Duplessis had done this once, in 1937—he wanted to fire his Minister of Public Works.

Dupuis came to see me because of our relationship: I was a kind of link between certain of these people [the Old Guard Liberals] and the new wing, the New Guard. I had insisted that Dupuis become a Minister at the same time as Sauvé.

When I saw him, Dupuis was mad and he was saying, "I'm not guilty. This is not fair," and so on. I told him, "There's only one solution. When the Prime Minister of this country in this system of government asks for your resignation, you have to give it to him." So he wrote this letter in my room, and I phoned Mike, and

I said, "Well, the whole problem is solved." After a long period of difficulties for Dupuis, he was pronounced not guilty. It was another so-called scandal.

YVON DUPUIS

I was not hiding. I was in Montreal. The police knew where I was; everybody knew where I was.

Maurice Lamontagne rang me from Ste Adèle and he said that he wanted to see me. So I went there to meet him, and he said, "Yvon, I know you're honest. I know everything." And he talked to me: "Mr. Pearson asked me to try to convince you that it's better if you resign." I said, "Okay, I'll give you my resignation." That's it. But I always regretted it after. I should never have resigned. As I was telling the Prime Minister, the fact that I was resigning was an admission that I was feeling guilty.

I regret that Mr. Pearson, who was a sincere man , an honest man, a great Canadian, had shown that lack of leadership, and I blame him for having put me in a very desperate situation without reason. That is something that I will reproach him [with] all my life, because he hurt me very very deeply. I could have died from that; it was terrible. I suffered deeply. If I had been guilty, I would have said okay, I'm guilty, that's all; let's finish with it. But I was not guilty. I had to fight without money. I had nothing to protect me, and I had all the newspapers against me.

TOM KENT

Whatever else one may say I don't think Mr. Pearson's handling of Mr. Dupuis could possibly be criticised. I emphasise again, not because I am passing judgement on whether there was in fact anything wrong, but undoubtedly there was indiscretion of the kind which could raise the suspicion of something wrong in a way that a Minister should not be exposed to.

Although he was denied his party's nomination, Yvon Dupuis nevertheless ran in the 1965 election. He did so because, as he said, he wanted to show everyone that he did not accept the treatment that he had received in court and that he was an honest man. The split in the Liberal vote allowed the Progressive Conservative candidate, Paul Beaulieu, to win easily. It was not till a couple of years later that Dupuis was exonerated after a new trial had been ordered by the appeal court. However, Parliament paid no attention to his acquittal.

YVON DUPUIS

So everything that I said in the House of Commons I proved in court. And I was expecting at least the Prime Minister to stand up and say, "Mr. Dupuis, who was a Minister was accused and now he is cleared by the court, and I want the House to pay attention to the fact that he was acquitted," or something like that. He never did.

J. A. Mongrain, the mayor of Three Rivers who became the Member for Three Rivers, went to him and said, "Mr. Prime Minister, it is my idea to talk about the fact that our colleague who was accused for nothing and had to resign [has been acquitted] and that the House should pay him tribute." He said, "No, don't touch that." Mongrain told me that.

As a matter of fact, if you look in Hansard you will see that one day Mongrain started to say that I was acquitted, and the Speaker stopped him. Mr. Pearson didn't do anything. It would have been the task of Mr. Pearson to say, "Let the Member speak. We accused a man in this House and now ... " Mongrain just wanted to put in Hansard the article of the newspaper or the copy of the judgement, something like that. It was Mr. Speaker Lamoureux who was presiding and he didn't permit Mongrain to go any further. I was accused unfairly, I had to resign unfairly, I won my case, and in the House of Commons nothing was done to repair it. So that's the type of democracy I have to face in Canada. I am still a Canadian.

Despite the fact that his government was being rocked by the scandals and other troubles, Mike Pearson was able to keep his sense of humour. Harry Hays remembered him answering a reporter's question on one of the most difficult days by saying, "We'll cross that bridge when we fall off it." The crisis winter of 1964-65 was a trying time for Prime Minister Pearson, and his behaviour with regard to Guy Favreau and others whilst it could be excused by Tommy Douglas as being in the British tradition of protecting the collectivity of the government and not the individual Minister, nevertheless distressed some of his followers and admirers. Tom Kent, who was probably the closest to him of his associates, had an explanation for Pearson's character, and Douglas Fisher pointed out that the scandals brought out the worst side of English-French relations in Canada.

TOM KENT

Mr. Pearson was a diplomat. His skill was in settling differences and sometimes that perhaps meant evading the expression of the differences. There was an element of escapism, and no question, Mr. Pearson could be an escapist. He found it very difficult to say anything unpleasant to anybody face to face, and most people who talked to Mr. Pearson tended to leave him thinking that he'd agreed with them. That was true even if the views of A and B in succession were rather diverse, and that sometimes left lots of problems to sort out afterward.

There was a great diplomatic skill involved, and often it was very important, very productive. There were, however, times when it could be very destructive. Obviously, it would have been better to have dealt with the situation [the Rivard affair] right away, and if it had been dealt with in a simple way, it could have been defused very easily. In fact, I think that's true of the whole so-called scandals. They became of significance, not because there was really anything of any real importance in the incidents, but because the handling of them was contorted and indecisive.

DOUGLAS FISHER

It was this race thing. And let's recognise that this is something that's alive today: it was alive in the wars; it was alive in the 1890s; it goes back to Riel's execution; it goes back to the reason Macdonald and Cartier got together—the two peoples. There isn't that great trust in each other.

The English people in Canada are always in a sense almost overwilling to believe that the French Canadians are corrupt, inept, full of chicanery, doing deals, in a sense prostituting Ottawa and what you might call the tax revenue's resources of the nation as a whole in their own favour. Pearson, of course, was making moves in his talk of co-operative federalism that jarred quite a few people in English-speaking Canada. And some of Pearson's Ministers didn't help anything at all.

The so-called scandals during the winter of 1964-65 were a bad time for everybody. As Lester Pearson said, they brought parliamentary democracy into disrepute, and, as most of those involved in the scandals happened to be French Canadians, they increased racial tensions across the country. There was no need for a royal commission to look into Rivard affair and pass judgement on the conduct of the Justice Minister. That was admitted to be a grave mistake by Mitchell Sharp; it was but one example of the way the whole situation was mishandled which gave the period much more significance than it warranted. Paul Martin described the scandals as a regrettable and tragic situation which brought about the deaths of Guy Favreau and René Tremblay. However, the worst result of all, in Douglas Fisher's mind, was the loss of Maurice Lamontagne; he had to resign after the 1965 election. Fisher said he was one of the finest men that Canada had had in twenty years, full of ideas, and he was removed and went for nothing.

It was a wonder, considering the circumstances, that Prime Minister Pearson was able to survive. The fact that he did was an achievement in itself.

9 1965 and the Quebec Triumvirate

AT THE END of 1964 Walter Gordon and Keith Davey, who had directed the Liberal forces in the 1963 election, began planning for a 1965 election, and Lester Pearson was certainly thinking of one because he spoke to Gordon about being in charge of his campaign again. On December 30, 1964, the Finance Minister wrote a long memorandum to the Prime Minister in which he put down the pros and cons of an election. Among the pros, which far outnumbered the cons, was Diefenbaker—he might not be around indefinitely and if they waited for his retirement, they might lose popular support. There was also a public-opinion survey that showed they could win a majority.

However, Pearson was hesitant. He didn't relish the thought of taking to the hustings again; Gordon realised this and put down as one of his cons that another national campaign was "the last thing in the world that you personally would wish to contemplate." Pearson was receiving contrary advice, particularly from Tom Kent, who was as adept at writing strong memos as Walter Gordon.

WALTER GORDON

There were a number of reasons [for an election]. First of all, 1964 had been an unhappy year for the Liberal government. There was the disastrous federal-provincial conference in Quebec in April of that year and the changes in policy that followed; there

241

was the long debate over the flag issue; there was the prolonged discussion of the pension plan and the changes in it; and then there were the difficulties that Guy Favreau got into and other members of the government.

Everyone was tired and fed up and discouraged, and a lot of people wondered why the hell they were living in Ottawa anyway. It didn't seem to be a very pleasant way to put in time. So there was a strong feeling that, if we had an election and won a majority, things would begin to fall back into place. And also, at that time we thought we could win a majority, and I think we probably could have. Those were the main reasons.

TOM KENT

By the latter part of '64 the government, in my view, was consumed by a death wish, and Walter [Gordon] among the Ministers and, of course, Keith Davey organisationally, were convinced that it couldn't go on as a minority government, that there had to be an early election. And there were great pressures of that kind. In fact, there was a meeting of the national committee around the Christmas–New Year period, '64–'65, which really was handled in terms of there's-got-to-be-an-early-election, by Walter, as chairman, and Keith, as organiser. I disagreed very strongly with that view. It seemed to me that it was just an escape from the problems of the government, not a solution to them.

In January, 1965, I wrote a very strongly argued memorandum to Mr. Pearson expressing the reasons why I thought that [having an early election] was a wrong and mistaken view. I also said that unless he made it very clear that he was not going to take the initiative in seeking an election, stated it absolutely firmly and laid it down specifically to Walter and Keith, then there'd be lots of talk about an election—Keith would be talking to everybody about an election, telling every journalist in Ottawa that there was going to be an election soon—and an atmosphere would be created in which there'd have to be an election, because if there wasn't, it would seem like cowardice, retreat, on the part of the government.

At the same time, I argued that the alternative was that we get very clear on our policy initiatives and put forward a fairly simple but coherent further program which didn't get us into a lot more contentious legislation but did have some firm administrative action which could be pushed through, which would do some good and be well received.

I remember so clearly Mr. Pearson wrote on that memorandum, "I agree. I will make this absolutely clear," and so on. And, of course, he didn't. Walter wanted an election and Mike never said in so many words to Walter or to Keith Davey, "Goddammit, don't talk about an election." I am sure he never said it to them, which was all that was required.

KEITH DAVEY

The polls showed that our fortunes were at their highest in the spring, and they began to go down. Quayle* advised us in the summer of '65 that "if you go to the country now you *might* get a majority. You'll certainly win the election; but if you leave it any longer you won't get the majority, and if Diefenbaker ever quits and they get a good new leader, you'll really be going." So we took a risk and went to the country in the fall of '65.

The criticism has been levelled at Walter and at me that we were sort of Toronto-centric urban politicians, and I guess we were. And in Toronto Diefenbaker was anathema, he really was, and he was extremely unpopular. He did disastrously there again in '65. I've never felt that I fully understood every part of the country; I think I do know the part of the country in which I live.

There was a hint that even then Lester Pearson had retirement in mind as he spoke to Premier Lesage of Quebec about joining his government with the idea of succeeding him. Obviously Pearson believed in the Liberal tenet of alternating the party leadership between French-speaking Catholics and English-speaking Protestants. He could not know that the Quebec triumvirate of Jean Marchand, Gérard Pelletier, and Pierre Trudeau were to run as Liberal candidates in the 1965 election, and that one of them would be his French Canadian successor. Both Prime Minister Pearson and Premier Lesage spent the 1965 New Year holidays in Florida.

---

*Oliver Quayle was the U.S. pollster who had taken over Lou Harris' polling organisation.

JEAN LESAGE

Mr. Pearson rang me, and I went to see him. He asked me if I would be interested in going back to the federal Cabinet, and he led me to understand that possibly my future would lie in his succession.

First of all, I wanted to stay in provincial politics. I felt that I had been given a mandate that I had to fulfill. Two: I did not think that there was much future for a premier of a province to go to Ottawa as a leader of a party. History was there to tell the contrary. It is different the other way around; a Cabinet Minister going to be the premier of a province. This has happened a number of times in a number of provinces, but not the other way around. So this has not been published, but it was in my mind because once you have been a provincial premier, it is reasonable for some people in the other provinces to think that you are committed and that you are biased.

At about this time Pearson was considering changes in his Cabinet, and he asked Gordon whether he would take another portfolio, and the reply was a categorical no; Gordon said that he wanted another two years at least as Finance Minister. In his memo calling for an early election, Gordon suggested that a prerequisite was a major Cabinet reorganisation.

PAUL HELLYER

I would say he [Walter Gordon] wanted an election to consolidate his power in the party, and perhaps, in the process, to enhance his own position, and at the same time to move to the side some of the others. I hope I'm not being unfair to him; I don't think I am. I think he felt that a majority government, which came from an election of which he was the principal architect, would be one in which he would have a stronger, more pre-eminent role.

WALTER GORDON

Not only Mike but everybody was reluctant to begin with because we hadn't got the results of the Dorion Commission [enquiry] into the Favreau affair. We certainly didn't want to have that come out in the middle of an election campaign, so it got put off. Also, there was certain legislation we thought would be desirable to pass before an election, like the Canada Development Corporation.* There were some other things—the Canada Pension Plan—I don't think it had gone through.

The House of Commons approved the Canada Pension Plan on March 29, 1965; the Dorion Report was submitted to the government on June 28, 1965. In the meantime Tom Kent was able to put forward the program that he had proposed in the memo to the Prime Minister: it was a combination of social welfare measures such as the Canada Assistance Plan, the Manpower Mobility Program, and the Company of Young Canadians. The program got the grandiloquent label of "The War on Poverty," and a co-ordinating secretariat under Tom Kent was set up in the Privy Council Office. Since Lester Pearson had never called off his election hawks, Walter Gordon and Keith Davey, the debate raged noisily among the Liberals. There were quite a few opposed, including James Walker, the government Whip; John Nichol, the new president of the party; and A. H. (Hammy) McDonald, a former Saskatchewan Liberal leader and Western advisor.

JAMES WALKER

I was opposed to that election. Keith [Davey] and I argued like mad, and I said, "Keith, you're crazy. As far as I'm concerned, Keith, as the Whip of this party I would rather be in a minority position where I can require the assistance of one of the four Opposition groups. I would rather operate in that minority position than have you give me three Members of Parliament, extra ones, after an election. That would give us a majority of one. Then the whole Opposition can confront us. You show me, constituency by constituency, where we're going to pick up a seat."

But at this time they were committed; mentally they were committed and they were going to go ahead. No, I was very much opposed to that election. I might not have been if I had not had the responsibilities of trying to keep that government in power.

*CDC was not established during Pearson's government.

The Opposition were great. Eric Winkler, the chief Opposition Whip, and I never double-crossed one another. And there were times when we consulted and I'd say, "Eric, do your crowd want an election?" And he'd say, "Hell, no." And I said, "Okay, I've got eighty-nine guys. That's all I can get for this vote today. Go down and see how the Tories and the NDP are going to vote." Stanley Knowles would send me to talk to the Social Credit group. They were all dickering and playing around, and by the time it's over my eighty-nine guys were there, and eighty-seven on the other side were there.

Believe me, most of the Members didn't want [an election]. They couldn't afford it. I had been through a '62 election and a '63 election, and here's another one in '65. And funds are getting harder to raise and you're digging into your pocket. Well, you're not digging into your own pocket; you're going to the bank and borrowing, and then taking two or three years to pay it back.

JOHN NICHOL

I was very cool on the '65 election. I felt that Mr. Pearson was being pushed into something which he was very uncertain about. But frankly, people were talking about the election; and I think I'm not breaking any confidences by saying that Keith Davey, who was then the national organiser of the party, and Walter Gordon really wanted that '65 election. And they were giving him heavy advice.

There was quite a bit of debate in the press about it. Now the debate wasn't arising from statements Mr. Pearson was making. I mean, Mr. Pearson wasn't saying, "I don't know whether I'm going to have an election or not. I don't know what to do." He was keeping his trap shut. But other people in the party were speculating out loud about it, and since they were related to him in a political sense, it was taken to be that he was speculating about it. He was speculating very quietly about it. And I think he made a mistake; I think he shouldn't have called it.

A. H. McDONALD

Walter Gordon invited me to come to—I don't recall whether it was Toronto or Ottawa—to discuss this election with him and one or two others, and that was when I was asked if I would head up the organisation in Saskatchewan for the election. I was opposed to the election then, and I told [Gordon] that I couldn't see that we would do any better in Saskatchewan; it just wasn't there. But he was convinced that the situation in Canada was favourable to elect a majority government.

Of course, I wasn't as familiar with Canada as he was, but I was certainly familiar with the situation in Saskatchewan because we had fought the provincial election the year before; and although we won it, we didn't win it with the majority that we thought we were going to have. We had been one year in power in Saskatchewan, and we were not making the political progress provincially that we had hoped we would make. It was a cinch that if we weren't making it provincially, it wasn't there federally. I was aware of that, and this is what I conveyed to Walter Gordon. But Saskatchewan is a very small puddle in a federal election.

However, those who were determined on an election, like James Coutts, the Prime Minister's Appointments Secretary, had greater access to Mr. Pearson.

JAMES COUTTS

Pearson asked me in his office one day whether I thought we should have an election, and I said I thought we should. I thought that the public would see that the programs that had been launched, and the ideas that had been launched, could be better implemented with a majority on the government's side. There was no doubt about it in my mind that it was the right thing to do to have the election. He did ask two or three people on the staff what they thought.

On July 19, 1965, the long-delayed federal-provincial first ministers' conference met in Ottawa's summer heat; on the second day Pearson announced a medical health insurance program, or Medicare as it became known, for the country. According to all reports, he and Walter Gordon emerged from the meeting bubbling with enthusiasm because only one provincial premier was opposed to the scheme. Premier Manning of Alberta charged that the Liberals were auctioning Canadians at fourteen dollars a head [the federal share of Medicare costs]. It was regarded as an election plank by the press, and the combination of Medicare with the Canada Pension Plan was considered an unbeatable welfare package.

In mid-August 1965 Mike Pearson went on a nine-day tour of Western Canada, which Walter Gordon and Keith Davey trumpeted as a pre-election tour. The Prime Minister had a brief holiday at a farm on Vancouver Island where he met his friends Bruce Hutchison, the editor of the Vancouver Sun, *and Stuart Keate, its publisher. There was some disagreement between these two distinguished observers as to Pearson's appearance.*

WALTER GORDON

We kept on talking about the election. Then in the summer of '65 Pearson went on a trip on his own to Western Canada, and it was looked upon as the forerunner of an election campaign. That's what it sounded like. Everybody thought from his statements that he was planning an election. By the time he came back, he was pretty tired—and he hated election campaigns anyway—so there was a good deal of backing and filling. And he'd put it off too late.

BRUCE HUTCHISON

Pearson was staying on a farm outside Victoria having a holiday, and I went out to see him one day—that must have been in the summer of '65. He did say he was considering an election, but he hadn't made up his mind and he didn't know.

I never saw him more relaxed. He was on a holiday in a nice country place. No, he didn't seem harassed or worried at all. He said this thing had been suggested, and he hadn't made up his mind and that was all.

STUART KEATE

I remember going out to the Woodwards' farm that day and asking for the Prime Minister. They said, "Well, he's out in the garden." From fifty yards or so away—he didn't see me approaching but I was watching him, and he was walking up and down, pacing up and down with his hands in his pockets and with a worried look on his face. I know this [election] was very, very much on his mind; and he asked three of us who were there, Bruce Hutchison and Arthur Irwin and myself, "What do you think about all this?" My recollection is that we said, "No, this is not really the time to have an election."

Even if Lester Pearson did not want an election —and there is evidence that he did not —he had to agree to one. There was no other option. He had not ordered Walter Gordon and Keith Davey to stop their election preparations, and the climate had been created where it would look like cowardice or a retreat not to go to the country. In fact, Kent, although opposed to an election, knew by the summer that there had to be one and joined those who were urging it. According to John Nichol, Pearson got himself into the position of looking like a very vacillating individual because the public debate was so intense on whether he was or was not going to have an election.

After the Prime Minister's return to Ottawa, the Finance Minister kept seeing him in his office or at his residence and encouraging him on the election prospects. Finally, before consulting the Cabinet, Mike Pearson seemed to agree to the inevitable and said that he would resign if they didn't get a majority. Walter Gordon said that he would resign too. When Pearson polled the Cabinet, all Ministers present said that they were in favour of an immediate election except for four: Paul Hellyer, Paul Martin, Maurice Sauvé and Watson McNaught from Prince Edward Island, who was most strongly opposed and said so.

MITCHELL SHARP

I was in favour of an early election, not on the grounds that I was convinced we would win as the opposite —I was fairly certain that if we didn't have an election we would lose more seats. Therefore I felt that the time to have an election was now, in order to check what I thought might be a continuing loss of support.

Perhaps I could reveal one Cabinet meeting, which had a certain element of humour in it. Mr. Pearson called a special meeting of Cabinet to discuss the question of an election. We met in the East Block, and the Cabinet room was just filled. We were all arranged in order of seniority, as is the rule. Mr. Pearson explained that he had called us together for our individual opinions on whether or not there should be an election. He said to Paul Martin, who sat on his right, "All right, Paul, now what's your view?" Paul Martin said, "I prefer you start at the other end." So each Minister in turn gave their views, and then it came back to Paul, and he said, "Mr. Prime Minister, I don't have a view."

I asked Paul afterwards, I said, "Paul, that was one of the funniest things I've ever seen." He said, "Well, you may have thought it was funny, but it was very serious." He said, "I knew that Mr. Pearson didn't want an election and that Walter Gordon was urging him, and I didn't think that he should have asked us individually to express our views. He should have decided whether he wanted an election or not, without consulting us, and therefore I didn't give him my view, and I didn't think any of you should have."

J. W. PICKERSGILL

I thought an election was desirable, but I didn't think it was absolutely necessary. But what did impress me was a quite different argument, which I put to the Cabinet: we were going to have a redistribution, and the act had not been proclaimed, but it had to be proclaimed quite soon. It was pretty indecent that, even as it was, it was delayed so long. Then once we proclaimed it, I got the best estimate I could from the Chief Electoral Officer about how long it would take before the redistribution could be completed, and there was a period of almost a year and a half, if you abbreviated everything—which I was sure would not happen, when the government would just be tied into that Parliament.

Now, I can't answer for the accuracy of all the details, but I do know that we were going to be in a position, which I regarded as very undesirable, when the government was not free to have an election if it needed to. And I was not so much concerned about whether we would want to have an election to improve our situation. I was concerned about the possibility, with a minority in the House, that we might reach a situation where no government would be possible in the country, and for technical reasons we could have no election.

I exposed this to the Cabinet at some length, and I think some of the Ministers understood, though it was very technical. And I suggested to the Prime Minister that, before we made a decision, he should verify these facts. He did so. While he thought maybe a few days could be shaved off, the brute fact was that there was going to be a long period, if we didn't have an election under the existing electoral map, when we couldn't have one at all.

PAUL HELLYER

There were four of us who thought that going to the people on the issue of getting a majority, when there was no compelling reason for it, looked silly. The government had just finished putting through all sorts of controversial legislation. It had survived in the House, and all of a sudden it was going out to tell the people that it can't govern. No one was going to believe it, and no one did.

PAUL MARTIN

I don't think there were very many who opposed [an election] in the final analysis. I was opposed to it right from the beginning. I had seen a poll that had been taken throughout the country, and it didn't seem to me that it was very logical, in the face of that, to have a test. However, my view didn't prevail. The election itself resulted in very little change—no change, practically, at all. Mr. Gordon had a right to make the suggestion and others had a right to support it. But the polls clearly indicated that there would not be much of a change.

Prime Minister Pearson told the Cabinet that he would make his decision on Tuesday, September 7, 1965, the Tuesday after the Labor Day weekend, and it was taken for granted that he would be announcing an election. Walter Gordon realised that Mike Pearson didn't really want to do this and that it was he, Gordon, who was more responsible than anyone else for making him come to this decision. In the notes that he made on the Cabinet meeting, Gordon wrote, "If we don't get a majority, I will have to offer my resignation from the government —whether Mike does so or not."

The election was called for November 8, 1965. Both Tommy Douglas and Gordon Churchill were shocked.

T. C. DOUGLAS

It was a complete surprise when he announced that he'd decided to dissolve Parliament and go to the country and ask for a clear majority. He had got along fairly well. He'd had these scandals and one thing and another, but there'd been no attempt to upset the government. I think it was the greatest political blunder of his career. And ironically enough, it went back to the same person, Walter Gordon. Walter Gordon, along with Keith Davey, had persuaded him that the polls were good—they were at 48 percent and this was the time to dissolve Parliament and go to the country.

Just imagine yourself as Prime Minister with all the experience that Mike Pearson had had, both in the House and prior to that in the public service, and with all the people he had around him like Paul Martin who had been taking part in elections for twenty or thirty years. And to take the advice of an individual who had never campaigned in his life until 1962 and who had never really had to contest a tough election. I mean getting elected in that section of Toronto was a lead-pipe cinch. If the financial community approved of you, you were away. If they didn't, you were a dead duck. And with the best will in the world, Walter Gordon really knew nothing at all about the nuts and bolts of political organisation. I don't suppose he ever canvassed from door to door in one of the poorer areas of Toronto or any other city. I don't suppose he'd ever gone out and canvassed from door to door in a farming community to find out what people think. And here is the man on whose recommendation you dissolve Parliament and call an election. It was sheer political lunacy.

GORDON CHURCHILL

That election took me by surprise. I didn't think that he would call it in 1965, and although Mr. Diefenbaker told me earlier in the year that there likely would be one, I couldn't see any reason for it because Mr. Pearson, although he had been in a minority position, had nothing to worry about with regard to the Créditistes. He had nothing to worry about with regard to the NDP, who were not going to support us under any circumstances. He was under a certain amount of pressure, as you are in a minority situation, but it wasn't that serious. I didn't know how the hierarchy of the Grit Party arrived at the decision.

I think they thought that we were very badly split in our party because of the troubles that had arisen—the dispute over the flag debate in 1964, the attempt of the executive of the Conservative Party to get Mr. Diefenbaker's resignation in March of 1965. I guess they thought that we were in such disarray that we couldn't recover, but we were able to miraculously unite our party in a very short time in '65.

The reason Maurice Sauvé gave for not supporting an immediate election was that the special people in Quebec—by whom he meant Jean Marchand, Gérard Pelletier, and Pierre Trudeau—would not be ready to run at that time. While he did not say so, it was obvious to the assembled Ministers at the Cabinet meeting that there had to be an infusion of new blood because of the effects the scandals had on the French-speaking Ministers.

Actually, the Liberals had been trying to get Marchand to join them since the early '60s and he had intended to be a candidate in the 1963 election but had refused to run when Pearson reversed the party's policy against accepting nuclear warheads. Guy Favreau, René Tremblay, and Maurice Lamontagne had kept in touch with Marchand while he was a commissioner with the Royal Commission on Bilingualism and Biculturalism, and in July 1965 Lamontagne talked to him about running in the coming election, which was fully expected although not yet called. During their discussion there was no mention of the other two; Lamontagne was opposed to the candidacies of Pelletier and Trudeau, largely out of loyalty to Prime Minister Pearson and the members of the Liberal caucus. Gérard Pelletier had been contemptuous of the party, calling it a garbage can in an editorial in the Montreal French-language paper, La Presse; *while Pierre Trudeau had asserted that when power beckoned Mr. Pearson, honour and principles were out, and he had written in* Cité libre *that "the leader of the herd having shown the way, the rest followed with the elegance of animals heading for the trough."*

However, Maurice Sauvé had no such concerns about Liberal sensibilities or the Prime Minister's amour propre; he saw Jean Marchand and suggested that he would carry more weight if he insisted on having Pelletier and Trudeau accompany him to Ottawa. At the same time there was still the problem of the nuclear warheads and Marchand wanted an assurance from Prime Minister Pearson that they would be removed.

MAURICE LAMONTAGNE

I remember, in July, I was taking a few days of holidays in Quebec City, and I met Jean Marchand one afternoon. He had really decided to run whenever we would have an election. He could not commit himself, however, at that time publicly because he was still with the CNTU, the labour federation in Quebec, and the moment he announced his decision to enter politics he would have had to resign. Since there was no date for the election he could not make any statement. I am quite sure that his decision had been made as a result of that long conversation we had in Quebec City. During that conversation I remember very well there was no question raised about Mr. Trudeau or Mr. Pelletier.

MAURICE SAUVÉ

The federal Liberals had gone through all these scandals, and men like Favreau and Lamontagne were very anxious to get into the party a man like Marchand who had a tremendous reputation — a labour leader, a member of the royal commission, an honest man. If Marchand would run for the Liberal Party, he would certainly not ally himself with corrupt people; he would not join Favreau, he would not join Lamontagne, he would not join Tremblay if those people were corrupt, because he was a pure man. And certainly his becoming a Liberal meant that they were okay. So they were seeking Marchand's participation to clear themselves.

I was conscious of that, and I saw Marchand, I remember, in his home in Cap-Rouge and spent an evening with him. I said, "Marchand, I think you should come in politics, but you should come in the same time as Trudeau and Pelletier. If you come, the three together, you will not be eaten by the system. If you come alone, you might be destroyed."

Finally, one day in July or August I got them, Pelletier, Marchand, and Trudeau, to come to my home in Outremont. And that evening the three of them said, "Fine, we will meet with Favreau and discuss our entry into the Liberal Party. Although we've been very critical of the Liberals, very critical of Mr. Pearson, we feel that there's an overwhelming reason for us to join the Liberal Party because of the threat to national unity. And with the scandals that have happened and so on, we want to join and work for the good of the party and the French Canadians in Canada."

JEAN MARCHAND

When the 1965 election was about to be announced, Keith Davey tried to convince me that I should run that time, and I should run alone. He said, "Favreau is there now. You wouldn't be alone. Lamontagne is there. René Tremblay is there. You will have this group that you were looking for." But I was not satisfied, not because I thought that those men were not good men—I think that they were. But I had great confidence in Mr. Trudeau's mind and in Pelletier's judgement too. Anyhow, I wanted them to run. This was the first fight, and Davey tried to just isolate me from the two others. But it remained a condition.

We went to see Mr. Pearson because the nuclear weapons were still there. He said, "As soon as we can do it, they will be gradually removed—unless there is an international war and we're involved, and you would probably be the first to agree [that they should stay]." He offered to put his promise in writing. But I never insisted on this because I didn't think that I should. I was not in the party. And I said, "We're ready to run. The least that we can do is believe the word of the Prime Minister which is not interpreted by somebody else but by the Prime Minister himself."

MAURICE SAUVÉ

I went to see Mr. Favreau and said, "I know now that Trudeau, Marchand, and Pelletier are ready to join the party, and I'd like you to see them." Favreau wanted to get Marchand, but he was opposed at that time to Trudeau and Pelletier. He said, "Pelletier has written editorials, Mr. Trudeau has been on the platform with Thérèse Casgrain against Maurice Lamontagne in the Outremont riding; he's written all sorts of things in Cité libre. It's not possible."

So I went to see Mr. Pearson and I said, "Here are three good men who want to join the party and there is some hesitation from Favreau." "Well," he said, "I'll speak to Favreau."

Then Favreau called a meeting of all the Quebec Ministers, I remember, in his office. And we talked about this. And all my colleagues then were in favour of getting Marchand, but were all opposed to getting Trudeau and Pelletier, for the same reasons. I got worried, so I went to see Mr. Pearson again, and I said, "You're going to have to do something if you really want those three men in. You're going to have to impose this on Favreau because the Quebec Members, both the Cabinet Members and the caucus, are not very . . ." And in the following days this all leaked into the newspapers. Was I ever mad! I don't know who leaked that, but it all leaked in Ottawa. Anyway, Mr. Pearson saw Favreau and he said, "You have to see them."

The political machinations reached a climax at a meeting in the Windsor Hotel, Montreal, on the night of September 9, 1965. Guy Favreau had called the meeting, and he, Maurice Lamontagne, and "Bob" Giguère, who was the Liberals' Quebec campaign manager, were there, as well as Jean Marchand, Pierre Trudeau, and Gérard Pelletier. So was Maurice Sauvé.

MAURICE SAUVÉ

I had been told of the meeting. And then on the day of the meeting I received a phone call from Favreau's office saying that it had been postponed. I said fine, and I decided to check with Trudeau; I phoned Trudeau and I said, "Pierre, when is the meeting we had proposed?" "Well," he said, "it's tonight at eight o'clock." And I said, "Are you sure?" He said, "Yes, at the Windsor Hotel, and the three of us will be there. Pelletier will be late because he's speaking somewhere. He's going to meet us around eleven o'clock." I said, "It's strange. Favreau tells me that there's no meeting."

"Well," he said, "Maurice, there's certainly a meeting. I'm going to phone him." So Trudeau phoned Favreau and said, "What is it? I understand that there's no meeting tonight?" Favreau said, "No, there's a meeting." Well, Trudeau said, "How is it that Maurice Sauvé was supposed to be there, and I insist that he should be there? Why is it not?" Oh, Favreau gave a strange reply. Anyway, I arrived there.

MAURICE LAMONTAGNE

Attending that meeting were Guy Favreau and Bob Giguère, myself, and Maurice Sauvé, who had apparently conspired behind the scenes during these last few days and had—at least this is what Jean Marchand told me afterwards—tried to convince Marchand if he were to come into politics to insist that the two others came. I think that Sauvé invited himself to this meeting. Then, of course, there were Jean Marchand and Pierre Trudeau and Gérard Pelletier.

We met in the evening and the meeting lasted until I would say about three o'clock in the morning. I think I was the leading questioner and did most of the talking on our side. Jean Marchand represented no problem, but he made it clear at the beginning of the meeting that he would be very interested in getting the two others to run as well. So that was the first time that this was really discussed.

I started the discussion and said, "As far as I am concerned, I certainly have no objection. We are Liberals and we can forget a few things. But I think that you, Pierre, and you, Gérard, you'll have some problems, because you have written all these articles against Mr. Pearson. I have not discussed this with Mr. Pearson at all, but knowing the man I know that he's quite prepared to put this aside and forget about it—but as far as you're concerned, you certainly have problems, because you have accused the Liberals during the scandal affair."

I said, "Well, you will join the party now. You will join us. How will you reconcile this with the former positions you have taken? You remember the opposition you had to the acquisition of nuclear warheads. Well, you will enter this party under the same conditions that you turned down back in 1963." The discussion was quite long.

MAURICE SAUVÉ

For about an hour and a half Lamontagne and Favreau and Giguère gave all the arguments why Marchand should join the Liberal Party and all the arguments why Pelletier and Trudeau should not join—they had written against the party, the press would bring this out, it would put them into an impossible situation, the caucus was not favourable to them, and so on. I was saying, "They have to join for the following reasons," and I was giving all the positive reasons why they should join. I was fighting like mad. In the meantime, before the meeting, Jean Marchand had announced that he was giving a press conference the next day at four o'clock to talk about his future, and in fact he had said he would join the Liberal Party. And I had said to Jean when he arrived at the meeting, "Why do you say this when you don't know what will happen to Trudeau and Pelletier?"

MAURICE LAMONTAGNE

At the end I said, "I think things will be very tough for you, not only outside the party but within the party, because we will have to convince all those that were insulted." Pelletier in particular had written quite a number of articles about the poor quality of some of our Members on the Island of Montreal. "Well, this is a question of honour and a question of reconciling your conscience with something which you have strongly objected to in the past." I said, "That will be a difficult period for you, and I think that you should really reflect upon it very seriously. You should go in the other room for a while and discuss this among yourselves, the three of you."

They went into the other room, and Maurice Sauvé made a move to join them, and Marchand told him, "Stay here." And he stayed with us.

MAURICE SAUVÉ

Finally Pelletier arrived, and we summarised the discussion, and at around eleven I said to Pelletier and Marchand and Trudeau, "Let's go into the other room. I want to have a talk with you." So I went into the other room with them and I said to Pelletier, Marchand and Trudeau, "Why don't you embarrass them and say you're willing to join, and it's for them to tell you that you should not join," because they were trying to convince Pelletier and Trudeau that they should not ask to join. I said, "Reverse that. Tell them that you are ready to join and you'll see what will happen."

We came back into the room, and they said, "We want to join."

Then Marchand said, "We're going to announce this tomorrow at the press conference that has been called."

MAURICE LAMONTAGNE

They discussed together for about an hour or so, and then they came back and they said, "We're ready to come in." So I said, "Okay," and Favreau, of course, said okay too. Then we had to communicate with Mr. Pearson, and Mr. Pearson agreed. I don't think at that time he was particularly pleased, but the three people in different ways were acquisitions, really, for the Liberal Party—and this has been a tradition in the Liberal Party, to seek new blood. So in spite of the immediate past, I think Mr. Pearson came to the conclusion that it would be a good thing.

GÉRARD PELLETIER

I know that when the decision was taken I started meeting with the already elected Members from Quebec, and some of them were just appalled that heretics like ourselves could come into the party. Others said, "Well, my God, these are people who have proven themselves as communicators with Quebec," and so on. So we weren't imposed on the totality of the Liberal caucus. It was split. I think it's only a minority, really, that were opposed to us, because the prize being Marchand, they were ready to tolerate the two others.

Duplessis had been saying for years that we were all Communists and I'm afraid that a few of the Liberals believed it. So surely some of them felt pretty desperate that this would be done, but it was done with the backing of Pearson and it was done with the backing of Favreau as well. Maybe Favreau was of two minds, I don't know. I didn't know the man well enough to read him. Lamontagne wanted Marchand.

JEAN MARCHAND

I was never a member of the NDP. And I don't think that Trudeau has ever been a member of the NDP. Pelletier was never a member of the NDP. The only thing that Trudeau did was to support Thérèse Casgrain, who was running for the NDP in Outremont.

Let me explain: I was for the last years the president of the CNTU, and the Canadian Labour Congress was supporting the NDP. And the NDP was supporting the Canadian Labour Congress against the CNTU in Quebec. So it was very difficult. And the NDP and the old CCF had no roots at all in Quebec.

The reason why we came to Ottawa—because normally I should probably have gone to Quebec and not to Ottawa—is because we thought that the separatist movement was gaining ground in Quebec very rapidly. After what happened to Lamontagne, to Favreau [as a result of the scandals], we said, "Well, there is a vacuum there, and if we believe in this country and we want to do something for the country, we have to do it in Ottawa—and we have to do it in the party which has a chance to be in power."

It's useless to start building a party with your neighbour and say, "Well, maybe someday in twenty or twenty-five years we'll have a good party representing exactly our ideologies." We thought that the NDP could not achieve power even if we had joined the party because a large portion of Quebec would have been opposed to us. We found that the proper instrument was the Liberal Party because we thought it was the most liberal organisation in politics in Canada, and we decided to join it. But I don't think that any of us had been members of the Liberal Party either.

Although Jean Marchand would not say whether he and Gérard Pelletier and Pierre Trudeau planned the take-over of the Liberal Party before they joined it, the three of them met regularly and did discuss the moribund state of the party or its Quebec section and the need for cleaning it up and getting rid of the Old Guard. It was more than an intellectual political exercise since they were concerned with the failure of the French-speaking Ministers in Ottawa and the effect that this was having on public opinion in the province and the encouragement it was giving the separatists. There was a lack of confidence in these Ministers and Pelletier asserted that while Favreau and Lamontagne were brilliant technocrats, they were not very well known in French Canada. The so-called scandals had created a vacuum in the Quebec wing of the Liberal Party, which was the power base, and it was clearly the intention of the triumvirate to fill this vacuum.

Once they were elected to Parliament—and Marchand became almost immediately the Quebec lieutenant or leader—they went to work. And in a remarkably short time their mission was accomplished.

JEAN MARCHAND

When I arrived I said, "Well, I'm going to do that [clean-up] job," and I did it. I had the support of Trudeau and Pelletier, but they were not directly involved or personally involved because they assumed that I was naturally the man to do this kind of job, having been involved in organisation for so many years.

I was suspecting a lot of things and I said, "I'm not the one who's going to spend half of my life proving that these people aren't clean" and so forth, and I just started from scratch. I never bothered to try to have any evidence on each of those persons, because many of them anyhow were entirely worthless from a political point of view. For me it was a good reason, and I didn't have to have any other kind of evidence.

How many? I think that it's probably less important in terms of numbers of those who were incited to quit than to be sure that all the new blood coming into the party was new—were people who really constituted renewal as far as the party was concerned. There were the headquarters, which had to be changed in Montreal and in Quebec City and they were changed. A few years after that you didn't see the same people. And this was important. Then there were the candidates—try to find new candidates and persons who were really representing Quebec and had a future in politics.

This was my work, and I was entirely supported by Pearson on this. He accepted almost everything I said, you know. Quebec was always a little bit of a mystery for him, and he had to rely on advice. I think that he trusted me. I don't remember him telling me, "You shouldn't have done that," or "You shouldn't do this." He just said, "Well, do the job the way you think you should do it," that's all.

GÉRARD PELLETIER

Many people thought that Trudeau and I would cross the aisle in Parliament after a month. They didn't know us, really, because what we'd been doing in our lives was to get into already existing organisations, like the CNTU. The Confederation of National Trade Unions was a very reactionary kind of outfit when Marchand got into it, and it still was when I got into it with Marchand and we worked from the inside and it became quite a progressive outfit.

We thought it would be ten years before we could accomplish anything [in the Liberal Party] and we were ready for that. But we knew that—because it's an experience that we had gone through with the CNTU—we could move an existing body to a more progressive stance. I think we did it with the Quebec people much sooner than we thought we could, because nobody had ever really thought—me less than others—that Trudeau would be Prime Minister three years later. This just happened.

Then there was the recruitment of Robert Winters, which Lester Pearson undertook himself—Winters had been a Cabinet colleague in the old St. Laurent government, and after his defeat in the 1957 election had become a big businessman in Toronto. It could be said that he was at the opposite end of the political pole from the other star Liberal recruit, the socialist-inclined labour leader, Jean Marchand. Paul Martin said that Pearson was anxious to get Winters to return to Ottawa, but Jean Chrétien, who had become the Prime Minister's Parliamentary Secretary, said that he had no great love for Winters and was doing this simply to please the business community. Certainly, he offended his friend, Walter Gordon, who was very suspicious of any commitments that Pearson may have made in order to get Winters to run.

PAUL MARTIN

I know that [Winters] didn't think that Walter should continue as Minister of Finance, but I don't know that Mr. Pearson ever agreed that that would be a condition of his running. I think Bob wanted to come back into politics. I think he wanted to serve in government again, and I never thought that he would become Minister of Finance. I thought he would become Minister of Trade and Commerce, and he was a very good one.

MITCHELL SHARP

I had kept in contact with Winters during the time that I was out of Ottawa. When I was in Toronto I usually saw quite a bit of him. However, my impression of Winters, which was confirmed later, was that Winters had a reputation as a good politician in business circles, and in political circles as a good businessman. It was very interesting; he was a very interesting phenomenon. I didn't consider him particularly outstanding in either.

I was one of those who spoke to Winters and encouraged him to run in 1965. I said I thought that he would be a good addition to our team. He was not likely to talk to me about what position he would have or anything like that. He did, however, obviously have some talks with Pearson, which I wouldn't have known about except anything that Pearson told me. But Winters, I'm sure, came back into politics in the belief that he would be probably given Finance, and would eventually become the Leader of the party. I'm pretty sure, knowing him as I knew him, that was what he would think were his just deserts.

PAUL HELLYER

Winters was considered extreme right-wing, and he was really brought back into the government by Pearson at a time when Walter Gordon and the party were in great disfavour with the business establishment. And Winters was the price of continued business support of the party. I don't know that his return was enough to overcome all their fears, but at least it calmed them to the extent that they would not jump ship, and that they would still support the party financially, which they did in the following election. So this was, I think, a strategic move on [Pearson's] part.

Now, one of the reasons Winters felt so let down later is that Pearson gave him the impression that, if he returned, he would be the heir apparent. But knowing the characters involved, if you had a tape recording of the discussion, if you analysed it, you would find out that he did not in fact say that; that it would be a hint in a tone of voice or in some way that would create that impression without ever having been explicit. Certainly Winters had the notion, the gut feeling, that when he came back that this was in recognition of the fact that he would be the obvious person to lead the party after Mike bowed out.

J. R. SMALLWOOD

Bob Winters was of course head of Brinco and helping to get the development in Churchill Falls, which was like blood to me and to Newfoundland. He told me that the reason he had come back into politics and entered Pearson's Cabinet was that he wanted to be Prime Minister, he wanted to succeed Pearson, and that Pearson had agreed. I don't remember that Winters told me categorically that Pearson had agreed, "Okay, you come in and I will support you and you will succeed me." But he certainly did tell me that Pearson understood that his ambition was to succeed him.

The 1965 election campaign got off to a bad start for the Liberals. Premier Jean Lesage had planned an extensive speaking tour of Western Canada to explain what Quebec wanted, and despite the fact that the election had been called, he would not put it off. Walter Gordon, the Liberal campaign chairman, protested, and so did Prime Minister Pearson, but to no avail. Lesage told his Western audiences that he was insisting on respect for the Constitution, by which he meant the return of powers that rightfully belonged to the provinces under the British North America Act and the means of exercising those powers. He refused to get into any discussions about the future of the French Fact and seemed to go out of his way to annoy reporters. As a result he got a bad press and all he succeeded in doing was to stir up anti-Quebec feeling and to increase the growing sense of alienation in the West. There were many reasons for the latter and they went beyond the general antipathy toward French Canada: bilingualism was not much more than a concept then.

Since his advisors knew that Prime Minister Pearson did not enjoy the hustings and had been in two minds about calling the 1965 election in the first place, they came up with a scheme whereby he would do less campaigning. Which may have been the reason why Tommy Douglas said that he seemed to be fighting the election like a man in a trance. John Nichol, who travelled with Pearson throughout the campaign, said he started late because the strategy was for him to remain in Ottawa and be "Prime Minister" as long as possible. It was not a very well-run campaign, and the Liberals themselves admit this. There was, for example, the tragi-comic breakdown of the public-address system at the mass rally in Toronto's Yorkdale Shopping Mall.

JOHN NICHOL

In the case of Yorkdale, because there had been so much ballyhoo, the failure of the public-address system was an absolute disaster. And there were accusations of sabotage and so on, which were all nonsense. In fact, Paul Taylor, a journalist who had heard the public-address system earlier in the day, mentioned to us that it was inadequate to the background sound level that would be in that place; and this was conveyed to the organisers in Toronto, but they assured us that it was properly done. The organisers of that meeting remain embarrassed to this day about it.

We tried a bullhorn, we tried yelling, we tried everything. But it was just hopeless. The sound level was beyond all that. The irony of it is that political meetings are a big fake, organised for the benefit of the press because the journalists love to count heads and say "big this" and "big that." The politicians soon learn to generate huge "spontaneous" meetings which inform no one about anything.

Even if the sound system had been working, I don't think there was anything very new going to come out of it. The trouble was that a place like Yorkdale is designed as a shopping centre. It isn't designed to hold 20,000 people. We had a situation where the window of a shoe store with eighth-inch ordinary glass was being pushed by 3,000 people, and it's a wonder that somebody's throat wasn't cut. I was really frightened. And all in the name of whooping up enthusiasm for the candidates. It was just terrible.

Pearson was tired and there was disappointment over this fiasco which lasted pretty well until he got back to the hotel. By then it was gone. Then the guys showed up that had put the thing together, and most of them were terribly dejected. Mr. Pearson, in his usual manner, then devoted himself to making them feel better.

Then there was the question of whether or not he should stick to the headquarters election plan and not reply to Mr. Diefenbaker's charges about the scandals.

WALTER GORDON

The election strategy was sort of elementary. You stick to your own issues; you concentrate on what you have accomplished and what you want to accomplish and you don't reply to the Opposition. But Diefenbaker kept on, in a very skillful way—not one that I admire, but a skillful way—suggesting that there were crooks all through the Pearson Government, most of them with French names. We'd advised Pearson not to reply. That was left to Mitchell Sharp to do. However, I think we were wrong. Mike, after all, was the Leader of the party and the Prime Minister, and he decided to reply to Diefenbaker. When he did on television, it was one of the best performances he ever made.

And there were complaints about his oratory, his style, that he wasn't aggressive enough—Mitchell Sharp wished that he had been able to project a stronger image, then he would have been more of a counter-attraction to Diefenbaker. And that was the trouble: Lester Pearson was always being compared with John Diefenbaker, who was one of the greatest political campaigners in Canadian history, if not the greatest. Actually Pearson was not as bad as he was made out to be, and he was certainly a better crowd pleaser than his Liberal predecessors, St. Laurent and Mackenzie King.

PAUL MARTIN

It was a political style that he lacked. He didn't want to emulate. He didn't want to be like William Jennings Bryan or Lloyd George. I said, "Well, try to be like Gladstone then." There's a very good book out on Gladstone; it talks about his oratorical style, and his style in Opposition. But that was it. I didn't want him to be like Diefenbaker. He couldn't be. But I wanted him to be able to respond with vigour.

I remember I was in Saskatoon and I watched Diefenbaker on the television. I was going to a meeting in Saskatoon where I was speaking, and beforehand he came on at seven o'clock or so and he was asking a bunch of questions: "I asked Pearson this, I asked Pearson that ... "

I sat down and wrote a whole bunch of questions for Pearson: "I asked Diefenbaker this, I asked Diefenbaker that ... ," a complete repetition. And I called Mike right away after this, and I said, "Did you hear him?" "No," he said, "how do I have time to listen?" So I said, "He put on quite an effective show tonight, and if I were you I would ask him these questions, and I would ask them in this same form. And here are twelve questions." "Oh, too many!" I said, "No! That's the whole point! The more the better. You just say, 'I asked Mr. Diefenbaker this, I asked Mr. Diefenbaker this,'" and I went on. "Oh," he said, "they'll be bored." I said, "They won't be bored."

And I knew damned well he wasn't going to ask the questions. It wasn't his nature. So he didn't, and I did. I got more attention over those damned questions than any speech I made in the campaign.

There were several reasons why the Liberals did not fare well in the 1965 election.

T. C. DOUGLAS

In two words, it was Diefenbaker and Pearson. First Diefenbaker. Diefenbaker was a charismatic and popular figure in Western Canada. We had never had a Western Prime Minister. It's true that Mackenzie King represented a seat in Saskatchewan, and R. B. Bennett was a lawyer in Calgary but we'd never had a Westerner who understood the West and who spoke the language of the West and expressed the views and the moods and the hopes and aspirations of the West. And consequently, Diefenbaker had a great hold. So that for anyone to take the West away from Diefenbaker would have been very, very difficult indeed.

The second thing is that Pearson, himself, didn't know the West and didn't understand the West. He was essentially an Ontario, university, diplomatic, intellectual type. That didn't mean that he wasn't a very manly person, you know. Everybody liked his interest in baseball and hockey and that he was sports-minded. But he didn't understand the psychology of the prairie farmer or the prairie people or the people in the pioneer communities, and I'm not sure that he took too much trouble trying to cultivate that. He had the blind spot that so many Easterners have of never seeing very much past the head of the Lakes.

JAMES COUTTS

I think there were a couple of reasons. First of all, there was Diefenbaker, and he had a very firm grip on the hearts and minds of Westerners. We did have considerable success in British Columbia—not enormous, but four seats and six seats. On the prairies, people believed in John Diefenbaker. He was their guy. He was from there. He had done things and said things that appealed to them, and they weren't about to forget him.

The other thing was, I think, the organisation of the party when it was rebuilt beginning in '58, '59, and '60. The core of the people who rebuilt the party were essentially urban and Eastern. You couldn't go into a town or a community in Ontario or Quebec where there hadn't been in that three- or four-year period of building half a dozen people who had never been in politics but who were attracted behind Mr. Pearson, behind the new structure of the party. That initiative which was two or three years in the making was not in the West.

CHRISTOPHER YOUNG

I think that Pearson's main objective as Prime Minister was to hold the two basic groups of the country together, the English and French speakers in Ontario and Quebec, and that did mean, undoubtedly, excluding and down-playing the Western Provinces and to a lesser degree the Atlantic Provinces. This appeared perhaps particularly obvious because of Mr. Diefenbaker being a Westerner and being such a dramatic spokesman for the West. Pearson and his advisors were not sufficiently sensitive to that, and of course it was a self-reinforcing failure because every time they had another election and got even fewer seats than before, they had fewer talents to pick from and they got to the point where they had practically nobody to use.

I used to think that they should send somebody, and Mitchell Sharp was the obvious person in my mind, to run in Winnipeg or somewhere. Mitchell Sharp came from Winnipeg. They could have parachuted in somebody such as him with some Western credentials to become a focus for some sort of respectable following out there. But really, the efforts were very feeble. They were totally preoccupied with Quebec and Ontario, and they always said if they could win a hundred seats in Quebec and Ontario, they could pick up enough elsewhere to get a majority.

MITCHELL SHARP

I was conscious when I was in the West of this particular problem of identification with the West. We found it very difficult to make that identification. Take, for instance, the wheat sales. It didn't matter how much wheat we sold. It had all started with Alvin Hamilton because Hamilton had created the impression that he had insisted, whereas we just sold it. It hadn't been done because the West was clamouring for more wheat sales; it was simply because we were skillful salesmen.

Those are two quite different matters. I remember—and probably it wasn't very good tactics on my part, although I don't know any other would have paid off—I simply said, "I didn't personally sell this wheat. That wheat was sold by the Wheat Board. The policies that we adopted, the trade policies and so on, helped the Wheat Board sell the wheat. But it is you on whose behalf the Wheat Board was selling this wheat." And the same was true of Alvin Hamilton. I said, "Alvin Hamilton never sold any wheat. He happened to go to Hong Kong at the time that a sale was being negotiated for China. If Alvin hadn't gone we would have sold the same amount of wheat." But that didn't go down particularly well.

Alvin Hamilton had pounded the desk and had insisted upon selling wheat to China, so he convinced the West. Whereas I was an Easterner, I represented Toronto, and perhaps under my direction the Wheat Board has sold more wheat, but that must have come about in the natural course of events. It couldn't have been anything to do with defending the Western interest.

A. H. McDONALD

We [in Western Canada] lacked support and help, financial support. Now I'm not talking about government handouts; I'm talking about trying to get money out of banks and other institutions in Central Canada to develop the province of

Saskatchewan in non-agricultural activity. And it was difficult. I can recall the efforts that the CCF made to bring a pulp mill to Saskatchewan, and they failed. Ross Thatcher was determined to bring a pulp mill to Saskatchewan, and he did. But he didn't bring it there with any help from the pulp industry of Canada or the banks of Canada. The industry was brought there by Americans, and we have found that in many instances, if we want help and assistance we have to go South rather than East.

This is one of the problems. And when this problem exists, a lot of people blame government, whether it is caused by government action or inaction or not. And there's a general mistrust of Eastern Canada, especially in the province of Saskatchewan. When you think of Eastern Canada, you think of Ottawa, and you think of the Liberal Party, because they have been the party in power. There's a whole range, a whole multitude of issues that have aggravated people over the years. Today people are better advised than they've ever been in their lives before because of modern means of communication. Everything that happens in Ottawa now, we know about it a tenth of a second after it happens, whereas it used to take two weeks. And so people understand the problems of Canada and of their own province better today than ever before. This has turned them more against the government of Canada, and the government of Canada most of the time has been a Liberal government, so it's turned them against the Liberal Party.

HARRY HAYS

I think Medicare hurt Mr. Pearson, and some of the unemployment insurance, social programs which he believed in were more apt to hurt him in Alberta than they would in other parts of Canada as I know Canada. Because in Calgary we were exposed to more Americanism. Forty thousand Americans live in Calgary, and they have top jobs in the petroleum industry, and they're on the university senate, and they're on the school board. And in the United States, they'll accept people with a great deal of material assets better and they'll look up to those sort of people. And Calgary accepts successful people more so than any other place in Canada. So they would be opposed to social programs ... Medicare, you know. If somebody wants an education, let him pay for it himself; and if somebody's sick, let him look after himself; and if your old mother-in-law can't look after herself, well, the government shouldn't have to.

CHRISTOPHER YOUNG

There were a group of us talking to Pearson and Gordon in the motel, and I remember asking the question why there was so little time being spent in Saskatchewan. I think there was one day for Saskatchewan in the remaining whatever-it-was weeks of the campaign, and days and days around southern Ontario and the suburbs of Toronto. There was a reason for spending a lot of time in those areas that were very heavily populated swing seats—good fighting territory, but still it seemed way out of proportion to me. And Walter Gordon said something to the effect that there were as many seats in metro Toronto or suburban Toronto as there were in all of Saskatchewan.

So it was a purely mathematical calculation on his part. Of course, I felt it was a terrible mistake, because it's not just mathematics, it's psychology, and it means that you're writing off not just seventeen seats in Saskatchewan, but a great big chunk of the West. And this attitude is why basically the West was so totally alienated from the Liberal Party and remains so to this day. Now, that's Walter Gordon and he's a Toronto politician, but I think that Mr. Pearson ought to have been a little more willing to reject the advice of people like Gordon and Davey and rely on his own judgement, which was extremely good politically, I think, but a little bit hesitant, perhaps because he came to it late.

A. H. McDONALD

I recall a little while ago talking to our new senator from Saskatchewan, Davey Steuart, and he talked about the Liberal parties in the West. He said that the Liberal Party in Saskatchewan is in Opposition, the Liberal Party in Manitoba is in hiding, the Liberal Party in British Columbia is nonexistent, and the Liberal

Party in Alberta is a protected species.* This pretty well sums up the position of the Liberal Party.

Now, that being the case, surely people in Ottawa, not only in government but people in Ottawa, Toronto, Montreal, better recognise this fact and do something about it. The Liberal Party is in that position because it has been the government of Canada throughout most of my lifetime. If it had been the Conservative Party or some other party and these conditions prevailed, they would have been anti-Conservative or anti-Social Credit or anti-NDP. There's got to be a change of attitude among people who live in the central parts of Canada. And until that attitude changes, whatever party's in power in Ottawa, it's going to be in trouble in Western Canada.

KEITH DAVEY

The party, as a party, was revitalised in Ontario, it was revitalised in British Columbia, it was revitalised in Quebec. It wasn't revitalised in the Atlantic Provinces but that really didn't matter because of the overplay between provincial and federal parties. In the West that never happened, and Mr. Pearson inherited, as the resident Liberal leaders, the remnants of the St. Laurent Old Guard. Too frequently in the West the party was in the hands of patronage lawyers. I think that was a big factor. The guard never changed in the West. I think Liberals in the West had become, even as early as '65, inured to defeat, and I think that the party in the West had become much too far to the right. I think that we became in Western Canada a pale carbon copy of the Tories.

I remember we could have had [Ed] Schreyer as a Liberal candidate in 1962, but the Old Guard in Winnipeg just wouldn't hear of it. Tory friends have said to me over the years, "You don't understand the West; we're much more conservative-minded out there." While these guys were telling me this, they'd gone on voting for the NDP. I think the problem is that our natural constituency, which is somewhere to the right of the NDP and to the left of the Tories, we've allowed other people to appropriate.

*Steuart was commenting on conditions in the mid-'70s when the fortunes of the Liberal Party in Western Canada had deteriorated even further.

Now, there's another factor, which I conceded once, and that was that the party had fallen into the hands of guys like me who had a far greater understanding of this part of Canada [Toronto]. I accept that fully and totally, and that was also a major factor. But again, if I'm not going to take all of the credit for the party's continuing success in the Toronto area—and I don't think I can take any of it because I think it's a sociological thing—then I don't think you can blame us in the West because it's the reverse sociological factors at play.

Election night, November 8, 1965, began well enough, and while the Maritimes were a disappointment, the loss of seats there was small, and the news from the populous central provinces was generally encouraging, with good gains in Quebec and Ontario holding firm. However, as the results came in from the West, with the loss of one of two seats in Manitoba and the total rejection of the Liberals in Saskatchewan and Alberta, it became evident that there was no hope of gaining a majority.* By midnight the small party in the Pearsons' suite in the Chateau Laurier had become a wake. Tom Kent was there, and Keith Davey, the members of the Pearson family, John Nichol and his wife Liz, and Mary Macdonald. Tom Kent said that Liz broke down and cried. There was a telephone call from Walter Gordon and, according to Gordon, Pearson said that he was going to resign immediately and expected him to do the same. Gordon, according to his own recollection, told him not to be silly and that he would see him the following day.

JOHN NICHOL

I was with [Pearson] when we received the election results. There was great disappointment on his part, and a feeling for a moment at least that he was going to quit. He didn't say he was going to resign, but he said something that implied that. I remember that some of us went into the other room and got a shirt cardboard out of his suitcase and wrote the notes down on it for

---

*In the 1965 election the Liberals won 131 seats, two short of a majority; the Progressive Conservatives, 97; the NDP, 21; and others (Créditistes, 9; Social Credit, 5; Independents, 2) 16. The results of the 1963 election were: Liberals, 129; PCs, 95; Social Credit, 24; NDP, 17. There were 265 seats in the Canadian House of Commons in those years.

what we thought he should say. It was what he knew he was going to say anyway, and that was that the electorate had spoken and that it wasn't all that he had hoped for, but that he remained the Prime Minister and that he was going to serve the people as best he could, and so on and so forth. Which is exactly, I believe, what he said.

But there was a moment when he felt pretty discouraged. It's a long, long way to go for nothing, that election. And that's what it turned out to be. Almost exactly the same number of seats.

10 *More Trouble*

IN THE AFTERMATH of the 1965 election, Lester Pearson's mood was described as one of bitter frustration. He had called an election, which he didn't want, largely because of the importuning of Walter Gordon and Keith Davey—he realised now that he should have ordered them to stop their election propaganda at the very beginning, as Tom Kent had suggested and as he had told Kent that he would do. They had given him the wrong advice but he had to blame himself because, as he said, he had to take the responsibility for the decision to go to the country. He should have had more confidence in his own political judgement, which his nephew, Christopher Young, said was usually right. It was particularly galling that he should have gone through all the agony of the election campaign which, he said, was not necessary, to end up in exactly the same position as before, even as far as the posture of his government was concerned.

The day after the election was, by his own account, gloomy for Mike Pearson; he was an unhappy man, depressed and glum, according to Vic Mackie, no longer the easygoing, affable statesman who got along so well with reporters. He was in such a dark mood that he put a stop to a practice that went back to Mackenzie King's days of members of the Press Gallery stationing themselves outside the Cabinet Room in the East Block of the Parliament Buildings and getting informal interviews with the Ministers and Prime Minister.

275

VIC MACKIE

Mike came out of his office and there must have been twenty-five press people and some radio people and a TV camera in the corridor. He brushed passed us and said he didn't want to say anything. I said to Dick O'Hagan, his press officer, "It's the day after the election, and he has got to say something, he's got to talk to us."

Dick agreed to send a note in to him and say that we wanted him to have a press conference after the meeting. The note came back with *No, absolutely no,* written on it, which shocked O'Hagan and me because we assumed that Mike was his usual self and able to get along with the press.

By this time word had got back to the Press Gallery that there was a crowd of newspapermen in the East Block and as the Cabinet meeting went on, more and more press people came over and another TV camera arrived and all kinds of radio people with their microphones and there was a fantastic crowd jammed into that corridor. I was in the forefront and I got hold of Dick and said, "This is madness; he'll never get through this crowd." Mike emerged from the Cabinet meeting and he was horrified to see this huge phalanx of press barring his way to the Prime Minister's office. He forced his way through the crowd, pushing and shoving, with the microphones being rammed in his face, and TV cameras being tilted sideways. It just looked like a football game with Mike bucking the line physically. I remember him being pushed and shoved—and he was furious.

We got into his office and Dick O'Hagan told me subsequently that he was just livid with anger; he announced that the press was barred from the East Block. "From now on we won't let them in." And we weren't. That was it. We were never allowed back in the East Block again because of Mike's sense of pique over losing the majority in that damn election.

The 1965 election was a watershed for Prime Minister Pearson. Walter Gordon resigned from the Cabinet, and Keith Davey quit as national organiser of the Liberal Party, and so many of his closest advisors were to go that it looked as if Pearson was cleaning house. But there was nothing deliberate about this; he did not decide to take on a new staff because of the failure of the old staff. Actually, he wanted Gordon to stay in the Cabinet, and offered him another portfolio, but Gordon would not agree to being anything but Finance Minister and insisted on leaving and leaving immediately.

WALTER GORDON

I had said I would resign. He had said he would resign. Well, he changed his mind. But I had said I'd resign, so I went out to see him, and he immediately raised the question of the Department of Finance again, which I had assumed was settled. So I said, words to this effect: "Well, you don't have to worry. Here's my resignation."

Mike was in a jam. I didn't know then but I found out later—he had told various people—that I would not be in Finance, and I presume he at least implied to Bob Winters that Bob was going to be Minister of Trade and Commerce. Well, Sharp was Minister of Trade and Commerce, so the presumption was that Sharp would move to Finance, but I don't know that. Anyway, I handed my resignation in and he put it in his pocket. I said, "No. You'd better read it." So he did. Now he offered me various things, you know. Did I want to go to Washington? Did I want to be Minister of ... I forget if it was Transport or something or other? But that wasn't the issue as far as I was concerned.

TOM KENT

Walter Gordon would always do the decent thing—there is no man of whom you could be more sure for that. It was right for him to offer his resignation. But in fact, Mike was as responsible [for the election] as Walter was. And the right thing, frankly, I think, would have been not to accept the resignation. I think Walter was entitled to expect that; while it was the right thing for him to do to offer it, it was equally the right thing that it not be accepted.

PAUL MARTIN

Mike offered him another portfolio, and Walter didn't want to take that. I called Walter about that and urged him to take the other portfolio. My recollection is that it was Trade and Commerce. I thought that Walter had a lot to offer and that he could continue to serve and make a contribution, but it was obvious that he had to go from Finance.

MAURICE LAMONTAGNE

Walter Gordon certainly expected that there would be more insistence on the part of Mr. Pearson for him to stay—that is for sure. Whether he would have stayed, I'm not too sure. I think that, in spite of what he had said during the campaign, Mr. Pearson had made a commitment to get rid of him as Minister of Finance.

I know perfectly well, directly from Mr. Pearson, that he had made a commitment to Mr. Winters. He told me this just a few days before the Cabinet was announced. I was trying to get a different portfolio for Jean Marchand, and I thought it might have been a good thing to send him to Trade and Commerce because he couldn't go to Labour and the Department of Trade and Commerce was a relatively small department, really, but it had a lot of prestige for the outside public because of C. D. Howe and all this. But I think this prestige was not supported by the reality of power. In any case, I remember at that time that Mr. Pearson had told me that he had made a commitment to Bob Winters to give him Trade and Commerce, and that meant really that there was another commitment to give Finance to Mitchell Sharp. So I don't think, under those circumstances, that even if Mr. Pearson had offered another portfolio to Walter Gordon at that time, he would have accepted it. That's probably what happened.

JAMES WALKER

Walter Gordon met some of his supporters among the Liberal M.P.s at the old Liberal headquarters in Ottawa—he didn't organise this; we organised ourselves. When he told us he was going, we wept. Strong men wept. It was a most emotional evening. We said, "Walter, stay. You're the heart and soul of the spirit of Liberalism in this party."

I went to Mr. Pearson and said, "This is just a terrible thing. He can't go. He's got to stay." And he said, "Don't worry, Jimmy. Walter will be back in."

Now, I interpret this as the quandary Mr. Pearson was in in

dealing with Ministers, the great majority of whom wanted Walter Gordon out of the Cabinet. Does he want a mass resignation? Some of them, I believe, were at that stage where they said, "It's Gordon or us"—"us" being a group of them. The worst thing in the world that can happen to a party is to have a mass resignation of Cabinet Ministers. The country's confidence is gone in your government. I think he was playing for time. He had met crisis after crisis of that kind internationally, and Pearson I think was playing for time.

KEITH DAVEY

It is my understanding that Pearson said [to Gordon], "Well, that's nonsense; I won't accept your resignation. But I am going to transfer your portfolio. You choose your portfolio, but you won't be the Minister of Finance." So Walter said, "Well, that's fine. That's an effective resignation because I don't want any other portfolio. If I'm not the Minister of Finance, I'm out."

I had dinner with him that night, and I said, "What happened?" expecting him to say anything but what he said: "I resigned." God, I was shattered. But he wasn't. Because that's not his style to be broken up. I'm sure he was, but again he's such a thoroughly civilised person—we joked and laughed and had a pleasant evening.

Prime Minister Pearson tried to get Keith Davey to change his mind and continue running party headquarters but again without success.

KEITH DAVEY

I went to Mr. Pearson the next day, and said that I would like to resign as well. He said, "Because Walter has resigned, that's absolutely no reason why you should resign. I don't think you should resign. I don't see why you want to. I'd like you to go away and just think about your position. Then come back at Christmastime and we'll talk about it. But I really don't think you should resign."

I came back at Christmastime, and I said, "I really do want to leave." He said, "Well, look, what you should do is talk to me about the BBG [Board of Broadcast Governors] and the CBC, about going into some appointment in the broadcasting area." I said, "May I say what I would really like?" He said, "Sure." I said, "I'd like to go to the Senate." And he said, "I think you're too young to do that. What do you want to go to the Senate for? It's a dead-end street." But he said, "If that's what you really want to do. I'll do it for you, of course."

Then the footnote to that story: On the 31st of January 1966, the executive of the Liberal Party of Canada was meeting in Ottawa, and I attended the meeting. We were going out to 24 Sussex in the afternoon. At the meeting I made my formal swan song. In the middle of my swan song, the phone rang, and my secretary came in and said, "There's a phone call for you; it's urgent." It was from Walter in Toronto. He said, "Look, Keith, I have reason to believe that Mike is going to call you and see you and urge you to stay on as the national director of the Liberal Party." And he said, "My judgement is you shouldn't do it. You should insist upon the Senate, and you should insist upon it now." I went back into the room and finished my swan song. And by God, how Walter knew to this day I don't know, but Mr. Pearson phoned me. And he said, "Keith, I'd like you to come and see me for a few minutes."

The executive meeting adjourned for lunch, and I went zipping out to 24 Sussex. We went up into his study on the second floor. He said, "I've been thinking a lot about your position, and I really don't know why you want to go to the Senate. I think I have a better plan. I am not going to run another campaign. I'm going to stay for a year or two, and then there will be a leadership convention." And he said, "I would like you to stay with me through those years and through the leadership convention, and then you can leave when I leave." He said, "We did this thing together and we'll leave together. I think that would be great."

I swallowed hard and said, "Look, I really want to leave." Because frankly the heart had gone out of me, mostly because of Walter [going]. I still had a great affection for Mr. Pearson. You can imagine how tough it has been on me when these two guys became in effect enemies. I found that extremely difficult. But in any event, I said to him, "Does this mean that I don't go to the Senate?" And he said, "No, no. Come on." We had an affectionate relationship. I don't want to overstate the case, but we were great friends.

So that afternoon I went back, and the executive all came out, and he paid a very fulsome tribute to me, and he said, "You may see Keith in other places in a few days," and so on. Everybody took it to mean the Senate. And I was subsequently appointed.

The resignations of Walter Gordon and of Maurice Lamontagne and René Tremblay occurred within a short time of each other in the aftermath of the 1965 election, but there was a difference. As Tom Kent put it rather brutally, Lamontagne and Tremblay were, for all practical purposes, thrown out. Prime Minister Pearson asked for their resignations. He spoke of them as honourable men of great ability but they had had difficulty defending themselves in Parliament, and thus their usefulness had been undermined. Allan MacEachen felt that if Walter Gordon had not gone, Maurice Lamontagne might have been able to stay. Pearson said that he dismissed Lamontagne and Tremblay because they were no longer effective; his treatment of them, in Jean Marchand's view, was in keeeping with what he conceived to be his role as Prime Minister and conciliator.

ALLAN MacEACHEN

I can only believe that Pearson accepted Walter's resignation because he thought it was politically desirable at the time. When Walter left for his "sins," the purists in the nation said, "Well, why shouldn't Maurice go?" So Maurice left. His resignation was accepted. I don't think at the time there was any sort of general purge, but I do think that probably Pearson was becoming more confident and wanted less people breathing down his neck all the time and telling him what to do, quite frankly. You know, the relationship between himself and Kent and himself and Gordon had been so close at a certain time that probably he had outlived that and wanted a little more freedom, manoeuvrability, instead of having to listen to the same advice. That would be my interpretation.

MAURICE LAMONTAGNE

Mr. Pearson told me that, because of the campaign, there was resentment, that there were people in the party who were saying that those scandals were partly responsible for the party not getting a majority. He thought that it would be better for the party and, perhaps, for myself to get out—at least temporarily. He was saying that it was a terrible thing to do, but that he felt that he had to come to that conclusion.

I told him at that time, "Well, I think that in view of the present situation, there are only two courses of action to take. Either we deal with these alleged scandals squarely and even go on the attack, and you will have to take the leadership on this, or as you say we'll still be on the defensive, and then I'm not really interested in staying because I will always be marked in that way without being defended by anybody." Because this thing had been raised during the campaign. There were all kinds of rumours again. I remember he phoned me during the campaign, and I was supposed to have received a donation of 50,000 dollars from somebody. Of course, it was completely false.

There was this kind of atmosphere of suspicion, and in view of our past relationship I could see that there was something there, this lack of confidence. I was not so terribly interested in politics that I decided also on my part that I should go. I said, in conclusion to my discussion with Mr. Pearson, "Here you have decided not to go on the attack, not to lead and deal with this squarely. I feel it's too bad. I think that these things will continue more or less, and probably one day they'll be after your own head. I hope I'm wrong in this forecast, but this is the scenario I'm envisaging." He said, "Well, I hope you're wrong too." That was it.

JEAN MARCHAND

As a Prime Minister he was playing with a certain number of forces. If one of them ceased to be a force for the moment, it no longer represented any interest in his game. I call it a game—in French I would use a different word—but in his way of governing the country.

He considered himself as the supreme conciliator of this country, not only between French and English Canadians, but between the group interests in Canada. When he was discussing [politics] and I would say, "What about consulting this fellow?" "Aw, he doesn't represent anybody; it's useless," or "He's not strong enough to do anything." The idea of strength was very important. This is probably a quality of a conciliator: just to forget about his own truth, what he thinks is the truth, and to see what is the truth that is going to be accepted by what we call the consensus. And the consensus sometimes has nothing to do with the truth.

This is not something exceptional, because all those who have any kind of success internationally are those who are behaving that way—trying to get together people who don't have or don't believe in the same things, and trying to find a common denominator or something, that they will live together for at least a certain length of time. That's why when Pearson was evaluating people—of course he had good friends—he would say, "Oh, it's unfortunate because he is so nice a man, but he no longer represents anything."

Besides Gordon, Davey, Lamontagne, and Tremblay, the others who left included Tom Kent, Dick O'Hagan, and Jim Coutts. It was a clean sweep of Lester Pearson's closest advisors, and yet, from all accounts, it was not planned. All of them had their reasons for wanting to go. In the case of Tom Kent, it was really a mutual feeling that they were getting on each other's nerves, and all of them felt that they should not remain in the pressure-cooker atmosphere of the Prime Minister's office in a minority government for more that a couple of years. But there was the fact of the 1965 election, and as Walter Gordon hinted, if Pearson had gained a majority in that election, it is doubtful if so many would have left him or that he would have allowed so many to go.

WALTER GORDON

Mike had a complex character and I don't know what was motivating him at the time. I think he was a thoroughly frustrated fellow, a very tired one, and getting pretty old. I would put it that it was an expression of frustration over his failure to win the election, and probably his poor campaigning because that had a lot to do with it.

TOM KENT

My going, I think, was a little different in the sense that it was the completion of a process that I had made very clear to Mike I was intent on carrying out long before the '65 election. At the same time, I think it was probably a little bit of a relief to Mike. He and I had a very peculiar relationship—very close in some ways, difficult in others.

After the problems of '63, the whole thing had been so distorted by Walter not playing the part that he was supposed to play, and I had really got into a position where I was doing far more than was reasonable for one person to do. Remember, the Prime Minister's office in those days consisted of Jim Coutts guarding the door, Dick O'Hagan and Hal Dornan handling the press, Mary [Macdonald] as the factotum. That was it, apart from myself, compared with a hundred or whatever it is now. It was an unhealthy relationship in the sense that I was really doing too much and really Mike was too dependent on me. And I think we were both under the sort of strain that arises from one side, from my side feeling, "Good God, why should I be doing that much?" And on the other hand from his side almost a resentment, and understandably, of being as dependent on me as he was. Remember Diefenbaker used to make cracks about the Leader of the Leader? That sort of stuff. Those things all hurt.

Our relationship survived a great deal of strain relatively well. But the fact remains that his approach to lots of things was very different from mine—all sorts of things on which he didn't take my advice, lots of things on which he took it perhaps all too readily. In any case, that is such an intense, exposed sort of position that nobody should do it for too long. You know, a couple of years is probably the most that anybody should be in that job. By April '65 it was two years. And I was very much concerned to move to something else.

KEITH DAVEY

I think that Tom was always very hard on Mr. Pearson. He was a very difficult guy for Mr. Pearson to deal with because Tom is an unrelenting worker, and he's not an easy guy. Mr. Pearson would want to take it fairly easy coming back from a rally at a particular place, and he would be on the plane, sitting with a drink in his hand, just trying to relax, and all of a sudden Tom would come up and sit down beside him and say, "Mr. Pearson, here's something I've worked on for tomorrow night." Mr. Pearson would never in God's green world say, "Look, Tom, get lost."

JAMES COUTTS

Both O'Hagan and I had made a decision early in '65 that we both had been at it long enough—Dick for a period of four or five years and me a period of three—that we should go. You can only do those things for a certain amount of time. We told Mr. Pearson in the late winter and spring of '65 that we wanted to go and we made arrangements as to where we were going to go. In both cases, he asked us to stay and to change those plans in the summer of '66. And on both occasions we said that we'd made our plans and we did want to go, and he said that was fine.

RICHARD O'HAGAN

I think many of us were tired and also felt a need to do something new, and I think in every instance that's what happened. Certainly in my own case, I went off to a very satisfying period of service in Washington at the Embassy, which was not intended to be and wasn't a patronage plum. I mean Mr. Pearson persuaded me to go there and do something that he thought was good for the country, but he thought, at the same time, having my own welfare in mind, it was good for me.

Two more Cabinet vacancies had to be filled: Harry Hays, Agriculture Minister, and J. Watson McNaught, Minister of Mines and Technical Surveys, had been defeated in the election. Mr. Pearson had some drastic changes in mind. As was expected, Mitchell Sharp replaced Walter Gordon as Finance Minister , and Robert Winters took over Trade and Commerce, the portfolio that Sharp had had. The Agriculture Minister was traditionally from the Prairies but the Liberals had elected no one in Alberta and Saskatchewan and only one from Manitoba, Roger Teillet, a French Canadian who was already Minister of Veterans' Affairs. Lester Pearson toyed with the idea of appointing Senator A. H. "Hammy" McDonald, former Saskatchewan deputy premier, as Agriculture Minister, but in the end settled on J. J. "Joe" Greene, an Ottawa Valley lawyer, for the post. He moved Judy LaMarsh out of Health and Welfare and gave her the Secretary of State portfolio that Maurice Lamontagne had had. He persuaded Jean Marchand, who was to become his Quebec lieutenant, to accept the Citizenship and Immigration portfolio that René Tremblay had had. Jean-Luc Pepin, who had been Minister Without

Portfolio, got Mines and Technical Surveys. Besides Greene and Marchand, the other new members of of the Cabinet were Jean-Pierre Côté, who became Postmaster General, and John Turner, Minister Without Portfolio. As Winters had been a Minister, he was technically returning to the Cabinet.

It was a thorough-going shake-up, and the "new look Cabinet," as Pearson called it, was sworn in on December 18, 1965. The Prime Minister asked John Nichol to replace Keith Davey at the Liberal Party headquarters.

HARRY HAYS

Mr. Pearson phoned me the night I was defeated, and he said, "Now, I don't want you to burn any bridges. I hope that we can get a seat for you and that you will continue on as Minister of Agriculture. In the meantime I want you to stay on," which I did until the end of the year. Three Members came to me and said, "Well, you can have my seat." There were two Ontario seats—Paul Tardif's was one—and one in Newfoundland. But I didn't think at the time that I should like—Paul's was a completely safe seat—[to run in the East]. That's how I happened to be summoned to the Senate.

J. J. GREENE

Living close by, I was able to go to Ottawa before most of the newly elected Members, and I camped on Mr. Pearson's doorstep. When I finally got in, he said, "Oh, you want to be a Parliamentary Secretary, Joe?" I said, "Parliamentary Secretary, hell. I want to be Minister of Agriculture." And he blanched at the thought. We had Bruce Beer [M.P. for Peel-Dufferin-Simcoe, Ontario], who had been Parliamentary Secretary to Mr. Hays, and I thought that I could do a better job than he could. I could see this was an opportunity to jump quickly from the back row, where my rear end was dunking in the Ottawa River, as I used to say, into the front. And I thought I could communicate with Westerners better than Bruce Beer could, really. I once persuaded the government, by a speech in the House, to give drought relief to the farmers of the Ottawa Valley. Then I pushed it hard in caucus—there had been a very bad drought — and I think he recalled that. You know, it's not easy for a back bencher to get something he wants, especially out of a minority government. This wasn't a great deal of money a few million dollars. On that thin base I bulled my way into the front benches, if you like. Now with some Prime Ministers it wouldn't have worked, But with Mr. Pearson it did.

The first notice I got was to be at Government House at nine o'clock on such-and-such a day for the swearing in. I got there at seven. The door wasn't even open. I think it was Esmond Butler [Secretary to the Governor-General] who came to the door and let me in. He said, "You might as well come in and sit down. There'll be nobody here for two hours."

JUDY LaMARSH

When I came back from a post election holiday in Jamaica Mike invited me out to see him at the Sussex Drive house, and told me that he wanted me to leave the [Health and Welfare] portfolio because there'd been a lot of stink about it. I said, "Who will you put in it?" And he said, "Allan MacEachen." I said, "Well, he's lazy; he'll never get it done." And he wasn't about to discuss that with me.

He said, "You can have a choice." I said, "Of what?" And he said, "Solicitor General . . ." Well, my father used to call it the hindest tit of all because it wasn't a full department and really had very little to do with anything, aside from commuting death penalties at that time. But he was in the process of beefing it up. And he offered me the Post Office—that graveyard—and I wasn't the slightest interested. Then, he offered me Secretary of State, and he mentioned the broadcasting and the Centennial. It was the Centennial I was interested in, and I thought, "Well, why not." I wouldn't have been interested in Secretary of State as it had been. But I was pretty incensed about all this and I said I would think it over.

He went off to Jamaica and I heard that he went to Rockefeller's island or something, and there was no communication, which was dreadful: nobody could reach him. Finally, MacEachen tracked him down. I don't know what connection there was between

Mike and MacEachen, but MacEachen was always very much like a son to him. At any rate, MacEachen went down to say that he didn't want to do Health and Welfare, that he didn't want to leave Labour. Mike was pretty mad that Allan had broken his privacy and didn't pay any attention to him anyway.

The next thing I knew was that Tom Kent came to see me and said, "The Prime Minister wants to know your decision." I said, "Well, that can wait till he gets back. I haven't made up my mind, and I'm going to let him worry about it." He said, "No, it doesn't work that way. He either wants your resignation or your announcement of which portfolio you want." So I had to think about that pretty fast, and I decided on Sectetary of State.

TOM KENT

He [Pearson] was fascinated by Marchand. He thought that Marchand could really change things. And that had an importance to me because I was given the job of persuading Marchand to take a major portfolio. Marchand was very reluctant to take a portfolio. I mean he wanted to be a Minister Without Portfolio. He didn't feel familiar enough with things that he was prepared to take on a major job. I had to persuade him that Ottawa wasn't like that. A Minister Without Portfolio didn't really have any role in Ottawa. You had to have a department behind you, and the thing to do was to do something new and creative. This idea of the [new] Department of Manpower in which I'd been involved [appealed to him] and the terms of which Marchand agreed to become Minister was that I should be his Deputy Minister. It was at that point, of course, that I left Mr. Pearson.

The conversion of the Department of Citizenship and Immigration into the Department of Manpower and Immigration was one of the changes that Lester Pearson made in the structure of the Canadian government. Jean Marchand could not become Labour Minister, for which he was so well suited, because he had been head of the Confederation of National Trade Unions, CNTU, and that portfolio would have appeared to create a conflict of interest as far as the rival Canadian Labour Congress (CLC) was concerned, and Mr. Pearson was moving some of the manpower branches of the Labour Department and amalgamating them with Immigration to form a new department. Tom Kent was able to persuade Marchand to take over this department with its manpower emphasis, but he was sworn in as Minister of Citizenship and Immigration because the legislation making the changes, including the change of name, had not been adopted.

The citizenship directorate was allocated to the Secretary of State's department, which had already acquired most of the country's cultural agencies such as the National Gallery, the National Library, the Public Archives, the museums, the National Film Board, as well as the Canadian Broadcasting Corporation. The Secretary of State's registrar functions and commercial divisions were put together in a new Department of Consumer and Corporate Affairs, whose first Minister was John Turner.

As a former bureaucrat, Pearson understood the working of the bureaucracy better probably than most previous Prime Ministers and he realised that there was a need for rationalisation and realignment of many of its offices and operations. One of his first acts on coming to power in 1963 had been to bring the Department of Defence Production, which was a hangover of the Second World War, together with the industry part of Trade and Commerce to form the new Department of Industry and Defence Production. However, this was not entirely a successful move and eventually the industry section was returned to its old department, but its separation had given it a greater status so that the department was renamed the Department of Industry, Trade and Commerce. At the same time, the remainder of Defence Production became the separate Ministry of Supply and Services.

Prime Minister Pearson recognised, long before the Arab oil embargo, that energy was of supreme importance for an industrial state such as Canada and that technical surveys were really part of the country's pioneer past. Therefore he, converted the Department of Mines and Technical Surveys into the Department of Energy, Mines and Resources and gave Jean-Luc Pepin the task of supervising the changes. Actually, the "resources" in the department's name came from the Department of Northern Affairs and National Resources, which was changed into the Department of Indian Affairs and Northern Development, thus concentrating its efforts on the welfare of the native peoples.

Lester Pearson's work in realigning the ministries and restructuring the federal government was considered by observers of the Ottawa scene to be among his notable achievements—comparable with such social welfare measures as the Canada Pension Plan and Medicare.

Some of the departments were too large and cumbersome and included bits and pieces of unrelated functions—they were more portmanteaus than portfolios. Justice was one, with its responsibilities for the police and penitentiaries as well as the courts, and Mr. Pearson decided to turn some of these responsibilities over to the Solicitor General's office which, as Judy LaMarsh had said, was hardly a department at all. However, the Prime Minister did nothing about Transport, which was the most overstuffed department, having under its jurisdiction the railways, shipping, airlines, and communications, plus all the agencies connected thereto, such as the National Harbours Board, the St. Lawrence Seaway Authority, the Northern Transportation Company, the Aviation Safety Bureau, and radio and telecommunication licencing bodies. The reason may have been that Jack Pickersgill, who was Minister of Transport, didn't want to see his empire broken up or disturbed in any way. In trying to modernise the creaking machinery of big government, Mr. Pearson had had to contend with the resistance of civil servants, particularly the top officials, to any kind of movement or change.

It was the unfortunate experience with Guy Favreau that prompted the Prime Minister to do something about lessening the burden of the Justice Ministry. He determined to move the Royal Canadian Mounted Police, the penitentiary services, and the parole board into the Solicitor General's office, thus making it into a bigger department than Justice. On July 7, 1965, he appointed Lucien Cardin Justice Minister to replace Guy Favreau who had resigned because of unfavourable comments about him in the Dorion Report. At the same time, he brought Lawrence T. Pennell, a bright young lawyer from Brantford, Ontario, into the Cabinet, and made him Solicitor General. The appointment of Lucien Cardin as Justice Minister was a grave error of judgement on Pearson's part. Christopher Young said that the obvious candidate was George McIlraith, who was a competent lawyer and good at defusing trouble in the House of Commons, but the Prime Minister decided that the appointment of an English Canadian to a post that was traditionally French Canadian would be considered an affront to the Quebec Ministers and the Quebec caucus. Cardin himself had grave doubts about taking the job because he didn't feel that he had enough legal experience, and it was only because of Pearson's insistence, and his assurance that it would be for a short time, that he agreed.

One of the problems that the new Justice Minister inherited was the case of George Victor Spencer, the Vancouver postal clerk accused of spying for the Russians. It had been said, originally, that Spencer would not be charged because he was dying of cancer, although there was some question that there was enough evidence to convict him. At any rate, Cardin described how he was tricked into appearing on the CBC program, "This Hour Has Seven Days," on November 28, 1965, at which time he not only confirmed the spy's name but said that Spencer would be under RCMP surveillance for the rest of his life. When the Twenty-seventh Parliament got down to regular business, the Opposition hammered relentlessly on the Spencer case and demanded that the little man be given a hearing which, they said, he wanted. Cardin asserted that there was no reason to give into Mr. Diefenbaker on this matter and refused to have a public enquiry.

LUCIEN CARDIN

I stood firm against the demand for a judicial enquiry. That was my attitude toward this thing. Then Mr. Diefenbaker started his insinuation that we had something to hide here in Ottawa and that was why we only fired the poor man and didn't want to do anything else with him. That came up over and over again. [George] Hees made that statement and other Members made that statement that we had something to hide. That caught the attention of the press, and people could have perhaps believed it. But it had always been the practice in Parliament of never divulging anything at all about a security case. That was sacred. You just didn't. The only exception was to inform the leaders of the parties [in confidence] what the situation was, so they could understand it. But you would never institute a royal enquiry into that kind of a deal.

LAWRENCE PENNELL

I took the position that the Cabinet ought not to be involved too much in the affairs of Justice. True, the law officers wore a double hat, but decisions such as whether to prosecute Spencer, for instance—I was very strong that they should not be a Cabinet decision. Whether a person is prosecuted is not a political decision. It's a matter of legal decision made by the law officers of the

Crown. When the great hue and cry went up, "Well, why wasn't Spencer prosecuted?" a lot of people misunderstood. It was said in the House that the Cabinet had [decided not to prosecute] for a number of reasons—one was because it might strain international relations with Russia. I can tell you frankly that it was a decision which Mr. Cardin and myself made, and I wouldn't countenance Cabinet making that decision.

However, Pearson was under pressure from some of his own Members to have a hearing.

J. W. PICKERSGILL

This Spencer business was a very curious business altogether. I don't mind saying, because my recollection about this is very clear, that I strongly advised Mr. Pearson to have an independent enquiry and to start the enquiry before Parliament met because, if I remember correctly, Lucien Cardin had been interviewed on TV and it seemed to me had just provided all the material that Diefenbaker needed to make a great civil liberties issue out of this thing.

I went down on the plane that carried Pearson for his official visits to the West Indies. He'd been at St. Bart's and we flew down to St. Martin, and we had a day there before Mr. Pearson continued on his journey. I told him about this broadcast, and I said, "In my judgement, if we leave this subject around for debate, we will have great trouble because it's just exactly the kind of issue that is right down Diefenbaker's alley. There's nobody who could make more of it. The thing to do is to have a judicial enquiry into this, and announce it before Parliament meets." And I thought he was quite convinced about this. In fact, he said he would.

I didn't come back until just before Parliament opened, and I was horrified to discover that Cardin had not liked this idea and that he'd decided not to do it. I was desolated because I had never been more prescient about anything in my life than I was about that. I just knew that we were going to be battered almost beyond endurance. I don't like to boast about how wonderful I was, but I think this is once when my judgement was right. If my advice had

been followed, I think there would never have been any
Munsinger.

BRYCE MACKASEY

I spoke to Mr. Pearson on several occasions about Spencer, that
he should be given a hearing. Finally I made a speech in the House
expressing some doubt about the government denying an
insignificant Canadian the right to a trial.

I can remember brooding about it and saying, "Well, I've
caused this embarrassment in the government. So what?" But
events started to move rather rapidly in the Spencer case. And I
remember going down the hall to Pearson's office, and I ran into
Pierre Elliott Trudeau. And he said, "Where are you going?" I
said, "I'm going to resign as Parliamentary Secretary," which
I was then. He said, "Well, I'll go with you and I'll resign as
well, because I felt what you felt." All we got was a good
tongue-lashing—if Mr. Pearson wanted our resignation he'd ask
for it, something of that nature.

*Friday, March 4, 1966, was a climactic day in Parliament and resulted
in probably the most serious crisis the Pearson Government experienced. It
was the day David Lewis of the NDP informed the House that he had a
telegram from George Victor Spencer stating that he did want a hearing. It
was then that Mr. Pearson decided to reverse the government's position and
allow an enquiry.*

DAVID LEWIS

After I had demanded an enquiry into the Spencer case, Jean
Marchand said, "You're making the demand; you don't even
know whether he wants a board. What right has the government
to appoint a board? What right have you to demand a board, if
Spencer doesn't want one?"

That sounded sensible to me. So I got on a long-distance phone
to Vancouver and spoke to Spencer's lawyer. The result was that I
received a telegram, which I had got over the phone, that indeed
he wanted an arbitration. And I rushed down to the floor of the
House with the telegram—I forget what rule I got on my feet to

read it. Pearson was there and said, "I'll tell you what. I'm going to telephone Spencer to ascertain whether he really wants a board myself. And the Honourable Member for York South is welcome to listen on an extension of that phone."

Those weren't the exact words but that was the effect of them. I was flabbergasted, and I remember saying something to the effect, "If I can't trust my country's Prime Minister to tell me the truth about a telephone conversation, we are really in bad shape. I'm not getting on any extension to monitor what you say."

Imagine the Prime Minister saying to a Member, "Get on the telephone with me to make sure that I am telling the truth!" This again underlined the kind of person Pearson was. Some people interpreted it as great weakness on his part. I'm not at all sure that it wasn't great shrewdness on his part. If I had agreed to listen to the telephone, he could say, "You see, he had all the rights and everything." If I didn't agree, as I didn't because I just wasn't going to put myself in that position of indignity of listening at a telephone, then he could say, "Well, I offered it to him." So I'm not so sure it wasn't negotiating shrewdness as well as incredible weakness.

JEAN MARCHAND

It's very difficult to understand, for a man like me, when I saw Pearson in the House asking the Leaders of the Opposition, Diefenbaker and David Lewis, to come to his office [and listen] on two phones while he would talk to the spy—how could you explain that? I was at the head of the labour movement and I would never have done that in my life! The only way to explain that was the temperament of the man. He thought, "If I can get everybody together by doing this, let's do it." I don't say that he didn't have principles because he was a man of principle; there is no doubt about that. He was an honest man and so forth. But outside that, he thought that all principles were quite flexible, and he was adapting them to the specific situation he was dealing with.

GORDON CHURCHILL

The Minister of Justice, Cardin, came into the House when the questions were being asked about Spencer and he refused to have the enquiry. He staked his future on it. He just would not give ground. He was being absolutely firm. And he had no sooner taken his seat than Mr. Pearson came in, and without speaking to Mr. Cardin or anyone else, stood up and announced that there would be an enquiry. He had received a letter from the NDP and pressure from them. He pulled the rug right out from under Cardin, and Cardin immediately submitted his resignation. It took about twenty-four hours of pressure on him by his friends to get him to withdraw it. Why Mr. Pearson did that, I don't know.

BRYCE MACKASEY

One of the rationalisations for not giving [Spencer] a trial was that he hadn't requested one, and I think Davie Lewis got up and said he had. Mr. Pearson and I talked about it, and he said, "Bryce, my instincts were the same as yours right from the begining. I let them overrule me in the Cabinet, persuade me", or whatever.

That afternoon we met, some of us, in the lobby. There was hostility toward me. It didn't bother me. Mr. Pearson called me over and he said, "What do you think?" And I said, "I think that you've got to reverse your position and give the man a trial on the strength of the fact that he has asked for one." He went away with Allan MacEachen and came back about twenty minutes later. I remember telling him I thought enough to resign if he stuck to his position. And he said, "Don't worry because it's going to work out just the way you want it, the way I want." And he even got up that day and reversed himself.

The reaction was immediate. There was open hostility to me. On Tuesday the Quebec caucus met, as it often did on Tuesday nights, with particular hostility from a lot of the Members. I defended Pearson, which wasn't easy to do, and what I succeeded in doing was to turn the hostility towards myself. I was what you might say "sent to Coventry" for about three months. In fact, it's happened to me many times. I just was determined I was not going to let it bother me—although it did, of course.

ALLEN MacEACHEN

I heard the Opposition making a plea for a hearing for this man who was dying of cancer. The man who made a very impressive speech was David Lewis. I went to the Prime Minister's office and said to him that I wouldn't want him as Prime Minister to have disregarded a human-rights issue, and that he really ought to consider appointing the enquiry. He said, "Well, of course, we can do it." He said, "We have to talk to Cardin."

I talked to Cardin and the Prime Minister talked to Cardin and my recollection is that Cardin accepted the idea of the enquiry. That is my recollection. Subsequently, the press reacttion and the reaction of the Quebec caucus was that the Prime Minister pulled the rug out from under Cardin. I have never accepted that interpretation.

LAWRENCE PENNELL

I had just finished making a speech in defence of Mr. Cardin's position, and I had given considerable thought to it. After delivering the speech, I sat down, and I had barely leaned back when I received a message that the Prime Minister would like to see me. I went to the Prime Minister's office, and Mr. Cardin was there. Mr. Pearson said, "You may be somewhat upset about this, Larry, but I'm going to inform the House that we will have some sort of enquiry into Mr. Spencer's complaint, his position and so forth. What is your reaction going to be to that?" And I said, "Well, if that's what you wish, that's what will be."

I know the press then carried the story that I was probably resigning, but it never even crossed my mind. It didn't disturb me at all, really. But I had thought that I'd made a very effective speech, if I may be forgiven and not disfigure these remarks with egotism, and I was rather proud of it. I was pleased that I had the opportunity to get it into Hansard. So I didn't feel let down particularly.

Later that day Cardin came to the conclusion that he could not continue as Justice Minister after the Prime Minister had given in to the Opposition in the way he had done. Maurice Lamontagne was not in the House that Friday and it was not till the following Monday, March 7, 1966, that he found out that the government was in serious trouble. After their resignation Lamontagne and Walter Gordon shared a desk — they called it the penalty box — in the front row but away from the treasury benches.

Both were writing books: Lamontagne was preparing a second edition of his book on federalism while Gordon was working on another of what he called his small books; he had shown Lamontagne a few chapters and they had agreed to meet and go over them that day.

MAURICE LAMONTAGNE

I arrived there that afternoon for the question period and immediately Jean Marchand came to my desk and said, "Well, I'll probably resign as a Minister this afternoon." I said "What?!" He said, "Can we see each other in the afternoon?" I said, "Yes. I have to see Walter and I'll manage to see you perhaps at dinnertime. Is it all right?" He said, "Yes."

I didn't know what was happening at all. I saw Walter and then I came back in the House. It was about four-thirty or five o'clock. Guy Favreau and Bud Drury came to my desk and they said, "Could you come along with us?" We went into Guy Favreau's office. Then they started to tell me the story, and they said, "Well, this is terrible because there has been this meeting between Cardin and Mr. Pearson. Apparently there was some kind of confusion there, but in any case, now that Mr. Pearson has changed his mind, Mr. Cardin has decided to resign, and if he resigns then Léo Cadieux and a few others from Quebec will do the same, including Marchand"—and then I understood the story that Marchand had told me.

JEAN MARCHAND

We had had Lamontagne and Favreau, and there was Cardin involved [in trouble]. Who was asked to defend this policy before the House? And who did it? And at the last moment Mr. Pearson decided just to drop it. So I was furious like hell, there's no doubt about that. And I said, "Well, if this is the way you're going to do business of course, I'm surely not [going to be around]." It's Cardin himself who would decide because I said, "If you resign on this, you're going to have my full support. But I'm not going to resign if you don't."

MAURICE LAMONTAGNE

They told me that they had tried to talk to Cardin without any success and they had come to the conclusion that I might be helpful. I said to them, "You should be the last ones to ask me to do that after what happened to me [in resigning]."

At about seven o'clock in the evening I called Mr. Pearson and said, "This is none of my business but I am with Guy Favreau and Bud Drury and they feel that I could probably be useful if I could speak to Cardin." Mike told me, "That would be most helpful, I'm sure." I said, "I'm prepared to do so, especially if you tell me that this will be useful, but I don't know where he is. I have been trying to get him on the phone without any success." He said, "Well, he's coming to 24 Sussex this evening at eight o'clock. Why don't you come along with Favreau?" I said, "Okay."

We went there. Both Favreau and Mr. Pearson left me in the small library so I could be alone with Cardin when he arrived. When he saw me there, Cardin started to laugh and he said, "I know the purpose of your presence here: to try to convince me not to resign. After what they have done to you, you should be the last one to be here." I said, "Well, this is life, and we have to forget."

He said, I know also what you will tell me—that I should not resign for the good of the country and all this." I said, "Well, that was what I was about to tell you." He said, "Don't forget that I was born in the United States." Certainly he was in an emotional state, and I'm sure he would not have said that very seriously. But after about twenty minutes I saw that there was no way to convince him, at least that night, so I went out of the library and met Mr. Pearson and Favreau, and I told them, "I didn't have any success, and I think my business here is over, so I'm leaving." I left and they remained, the three of them.

On my return to the Parliament Buildings, I saw Marchand. It was later than we had anticipated, but Marchand confirmed all these things and he told me, "After what has been done to you and to Tremblay and all the others, I will not tolerate going through another period like this. If Cardin goes, I'll go, and I won't be alone." He was mad too. I said, "There's no necessity for you to go. After all, you don't know Cardin very well. You'd never met him until you became a Member of Parliament." He said, "It's a matter of principle, and I've decided to go." I realised then that it was really serious, but I felt that I had done what I could.

The next day, all kinds of discussions continued but without any substance. At about six o'clock in the evening or seven o'clock—I don't remember exactly—on Tuesday evening I received a call from Mary Macdonald telling me that Mr. Cardin was having dinner with Mr. Pearson at 24 Sussex, and he had brought his letter of resignation, and that was it. She asked me whether I was prepared to make a last effort. I said, "If you think that this is acceptable and useful, I am prepared." I waited for an hour and a half or so, and then I think it was Mrs. Pearson who phoned me, telling me that Cardin had just left 24 Sussex and had agreed to come to my office. I had phoned Marchand. The press was always following Cardin but I had a very small and isolated office on the third floor just above the Speaker's apartment, and Cardin succeeded in coming without being noticed. I decided that I would invite Marchand to come to my office, and Walter Gordon.

WALTER GORDON

Lamontagne said that Cardin was going to resign and if he did, Marchand would go too, and that meant that practically all the French Canadian Ministers would go. Mike couldn't let that happen, and Mike would have to go and we'd have to pick a new Leader in a hurry. So would I come and help him talk Cardin out of it. Well, I said, "God, I am not a member of the government. Surely this is a Quebec thing." "No," he said, "you and Cardin hit it off, so come along." So I did, and there were the three of us and Marchand.

MAURICE LAMONTAGNE

I organised the scenario, and when we were all together, I said to Cardin, "I think that you and Marchand have a few things to say to each other. Of course, Walter and I are outside of it. We are interested in the Liberal Party and maintaining the government, but that's not for us to decide; it's for you, both of you."

So Cardin started to speak to Marchand and to tell him, "I've been in politics now for fifteen years. I've done my job. I'm tired, I'm fed up, I want to do other things in life. Let me go. Because after all, you people have been saying for months now that you would do miracles in Ottawa. You have just arrived, and you want to resign. Why? Leave me in peace, and let me go." He pushed and pushed. Marchand was always saying, "This has happened to these guys; I don't want this to happen to anybody else," and all this. But I think that in the course of the conversation, when Cardin saw that Marchand was quite determined to leave, that shook him a little bit.

I said to Marchand at that stage, "I think you might go now, and we'll remain with him." I asked Walter, after Marchand left, to speak to Cardin. Cardin had a very great admiration for Walter, and I think he listened very carefully to what Walter had to say—which was more or less the same message as mine. Then Walter left, and I remained alone with him [Cardin].

I told him, "You have a very serious responsibility on your shoulders." Cardin was supposed to have said to Mr. Pearson when he told him that he was now prepared on the basis of human rights and all this to have an enquiry, "Okay, you're the boss," and then left. Apparently "Okay, you're the boss" [did not mean] "Okay, make your own decision and I'll make mine, and I'll resign." So there was that kind of confusion. I was always coming back to this with Cardin and I said, "I think that you have made a mistake too. In your conversation with Mr. Pearson, you should have gone on and said, 'Okay, you're the boss; but if you take that decision, I'll resign.' But you never said that to the Prime Minister."

Then I said, "As a result of that confusion, are you prepared to face the future, to see the Pearson Government go down and somebody else come? You'll have to live with that for the remainder of your life. And unfortunately now, as you can see, your destiny is linked with Marchand and a few others, and indirectly perhaps but in a very real sense you will also be responsible for the termination of the political careers of these people. Will you be prepared to live with this?" I was always coming back to this.

So at about two o'clock in the morning he said, "Okay, Maurice, I'll stay." We shook hands, and I had just a little bit of rye in my office, and we both took a drink and left.

At about nine-thirty the next morning, it was the morning of the caucus, on Wednesday [March 9] I asked to see Mr. Pearson in his office, and of course I was granted an interview much more quickly than even when I was a Minister. I told him about the previous evening, and I said, "Everything is solved. You're safe now." Mike began to cry a little bit. I said, "Can I recall our conversation of December 1965 and remind you of what I told you at that time—that they would eventually go and seek to get your head?" And he said, "Yes, I remember." And I said, "I was not expecting at that time, though, that I would be the one to save your head." We shook hands.

ALLAN MacEACHEN

I went to [Pearson's] office in the morning before he went to caucus. He was sitting behind the flower in his lapel and very relaxed, and I raised the question of the caucus and said, "You know it is going to be difficult." He said, "Well, Allan, they think they have me in a trap. But I am not staying in any trap." Maybe he knew Cardin wasn't going to resign, but he didn't say that to me. But he had fixed in his own mind at least his solution to the question. Certainly it worked all right.

But it was a bad caucus for him. It was the first time that I ever heard it suggested that the Prime Minister consider leaving his post because his days were numbered or his months were numbered.

MAURICE LAMONTAGNE

I rushed to the Quebec caucus, which was in arms. They were all prepared for revolt. And Cardin wasn't there. The main caucus was starting at about eleven o'clock. I was not able to say anything at that time about my conversation with [him]. I kept saying, "Be patient, wait until Mr. Cardin comes in." Then, fortunately, he came in and announced his decision to the Quebec caucus. That was a great relief, and everybody started to applaud.

Then we went to the national caucus, and again Cardin made his statement, and Mike spoke, and there was unity again. And after the caucus we went to Cardin's office just next to the caucus room—with Mr. Pearson and Guy Favreau. And we opened a bottle of champagne.

It was on March 4, during the heated debate on the Spencer case, that Cardin blurted out the word "Monseigneur," which he said was his mispronunciation of "Munsinger." Actually the revelation of the Munsinger case that day came before the events that led to Pearson's agreeing to the demands for an enquiry into the Spencer case and Cardin's subsequent decision to resign. The Friday sitting of Parliament began with Opposition Leader John Diefenbaker attacking the Justice Minister for his handling of the spy issue and repeating his charges of evasion and deception. Cardin fought back and asserted that Diefenbaker should be the very last person to give advice on a security case. Then he challenged "the right honourable gentleman to tell the House about his participation in the Monseigneur case when he was Prime Minister."

At the time it was reported that Guy Favreau had prompted him with the word "Munsinger," which would indicate that Lucien Cardin didn't know much about the case. However, there was so much noise in the Chamber that it was difficult to make out an aside such as this; furthermore, Cardin said that he was absolutely sure that nobody had whispered Munsinger to him — he had mispronounced the name because he had never seen it written but he knew all about the case.

At the time of the Rivard scandal in 1963 Prime Minister Pearson had asked the RCMP for "information indicating any impropriety or anything of a scandalous nature involving any MP or any party over the last ten years," and the Munsinger file was delivered to him at the beginning of December 1964. This was Canada's own "Sex and Security" scandal, involving the liaison of Diefenbaker's Associate Defense Minister, Pierre Sévigny, with Gerda Munsinger, a good-looking German woman of dubious background. The RCMP had not proved that there had been any security leak, and Diefenbaker had reprimanded Sévigny but had not dismissed him from his Cabinet post. After reading the file, Mr. Pearson had written a letter to Mr. Diefenbaker expressing concern that, as Prime Minister, he had taken no action in the matter. Gordon Churchill had advised the Opposition Leader on how to react to this letter. The Munsinger file remained in the Prime Minister's office for more that a year before it was turned over to the Solicitor General, Larry Pennell.

GORDON CHURCHILL

The allegation was that this was a security case, this Munsinger case, which it wasn't. Mr. Pearson wrote a letter to Mr. Diefenbaker outlining what he proposed doing, and said, "Now, if you have any information to supply, you might let me know."

Mr. Diefenbaker called me down immediately to his home, and I said, "Don't write a letter of reply to it. Put nothing in writing. Go and see him and tell him that you got the letter and that you quite approve of the idea 'provided you extend the investigation to twenty years and not just ten'." I said, "That should scare him off." So Mr. Diefenbaker did that, and Pearson held back then for quite some time.

But he got the RCMP to produce the Munsinger file, and kept it in the Privy Council Office for fifteen months or so. The Liberals were going to make use of it in the 1965 election campaign, and didn't, and then raised it in the House and had the enquiry and all that terrible garbage. What good did it do? They were trying to destroy Diefenbaker. But it didn't destroy him and it cast doubt on Mr. Pearson's judgement. It was most unfortunate.

T. C. DOUGLAS

I think a Prime Minister is perfectly justified—and so is the Minister of any department—in saying, has there been any conduct in past years by previous governments, including my own political party, where national security has been endangered, or where there's been any question about propriety with respect to handling public funds and public property. That's one thing that I think is legitimate, perfectly legitimate.

I think it's not legitimate to say to the RCMP or any other group within the government, "You do a research job and see if you can dig up any dirt on our political opponents." It seems to me that this is an improper use of the security forces of the country and of the administrative machinery of the government. If you push it far enough you get a Watergate, inevitably, and all this coming out in the United States now about the horrendous things which the FBI did, including spying on the president and spying on the members of cabinet and keeping dossiers on all the members of important congressional committees, so they could use it if they got into trouble. Let's face it, this has been done for years, always I suppose under the guise of security. But it's a different thing, I think, for a Prime Minister to say, go out and deliberately get me anything you can that I can keep in my top drawer against the possibility that I may need it as a counterpunch.

LAWRENCE PENNELL

The [Munsinger] file was brought to my office. I never opened it, I never looked at it. I wanted to be able to stand in the House and say I'd never seen it, and I never did. I never touched it and never opened it, and I did not speak in the Munsinger affair.

Did Lester Pearson agree to let Lucien Cardin strike back at John Diefenbaker by revealing the contents of the Munsinger file? Was this a condition of his withdrawing his resignation? Certainly many Conservatives believed that it was, and Erik Nielsen and Davie Fulton are quoted as saying so in my book, Diefenbaker: Leadership Lost. *Fulton criticised it as a very weak decision to placate Cardin. However, Maurice Lamontagne maintained that there was no such deal and asserted that he was more at the centre of decision with regard to Cardin than the Prime Minister; Lamontagne said that he had never raised the Munsinger case with Cardin because he didn't even know about it. And Cardin himself, in describing how he got little or no sleep Wednesday night agonising over what he was going to say at the press conference on Thursday, March 10, 1966, said that he knew that Mr. Pearson did not want the Munsinger case to be divulged (see* Diefenbaker: Leadership Lost, p. 151).

Whether or not Cardin had actually seen the Munsinger file, Guy Favreau and others had seen it and wanted to raise the issue long before Cardin blurted out "Monseigneur" in Parliament. At the time Walter Gordon had told them that if they did, he would resign from the government, that he hadn't come to Ottawa to get involved in that kind of dirty stuff. However, he excused Cardin, whom he described as a gutty little guy, for letting it out because he was being badgered to death. On February 24, 1966, Guy Favreau had called Davie Fulton to his office and warned the former Justice Minister that, if the Conservatives continued attacking Cardin over the Spencer affair, there might be developments that the Tories would regret. Fulton took this to mean that there was pressure on the Liberals to expose the Munsinger thing, as he put it (see Diefenbaker: Leadership Lost, p. 147).

At the press conference on Thursday, March 10, 1966, Lucien Cardin mixed information and misinformation about the Munsinger case, which he described as worse than Britain's Profumo sex and security scandal; he said that Gerda Munsinger had died of leukemia in East Germany; and he admitted to a working arrangement between the Prime Minister and himself and other Cabinet Ministers as to what they were going to do. Then, the Justice Minister outlined the charges he was making against John Diefenbaker in a sworn affidavit and a letter to Prime Minister Pearson.

The Toronto Star found that Gerda Munsinger was alive and well and working in a bar in Munich; the news caused another angry outburst in Parliament, during which Gordon Fairweather described Cardin as a frustrated Minister who wanted to commit hara-kiri and was willing to take other people down with him. After a short but heated debate an enquiry was ordered and Mr. Justice Wishart Spence of the Supreme Court of Canada was appointed a one-man commission to look into the Munsinger case. David Lewis felt that, if a judge had to be involved in such an investigation, it should have been another one. Pierre Sévigny admitted to the liaison with Gerda Munsinger but angrily denied that he had betrayed any secrets. (His side of the story is recounted at length, in his own words, in Chapter 9 of Diefenbaker: Leadership Lost.*) Davie Fulton agreed that Sévigny, with his distinguished war record—he had lost a leg in action — was not a security risk; there was no security involved and it was no more than a sex scandal. Pierre Sévigny was the main victim of Lucien Cardin's revenge, but the Munsinger case did nobody any good and certainly redounded to the discredit of those who had resurrected it for political purposes.*

DAVID LEWIS

Of all the judges [Prime Minister Pearson] could have chosen, he chose Spence. If I had been in his place, I'd have taken a man like [Emmett] Hall, in the absolute confidence that he would be fair. Because Hall would call it as is. And there were others in the Supreme Court of Canada whom one could have confidence in [regarding] their absolute objectivity. Now, Spence was undoubtedly objective within his framework, but he was so much a Liberal. A really smart politician would have appointed an ex-Tory, unless he didn't have a case, unless he knew his case was darned poor.

LAWRENCE PENNELL

When the big debate was on about setting up the commission under Spence, I was attending the Commonwealth Attorney

Generals' Conference in the U.K. LaMarsh is in error in her book when she makes the suggestion that I put forward the name of Justice Spence. I was in the U.K. at the time, and I know who did suggest it; I'm not going to say, but I certainly had no part in it and had nothing to do with it. I went down to Canada House to find out what was happening myself. So that indicates my knowledge of the decision to set up the Spence Commission.

I'm very much against [a Supreme Court Justice heading a political enquiry]. One might say that I'm now using the wisdom of hindsight, but had I been there I would have very much opposed the Spence Commission. I think that it's not for the judiciary to pass judgement on political decisions. Whether the government acted rightly or wrong, that's for the people to pass the ultimate decision at the ballot box. And so I think that it was perhaps not the most prudent approach. I'll put it that way. I would not have recommended any justice doing a commission as to whether a government had acted properly or not, in that particular instance, whether the Minister should have been relieved of his duties or not. That was a decision for the government to make.

J. W. PICKERSGILL

I don't think the fact that he was a Supreme Court judge makes any difference. Whether you should appoint a judge at all — I would be inclined, on the basis of these experiences, to say, No.

DAVID LEWIS

Personally, I thought that the Liberals were lower than low in raising it. I think it was one of the shabbiest pieces of political skulduggery that I have known in my life — not the Munsinger case but the Liberals using it the way they did. I'm not sure that Diefenbaker was wise in jumping at it, in not ignoring it, but then Diefenbaker is not likely to ignore anything like that. So it's asking for the moon to suggest that. I had no use at all for what the Liberals did in that situation. I think they knew the truth, I think they knew that Sévigny had been indiscreet, but they also knew that it didn't affect the security of Canada. I can't imagine that rather ineffective person, Sévigny, affecting the security of anything. So he dallied, but they knew perfectly well that it had nothing to do with Canada's security. I'm sure they also knew that the Munsinger dame was much closer to being a prostitute than to being a spy.

I have great respect for the Soviets and I have great respect for what they do, for their competence, and I'm sure Pearson did, and to imagine that the Soviets would use a woman like Munsinger in the way they suggested was crazy. And I'm sure Pearson knew it was crazy. So that I had absolutely no use for what the Liberals did, and it ended up in nothing. It was a whimper. Even the judge's report, which was really scandalous — Diefenbaker was absolutely right in raising the roof over it. You know, it was a dead issue. Digging into the past over somebody's peccadillo! What the devil good does that do Canada or Canadians?

DOUGLAS FISHER

If I look back now at what I think was the most shocking of the scandals in terms of there really being nothing there, it was the one the Liberals created themselves. It was the Munsinger thing with Sévigny. There's no way you can look back on that and take it with enormous seriousness. I mean, the enormity of what Sévigny did was naught, really. And Pearson was stupid to let that thing roll out. And it was a French Canadian, Cardin, who released it. And it really hurt most of all, I suppose, Sévigny, who was another French Canadian. He was gone. There was no point. It was just silly. On reflection, Diefenbaker behaved, I thought, fairly well; and I think Davie Fulton, who in a sense was the key guy—he wasn't satisfied with the way Diefenbaker handled the Munsinger thing, but he went along with it.

You just can't see it in perspective as being terribly responsible. It sounds to me very much like Pickersgill put the cast around that interpretation, that he convinced some of the Liberal Cabinet Ministers that here they were sitting on a bomb that they could throw at Diefenbaker that would blow him up. Instead, all it did was make the whole political scene look bad, and French Canada in particular. Who emerged when that came out as having the mistress and all that stuff was another French Canadian. It was kind of an irony.

On May 18, 1966, a real bomb blast shook the Parliament Buildings. Jack Nicholson, who was then Minister of Labour, was on his feet answering an Opposition question when he was interrupted by a terrific noise, as he described it; his first reaction was that a boiler had exploded. He never finished his sentence because the House of Commons was adjourned immediately. The bomb had gone off in a lavatory above Nicholson's office and the blast was severe enough to knock an oil painting on loan from the National Gallery and break off a corner. It killed Paul Joseph Chartier; only minutes before he had asked somebody to keep his seat in the public gallery opposite the Speaker's Throne while he went to the toilet. It was assumed that he was priming the bomb when it went off and that he had intended to throw it into the Chamber. I remember the incident well because I had returned to the Parliament Buildings from the Spence Commission hearings on the Munsinger case to find the corridors full of smoke.

It was not till April 4, 1967, some six months after Mr. Justice Spence delivered his report, that Lucien Cardin left the government as his first step to retirement from politics; he was not a candidate in the 1968 election. On the same day Guy Favreau resigned as President of the Privy Council for reasons of health. Cardin was replaced as Justice Minister by Pierre Elliott Trudeau.

II The French Solution

THERE HAD BEEN promises enough about increasing bilingualism. Back in February 1965 the preliminary report of the Royal Commission on Bilingualism and Biculturalism had warned that Canada was "passing through the greatest crisis in its history" and that something had to be done urgently to prevent the country from breaking up. That something, in the context of the commission's terms of reference, was to give bilingualism a real meaning. Maurice Lamontagne, when he made his maiden speech in the House of Commons on June 25, 1963, had said that the government wouldn't wait for the recommendations of the B and B Commission, which hadn't been appointed then, before taking action. He had described their goal as "perfect equality for the two official languages" in the Ottawa administration "as soon as possible." Yet, it was not till April 6, 1966, that Prime Minister Pearson announced that his government had taken the first steps to make the federal civil service bilingual.

In his statement to Parliament Mr. Pearson said that it was important that all Canadian citizens, whether English-speaking or French-speaking, should have a fair and equal opportunity to participate in the national administration and to feel at home in Ottawa, the national capital. To that end, the government had adopted a number of measures that would make it possible, within a reasonable length of time, for both languages to be used within the civil service and to allow for

309

communications with the public in either English or French. Up to then, the working language in almost all government departments had been English, and communication with the public, even in Quebec, had been mainly in English. Beginning in 1967, university graduates recruited for the civil service would have to be bilingual or be willing to acquire a reasonable proficiency in both official languages; by 1975, promotion would depend on bilingual proficiency or willingness to acquire it. However, Mr. Pearson pointed out that bilingualism was required only for positions where a need existed for both languages, and did not apply to technical, professional, and scientific categories. A great effort would be made to teach civil servants French, and the present program of language training would be strengthened and expanded. The Prime Minister also said that "each year some twenty English-speaking civil servants from the most senior categories, plus their families, will spend a twelve-month period in a mainly French-speaking city, while some ten French-speaking civil servants and their families will spend a similar period in a mainly English-speaking city, to study the other official language and gain an understanding of the cultural values of the group they are visiting."

Mr. Pearson gave assurances that the merit system would be maintained, and asserted that "bilingualism must be introduced gradually over a period of years in a manner which will not lead to injustice or misunderstanding," and that "the careers of civil servants who are not bilingual and who have devoted many years of their lives to the service of their country must not be prejudiced in any way by measures to develop bilingualism." Opposition Leader Diefenbaker, while welcoming the objective of the Prime Minister's statement, dismissed the assurances as so many pious words. Mr. Diefenbaker said that there had to be greater guarantees "that those who are today in the civil service will not, as a result of changes made after their entry into the civil service, be prejudiced in any way."

There was a lot of discussion in the Cabinet on the subject of bilingualism, of making the civil service bilingual, and, according to Mitchell Sharp, Lester Pearson was impressed by the views of his French Canadian Ministers, Guy Favreau, Maurice Sauvé, and the newcomer Jean Marchand, who had been on the B and B Commission. (Maurice Lamontagne, the original advocate of the bilingual policy, was no longer a member of the Cabinet.) All of the Ministers were in favour of the promotion of bilingualism with one notable exception.

PAUL HELLYER

I don't think at that stage that there was an adequate realisation of what the full consequences might be. When you're talking about something in the abstract, it's quite different than looking back on it and saying there was no way that we could have foreseen precisely how this would develop. And don't forget that Mr. Pearson, in all of those discussions, always talked about the safeguards. No one's career would be put in jeopardy. Well, how can you argue with that kind of policy? If it's not going to hurt anyone, and it's going to help somebody else, who can be against it? So I think that was the general tone of the discussions at the time that the policies were being evolved.

E. J. BENSON

Mr. Pearson was the first one to really have a French presence in the Cabinet. And as part of this [plan] trying to get Quebeckers to look away from Quebec City and look to Ottawa, the capital of their country, he felt that there needed to be communication in their own language with Ottawa. And thus he developed the scheme that at least the senior public servants and those in day-to-day contact with Quebeckers should have the ability to communicate in both languages.

Personally, I was very sympathetic to this. There are so many people in Canada who just can't comprehend that there are a great many people in Quebec that don't speak English. It seems un-thinkable to them. But all you have to do is to go fifty miles east of the Ottawa River in the bush, and there are lots of people there that can't speak English. They had no grounds or basis of communication with the government in Ottawa. They looked automatically at Quebec City. Mr. Pearson felt that if we were going to hold the country together he had to start changing the attention, the focus, from Quebec City to Ottawa on national matters at least, on matters that fell within the federal jurisdiction.

LAWRENCE PENNELL

It was my understanding that this was a start. He said, "Government's got to give an example. If government doesn't lead, who does? And that's one of the matters we have to concern ourselves with—bilingualism." And I think he took that as the starting place. He was well aware that he was going to receive a lot of criticism for it, and he said, "This is going to be very difficult to handle politically." He was aware of it and he said, "It may very well hurt us at the polls." But my impression is that this was merely a starting place for him.

J. R. NICHOLSON

I was born in northern New Brunswick and so many of my friends had French as their mother tongue, I felt that there were inequities that had to be corrected. One or two others from different parts of Canada felt differently, but there was never any serious disagreement in the Cabinet.

Maurice Sauvé was the notable exception to those in favour of bilingualism.

MAURICE SAUVÉ

Mr. Pearson surveyed the Cabinet members on their reaction, and everybody was favourable, and I was the only one who was unfavourable. He had to insist that I should speak because I had not said a word. All the others were so enthusiastic that I felt it was not necessary for me to speak. But he noticed because I was sitting across the table from him. He wanted my views because I was a Quebecker. And he said, "What do you think about this?" I replied that I was opposed to this suggestion of his. He couldn't understand; he said, "You're a French Canadian, you're from Quebec; why wouldn't you support bilingualism in the civil service?"

I said, "I know your motives, I know your intentions are all good, but you won't achieve what you want to achieve through that. The consequences of this will be that you're going to have a large number of English-speaking Canadians learning French, and all or practically all of the French Canadians who are coming into the civil service are already bilingual, and you will increase competition for the better jobs in the civil service if you have this type of program. We now have a system whereby if you have two competent persons and one is bilingual and the other one is not bilingual, you give preference to the bilingual one, just the same as you give preference to a veteran."

And I said, "Many of the higher jobs in the civil service have been given to the French Canadian because he was bilingual. You will increase competition for the French Canadian and the net result will be that eventually you will have less French Canadians in the top civil service jobs, and that's not what you want to do." And I went on: "I don't think that this is the policy that you should follow. I think that if you want to have more French Canadians in the top civil service jobs, you'll have to appoint them to those jobs, especially the ones which are an appointment by order-in-council and the ones for which you are directly responsible."

I said, "I'm so much convinced of this—that what you're doing now will not bear any fruit, will not satisfy Quebeckers and will antagonise the rest of Canada—that I want for the first time my objection to this policy to be recorded in the Cabinet minutes."

J. W. PICKERSGILL

It seemed to me that if we really wanted to make French Canadians feel they were a genuine part of the country and not a tolerated minority, that we had to make the government functionally bilingual. Therefore, I was very much in favour of anything that would really work toward that end. But some of the ways it's been carried out perhaps would have disappointed Pearson in his own objectives. Mind you, Pearson was not an administrator. That was not his talent at all. And I don't think he would have perceived very readily just how you work out the mechanics of these things.

But I've always felt, for one thing, that far too much emphasis was placed on speaking the language. It seemed to me that what was really important is that if you go into an office and want to speak French, the person you're talking to, or someone that can be got readily—it doesn't have to be the very first person you accost but somebody who can be got readily so you don't have to wait for half an hour—will be able to understand you, and if you give him the document to read he'll be able to read it without sending it to the translation bureau. In other words, you will have a real bilingualism—not a total competence in one language or the other. A lot of this could have been achieved at very much less cost, and I think this was what Pearson originally really had in mind. I think that was one of the reasons why he emphasised, perhaps even overemphasised, the undertaking that this would not disturb the comfort and convenience of the unilingual Anglophone bureaucrats.

In making his announcement Prime Minister Pearson had indicated that the officials would be in charge of the bilingualism program in the civil service; a special secretariat within the Privy Council Office would be responsible for the implementation and development of the policy. Opposition Leader Diefenbaker wanted a debate in Parliament and regretted the way the government had allowed the Civil Service Act to be changed "by interpretation on the part of the Civil Service Commission." Maurice Lamontagne blamed the excessive zeal of the English-speaking civil servants for wrecking the bilingual policy. It was estimated that it cost the treasury between 70,000 and 100,000 dollars to support a Deputy Minister and his family on a year's language-training course. Tommy Douglas quoted one official as figuring 92,000 dollars to be the price for his year in Quebec City; he had no use for French in his job and had only six or seven years to go before retirement. The bilingual policy applied to government agencies and the CBC was busy spreading the French network across the country.

MAURICE LAMONTAGNE

When I left the Cabinet, the English-speaking bureaucrats or top civil servants took over. They became converted to the new faith, or the new national goal, and they went at it with a vengeance, with the vengeance of the newly converted.

I remember very well two persons—John Carson, whom I had appointed as chairman of the Civil Service Commission, and Gordon Robertson who was the clerk of the Privy Council Office at that time—they started to develop a scheme. I do not believe that this plan was developed by Ministers. It was developed by these people. They had the idea of buying twenty or twenty-five houses in Quebec City, about ten or fifteen in Toronto, and to send the top civil servants to these two cities to learn either French or English. It all started at that time without any, I think, ministerial control and without any idea of the political realities of the country.

These people had been civil servants most of the time, especially Gordon Robertson, who was a great man and a great friend of mine, but they didn't have any idea of the possible English-speaking backlash. They thought that the French-speaking Quebeckers were putting a very top priority on this. I think that they were wrong. The program started to develop, and the English-speaking Ministers were reluctant to protest because they didn't want to be identified as bigots, and the French-speaking Ministers were saying, "Well, gee, this is very nice and most acceptable."

This is how the whole program—this is my own interpretation—got out of hand and became completely unrealistic in the sense that we have disturbed the career of older civil servants who couldn't possibly become bilingual by going to a school to be immersed in French. When they had to go—and they were more or less forced to go—in their absence either they would be replaced by somebody else because their absence proved that they were relatively inefficient, or the department where they were functioned less efficiently.

I mentioned that Gordon Robertson had the idea of buying these houses in Quebec City. He was the top civil servant at that time. And he wanted to be the first to go to Quebec City, although he was already fluent in French. And I thought that because of the talents of Gordon Robertson, his strategic position, it was a loss of time and money. So I said in the caucus that day, denouncing the buying of these houses, that Gordon Robertson had received the highest scholarship that could be obtained throughout the world, because he was going there with his house and his full salary. And that determined the trend which developed later.

I don't think that the houses in Toronto were ever occupied; I don't know because most of the French-speaking people who had joined the civil service at that time were fluent in English. And they had agreed to go to Ottawa, but Toronto—they were quite reluctant to go into exile in Siberia. I think it was a very bad strategy and, until I'm proven wrong, I would say that this was developed by civil servants.

JEAN-LUC PEPIN

I can't comment on that, except to say that one could take exactly the opposite view and make as much sense. I've no reason not to believe that the top civil servants took these courses in Quebec, but the fact they did could have been justified by their eagerness to set a good example to the others at lower levels. People can very well say, "Well, if Robertson is convinced, as he appears to be, that bilingualism is the order of the day or is the thing of the future in this country, I might as well also [go along]."

JUDY LaMARSH

I think we threw an awful lot of money away in buying houses in Quebec and buying houses in Toronto or Ottawa or wherever they were, and taking senior civil servants out of their positions for a whole year and bundling them up and sending them off to other parts of the country to learn the language. I don't know how successful it ever was. I never heard Gordon Robertson speak French. And he was the Secretary of the Cabinet, and they sent him away for a year.

They stopped at the top, and I always thought it kind of unfair that Members could be there representing the people and didn't have to speak in both languages, and the civil servants had to. As a matter of fact, I've always had a funny feeling in my head, that if Diefenbaker had not brought in instantaneous translation in the House, the House might have become bilingual. But once that happened, it never did. Even the ones who were not lazy, who wanted to study French, didn't use it very often, except as a kind of parlour trick.

T. C. DOUGLAS

You give a bureaucrat an objective—see, this is what we ultimately hope to work toward—and he sits down and he draws a straight line from A to B. He has never learned the basic things that a politician has to learn and that is that you can only move as fast as people are willing to go with you, and in order to do that you must keep in constant touch with people. How far will they go? How much do they agree with? If they don't agree with you, explain why, and when you've finally persuaded them, then you move. You don't move until you've explained it. You take people with you. But these people say a straight line is the shortest distance between two points, so here we go and crash through and they've really, I think, set the whole idea of bilingualism back rather than helping it.

PAUL MARTIN

Perhaps there has been too much zeal in unnecessary places. I'll give you an example. We have now established a French television station in Windsor, where I live. I'm very happy; I worked hard for that. Long before the bilignual commission came into being, I was trying to get a French television station because we have a substantial Francophone population. Now we have a French television station and it's making a good impression; it's popularly received not only in Canada but, by the way, in the United States.

But they've also established a French television station in the city of London. When I heard that, I said, "No wonder we're having our problems with the bilingual program." The French population of the city of London is about 1 percent, if it's that large. You can understand, with the state of the Franco-Anglo relations in Canada, how provocative that kind of thing is. It's just absurd to have done that. Now the government didn't do that, I'm sure. These things are not done by the government. The corporation [CBC] is a private corporation, but I think the government should have been made aware of it, and not allowed that kind of decision to be made and promulgated.

ALVIN HAMILTON

When the civil servants got control of it, they simply made it a great patronage system for the civil servants, and that has really upset Canadians all across the country. The people in Lac St.-Jean, Quebec, have no opportunity to hear English spoken. Why should they have a bilingualism program stuck down there?

There are a few French Canadians in my constituency [Qu'Appelle, Saskatchewan], and you upset them terribly by putting in French-language television stations right in the middle of a 90-percent-English area which dominate the airwaves. It embarrasses these French Canadians. They've learned to speak English long ago because that's the *lingua franca* of Saskatchewan. They still go to their churches, they still speak French among themselves. They love to hear French, but it's very embarrassing to have all this pressure. They get along fine with their neighbours, and likewise the English-speaking people in Quebec in the Eastern Townships. They've learned to speak French in some measure.

But to take a group of people in Lac St.-Jean and say, "You bunch of people have to learn to speak English in case some Englishman asks for service in a federal department"—that's going a little far. And in all our border customs stations they have them filled with French Canadian people, where they never hear French from an American crossing over at all. It's just really a farce. I would say that the abuse of a worthwhile program has been one of the main divisive factors in Canada.

MAURICE LAMONTAGNE

I remember having quite an argument one evening with Doug Fullerton, who was so close to the position adopted by René Lévesque. I said to him, "You are a traitor to your own group, and you're more pro-French-speaking, you support the causes of French-speaking people or Quebeckers more than I do." But I think that Doug Fullerton was in that kind of movement, that kind of conspiracy of English-speaking bureaucrats to develop this program. If all these people had not been very honest and efficient and very devoted Canadians, I would be tempted to say that perhaps it was a conspiracy of the English-speaking bureaucrats to have the policy fail. But I don't say that because I know it's not true.

Aside from the inevitable extravagances, such as houses in Quebec City and Toronto, it would have taken a lot of money, in Ben Benson's view, to introduce another language to the Canadian civil service. Maurice Lamontagne never advocated this; all he wanted was an institute, as he called it, to which all officer recruits would have to go.

MAURICE LAMONTAGNE

My basic proposal would have been to set up an institute. The program of the institute would have been to have immersion courses in either of the two languages, of course. People would have stayed at the institute for about five months. All the graduates of universities, having secured a job in the federal service, would have had to go through that institute.

We will never make a Deputy Minister who doesn't know any French bilingual unless we are prepared to pay a terrific price, not only in terms of money but also in terms of manpower. So this was my proposal: let's make sure that the young graduates of universities coming into the federal service will be not only bilingual but will understand what Canada is about by having a good course on Canadian economic history, the sociology of cultures, the principles of political administration, and all this; because it's not good enough to learn a second language if you don't understand the culture. I know some English-speaking Canadians who can speak French quite fluently, and hate the French Canadians in French. This would not have been very expensive. I don't think it would have produced all kinds of side effects as well.

One of the problems we have in the civil service in recent years is that it's too big: people don't know each other anymore. I remember twenty-five years ago, everybody knew each other and we could phone each other in whatever departments we were, and we were on a friendly basis. This kind of co-existence in that institute for five months would have inevitably produced friendships and some kind of common background, which would have had quite a good effect on the morale and the working conditions of the whole civil service.

Then, as another proposal, it would have been quite easy to get elementary courses for those who have contact with the public—to teach a janitor working on an elevator here to learn how to say *oui* and *non,* and to learn a few words like *cinquième étage* and things like that. This would have been quite simple.

There was an ambivalent attitude on language training. The Pearson government wanted middle-aged civil servants, even postmen, to learn French—something that Lamontagne never proposed.

ERIC KIERANS

Around this time my wife and I were spending a weekend at the Seigneury Club, and on a Sunday afternoon a group of senior civil servants—I recognised one of them but he didn't recognise me, thank God—came down for lunch with their wives. My back was to them, and I was listening to one of the most hideous conversations that I've ever heard of, and it related to Mr. Pearson's efforts to instill some percentage of bilingualism in the civil service. Some of the statements that were being made were libelous, but that aside, I thought that these people are civil servants, they work for a government in a country that calls itself federal and has two official languages, and refuse to recognise the rights of at least 25 percent or 28 percent of the population. And it wasn't only that they refused to recognise it; they were bitterly hostile to it.

T. C. DOUGLAS

What does bother people is this feeling that it's being forced down their throat. They've got neighbours, postmen, people in ordinary walks of life, who tell them, "I'm being told by my superiors that's it's only a matter of time until I have got to either learn French or get off, and I'm fifty five years of age and there's no way I can learn French. I've enough trouble with English and I'm liable to be out of a job." And the whole insecurity in the Anglophone civil service has seeped down into every community, not just with senior civil servants but ordinary people—postal workers, customs officials, policemen, everybody. They've pushed the thing so hard.

GEORGE HEES

I have never opposed the idea [of bilingualism]. Now, from hindsight, it seems that trying to teach people in their fifties a second language is something that just doesn't come off. I think that the thing has been carried too far. I think it's been unfair to make it obligatory for somebody to be bilingual in order to become a Deputy Minister, which is in fact what is the case today. Because an awful lot of people who have done very well in the civil service, who were dedicated to it for thirty years, got up into their middle fifties and then were in fact denied the prize at the top, which is a deputy ministership. So in practice the whole idea of bilingualism has gone rather astray as far as the civil service is concerned. In theory and at the time when Mike Pearson brought it in, it looked fine. In practice, it hasn't worked out very well.

JEAN MARCHAND

It may look funny, but sometimes I had to tell him [Pearson] not to go too fast. Because as a great believer in bilingualism as far as Canada is concerned, at the same time I was thinking of the vested rights of the civil servants. That means that I always said, "Well, if I was representing those people in a union, I would fight like hell against this policy you're proposing." Because you don't come to a man who's been hired, say, twenty-five years ago, and who was not required to speak French or understand French, and, at the moment that he's going to get his last promotions before he retires, which are very important years, and you say, "Well, from now on you will have to speak a second language." I think that we're cheating. It's unfortunate not to have told those men at the beginning to be bilingual if they wanted to go to the top. But you cannot blame those persons themselves.

So this is the part where I played a role—it may look funny but I still believe the same thing. As strongly as I support bilingualism, as strongly I support the right of those who were never required to speak a second language, who never knew the rules of the game.

Walter Gordon described how the French-speaking Ministers did not want him to learn French, and Judy LaMarsh said that the working language of the Cabinet was English.

WALTER GORDON

I used to say to my friends in the Cabinet who were French and who were closer to me than most other people in the Cabinet, Favreau and Lamontagne and Marchand, "Tell me, do you want me to go and learn French? I'll go down and take a Berlitz course."

"God, no," they said. "So-and-so has done that. That doesn't mean he can communicate with us. You don't have to speak French." So the four of us would go and have lunch together, and I would say, "Now look, you so-and-sos, I am not going to go out and have lunch with you and then sit there silently while you all talk French. You have to speak English." "Oh certainly, Walter, we'll speak English."

Then we'd sit down at the table and they'd all start speaking French, and after awhile, I would say, "Now, look, you idiots, I don't recognise that kind of English, and apart from that you said so and so and so and so, and I don't go along with that. Don't think you can get away with that in my presence just because I don't speak French. I never said I didn't understand it." So we'd have a fine time, you see. Those days were quite different from now. They'd think this was very funny then.

JUDY LaMARSH

When we began, Lamontagne and Cardin and Favreau would occasionally speak French, and Tremblay, amongst themselves. I don't remember any Cabinet papers being presented ever in French. But that [French] disappeared, people just stopped using it. When Pierre Trudeau came in the Cabinet, he started again. He and Marchand would often speak French. But I don't remember that any of their papers were prepared in French either, for distribution to the Cabinet. But I remember Pierre talking to Marchand and others often in French, but kind of asides. It just never was the working language of the Cabinet. I wouldn't expect it is today.

Millions upon millions of dollars were spent in fruitless attempts to make a unilingual English-speaking bureaucracy bilingual. In the end, in order to fill the designated bilingual positions, of which there were more and more, French Canadians had to be recruited and given preference.

C. M. DRURY

A number of devices were sought [to have French spoken in the civil service]. One was to recruit more people whose native language was French so that those who had learned this new skill

[French] would have somebody natural on which to use it rather than two guys who'd been away for a year practising their French in a corner, which is just so bloody artificial and unreal that it just doesn't happen. We had an occasion when the Public Service Commission was out giving preference to Francophones, and this produced quite a howl. But the purpose of that was to establish a teaching framework, if you like, in the public service and not, as suggested by the Opposition, to give the Francophones the positions of power which they didn't really merit. Then, secondly, and at some expense, setting up these communicators in French in each department—at least they were French-speaking by nature, by mother tongue, to whom the Anglophones could have recourse to brush up on and keep on going with their English.

Now we haven't enlarged the number of Francophones as communicators because it is artificial, and hasn't been really as productive as one would hope. In this sense, the investment is not being made best use of, because we haven't got enough Francophones who'd like to talk French in the public service.

GÉRARD PELLETIER

We were trying to attract Francophones from all over the country, including Quebec, into the civil service. I think we haven't been as successful as I thought we should have been for a number of reasons that it would take too long to analyse. But there is progress on that account as well, and I think you could say now that there is a French—I wouldn't use the word "establishment" because it's pejorative—there is a Francophone milieu in Ottawa. You don't feel that you're isolated from your home base. There are lots of [French-speaking] people around, and in most departments, if you go to a reception or a cocktail party, you're not alone of your species.

TOM KENT

It almost seemed that every senior public servant had to spend a year or two being immersed in French or he had no future in the public service at all. Otherwise, people who were bilingual had enormous advantages, irrespective of all other considerations, for senior positions. There was a great deal of duplication going on in the public service in order to have a lot of people learning to be bilingual and yet have enough people to do the work. I don't think there is any doubt at all that, like so many things [that are] right, once begun, it got a sort of momentum of its own which was excessive. Everybody tried to do it too soon. So I don't think I would change at all the view that I think we all took at that time that it was right to move toward bilingualism in a real and definite way, but I think we assumed more gradualism than there has in fact been.

GORDON CHURCHILL

The waste of those millions of dollars attempting to teach adults the use of another language can't be defended at all. It's ridiculous. There are some adults who are adept at languages and can learn them readily. But with most adults, no. I think it upset the civil service terribly and it was a waste of time. When you really consider that a person with his family would be relieved from his normal duties to take a course in Quebec or some immersion course in the French language somewhere, and then returned to his job and find that he never had the opportunity to use it, it seems to me to be the height of folly. It's nice to have a second language and a third language, but it has to be done normally at a very early age. It's easy for young children to learn a second language.

But to try to transform the civil service into a bilingual service I think is ridiculous. And it's caused nothing but trouble, nothing but resentment. Anyone who objects to it is of course a bigot or a red-necked racist or something like that. It's something that arouses the emotions. People can't discuss it without getting a bit angry. But it's done nothing for Canada except create disunity, and intense disunity, which is unfortunate.

DOUGLAS FISHER

It was the advent of Marchand and Trudeau that began to accentuate it and led to all the bitterness we've lived with in Ottawa. Most of us who have any feel of the whole country don't give a goddam about Ottawa and what the civil servants feel. I mean, the civil servants of the federal apparatus are not Canada. But what you *do* have to feel about is the people. Now what's happened in Ontario, a province that has perhaps the most costly and expensive and thorough school system in the world for an area this big with this big a population? What's happened? French dropped right off in the high schools. Where school boards put it in in the grade schools in Ontario, it's been doing very well. But in high schools, a drop-off. Ontario universities? It's no longer a requirement. Well, what kind of fools sit here in Ottawa talking about bilingualism when that's happening?

GEORGE McILRAITH

I think that's a wrong use of public money. It offends my sense of trust to a taxpayer to use such volumes of money in such a way [year's immersion course in French]. If you took the money that was spent on one person for the winter—and remember, the program has been extraordinarily unsuccessful—if you took that, do you realise that would have provided two teachers for our schools here [in Ottawa] where they can't get teachers; they're begging for them. Those teachers would have taught probably eighteen or twenty [students] per class, and made them thoroughly bilingual, and you would have had thirty or forty children bilingual. That's where the development should go. In this area you've got the extraordinary situation of the confidence of the civil service being destroyed on this subject, at the same time as you have parents coming to you and asking and making representations: "Can you get any of this money that is being spent diverted to our school board or our school to provide a teacher, so that we can make our children bilingual or give them the full opportunity of becoming bilingual?" The policy has been accepted, but its application has been extraordinarily insensitive and inept—insensitive both to the use of the taxpayer's money and in regard to the handling of people and understanding of people.

JEAN LESAGE

I might as well say it. It is a personal opinion, and might not be shared by others, but I believe that governments should avoid legislating on two matters—very important matters—which are language and religion. The history of the world tells us that there always has been more harm than good that came out of any legislation touching either language or religion. These are things which are so personal, so deep inside each individual, that they are a very basic principle of individual freedom, which should not be touched by legislation.

On the other hand, that some facilities, in providing services to the people, should be offered to them in their language is part of that freedom to which they are entitled. So I am not that critical of the federal law on bilingualism. Maybe they pushed it too far. Maybe they pushed it too far in their efforts, but I believe that it is part of the exercise of the individual's freedom to be able to receive the services given by their country in their language. But to impose a language on an individual, this is denying his freedom. I hope I make myself clear on this distinction.

As Lester Pearson indicated, bilingualism in the federal public service was the first step toward increasing the use of bilingualism across the country or, as his followers were to put it, toward making the French Canadians feel at home from coast to coast. The Prime Minister had said, in his House of Commons statement, that the policy of making the government bilingual was based on the principle that "the achievement of bilingualism is in itself a desirable objective for any Canadian citizen." Thus, Mr. Pearson's announcement on April 6, 1966, led inevitably to the Official Languages Act under his successor, Pierre Elliott Trudeau, and the extraordinary effort to make Canada a bilingual country in fact as well as fancy. British Columbians and Newfoundlanders and other English-speaking Canadians who had never heard French spoken were to learn about French from bilingual packaging, bilingual signs, and the extension of the French television network. All of which was costly —but the cost was justified by the claim that this was needed to keep Quebec in Confederation.

But was that Pearson's motive in making what was admitted to be changes in the Canadian Constitution, the British North America Act? Jean Chrétien, who had been his Parliamentary Secretary, felt that he was just a good guy who wanted to be fair and that his aim was merely to make French Canadians feel that Ottawa was their national capital.

Jean-Luc Pepin was convinced that bilingualism was the unifying element that kept Canada together, and so was Jean Marchand, who was expressing the view of the Quebec triumvirate. Robert Satnfield and others believed that bilingualism was not the whole answer to holding the country together.

JEAN CHRÉTIEN

He [Pearson] was worried about separatism, but I don't recall that we discussed that in the light of bilingualism — the program of bilingualism was perhaps of a different context at that time. It was really to make the institution more acceptable to the Francophone and to develop a Canadian identity of which he was very preoccupied, and it is in that light that he fought for the flag and was talking about the national anthem and so on. He was very keen on developing a national image identity in which the Francophone can find a home more than before. At that time the separatist movement or the Quebec surge was a different kind. It was very much of a radical movement of the FLQ which was a guerilla-type organisation, people who were very Maoist in their outlook, and terrorists. I think that Mr. Pearson felt at the time that it would have been good to make Canadian Institutions more acceptable to the Francophone.

Yes, the desire that he had to see all Canadians learning both languages was very much in his mind, and he said that to me. He said it was crazy that we were not forcing all the kids to learn both languages.

JEAN MARCHAND

I think that even if he was not speaking French very fluently, he thought that it was a very important problem, and he made a very elaborate statement in the House on bilingualism — how it was going to be implemented and so forth. And I think that he was convinced that it was essential to the survival of this country. And it was according to his temperament and his culture, if I can say, because as a diplomat he was used to this kind of problem, this kind of tension, and he was working at them with passion and interest.

ROBERT STANFIELD

I believe that the policy of recognising that Canada is a bilingual country, the policy that offers English-French equality in the institutional sense, is essential. But I would like to equally emphasise that while bilingualism is essential, it's—for many Canadians—not a unifying factor, so that it would be nonsense to pretend that we can unify Canada on the principle or slogan of institutional bilingualism. We cannot. Bilingualism—the institution of bilingualism—is widely misunderstood. But quite apart from that, it's divisive for some Canadians, and if Mr. Pearson ever felt that he could unite Canada on bilingualism, that it would bring us all together, that's absurd. And that's been proven to be absurd. That's one thing that has been proven clearly—that it would be impossible to bring all Canadians together under a policy of bilingualism.

In other words, in summary, we have to have bilingualism to hold the country together but bilingualism by itself is not going to hold the country together.

ROBERT FOWLER

What is needed to hold this country together?—if it can be done, and I think it can. The essential problem I don't think is economic. I think it's political, cultural, strategic, and it's very much a question of attitudes and sympathies, understanding.

JEAN LESAGE

As far as bilingualism is concerned, the federal law really gives much more protection to the French minority in the other provinces. To the French-speaking people in Quebec, it doesn't apply very much. I believe everybody will realise that. So, as the Quebec premier, it was good as far as my interests for the minorities, the French-speaking minorities, outside Quebec are concerned, because I have always been really concerned about the faith of those pockets of French-speaking people outside Quebec. But as far as Quebec itself was concerned, this preoccupation of bilingualism was not the priority in my mind, as Premier of Quebec.

However, Maurice Sauvé and others were insistent that Quebec's problems were economic rather than cultural. And there were others, not all New Democrats, who believed that prosperity was the real cure for separatism.

MAURICE SAUVÉ

As long as our political leadership in Canada, at the federal level or at the provincial level, especially from Quebec, believe that our problems are cultural instead of being economic, we're going to have the same difficulties. The English-speaking Canadians will be generous in terms of culture and language and so on, but we will never be satisfied. So what's the problem?" We're not supporting bilingualism in Quebec because we realise that if you want to go outside of Quebec you have to be bilingual, you have to speak English. After all, we're living in an environment of 225 million Anglophones, and we have accepted that. And we say in Quebec we want to live in French and speak French, and we don't want to have bilingualism being forced on us. We know that out of Quebec we have to be bilingual, and in Quebec we want to be unilingual. I don't share that view, but that's the majority sentiment. People say, "Let's speak French here; we don't need to speak English."

I understand very well the resentment of the rest of Canada. Why should they learn French when they don't use it? And they already have enough trouble supporting their own English culture that it's an added burden to try to be cultivated in French also. This should be limited to a small number of people, the people who want to do business in Quebec. Otherwise, it's quite acceptable that they be unilingual.

JOHN ROBARTS

Bilingualism and the language question was perhaps the focus, but I don't know that it was necessarily what they were after. I think I made the comment back in those days that I saw few problems between French Canada and the rest of Canada that a good 15 percent increase in the standard of living wouldn't cure. And even in those days, I must say, I was conscious of jealousy on the part of French Canada for the material success and the prosperity that Ontario had. And I quite understood that; it's completely understandable that you want what your neighbour has, I suppose. And I was aware of it in those days.

T. C. DOUGLAS

Let us not fool ourselves—bilingualism is only part of the problem and solving bilingualism, if we ever get it solved, will not necessarily mean peace with Quebec. The economic disparities of Quebec are really the fundamental and underlying cause of the discontent in Quebec, and this nobody has faced up to yet.

ALVIN HAMILTON

What's killed the affection of French Canadians for the rest of Canada is the fact that they are at the bottom of the totem pole economically. It's a disgrace that French Canadians living in a province as rich as Quebec should be down near the level of the Indians on the reservation. That doesn't mean to say there are no French Canadians who are well off, but the great majority are below the economic level of the other ethnic groups living in Quebec. Now there are many reasons for that, but that's not the point. The fact is the fundamental reason for alienation is economics.

Pearson had told Bryce Mackasey that he was racing the clock, and there were some observers, among them Doug Fisher, who were of the view that he realised that there was no solution and that all that he was doing was gaining time.

DOUGLAS FISHER

What does bilingualism federally do? It seems to me that it stretches out the length of time in which we continue within this [present] arrangement. It gives us more time to develop adjustments and face up to it without going to the rifles and so on.

Why do I think this? Well, I talked about this with John Turner often, and it's possible to reduce matters such as this to very blunt, simple questions, no-nothing questions. When I made the point to Turner before he became a Cabinet Minister, because he and I used to talk a fair amount about this problem, I said, "John, Pearson has already decided that he will not fight to save Confederation." "What do you mean, fight?" I said, "Well, Lincoln fought. There were politicians in the United States, Lincoln was one, and Lincoln had been a compromiser for years, who said, 'The Union is indissoluble. It's a fighting matter.'"

I made this point when [Gilles] Grégoire became the first separatist M.P. I made it on TV and in my column that there's the indication of something I've known for a number of years. We won't fight. It's okay to advocate treason in this country— because what Lévesque and Grégoire advocated could be seen as treason. But it wasn't.

The bilingual program was particularly unpopular in the prairies and the West. After Agriculture Minister Harry Hays was defeated in the 1965 election, Lawrence Pennell, the Solicitor General, was asked to fulfill a speaking engagement in Saskatchewan. He did so and sensed the resentment in the West to the bilingualism program.

LAWRENCE PENNELL

I was sent out to Saskatchewan to talk to the farmers. I remember that, right after the 1965 election, a Cabinet Minister was very hard to find. Harry Hays had made this commitment, and Mr. Pearson called me and asked me if I would take it on. And I said, "They'd think it rather strange, would they not, that the Solicitor General should be talking to farmers." However, the Minister of Agriculture wasn't prepared to go, after his defeat, and I filled in at the meeting.

That was when I really found out that bilingualism was going to be a matter of controversy. I wasn't going to talk about farming, because I didn't have the background or the knowledge, and so I decided to broach the subject of bilingualism. The reaction I got—I felt one might easily have caught pneumonia from the coolness that emanated from that meeting. At first I was well received and got a round of applause, and then I got on to that subject, and a great hush came over the meeting. I sensed [the opposition] then. I really did. And that was in '65.

Everyone from Tommy Douglas, himself a former premier of Saskatchewan, down to the newest Western M.P. said that the bilingual program was misunderstood, and the reason for this was that few if anyone had bothered to go out to the prairies and explain what the government's policy was and that it was not to stuff French down anybody's throat, as was generally believed.

J. R. SMALLWOOD.

I think that, in the eyes and ears of most Canadians, this was an attempt to ram French down their throats—everybody has to start learning French. That it was badly sold—it wasn't sold at all, it was anything but a professional job, a competent job, an efficient job. There shouldn't have been all those misunderstandings. They ought to have been anticipated, and they weren't. And so there's a horrible misunderstanding.

A. H. McDONALD

I have no doubt that on every occasion when Mr. Pearson flew into Saskatchewan somebody was putting the bird in his ear and advising him that this program was causing problems in the West. It wasn't so much bilingualism that many Westerners were opposed to; it was the approach that was being used. They felt that bilingualism was being shoved down their throats. Many Westerners were convinced that they were going to have to learn to speak French, which was never the case. That didn't stop people from believing that they were going to have to learn French. And they resented this. They resented even signs being put up on the post office or the RCMP or other federal institutions. This annoyed many people in the West. I'm not saying that was right, but that is a fact, and I think it continues to be a fact.

Many Westerners feel that the bilingualism program was ill conceived and the wrong approach. Many Westerners resent the amount of money that has been spent trying to teach people my age the French language. Many of us feel that if you're going to have bilingualism, then the first thing that ought to be done is to see that there are sufficient French teachers to teach the French language in every school in Canada to the children.

BRUCE HUTCHISON

Bilingualism was not greatly supported or certainly not much understood in the West. I personally believe that the bilingual legislation is sound and essential—that is to say, it's essential to give the French Canadian people the right to speak in their own language to the government of Canada, and in any part of Canada where there was a reasonable group of French Canadians. That was sound and essential and just—and outrageous that it hadn't been done before—the government made a complete botch of explaining that policy, such a botch that many English-speaking Canadians still believe, incredible as it may seem, that the government's trying to make everybody in Canada speak two languages, that if you're English-speaking you must learn French, if you're French-speaking you must learn English. There was nothing in the law to suggest anything of the sort. But for reasons that I could never understand, the government never was able to get those simple facts over to the public. Perhaps they're beginning to get them now.

But for years bilingualism was completely misunderstood in English-speaking Canada, and it doesn't appear that it had much effect in Quebec in conciliating the French Canadian people. Bilingualism in itself wasn't enough to solve this problem.

JOHN NICHOL

There are always going to be people who become infuriated when they meet a French sign in the airport in Vancouver. I know them; very intelligent people—educated, intelligent, adult, or seemingly adult people—who get in a rage when they see a sign in French at the Vancouver airport. I don't know why it infuriates them. And the thing has been badly distorted. They all feel they have to learn French. I don't know. Let's not go into all that mess.

James Walker, the Toronto Member who was the Liberal government's Whip for much of the time that Pearson was Prime Minister, asserted that the poor publicity or lack of publicity with regard to the French-language policy was after Pearson had resigned—but it probably began in the Pearson days.

JAMES WALKER

I don't think they [Westerners] are mad at Quebec at all. They may be very annoyed, not at bilingualism, but at the way it has been handled, to the extent that people think, and I've heard it said, "They [Ottawa] are going to shove French down our throats." Nothing's farther from the truth, but there's been no real effort to contradict that ridiculous statement. Nobody in this country has to learn the other language if they don't want to—nobody. But this is a very commonly and firmly held belief—that if they're not careful, that again Ottawa is going to put us all in a camp somewhere and drill another language into our system. How you correct that, I don't know. I do know that that particular belief, that "they" are going to shove French down our throats, didn't appear in Mr. Pearson's [days] because of what Mr. Pearson did; he handled it in a different way.

Jean Marchand blamed the English-speaking Ministers for not pulling their weight on bilingualism and seemed to suggest that they did this deliberately and were out to sabotage the program.

JEAN MARCHAND

I noticed that as long as we were talking about bilingualism in general terms, people all agreed, "Oh yes, that's a good thing, it does exist in Europe." But when you say, "You have to learn French" or "This job has to be done in both languages," that's when you strike professional interests or personal prejudices. There, of course, you start trouble.

My conviction is that probably too many English-speaking Ministers didn't do the selling job in their own part of Canada. We had to sell Ottawa to Quebec, and personally I felt like hell doing that. And God knows at what cost. This will be part of my book. I'm not going to give it to you now. But anyhow, this was our job. I assumed that the job of my colleagues was to do the same thing, say in Vancouver and in Alberta and so forth. The fact was that they were not all willing to do this or not all able to do it.

One of the most difficult things to get through was the simplest thing—and that was to convince the new Canadian or the Canadian of different origin to the British and French [of the need for bilingualism]. It was easy for any English Canadian to say, "If we give that [language rights] to this minority in Quebec, why shouldn't the Ukrainians have that?" They'd say, "Yes, why should they have privileges that we don't have?" But the problem of languages is not a problem of principle; it's a problem of fact. Why are there Frenchmen and Flemish in Belgium? There's no principle in that. It's just because they are there.

Now, find me a minority in Canada which controls a territory, which controls a government, which has its own institutions— universities and so forth. It's not the fact that they were here first. Some French Canadians used to use this type of argument, which I find silly, because if this is an argument I don't see why we don't all speak Indian or Eskimo, or Cree, you know. It is a simple fact. One day I heard Trudeau saying, "Do you know why it's important? Because Quebec can break the country. And any group who can break the country is an important group."

But why this situation in Quebec? It's just because they [French Canadians] happen to control a territory and a government and some important institutions. And it's not a matter of principle. If they say, "Well, there are a million people of German origin in Canada"—they are spread all over the place. But if you put them all in Manitoba, you may have a problem tomorrow.

These are simple arguments. I'm not inventing anything. And they all agreed. Even when I made speeches in the West on this, there was no discussion at all! They agreed very easily.

A by-product of Prime Minister Pearson's drive toward bilingualism was the effort made to have bilingual names. It began with a Private Member's bill in Parliament to change the name of the national airline from Trans-Canada Airlines to Air Canada, which was a similar nomenclature to Air France. Soon the government departments and agencies followed suit: the Department of National Revenue became Revenue Canada, the Dominion Bureau of Statistics became Statistics Canada; there were Agriculture Canada, Health and Welfare Canada, Supply and Services Canada, Transport Canada. The multi-nationals quickly got into the act with Shell Canada, Bell Canada, Texaco Canada. The "Franglish" reached the extent of Hockey Canada, Team Canada, Skate Canada.

DOUGLAS FISHER

Jean Chrétien got his first real notoriety of a favourable kind out of changing the name of Trans-Canada Airlines to Air Canada. I helped him as that Private Member's bill was not going to go through. There was no deal that had sold all the Tories. I managed to get Rod Webb and another Tory who was sitting there in Private Members' hour out of the House and into the lobby on a fabricated excuse when the bill was to go on. It was the second reading to be accepted. Then the thing just flew through, so we had the name changed.

TOM KENT

I think at the time the attitude as I recall it—certainly my own attitude—was Trans-Canada is rather clumsy. Air Canada, that's rather a nice name for an airline. But then, by no conscious process that I am aware of, the thing gathered a sort of momentum and reached the rather ridiculous position that it now has. I suppose that happened just by a process of the precedent of Air Canada having been set. Various people, French Canadian Members and Ministers and so on, wanted to follow the example and nobody thought it worth opposing.

Bilingualism, which always had a touch of binationalism about it, resulted in a change in the public display of Canadian heroes—at least in Canada House, London, where Lionel Chevrier was High Commissioner.

LIONEL CHEVRIER

One day we were going up the staircase of Canada House and I said to Pearson—there was a monument of Wolfe there—"Don't you think he looks lonely?" And Mike said, "What do you mean?" I said, "Well, I come out here every day. People come out here from all over Canada. Wolfe is a great soldier, but it seems to me that there should be a bust of Montcalm as well."

Well, he just couldn't jump on it quicker. He said, "Of course there should be, Lionel. Why didn't somebody think of it before?" And I said, "If it's an offence to Wolfe, then let's put Laurier's monument with Macdonald's." But he agreed with me at once. So I took it up with External Affairs. They had to get hold of Hébert, who was a sculptor in Quebec. He did a sculpture of Montcalm, and if you walk into Canada House now, they're not at the staircase above but they're down in the main hall as you come in, one on one side and the other on the other side.

Bilingualism also brought about changes in the Parliamentary Press Gallery.

VICTOR MACKIE

I can't remember what year it was—it was during Pearson's regime that the stationery of the Press Gallery was changed to have not only the Press Gallery in English but to have it in French, on the envelopes and on the stationery. But it came about very generally and there was no upheaval, no uproar, no nothing.

The Gallery always made sure that a French Canadian got elected to the executive and always tried to promote a French Canadian up to the point of being president, if he or she was prepared to take it on. The French Canadians who were in the Gallery were always very fluent, bilingualists, so they were quite capable of handling the job of being president because they could speak English almost as well as they could speak French. We had no problem there but the difficulty was in finding enough bodies; there were not that many people in the Gallery who were French. But when there was a man or woman who was capable of, and wanted to take on, the position of responsibility, then the Gallery would go out of its way to get them elected to executive office.

There were great expectations of what bilingualism could do to Canada, and they were held not only by French Canadian intellectuals such as Gérard Pelletier but by English-speaking intellectuals as well. In an interview some time before he left the government, Pelletier envisaged the day when every well-educated Canadian would speak both English and French.

GÉRARD PELLETIER

What I said was that any person with higher education—and I was limiting that to Canada really—would feel uncomfortable without a second language, because we're going in that direction universally. For instance, look at the French who were remarkably unilingual a generation ago, when I was there after the war. Now I meet my friends of that time and they've learned a second language—those who have higher education, of course. I think that with the internationalism and the communications developing the way they do, highly educated people, who had access to university, want to increase their capability of communicating with a culture which is not theirs out of curiousity or intellectual interest or what have you.

Most of his associates felt that Mr. Pearson would have gone more slowly, that there would have been a more gradual approach, and that the bilingualism policy would have been allowed to mature over a long period of time. But perhaps, because the expectations were too great, the government pushed too hard and aroused so much resentment and hostility that the cause of bilingualism received a bad setback. At any rate, all of this excessive zeal was not considered to be Pearson's fault.

PAUL HELLYER

I'm not the least bit sure that if Mr. Pearson's undertakings [that no one would suffer from bilingualism] had been lived up to in full, that there would have been much of a problem. But they have not been. The rules have been changed since. And the general *carte-blanche* undertaking that he gave has not been fulfilled, and this has created problems.

JOHN TURNER

I don't know the conversations between Favreau and Lamontagne and Tremblay with Mr. Pearson in '62-'63 on bilingualism, or between Mr. Pearson and Marchand and Pelletier and Trudeau on bilingualism. Undoubtedly they had something to do with the development of his opinions, because he relied very much on his French-speaking lieutenants, but it's impossible to divine what he would have done as that policy of bilingualism matured. He might have had an easier time implementing it because he was an English-speaking Canadian. I suspect that he might have been more flexible on federal-provincial relations, but one never knows.

TOM KENT

Certainly, Pearson saw the country as becoming a bilingual country, but he saw it becoming bilingual over a generation or two. I don't think he saw the civil service in Ottawa or the process of government in Ottawa becoming bilingual in the course of a decade. He saw it in the course of a generation.

YVON DUPUIS

Mr. Pearson I don't think would have gone as far as Mr. Trudeau went. He was for the respect of bilingualism in Ottawa in the federal field as far as the central administration of the country is concerned, but to extend that idea as Mr. Trudeau did, I don't think Mr. Pearson would have gone as far.

12 *Unification and Inflation*

BEFORE HE BECAME *Prime Minister, Lester Pearson had mentioned the unification of the armed forces in a couple of speeches, although Paul Hellyer wasn't sure that Pearson knew exactly what he was advocating. There had been some progress made toward the integration of a few common elements, and the need for integration was generally accepted, but unification went much further and meant, as the term implied, the amalgamation of the army, the Royal Canadian Air Force, and the Royal Canadian Navy, into one service that would have the same uniform and the same rank designations. This would be a unique reorganisation since no other country of Canada's middle-power size had been able to unify its armed forces. As might be expected, there was strong opposition and resistance to this move.*

Unification was the achievement of Paul Hellyer, and probably no other Defence Minister would have done it; Hellyer was only old enough to get in at the end of the Second World War and never got overseas or higher than the rank of corporal, so that he was bound by no loyalties, no traditions, no encumbering trails of glory. The bill creating the single military service was enacted at the end of April 1967. So that Canada celebrated its hundredth anniversary with a united armed force.

It all began on March 26, 1964, when a White Paper was tabled in Parliament calling for the unification of the entire defence establishment, to be accomplished in three stages. The first step would be to eliminate the

340

chiefs of staff of the three services and the separate army, navy, and air force staffs, and put in their place a single chief of the defence staff and a single defence staff. This would result in a reduction of headquarters personnel in Ottawa by 30 percent or about 1,000 officers of the rank of major to general. The money saved would be available for the purchase of new equipment, and thus there would be no need of an increase in the defence budget. Paul Hellyer said that the purpose of the whole exercise was to get "a bigger bang for a buck." The White Paper asserted that Canada's major defence contribution would "continue to be participating in collective defence arrangements, notably the North Atlantic Treaty Organisation." The White Paper also noted that this country was one of a small number of powers capable of and eligible for United Nations peace-keeping tasks.

PAUL HELLYER

When I went to the Defence Department I was not what I would now call a unificationist. I was probably an integrationist. I felt that the common services should be brought together. This was pretty generally accepted. But after being at the department for some weeks or months, I came very quickly to the position that the three traditional branches should be in one corporation.

There were many reasons for this. They had different strategies for war, there was no co-ordination between those strategies, the Chiefs of Staff Committee was not functioning in the way people on the outside expected it to. More precisely, it didn't set military priorities. They engaged pretty much in back-scratching, and the kinds of things they decided in committee were trivial, and the things they didn't decide, which were important, they dumped in the Minister's lap. They all had direct access to the Minister, which meant that the Minister, who is a layman, might be caught in the position of committing the money to the least important priority on a nice morning when somebody caught him off-guard. For many, many reasons I came to the conclusion that, of the various solutions to this organisational problem, the one making the whole apparatus into a single corporation was theoretically superior to other solutions.

So I began to write the White Paper, which I did personally.

The first draft was written in longhand; and then when I had finished it and had it typed I took it to Mr. Pearson to get his reaction because there was no way that I was going to recommend the unification of the armed forces, even in a single sentence as was the case in the White Paper, and then have him turn around and say that he wouldn't support it. So I, in effect, got pre-clearance on that proposal. After that the White Paper, of course, was subjected to the usual inputs from External, and Mr. Pearson himself took a hand in the drafting of some of the External aspects of it and rewriting a few paragraphs that he was particularly interested in. If you compare the final version with the original, I don't think you could easily tell where the differences occurred, if any, but everyone has his own choice of words. Ultimately it was submitted to the Cabinet Committee on Defence and External Affairs, and approved, and then to Cabinet and approved, and then made public.

The first step toward unification went smoothly enough, with the bill setting up the unified defence staff being adopted in the summer of 1964. Most of the cutbacks at headquarters were accomplished by the normal process of retirement, and only a proportionately small number of officers received the "golden handshake," as the press called the special cash bonus for those involuntarily retired as a result of the re-organisation.

In his efforts to rationalise the military establishment — to make it the very model of the modern armed force, as Paul Hellyer would have put it — the Defence Minister was assisted by Group Captain William Lee, a young staff officer who was actually about the same age as the Minister. Bill Lee had been such a success as director of public relations, RCAF, that he was seconded to External Affairs to help stage the NATO Conference, which was held in Ottawa in May 1963. It was at this conference that he came to the attention of Paul Hellyer. He became the newly appointed Defence Minister's chief aide, and many believed that it was Bill Lee who interested Hellyer in unification because he had long been an advocate of this and had written a briefing paper for the Air Council on this subject when he was a wing commander with the RCAF. At any rate, officers opposed to unification regarded him as the evil genius behind the Minister. Hellyer also consulted Lord Louis Mountbatten, who was then the chief of the United Kingdom Defence Staff, and Robert McNamara, the Secretary of Defense in the United States.

PAUL HELLYER

I talked to a lot of people about it. I don't think there's any doubt that Bill Lee had an influence. Some people accuse him of being the instigator. Unfortunately, I can't hold him responsible. The way we did things in that office, he often gave me his advice, and often I accepted it and sometimes I didn't. That's the way these relationships are supposed to work. And we had a very close relationship and still are good friends. He was of particular assistance in the implementation, where without his connections in the armed forces I think it would have been much more difficult than it was. And it was virtually impossible, even under the best circumstances. But I have to accept the major responsibility for the policy. It was one that I believed was right after studying all of the alternatives and talking to numerous people.

I discussed unification for literally dozens of hours with dozens of different people of all ranks and with both military and civilian experience, and retired people and active people, and tried to draw them out and get their views on it, right down to the wire ultimately when the final bill was introduced.

Just before that, I was concerned about it, as a result of all the public flak; I had thought to myself, "Is there something that I've overlooked?" I got together a group of senior officers and said, "Now, look, if there's something I've overlooked, you tell me." After three hours there was nothing, really. The only objection was primarily an emotional objection. So it was basically what I believed to be a rational solution to cope with technological changes which had taken place in the previous thirty years, and I believed it was the right solution then and I still think so.

Mountbatten and I discussed this [matter] on many occasions, and he was totally in accord. He asked me to keep him informed during the whole process, which I tried to do. It is what he would have liked to have recommended in the United Kingdom but which was politically impossible. His Minister at that time, who was Dennis Healey, said, "Of course you're right, but if you think I'm going to go through the kind of political hassle that this would raise, you're crazy." And I think that that was a realistic political appraisal—that when you start dealing with emotional issues like that, you're asking for trouble. And, of course, that was my experience.

McNamara took the same position. He thought it was a very courageous act. He couldn't say enough good about it. And then he said, "Within the next thirty years or so, all of the countries in the western world will follow, but the United States will be last," the reason being that they have more retired admirals and more admirals' clubs and more establishment, the so-called military industrial group, than any other country.

The first stage of unification was completed by the end of 1964. The second stage, which began in 1965, was the integration of the eleven field commands in Canada into six functional commands—mobile command, maritime command, air defence command, transport command, and two commands for material and training. The final stage, which started in 1966, was the elimination of the three services as separate entities and their unification into a single armed force. During 1966 there was a prolonged debate in Parliament on this whole question. Paul Hellyer had to admit that more than 26,000 persons had left the armed forces in the eighteen months up to the end of 1965, and fully half of them had quit at their own request before completing their terms of service. These revelations brought charges by the Opposition that unification was undermining the morale of the Canadian armed forces personnel. The Defence Minister had also promised that unification would bring about a considerable saving in money, which would be spent on new equipment, but both he and Léo Cadieux had a difficult time justifying this. Cadieux was Associate Defence Minister during most of the stages of unification and succeeded Hellyer as Minister after passage of the unification legislation.

PAUL HELLYER

Unification—and here we ought to differentiate between the integration process and the unification process—unification was really the ultimate organisational aspect of (a) making savings in money and (b) increasing the operational effectiveness of the forces. And I don't think you can separate these two things totally. But as long as you had three separate forces, then the question of combined operations was always a problem. Who would command the combined operation, and how would they get the collaboration of units from other services? And there was always a hassle. So we had to not only combine common services, but then we had to have an organisation which made it possible to appoint a commander who didn't ask politely at a table from a committee if he could borrow a unit but who, on the basis of advice from the various technical people around him, would decide what he needed and then issue the necessary instructions.

I don't think there's any other way that it could have been done. And this, incidentally, was the strong view of some of the great wartime commanders, namely Eisenhower and Mountbatten, who both had the precise problems of getting people to work together that you found in a smaller scale in even our own national combined operations.

GORDON CHURCHILL

There's one thing about that particular proposal—it had nothing to do with any pressure from any segment of Canada, and it had nothing to do, as far as I could see, with promoting any advantage for the Liberal Party. It was an idea conceived by Paul Hellyer, supported by Mr. Pearson obviously. It did no good at all. It didn't save the money that they said it would; and it weakened the armed forces; it created dissent, disunity in the country. And they're creeping back now to distinction between the navy and the army and the air force, as it used to be in the past.

Why Mr. Pearson went along with that I don't know, but Mr. Paul Hellyer, with whom I'm not unfriendly, was pressing things pretty well. He had leadership ambitions, and Mr. Pearson was not as popular as he had been earlier. Mr. Pearson was accused of indecisiveness and being a wobbler—Paul Hellyer was posing as the strong man who could make decisions. We had a very spirited debate with regard to integration and unification. If it had stopped at integration, which means getting the top-ranking officers, navy, army and air force, working together so they'd become familiar with each arm of the service, that would have been dandy. We didn't oppose that at all. But to make navy, army and air force personnel all the same—put them all in the same uniform and give them all the same ranks and make them all the same as if they were interchangeable—is ridiculous.

As we said to Mr. Hellyer, "A cook working for the air force or the army might very well serve as a cook on board a ship, but what's a master mariner to do? Where do you put him in the army if you take him off his ship? What about a man with some specialised knowledge? Can you shift him around to the air force and then into the army or back to his ship? It's just ridculous; it can't be done." But at any rate, unification again was forced through, and no good came from it at all, and no saving of money. The only way money was saved was by the reduction in the number of people employed in the armed services. If you knock off 20,000, you're going to save a pile of money, and of course that's what's been done.

PAUL HELLYER

A lot of the equipment that the forces had was old and out of date, and I actually contracted to buy more equipment for them than anybody in recent history. Without it they wouldn't have had anything like the effectiveness that they have had these last few years. They're desperately in need of another infusion of that sort, but we had a re-equipment program which was long overdue, and which made quite a difference to the potential of the forces, both active and reserve.

LÉO CADIEUX

When I became Minister of Defence, I was asked about the savings from unification: "After all is said and done, what did you save?" My answer had to be a negative explanation: there was an inflation factor of something like 3 percent in the economy at the time—it was 8 percent in the case of the armed services because of procurement and all that. We were still doing the same jobs; there had been no change in the assignments. And we had 20,000 to 25,000 people less to do them. We were spending the same amount of money, so I couldn't say that we had saved anything—but I could prove in a negative way that we didn't spend any more.

I felt that this showed that there were some very definite advantages to integration or unification. I was not there at the inception of the program but it seemed to me that, with the old way of three services competing with each other, it would have been much worse, and much more would have had to be spent. So there was a saving, but it was difficult to prove.

The unification debate reached its climax in the summer of 1966 with the so-called "admirals' revolt." The battle was joined in the Commons Defence Committee where Rear Admiral William Landymore launched several broadsides against Paul Hellyer's concept of rationalising and modernising the armed forces. Landymore, a much-decorated war hero, refused to resign and was ordered to relinquish his post as chief of Maritime Command in Halifax. Several other admirals, air marshals, and generals joined Admiral Landymore in attacking the unification proposals at extended hearings of the Defence Committee; they followed him out of the services although none of them carried the protest to the extent of refusing to resign as he had; Landymore was the only admiral to be fired. Throughout the storm Paul Hellyer remained adamant; he was so resolute and unyielding that Opposition Members began to suspect that he had already begun his campaign for the leadership of the Liberal Party.

PAUL HELLYER

Partly the problem arose from the fact that the senior naval officers were all about the same age, and consequently there was no way to bring in new people one at a time, as happened with the air force. The air force officers had staggered ages, and consequently as each one came up for retirement it was possible to bring in someone who was more amenable to changing the organisation. But this didn't happen in the navy, so there was, as a consequence, the greater upheaval in trying to get them to go along. Consequently it got more publicity and established in the public mind that the opposition was concentrated largely in the navy. Well, this was true. Probably if you had a thermometer which could read these things down to the individual degrees, the difference between the opposition in the three services was not nearly so pronounced as the public would have guessed.

GEORGE HEES

What was the reason for unification? It was because a fellow called Bill Lee, who was Paul Hellyer's executive assistant, sold him on the idea that this would be a great white charger on which Paul could ride into the leadership of the Liberal Party, something innovative, new, dashing, daring, bright, exciting. I am told that

that is the sole reason that the armed forces were unified. There was no military reason for doing it at all.

Was I opposed to it? Very much so, because I could see this hurting morale very greatly. After all, in the armed forces, symbols and history and tradition, battle honours and all the rest of it, are of great importance to morale. To take them away and put everybody in jolly green jumper suits is something which I think did the armed services a great disservice.

Lord Louis Mountbatten had been in full accord with the Canadian plans for the unification of the armed forces, as Paul Hellyer said, with one exception, and that was that he didn't think there was any need for a single uniform "unless it were to be navy blue with brass buttons." However, the Defence Minister insisted on a single uniform to get away from the counting of uniforms that went on at staff meetings in Ottawa so that each service would be sure that it was adequately represented. Paul Hellyer's objective was what he described as the special forces concept, the elite marine corps type of unit, which was how he envisaged mobile command, but he left the choice of a uniform to a committee.

PAUL HELLYER

Now, the actual choice of uniforms was not mine. This was done by a staff group, headed by an airman, so that the actual uniform is really a green version of the United States Air Force uniform that appealed to them. It was really a functional uniform based on comfort. No belts, no buckles, nothing really except one uniform that you can wear year round and slip on and off easily. And whether that's the right decision or not, this was a staff decision.

My total input into that was the shoulder badge: I suggested they continue to use the Canada shoulder flash, because although they said, and I agreed, that it was unique in a sense, it was unique at home but it wouldn't be unique if they were in Sweden or Switzerland or somewhere else where people might not know the background.

As might be expected, the reorganisation of the armed forces and their unification was accompanied by a complete overhaul of the militia. The

Newfoundland Premier Joey Smallwood and Jean Lesage at the
federal-provincial conference in Quebec City, April 1964.
(Public Archives Canada PA-117105)

Ontario Premier John Robarts at a press conference after the Quebec
City conference. *(Public Archives Canada PA-117111)*

Pearson with his Policy Secretary Tom Kent, April 1965.
(Public Archives Canada PA-117098)

Pearson with Defence Minister Paul Hellyer and Air Marshal Frank Miller, June 1965. *(Public Archives Canada PA-117109)*

Pearson and Keith Davey with John Nicol at pre-election rally in Ottawa, September 1965. *(Public Archives Canada PA-117103)*

Election night, November 8, 1965. From left to right: Press Secretary Richard O'Hagan, Senator John Connolly, Pearson and Jack Pickersgill. *(Public Archives Canada PA-117100)*

From left to right: Lucien Cardin, Lawrence Pennell, Jean-Luc Pepin, Watson McNaught, and George McIlraith. *(Public Archives Canada PA-117014)*

Mike Pearson and Maurice Lamontagne. *(Public Archives Canada PA-117115)*

Jean Marchand and Guy Favreau with Pearson, fall 1965.
(Public Archives Canada PA-117099)

Pierre Sévigny and his wife during the Munsinger enquiry, April 1966. *(Public Archives Canada PA-117120)*

Bruce Hutchison of the Vancouver *Sun*. *(Public Archives Canada PA-117113)*

Governor-General Roland Michener. *(Public Archives PA-117119)*

David Lewis, Tommy Douglas, and Stanley Knowles, November 1966. *(Public Archives Canada PA-117125)*

Robert Stanfield, who became Leader of the Opposition in November 1967. *(Public Archives Canada PA-117117)*

Pierre Trudeau, John Turner, Jean Chrétien, and Lester Pearson, April 1967. *(Public Archives Canada PA-117107)*

March 1964 White Paper confirmed that the part-time and reserve troops would continue to provide support for the regular forces but gave them other duties. They "would be required to form the framework for logistics and special units" as well as look after training and internal security and assist in survival operations. A second part of the White Paper, which was released some seven months later in November 1964, forecast drastic cuts in the militia establishments and a reduction in total strength to about 30,000 officers and other ranks. Every effort would be made to increase physical fitness and reduce the average age, as the militia had, in the years since the Second World War, tended to become veterans' clubs. As a result of unification, several famous regiments were reduced to militia units or eliminated if they did not have reserve battalions.

PAUL HELLYER

It [reorganisation of the militia] was really to do two things: to get a more streamlined force, and by that I almost mean it literally. The militia, the reserve forces, generally were commanded by people with wartime experience. Some of them were getting just a little long on the tooth, and some of them had put on a few pounds. And after reviewing the state of the militia at the beginning of the previous war and learning that no militia commander had taken his unit into battle because of age and physical condition, I decided that it would be better to try to streamline them a little bit. And also I had the requirement to save a certain amount of money.

I spent probably more time on that than I have on any other policy, any other comparable policy in my political career. I think I had twenty-two three-hour meetings on the militia reorganisation. And I consulted all of my senior colleagues in Cabinet, all of the provincial representatives in the Cabinet, and a lot of people to try and avoid the inevitable political pitfalls. So it was a massive reorganisation, which took a tremendous amount of time and effort, and that I think paid off. Although there was considerable flak from a few of the units afterward, it was mild compared to what I had been warned might happen.

Our aim was to reduce the number of units as well the age qualification for certain ranks, and the introduction of some new concepts such as the service battalions and a number of things all wrapped into one package to accomplish the two things of fewer units and more compact, streamlined units.

LÉO CADIEUX

I was very keen on the reserves. But it was not easy because the reserve units don't grow like mushrooms. Some of them were almost abstract units—they had no members. There were many cases like that. There were those with so few members they were very expensive clubs. The Minister is advised by the the Reserve Association and I reinforced that advice by naming a major general from the militia as a special advisor.

I had to disband some regiments. This was the greatest problem of my whole life. Me, disbanding the Black Watch! Me! A French Canadian! But there was no other way. I tried to have that settled by the regiments themselves. Nobody would give way. The regiment that was strong wanted to stay. The one that was borrowing from everywhere wanted to stay also. So somebody had to make a decision. The obvious solution is what I did. My executive assistant was a Black Watch, on top of that. And I said, "Look, I have to disband your regiment, and I guess I'm going to have to demonstrate to you that there is no other way but to go back to the original three regiments, the oldest regiments, the R.C.R.s, the Princess Pats, and the Vandoos [Royal 22nd]. Each with three battalions, and then you have the nine battalions [that we need]."

At least the Black Watch had a strong militia unit and could continue in the militia, which wasn't so bad, but some regiments didn't have militia units. The Canadian Guards had no militia unit, so it meant disappearance. Well, what can you do?

Although bilingualism was not a factor at all, as Paul Hellyer asserted, in the unification of the armed forces, there was no doubt that it was aided by the modernisation of the Canadian military establishment. The Defence Minister himself did make an effort to increase the use of the French language among the troops. Such a move was related to the general thrust of the administration, and while Hellyer did not remember any specific directives, he believed there may have been a policy paper on the question. While he was Defence Minister, General Jean Victor Allard became Chief of the Defence Staff, succeeding Air Marshal Frank Miller, who was the first to be appointed to this post after the amalgamation of the separate army, navy, and air force staffs. Hellyer said that he had put General Allard in the top job partly because he was willing to go along with unification, although he wasn't a great enthusiast, and partly because he was a leader of men—General Allard had an outstanding war record. The fact that he was a French Canadian also helped. Some observers believed that his appointment was a sign that future commanding officers would have to be bilingual.

The unification of the armed forces was an example of the way that Pearson dealt with matters in which he had little or no knowledge or interest. He gave Paul Hellyer a free hand. It was only when the unification project ran into trouble, and friends took him aside and complained about how bad it was for the troops' morale, that Pearson began to have second thoughts and wanted to postpone the whole scheme.

PAUL HELLYER

I don't think anyone can deny the advantage of fluency in two or more languages; but I don't recall any specific direction, policy, or discussion at that stage which said at some future date, however remote, every officer above the rank of colonel or brigadier general or what have you has to be bilingual. If there was anything of that nature, I have no recllection of it at all.

I was more concerned about unilingual French-speaking people having an opportunity to learn trades and to enter branches of the service which had previously been pretty well blocked to them because of lack of technical expertise. And this was a fact, that it was more difficult for a young French Canadian to become an airman or a sailor than it was to become a soldier. Because the Royal 22nd was always there, and they could get shuffled off into the infantry and there was a place for them. Whereas, if they preferred the sea or the air, every possible obstacle was put in their way—if not deliberately, at least through the way the system operated. I felt that they had been denied fair shakes in getting the rudiments of military training while they were getting their language training and that a number of steps had to be taken to redress that balance; and some were [taken] then and some have been since.

LÉO CADIEUX

We were trying to pursue the promotion of suitable officers for the command posts, but not as French-speaking officers—as Canadian officers with equivalent qualifications. But you had to accelerate some [Francophone] promotions as a beginning. This is the seemingly unjust part of it. One has to start, otherwise it's going to take a few generations and people are not that patient. I think we managed to cover this difficulty with care, with prudence, and not to be unfair to anyone.

I had the impression that, consciously or not, the English element so dominated the military activities that there was no chance of promotion, of even in some cases acceptance in some of the services. I thought—and I used that expression at the time and I still think it was apt to describe the situation—we were in the dead end of infantry. The only unit really open to French Canadians was an infantry unit, the Royal 22nd.

I thought we should try to make a beachhead in the navy, in the air force, and in the technical trades. This is why I suggested the creation of one unit—eventually it became, I think, a squadron of ships—in the navy where the language of work would be French. In the air, just the same. I presented the plan to Mr. Pearson, and he was so receptive to the ideas. He had that perception that really, honestly, this was the thing to do. So this is why I have such a high regard for Mr. Pearson.

In order not to make this unit an exclusive club and also to provide an opportunity for the English-speaking Canadian who wants to learn French, an eighty-twenty structure was envisaged. The so-called French-speaking unit would have 80 percent of personnel if possible French-speaking and 20 percent English-speaking, but the language of work would be French.

To begin with, we had HMCS *Ottawa* as the French-speaking unit in the navy, a French-speaking interceptor squadron at Bagotville [Quebec] and the Three Rivers Armored Regiment, as well as a French-language technical school at St. Jean [Quebec].

GORDON CHURCHILL

Naturally it would be helpful if you could operate the armed forces with bilingual personnel, but very, very difficult and very expensive. I don't know enough as to how the forces are getting on that way. I would think they intend to live separate and apart from each other. Mr. Cadieux, when he was Minister of National Defence, struck the Fort Garry Horse, my old regiment, off the list of regular regiments and substituted a new regiment, a new tank regiment, in the province of Quebec, which would be all French-speaking. I objected very, very strenuously to that, but that's what was done. And I think they have a ship where it's all French that's spoken, or something like that. So you really have two [language] divisions within the armed services. I wouldn't call them bilingual. I'd hate to be under active service and not understand the commands that were given in the language with which I was unfamiliar. Not for me, thank you very much. So I don't know how it's working out in the armed services.

GEORGE HEES

I was in the Second World War and I was on the staff of two different brigade headquarters. Each brigade had one French regiment and two English-speaking regiments. They all got along fine. We didn't need this unification or new linguistic policy or whatever. All those regiments got along just fine. They worked together and they fought together and they got along well together. There was no problem.

PAUL HELLYER

Pearson himself said he was influenced by the last book he had read or the last person he had talked to. And I don't think it's doing him an injustice to say that this was, in fact, true in many cases. There were actually incidents where Cabinet took a decision and someone would follow him into his office and chat with him for twenty minutes, and they would reverse it. I think that happened on a couple of occasions because of the concentrated argument on one side, so that this tendency to change his mind brought the charge of vacillation. I went through it on the unification [issue]. I think he changed his mind many times after the crunch came; and that notwithstanding his backing of the principle, that when it became politically difficult he almost backed off. I put a stop to that by threatening to resign.

When he wanted to postpone completion of the bill, for
example, in the spring of '67, I said that he was the boss and he
could postpone it till the next session if he wanted but he'd have to
get a new Minister to do it. And I did this because the thing was in
such a state of flux that it had to go one way or the other; it just
couldn't stay in the position it was in at that time. And the worst
possible thing for the forces would have been no decision. So I
took a very tough stand and he responded to that by backing me
up. But even then that wasn't the end of it. There were two or
three times I had to go through that ritual again.

*The fact that Admiral Landymore was fired went far to break the
resistance to the unification of the Canadian armed forces. If he had not had
the power to dismiss a rebellious officer, Paul Hellyer quite frankly
admitted that a major reorganisation of the kind that he had instituted could
not have been undertaken; and he went on to point out that there was no
similar power as far as the civil service was concerned. That was why he
despaired of any politician ever doing anything about an unwieldy civil
service, as he put it—he had learned to his own sorrow that it was
impossible to fire a high-ranking civil servant.*

*However, security of tenure was not confined to the higher echelons of
the civil service—all public employees were assured of their jobs. Despite
this, the Pearson Government granted them the right to collective bargaining as well as the right to strike. It all began in 1965 when Arnold
Heeney, a prominent civil servant and former diplomat, submitted a report
on the question of collective bargaining and the civil service. There was
evidence, at the time, that some of the civil service associations, while
favouring compulsory arbitration, did not want to go as far as having
the right to strike. However, by the time the issue came up for
consideration—the legislation was not passed till February 1967—Jean
Marchand was a member of the Cabinet. Marchand was very much
opposed to compulsory arbitration for a variety of reasons, one of them
being that the arbitrator was not elected and was taking the responsibility
of those elected Members of Parliament in committing the government to
expenditures, and he insisted that civil servants should have the right to
strike.*

MITCHELL SHARP

Heeney made a series of recommendations on collective bargaining that we had no trouble accepting. When it came to the question as to whether the civil servants should have the right to strike in order to achieve their purposes, Heeney was much less definite and he presented us with the arguments pro and con, and he came down in favour of giving them the right to strike, but only marginally, as he recognised that there would be opposition and that it had dangers.

The argument in Cabinet was long, and there was a great division within Cabinet as to whether we should go this route or not. I don't think that any Minister had any great influence. We did look to people like Jean Marchand, who had had experience with trade unions, and I don't now remember exactly what he said, but I think I could say that his general attitude was "there will be strikes whether they are legal or not, and therefore it is better to legalise them than to deal with illegal strikes." That is my recollection of how the argument went.

In retrospect, I'm inclined to think that we moved a little too quickly, and this is the judgement of people whose opinion I respect, who have had a lot of experience in this field. It would have been better to have proceeded in two steps—to have given the right of collective bargaining but not the right to strike; and after there had been experience in the collective bargaining, then to have considered whether the right to strike should also be added. A great deal of difficulty we have had is that these groups haven't had experience in collective bargaining, and they've embarked upon a strike action without a full understanding of its consequences and its limitations. Now, that's an opinion in retrospect. At the time we were not as aware of that particular issue. If we had [been], I think we probably would not have granted the right to strike then. We might have done it later though.

JEAN MARCHAND

I don't think that you can remove the right to strike from anybody. You can do it legally, you can pass a law and say, "You don't strike." And if they do strike, what do you do? If the railway workers go on strike, you say, "You're not permitted to go on strike." "We stay on strike." What do you do? So I don't think that you can say to a group of people, "You don't have the right to strike." I think that what you can require is that certain services be maintained.

I said to the [Quebec] hospital workers, "I agree with the right to strike; but if ever you abuse this right, you're going to die with it, your organisation is going to disappear with it." The right to strike in the public services is something which should be of a special nature—just to draw the attention of the public to your problem; that's all. You cannot deal with the government the same way you deal with an employer. It can hurt if the Aluminum Company of Canada has to shut down its plants for a year. Nobody's going to die. But you cannot close down the government for a year. It's not possible.

J. W. PICKERSGILL

I have already said publicly that I dissented from that particular piece of legislation. And I say it again. I do not think that you can have bargaining when one side has nothing to bargain with. My view is that we should try, if we can, to stop this so-called bargaining over wages, which is not bargaining but is inevitably blackmail. I don't mean blackmail in the criminal sense, but when a group of public servants can say, "We won't do our job unless we get so much," knowing full well that their employer can't go broke as the Ford Motor Company can go broke or as a supermarket can go broke. That acts as a restraint and the bargainer in the supermarket, the boss of the supermarket, can say, "Well, I'll close up the shop rather than pay you that," and therefore they've got to think twice. But in the public service it seems to me that the standard we tried to follow in the St. Laurent days—that we paid for the comparable work what good employers paid, but that this was determined by the government through objective standards—is the right way to determine the pay of public servants.

I do think that they ought to have the right to form associations, call them what you will, to deal with the conditions of work and grievances and that sort of thing. No, I disagreed with Pearson about this, and I think I was right.

E. J. BENSON

My view with regard to the right to strike in the public service is that it doesn't make much difference; if they can't reach an agreement of some sort that's reasonable, they'll go out in any case because we have that experience with the postal workers. The strange thing is, I don't really think that the Public Service Alliance at that time wanted the right to strike to be put into the legislation. The attitude of the Cabinet, as I recall it, was that if you don't give people the right to strike, you aren't really giving them full collective bargaining.

The people who can strike are, of course, the people in vital functions in the government. We've ruled out the ones that effect safety and security, such as prison guards and so on; they haven't got the right to strike. The ones that are most like industrial unions do strike—postal workers, air traffic controllers. These are people who have vital functions that really affect the country.

The worst negotiation I had was before they had the right to strike. This was in 1965 when Parliament had adjourned and the postal workers all went out. A decision had been made at that time that they were going to call an election and Mr. Pearson didn't want to reconvene Parliament. That was a terrible negotiation because the union had no strength. It really had no one leader. There were these people from all over the country and they came in and you'd make an agreement with them and then they'd walk out and go back and convince the people not to sign it even after they had agreed to the conditions under which they'd go back to work. These people all went on strike and they didn't have the right to strike. You can't go out and fire 12,000 people or police 12,000 people by the military and this sort of thing. It doesn't work.

MAURICE SAUVÉ

I was in favour—mind you, I think it was a mistake—but I was in favour then on the grounds that if you recognise the unions you should not deprive the unions of their right to strike. Also, I was quite sure that with the mentality that was then developing in Canada, no matter if you gave people the right to strike or not, if they wanted to strike they would strike just the same. It was not because it was allowed or not allowed that the people would strike. We've seen this with the policemen. The mentality was changing, and the people were deciding to take their own affairs in their own hands, irrespective of what the authority in the government would say.

J. J. GREENE

I had great qualms about it. But this was so much a part of the new Liberal politics, Walter Gordon's type of liberalism, that we have to appeal to the urban worker, to the organised worker. We can't leave that all to the NDP because there's only room for one Conservative Party in this country, and if it comes to a choice they'll choose the original Conservative Party, so we've got to become more liberal. Any instincts I had the other way, I thought I'd better submerge them in the interests of the fact that this party is now becoming an urban party, a party that's competing more with the NDP than with the Tories. And if I feel so strongly we shouldn't be [doing this] then maybe I shouldn't be in this party at all. I'd better go along with this sort of thing. Gordon had a great personal appeal, and was very good to me in every way he could, and if he believes in that I'd better go along with it.

I had great qualms. I think it was a trend that probably was inevitable. It's not as easy a game, mind you. In the old days you went into the public service and understood that when you went in that's one of the rights you didn't have. Just as when you go into the Cabinet you don't have the right to wheel and deal and make a dollar on the side.

J. R. NICHOLSON

There are certain civil servants who shouldn't have the right to strike. There should be compulsory arbitration or something else. You wouldn't permit the army to strike, you wouldn't permit the Mounted Police to strike, but yet we've given it to other civil servants in key jobs, hospital employees in the Far North, for instance—they shouldn't be allowed to strike. Instead of allowing the unions to make the choice, we should have said that in certain categories they would have to go for compulsory arbitration and wouldn't have the right to strike. When they join the Mounted

Police, when they enter the army, or a firefighting department out at the airports, when they accept these jobs, they'd know they're not going to have the right to strike. If that's made clear to them in the first place and they go into the service with that knowledge, there's no harm done. But the trouble is they've got it now, and once you give something to somebody it's pretty hard to take it away from them.

During the debate in Parliament the Conservatives warned the government of the danger of enacting the right to strike for the public service. Patrick Nowlan, a Nova Scotia Tory Member, said that compulsory arbitration was one thing but he could not agree with legislation that would allow government employees legally to walk off the job. Jack Horner, at the time an Alberta Conservative, pointed to the serious difficulty that the Quebec government was having with essential services being tied up. Gérard Pelletier, who appeared to be the government spokesman in the debate, said that he was in "total disagreement" with the Conservatives and that it was "absolutely normal" that the civil servants should have the option of the strike weapon.

The former civil servants in the Cabinet—and they included Lester Pearson, Jack Pickersgill, Mitchell Sharp, and Bud Drury—did not believe that civil servants would want collective bargaining, let alone the right to strike. They may have thought, because they had all been top officials, that they were out of touch with the mass of government employees, and thus they should let a former labour leader like Jean Marchand, who had got the Quebec public servants the right to strike, show the way. There is no indication that Marchand had explained to the Cabinet that the right to strike in the civil service should be limited to one- or two-day walk-outs. That appeared to be an afterthought on his part.

JEAN MARCHAND

When they [government employees] tell me, "You know, we never discuss on an equal footing with the government," I tell them that they are right. They are not on equal footing, because we have the right to pass laws, and they don't. So if you have a gun and I don't have, I cannot be on equal footing. It's not possible. But what I think we should allow them to do is to paralyse a service for a moment. Then people will say, "Hey, how come? Why are we paralysed? Why are we deprived of this service, which is very important?" It gives the employees an opportunity to explain to the public what the government is doing to them, and to go back to work. But not to say, "We're here to fight to death with the government of Canada." This is not possible. This is not even possible in a province.

What I'm suggesting is a one- or two-day strike, the purpose being to inform the public. If the strikers are right, and if the people say, "They are right, those people. They have only two weeks' vacation per year, while the average in Canada is three and four weeks. Why? Is there a bad administrator?" So this is why I supported this principle, and I still support that, but within those limits. Which were not explained, of course.

MITCHELL SHARP

All of us who had been in the public service found it absolutely astounding that civil servants would want the right to strike. I'm being perfectly frank. Of course, we had been civil servants at the top, or at least we were in elite groups. We had no interest in strike action; indeed, very little interest in pay. Even collective bargaining struck us as very strange, that civil servants should want to gather together to bargain with the government about their wages. We were inclined, I think, most of us, to say the system as it worked gave civil servants about as much as they would get by collective bargaining, and I think that's probably so.

The rule that the Treasury Board followed was that they awarded increases in wages similar to those being granted in similar occupations outside. That was the basis upon which we had all served in the public service. Until you get up to the upper reaches, and then there is nothing to compare. So my attitude toward it was that it was a strange phenomenon, and I think Mr. Pearson took much the same view.

JEAN MARCHAND

Why did Mr. Pearson seem to give in so often? I think it was in his very nature. It's the way he used to proceed. It was not a matter of honesty or dishonesty. It was a matter of procedure. His job was to keep people together. So sometimes he had to push somebody around a little bit to get the other one to accept something else, and so forth. And he was playing this type of game all the time. It was in the very nature of the job that he occupied before becoming Prime Minister.

In this job of diplomacy or conciliation, even in the labour field, the truth is the agreement. What do I mean? There is no objective truth. The truth is when the two parties agree together, provided they don't agree on the back of a third party. But if they do agree, the man who's the conciliator says, "I succeeded." "At what did you succeed?" "Well, it doesn't matter, I did succeed." Remember the settlement of the Seaway dispute.

June 17, 1966, was the date set for a strike by the St. Lawrence Seaway workers which would have tied up shipping in the Great Lakes system at the height of the summer traffic. The workers had rejected a conciliation board recommendation for a 14 percent wage increase; they were demanding 35 percent, which would have brought them level with the earnings of their American counterparts on the inland waterway. On June 9 Senator Norman A. "Larry" MacKenzie, a former president of the University of British Columbia, was appointed mediator and, within hours of the strike deadline, he was able to announce a settlement. The workers were to get a 30 percent increase, 20 percent immediately retroactive to January 1, 1966, and a further 10 percent on January 1, 1967.

It was an expensive agreement with far-reaching consequences. Jack Nicholson, the Minister responsible as Minister of Labour, blamed it all on Quebec. The workers there were holding the country up to ransom over completing Expo, the Montreal World Fair, on time for the opening in centennial year. There had been awards of a 50 percent increase in wages over two years and one of 70 percent over thirty months, Nicholson said. Stu Keate asserted that the Seaway settlement brought an unrealistic atmosphere into labour negotiations, by which he meant that a pattern had been established whereby conciliation and the normal process of negotiations would be regarded as a preliminary step before an appeal to government and Parliament. The 30 percent Seaway settlement also triggered inflation.

J. R. NICHOLSON

The employees on the Seaway had been asking for parity with their counterparts in the United States—in some places they were working only a few hundred yards apart, they played bridge together at different places along the Seaway, and their children played together—they felt the Canadians should be getting the same pay as those on the American side. Larry MacKenzie conducted a very thorough investigation, and the only report that I got was that he was hoping to bring about a settlement that would be acceptable to the government, but he'd make no guarantee. Finally, in the early evening of the day that he had his final meeting [with the representatives of the Seaway workers], he said to me, "I am recommending 30 percent increase over two years. It will still be less than what they were asking for, less than what their counterparts in the United States were getting, but it's in line with the settlement that's gone through for the waterfront workers in Montreal and Quebec." Even at that, we nearly had to order them back by an Act of Parliament.

When you consider that the waterways had been locked up virtually as a result of the strike of the dock workers in Montreal, if that had been followed by a strike in the Seaway, with coal and iron ore needed in the steel mills in Hamilton, it would have been iniquitous. The recommendation of an experienced and highly regarded mediator, Senator MacKenzie, came up in Cabinet; we debated it at length and the Pearson Government accepted it.

PAUL HELLYER

Dr. MacKenzie of the University of British Columbia was appointed conciliator or arbitrator—I can never remember which. And he bought the argument of parity between the Canadian Seaway workers and the U.S. [workers]. On what grounds he did it I never knew and still don't know. He recommended that [30 percent raise] to the government. The Cabinet was called into emergency session to consider the report.

Everybody in the Cabinet knew it was dynamite and practically everybody in the Cabinet knew it was the wrong thing to do. The decision was ultimately taken by the Prime Minister himself—

this after having been warned by nearly everybody that it was wrong and that the real thing to do was for the government to grasp the nettle and just say that we wouldn't go along with it.

E. J. BENSON

Although people say it [inflation] came from the Seaway settlement, the pattern was not established there, in my opinion. The pattern was established at Expo, where in order to get a certain [no-strike] agreement they gave very high increments. When the Seaway dispute came along, it was an unfortunate example because you had Canadians and Americans working on the same locks and the Americans were getting much more than 30 percent more than the Canadians. It was a case where there needed to be a basic adjustment in the income of the people doing that particular kind of work.

But when a government does that, it's never viewed as that, and I think that's what caused the difficulty. Certainly it meant that other people wanted more wages and more equality with American workers and this moves through the economy until it's at our present stage where perhaps our productivity is lighter than the Americans and our wages are as high or higher, and that's going to cause trouble in the long run. It has to.

JEAN MARCHAND

There was pressure on the market because of Quebec Expo and the building of the subway in Montreal. But this is a normal pressure and the only thing that you have to do at that time is to resist—that's all.

But if we focus on Mr. Pearson, it was inside his logic, because the one who presented the Seaway settlement to him said, "The parties agree on that." This was a very strong argument as far as Mr. Pearson was concerned. There was a dispute and the parties agreed.

He told me, "We agreed to 30 percent." I said, "I don't know. I'm very happy as a former labour leader, but I think that you're starting something very dangerous." "Well, this is an agreement." It was his very nature.

BRUCE HUTCHISON

The inflationary explosion preceded the Seaway dispute. It started on the Montreal waterfront. That was when the first breakthrough occurred, and they got x percent. So the Seaway workers said, "We're just as good and we want the same." Then we went on from there into the inflation.

But Pearson as a conciliator? In any free country, any democratic country, the primary function of a leader and of a political system itself is to conciliate and adjust, accommodate, compromise conflicting interests. That's what politics is all about. And the first duty of a leader in a free society is to attempt to bring about that sort of working agreement. It's never logical, it's always untidy, and it's always having to be changed. But to say that Mike didn't care about what happened as long as he got the boys together—I think that's stretching it too far. He made a mistake, probably, in the Seaway agreement and in many other aspects.

Our three great Prime Ministers, in my book, were Macdonald, Laurier, and King. Whether you liked them or not is not the point. What were they doing all the time? What were they but conciliators? Macdonald was the supreme conciliator, and he conciliated the various elements of this nation into Confederation. And Mr. King managed to hold the thing together in his time, and Mike tried to do the same thing.

13 *Vive le Québec libre*

IT DIDN'T REQUIRE much argument to persuade Lester Pearson that he should stay on as Prime Minister during Canada's centennial year; any idea that he had of quitting because of the disappointing results of the 1965 election was completely unrealistic, and he was quick to appreciate this. He knew that scores of heads of state would be visiting Canada that year and he was told that it was his duty as a world figure and the only Canadian to win the Nobel Peace Prize to welcome them and to preside at the opening of Expo, Montreal's World Fair, and other celebrations marking the hundredth anniversary of Confederation.

Furthermore, Pearson had a birthday present for the Canadian people: the universal health insurance scheme known as Medicare. This was the ultimate welfare project, and Allan MacEachen, who was a great proponent, called it the major federal-provincial program after the Canada Pension Plan. It had been promised in 1919, at the Liberal Party convention that elected W. L. Mackenzie King as Leader, and Stanley Knowles saw Medicare as the final winding up of the Mackenzie King estate, a thought that might have appealed to Pearson's historical sense.

At the time it was estimated that the cost of free medical services across the country would be a billion dollars of which the federal government would pay half or 500 million dollars. However, the provinces would have to subscribe to a set of four criteria or principles before they would receive the cost-sharing grants: (1) the Medicare benefits had to be portable and apply in any province, (2) there had to be universal coverage, which

365

meant that everybody was eligible, (3) comprehensive physician's services had to be provided, and (4) it had to be administered publicly and not by any private plan. In the spring of 1965 work started on a Medicare program that was to go into effect on July 1, 1967.

When the provinces were told about the proposal at the federal-provincial conference on July 19, 1965, they objected, but it was quite evident that Ottawa was going to go ahead with it. The way that Lester Pearson sprang the Medicare proposal on the provincial premiers and representatives infuriated Eric Kierans, who was then Quebec Minister of Health. This was typical of the arrogance of the federal bureaucrats and their determination to be the initiators of anything new, Kierans said, and added that it had a tremendous effect on René Lévesque, who was a Quebec minister and a delegate to the conference.

ERIC KIERANS

At the end of the conference, while the officials were working in the back rooms on drafting the communiqué and translating it and getting the commas right and all the rest of it—which takes two hours—everybody was making small talk. The final two hours are always just gossip. Then, just in this period, Mr. Pearson announces that there's going to be universal Medicare. Well, there wasn't anybody around the table who had ever heard of this before. Nobody had been consulted.

Put yourself in the position of the premiers: within an hour they're going out to face the press. I can't remember what else was decided at that federal-provincial conference—it was all going to be included in a blasé communiqué that didn't say very much. But, certainly the thing that was going to capture the attention was Mr. Pearson's announcement that there was going to be universal Medicare.

Now, Mr. Pearson didn't know how much it was going to cost. All he said was that it was going to cost about a billion dollars and that he was going to pay for half. So very quickly we, in Quebec, figured out—well, we'd be 25 percent of the 500 million dollars for the provinces—that's 125 million, somewhere around that. I remember Mr. Lesage saying to me, "Well, I'm going to fight an election on this next year." Even Mr. Lesage didn't know that Pearson and Walter Gordon intended to fight one that fall on

Medicare too, in order to get a majority government. It was completely opportunistic.

Anyway, Mr. Lesage said, "What do you think?" because I looked very dubious and I reminded him that the previous week we'd had a very difficult Cabinet meeting in Quebec because we had been living high, wide, and handsome on the credit of the province, and investors in the province were beginning to say, "Well, look, not so fast," and so on, and that this had resulted in our putting a ceiling on our expansion for the year '66.

I reminded him of this, and I said, "This is going to be another 100 or 125 million. It's going to have to come out of what we're doing if this is introduced. So what [program] are we going to stop?" I remember Gérin-Lajoie's quick reaction as soon as he sensed this—125 million more going to health meant it would be that much more difficult for him [he was Quebec education minister] to get whatever he wanted for an enrichment of education.

Here was somebody from Ottawa spending 125 million dollars of our money without even asking us! And putting us in the position of looking like eighteenth-century reactionaries if we said, "Well, wait a minute. We're not able to take part in this right now because we have x, y, and z to do first." Now, you look at it from the point of view of people whose own planning is all upset, and you try to cool them down, and what answer have you got when they say, "Yes, but they didn't even have the courtesy to ask us what we thought about it before they'd spent the money?" Now there was an awful lot of this that went on.

JOHN ROBARTS

There was one province that wanted the Medicare scheme. That was Saskatchewan because Tommy Douglas had introduced the plan and all they had to do was hold out their hands and get paid for what they were going to have to do anyway.

We had developed a plan here in Ontario. It was a combination plan as we had gone through the private insurance carriers. I think anybody will admit today, even though many wouldn't in those days, that a government just can't do anything in that sort of area as efficiently as private enterprise. I think all you have to do is look around. Our plan was accepted in our legislature after much debate and was working well for Ontario, for the type of society we had. We were simply told that the federal government had a plan, and that they were going to take 125 million dollars out of Ontario, and if we didn't join their plan and scrap our plan, they'd take the 125 million and distribute it over the rest of Canada and none of it would come back into Ontario. Well, that's a lot of pressure to put a government under, and, of course, I had to yield.

Some time after that federal-provincial conference Mr. Pearson had a dinner party at 24 Sussex. By then the bill was passed, and it is one of the most rigid pieces of legislation that ever went through the House of Commons.* There's no provision in it for regulations, so there was no flexibility whatsoever. I recall his sitting at a fireplace in his own drawing room and saying, "Now, I think I'll poll all the provinces to see who wants Medicare." I recall it so well because he said in his own inimitable smiling fashion, "I think I'll start with my friends first." So he started with the Liberal provinces, and there was [Louis] Robichaud of New Brunswick and Joey Smallwood of Newfoundland. He polled every province, and there was one that said yes, and as I said, that was Saskatchewan. Well you know, he was ashen.

When we left he walked into the hall with me and he said, "John, what can I do? If I try to change that legislation, I've got to take it to the House of Commons. My government will be defeated." And I said, "Mike, I guess the only thing I can say is, that's your problem."

ROBERT STANFIELD

On the question of Medicare, I was in on those negotiations, and Mr. Pearson was pretty tough again. Now the impression of Mike Pearson as an easy-going fellow who gave in all down the line is quite a wrong impression. He kept saying, you know, that "We're here to consult," but my recollection is on Medicare there were four principles that were really non-negotiable and the provinces virtually had to take them or leave them. Many of us were concerned in those days that we were going to be lured into

*Although the Pearson Government had decided on the broad outlines of the Medicare legislation at the time of the 1965 federal-provincial conference, "An Act to Authorise the Payment of Contributions by Canada toward the Cost of Ensured Medical Care Services by the Provinces" did not receive Royal Assent till December 21, 1966.

these programs on the basis of the federal government accepting a certain financing role and then later on the federal government would withdraw in whole or in part, and of course that's precisely what happened. Mr. Pearson didn't withdraw, but Mr. Trudeau has changed very substantially the federal financial role in these plans. I think it's a gross betrayal, but that relates to Pierre Trudeau, not to Mike Pearson.

ALLAN MacEACHEN

I remember that the premiers would argue that consultation was meaningless unless their views were accepted. Well, in some cases—certainly in the case of Medicare—we had to move ahead of some of the provinces, but it is to me a legitimate use of the spending power of the federal government. This was probably the major federal-provincial program after the Canada Pension Plan. It was put through the House while I was Minister [of National Health and Welfare], but the House of Commons was generally supportive of the over-all commitment to Medicare.

Although Walter Gordon and Maurice Lamontagne were no longer in the Cabinet, they still had a great deal of influence on the government. They were seat mates in the House of Commons "penalty box," which could be said to have been the source of a number of power plays. On three or four occasions, according to Lamontagne, their participation in the caucus deliberations served to divide the Cabinet. Certainly, they played a major role on the question of Medicare, which was hardly surprising since health insurance had been one of Walter Gordon's priority projects. The legislation that would have had Medicare come into effect on July 1, 1967—a symbolic date because it was the nation's hundredth birthday—was making its way through Parliament when Finance Minister Mitchell Sharp said that it would have to be deferred because of the economic situation. Allan MacEachen asserted that the original effort was to defer it indefinitely. There was an uproar in the Liberal caucus with Walter Gordon, Maurice Lamontagne, and their followers, who included Pierre Trudeau, attacking the government. Sharp agreed to a postponement for a year, and it was suggested that the Finance Minister might be able to let Medicare begin earlier if economic conditions improved. However, this was not a satisfactory way of doing things, and

Sharp insisted that the starting date had to be put off till July 1, 1968. Walter Gordon was afraid that any deferment would become indefinite, and Jean Marchand was on the point of resigning but accepted Mike Pearson's assurance that the plan would really begin then and would not be put off again.

In opening the Liberal Party's policy conference in Ottawa on October 10, 1966, the Prime Minister announced that the firm date for Medicare was July 1, 1968. It was at that conference in the ballroom of the Chateau Laurier that Mitchell Sharp and Walter Gordon had their decisive debate on Medicare and the question of economic nationalism.

MITCHELL SHARP

There were two issues that dominated the convention, and I was concerned with them both. One of them was Medicare, and the second was economic nationalism.

On Medicare, in the interests of maintaining our financial stability, I was very much in favour of a one-year delay in the implementation of Medicare. Walter, I think, was opposed to that; he was on the side of those who wanted an immediate implementation. But those cudgels were taken up more strongly by other people at the conference including, if I may recall, John Munro, who was then a young Member of Parliament and who took me on in open debate at one of the sessions, and it was quite a clash. However, the convention finally approved a resolution endorsing the one-year delay, which I was very grateful for although it was a very awkward and difficult period for me.

WALTER GORDON

Medicare was to come into effect on the 1st of July, 1967, Confederation Day. Mitchell wanted to postpone it or to dump it, and he had various reasons for this, which changed from time to time. Eventually, it was decided that it would come into effect one year later. That was the subject of debate at the convention. In the end, the resolution was something to the effect that the delegates were sorry that it had been postponed, but it was agreed it had to come in on the 1st of July, 1968. But that wasn't the end of the discussion. There were many more attempts to put it off.

E. J. BENSON

Walter Gordon didn't want to put Medicare off a year. It was there; let's go. I wanted to proceed, but I was of the opinion that the economy would be better off if we didn't proceed for another year. Walter, I think, had a fear that if it was put off one year, it would be put off another year, and you just wouldn't get Medicare. That wasn't going to happen as far as I was concerned. I told the meeting that if it weren't proceeded with in 1968, I would resign.

MITCHELL SHARP

The other issue was economic nationalism. There were two organised groups in that convention: there was the Walter Gordon group, who wanted to bring in a resolution advocating a policy of economic nationalism, a fairly substantial resolution committing the government or committing the party to particular things; and there was another group from Western Canada who were strongly opposed to Walter Gordon. I was approached by both.

The first approach came from Donald Macdonald, who was the chief spokesman for Walter Gordon; he came to me with a draft resolution and said, "We would like to reach an agreement with you on the wording of a resolution." I looked at it and I said I didn't agree with it, and I didn't think I would be honest if I started negotiating on the terms of that resolution. I said, "Fundamentally, I don't agree with it and therefore I would prefer not to have anything to do with it, I'm sorry." So that was the first approach.

Then I was approached by the Western group, who were opposed to Walter Gordon's views, and there I found myself at odds with them, too, because they wanted to advocate free trade with the United States, with which I didn't agree. I was in neither camp in that sense, although there was common cause with these Westerners over the economic nationalism resolution. So I met with some of my close advisors and drafted a short statement of my position and of what I thought should be the position of the Liberal Party.

I went to the open meeting where this was to be discussed. There were three microphones—one, two and three—people were invited to speak, and the chairman said, "I'll recognise microphone number one first." Donald Macdonald got there first. I lined up quite a way back because I was not a protagonist. My view was what I thought represented the views of the Liberal Party; but it was a statement, not a motion. Donald had only three minutes and all he had time to do was to read this resolution.

Then the second spokesman got up from British Columbia, and he said he had a resolution to put, and the chairman said, "Well, I'm very sorry. Mr. Macdonald has a resolution on the floor now for debate." But this fellow said, "I don't agree with it." The chairman said, "But it's there." He said, "What can I do?" "Well," he said, "you can move that it be tabled." He said, "I do."

Somebody saw me and knew that I had some views on this, and asked me to come up to the microphone very shortly after that. And I made my little speech, which got overwhelming support, and Walter Gordon's resolution was voted down by an overwhelming majority. Then the Walter Gordon people—I think it was Maurice Lamontagne who approached me—said, "Now we must get together and work something out," which we did. So I always looked upon myself, not so much as opposing Walter Gordon, as proposing a line that I thought the Liberal Party could support, which was true. And the resolution that came forward reflected a more moderate view on these issues.

WALTER GORDON

I was resigning my seat anyway. I thought I'd have one last attempt to do something primarily on the independence issue, not the Medicare issue. The independence issue was particularly a fight with the Western Liberals under Ross Thatcher. Andy Thompson [former Ontario Liberal leader] was going to organise the Ontario delegates to come and support my point of view, which they believed in. He got sick and wasn't able to do it. He came down to the meeting himself, against his doctor's orders, and I thought it was going to kill him for a while, but he survived.

But we didn't have the organisation so we didn't [win]. The impression was that I had lost and that Sharp had won. Well, to be perfectly honest, it didn't make any difference to me, because I was getting out anyway. I was sorry that the delegates hadn't supported the independence moves forthrightly, but that was going to be up to somebody else because I was getting out. It didn't have anything to do with my resigning my seat. That was settled beforehand.

The overwhelming defeat of Walter Gordon at the Liberal Party's policy conference on October 10, 1966 seemed like his final political destruction, as Bruce Hutchison proclaimed in the Vancouver Sun. *Hutchison saw him as the cause of dissension and disunity in the government and said that now that he was gone, the Prime Minister must be relieved. However, some few weeks later, there were talks about his becoming a Minister again, and by the end of December 1966 Walter Gordon was back in the Cabinet. The negotiations for his return were circuitous and indirect since they were conducted mainly by his friends. Lester Pearson was alarmed to learn that Walter Gordon was serious about resigning his seat in Parliament—the Prime Minister had to worry about the minority state of his government—but he resisted the importuning of people like Keith Davey and Jimmy Walker. Pearson's attitude was ambivalent, and Paul Hellyer noted that he seemed to be far more his own man when Gordon was not in the Cabinet. In the end it was politics that decided the issue. Pearson knew that, if he didn't make him a Minister again, Gordon would not continue as a Private Member; furthermore, there was every indication that he would not leave quietly but would blame his departure on right-wing anti-nationalist forces having taken over the Liberal Party. This was something that a minority government could not face.*

So Walter Gordon returned to the Cabinet, as Minister Without Portfolio first and then President of the Privy Council, and for a time it looked as though the differences between him and Lester Pearson had been resolved. But there were further misunderstandings, which led to the final break. While Gordon got back, Maurice Lamontagne was not reappointed a Minister.

WALTER GORDON

Pearson had talked to me about coming back to the Cabinet during the summer or early spring, but nothing came of it. He didn't follow them [the conversations] up as he said he was going to do. But it was all right. I was pretty fed up with politics at that time, so I just decided to get out. When everybody realised I meant it—I was going to resign my seat—then there were a lot of pressures on Pearson to do something about it. He and I had one or two conversations. During the first one he said he couldn't do anything about it. I said, "Well, that's fine. I wasn't asking you to. You asked me to come down and have lunch with you, but I am not asking for anything."

Next, he called me and said he'd changed his mind and would I come back to the Cabinet to do various things. It was an impressive list: I was to control the work of the Cabinet; to be on a committee with three other people or four other people to control the work of the House; I was to have a lot to do with the organisation of the party, which had gone to pot in the meantime; and a number of other things that I found interesting. In addition, I was to be chairman of a Cabinet committee to do something about the independence issue. So on those terms I went back.

PAUL MARTIN

Mike asked me what I thought, should he bring Walter back? I said, "That's pretty well up to you. I think it would not be a bad idea." I knew how keenly he felt about Walter Gordon being out. They were very close friends. He was dependent on Walter Gordon to a very great extent, and I knew that it would ease his mind if his friend were back in the government. And after all, Gordon was an able man and an experienced man of business. So he said, "Well, would you speak to Walter?" And I said, "Certainly," and I did.

I said I just wanted him to know that if he came back it would be with my strong approval. Others didn't feel that way; I know Bob Winters felt the opposite. I think that Mitchell Sharp didn't feel that way either. But Pearson had asked me what I thought, and I acted accordingly.

MAURICE LAMONTAGNE

I remember Mr. Pearson told me at the Christmas party for the Members that he wanted me to return to the government—there were two or three newspaper people there when he talked to me and he said to them, "Well, here's the guy, I'm trying to convince him to come back to Cabinet and he won't accept." In the meantime Walter had more or less decided to go because he was not going to come to Ottawa indefinitely as a Private Member and leave his family in Toronto. He would resign his seat. There was some pressure on Mr. Pearson to take him back, but as far as I was concerned, when I left for Guadeloupe for the Christmas holiday, Walter was going, and of course, I was not coming back to the Cabinet. From Guadeloupe, we went to the Virgin Islands. On our way home, I read in the paper that Walter Gordon was back in the Cabinet. Some reporters had asked about me, and Mike said that he had no immediate plans for me. I did not understand the situation very well, so when I got back to Ottawa, Walter phoned me and said, "Did you receive my telegram?" I said, "No." He had sent the telegram to Guadeloupe after we had left, and I never got it. In any case, he said, "I'm back and I'm very surprised that you're not back also. I've written to Mr. Pearson about this and he has told me that it was because Jean Marchand objected to your coming back."

I couldn't believe this because Marchand kept saying, "We must get Lamontagne back. He is used to working with the civil service. I'm more of the politician. He would reinforce the team." I went to see Pearson and asked what happened. He said, "It's because of Marchand. He's opposed." I said, "Well, I'm afraid I don't believe you." In any case, I said, there was only one way to find out, and that was to have a meeting, which we had at 24 Sussex. Pearson asked the question of Jean Marchand, when I was there, and Marchand said, "I'm against this. There's opposition in the Quebec caucus, and I cannot say more." So that was it. We came back together in the same car, Mr. Marchand and I, and I asked him a few other questions, and he told me that he couldn't say any more.

WALTER GORDON

We had several conversations and very easy, pleasant ones. After all, Pearson and I knew each other pretty well, and we liked getting together. He told me the various things that he wanted me to do; which he had said to Keith Davey, or Davey had reported to me, and that it would mean I would be Deputy Prime Minister in all but name. They were things that I was interested in.

I said, "Now, we mustn't have any misunderstanding about this. If you like, I'll write a letter, the kind of letter that you will write me." That was fine, so I did that. He said he approved the letter. He also confirmed this with the so-called go-betweens. I think there were Benson and Pennell and MacEachen, but there may have been somebody else. Eventually he did write me a letter. It was not quite as specific as my phrasing, because we write differently, but it covered the points. He added some other things at the end that I thought dealt with something else altogether, but he covered the points we had agreed to.

PAUL HELLYER

I think that the feeling in the Cabinet was as mixed about Gordon's return as was the party's. Gordon had his people in Cabinet. And there were others that would have been as happy if he never returned. Gordon's people were never in the majority, they were always in the minority. And the fact that the minority carried in every controversial issue, I think, was a matter of some annoyance to the others.

The Prime Minister seemed to be far more his own man without Gordon. He took charge to a far greater extent when Gordon wasn't there. When Gordon was there, he was sort of the crutch. When he wasn't there, Pearson acted more like his own boss.

WALTER GORDON

I had gone back into the Cabinet and found I had nothing to do. So of course I was frustrated. I had gone back expecting to do a lot of things that would have kept me very busy. One of them would have been to organise the work of the Cabinet, which was in a hell of a mess.

I said I couldn't do the job of running the Cabinet properly without a staff. If I was going to be President of the Privy Council, I wanted the Privy Council staff, which had previously reported to Pearson. That was never resolved, and I never got the staff. I am not complaining particularly. I think Pearson probably had his difficulties, but he never found it easy to say to people, "Look. I promised you this, but I can't live up to it, for these reasons." That was one thing that he found difficult to do.

I naturally went to him periodically and said, "When the hell are you going to implement the various things that were the basis of my coming back to the Cabinet?" But it got put off and put off, and finally I wrote him a formal letter and said I would like him to implement these things or tell me why he couldn't. I ran into him one day and he said he was finding it difficult to reply to my letter. Eventually he replied in general terms, but he didn't give me an answer. I think he was finding it difficult with his colleagues, some of whom were displeased that he'd asked me back and that they hadn't known about it. They were the conservative elements in the Cabinet, and I think they felt that I was trying to push a more progressive line than they agreed with, and they were upset that I was back in the Cabinet.

I think he felt, perhaps, that if he pushed his agreement with me through, that one or two of them might have been annoyed—I don't think they would have resigned, but they might have [been annoyed]. I don't know. You would have to ask Mr. Pearson, and it's too late to do so now.

Although Lester Pearson got Walter Gordon, to whom he owed so much, back in the Cabinet in time for Canada's centennial, he wasn't able to do the same for Maurice Lamontagne, who had served him so well, because of opposition in the Quebec caucus. However, at Gordon's suggestion, Pearson had Lamontagne summoned to the Senate in April 1967—a happy solution since Lamontagne seemed to want to go there. His appointment of Judy LaMarsh as Secretary of State and the Minister in charge of the centennial celebrations turned out to be a stroke of genius, although he could hardly claim credit for that because all he wanted to do at the time was to get her out of Health and Welfare. He had offered her what were three minor portfolios and she had chosen Secretary of State because of the centennial. Still, he gave her a free hand and let the 1967 party roll along, which Douglas Fisher felt was rather courageous of him.

On March 5, 1967, Governor-General Georges Vanier died. He was the second Canadian to hold this vice-regal post and the first French Canadian. General Vanier had been a popular figure and, despite the bitterly cold weather, grief-stricken crowds lined the streets of Ottawa for the state funeral on March 8. Prime Minister Pearson had made preparation for a successor to General Vanier although he had hoped that, despite failing health, the general would continue in office throughout the centennial year. Pearson intended to appoint a former Speaker of the House of Commons, Roland Michener, an old friend from Oxford days, to the country's top post, and, in 1964, had sent him as Canadian High Commissioner to India to give him diplomatic experience. On April 17, Roland Michener was sworn in as Governor-General of Canada.

JUDY LaMARSH

I think Pearson was kind of astonished at the centennial. He was afraid Expo was going to be a disaster, and he couldn't get any Minister from Quebec who really would take hold of that [World's Fair] and finally he dumped it on Bob Winters. But it had been through about three Ministers from Quebec before that. The centennial, he thought that was going to be an unmitigated disaster; there were all kinds of trouble in that Centennial Commission when I took over. But he got enthusiastic with things like the blazers. He thought they were a real gas. And he was delighted as a child over Expo when it went.

But he got very bored with his role in meeting all these people and all the folderol on Parliament Hill and all these dinners and lunches and stuff. He didn't get nearly as bored as I did because at least his career had sort of prepared him for some of this. But I was the one who was bobbing up and down to curtsey and running around presenting flowers to governor-generals' ladies and things like that, which Mike at least didn't have to do.

ROLAND MICHENER

Pearson used to complain about having to eat so many dinners. He had to come to my dinners. He was duty-bound. And I gave a dinner for every head of state, so there were about twenty dinners. If it wasn't a head of state, I gave a lunch and Pearson gave the dinner. That was the protocol. So that he had to eat two meals for every guest, and I had to eat only one. I didn't have to go to his lunch or dinner, as the case might be, but he had to come to mine.

I remember one night we were having dinner, and I always had the wife on my right and my wife had the visiting head of government or state on her right, Pearson on her left, and Maryon Pearson on my left. They brought in a beef Wellington, a great big chunk of beef all covered with pastry, and he said, "Oh, Your Excellency, not again!" He said, "I love it, I can't resist it, but I eat too much for my country."

No, he enjoyed it when he was there. Mike was a convivial man. I don't think it was his preference. If he'd had a free choice he would not be engaging in a seven-course dinner and talking small talk or whatever was on, because these dinners are not arranged as conferences. You usually have a lady on each side instead of the man you want to talk to. If she's charming enough that's some compensation, but they're not the best use of time. And I think he felt the strain of them.

I'll tell you one thing about this: my wife, in consequence, sat with Pearson through the fifty-two meals that were eaten in Government House and had much more conversation with him than I had. I know for one thing he always said to her, "How are you getting on with the restoration of Government House?" because he had urged her and encouraged her from the very beginning, and she set right in to rehabilitate the place. One of the first things was the ladies' washroom—it was an awful dump. It had pipes all through the top, and it wasn't adequate in size. So my wife got that all fixed up with the honeycomb ceiling and beautiful lights and decorated, and some paintings and carpeted and everything—really, it was quite presentable. That was one thing there was a lot of comment on. You wouldn't think that aspect of Government House would be so important, but there it was.

Then she got carpets throughout the areas where there were just scattered pieces of carpet. You know, the government had been pretty parsimonious, I think, with my predecessors; but Pearson said, "Now, Nora, the government doesn't mind the expense for our centennial celebration, so now's your chance to get everything done." So she got busy and made very considerable improvements. No big structural alterations, but all these little things. It was a sidelight on Pearson that he was so keen about that. He wanted Canada to be well represented.

Aside from the centennial, Judy LaMarsh's main preoccupation was broadcasting. She was the Minister through whom the Canadian

Broadcasting Corporation reported to Parliament, and the CBC was extremely unpopular with the government and the official Opposition because of a TV public affairs show called "This Hour Has Seven Days," which many M.P.s and Ministers considered distorted and vicious. There was to be a new act governing television and radio and the Secretary of State had to look after this. It was over broadcasting that Judy LaMarsh came to a parting of the ways, as she put it, with Mike Pearson, who was by this time tired of disruption. She was surprised to find that the Prime Minister had a special interest in broadcasting and had been a supporter of the Canadian Radio League, which became the Canadian Broadcasting League (a public broadcasting lobby), from its earliest days.

JUDY LaMARSH

Mike was the chairman of the Broadcast Committee of the Cabinet. At first he was pretty crazy about its work. Then he just got too busy and he stopped showing up. Finally I said to him, "You know, there'll never be a broadcasting act unless you just move over and let me call the meetings when you're not available." He did.

The first several meetings he called in his office, not in the Cabinet committee room. Several bodies that wanted to talk to the Cabinet committee, he had in, like the Canadian Broadcasting League. Again, it was a very complicated business. He simply didn't have the opportunity to have the kind of input that he wanted.

He was very mad at "Seven Days," I remember, when the program was on. He told all the Cabinet Ministers that we couldn't appear on it because they had done a very unfair job on Favreau when the troubles in Quebec were being bruited about. They had edited it very unfairly. Mike was actually furious about that, so he told us all we couldn't appear on it. They went after everybody, of course, but I didn't pay any attention to that.

Whenever the government changed in Canada, which was not very often in recent times, the broadcasting act was rewritten. It was the Conservative government of Prime Minister R. B. Bennett in the early '30s which established the first public broadcasting body, the Canadian Radio Broadcasting Commission. When the Liberals returned to power under Prime Minister Mackenzie King, the CRBC was transformed into the bigger and more powerful Canadian Broadcasting Corporation. Some twenty-two years later the Progressive Conservatives led by Prime Minister Diefenbaker withdrew the regulatory functions of the CBC —the private broadcasters had complained that it was unfair for the corporation to be both competitor and regulator—and gave them to a separate agency, the Board of Broadcast Governors. Now that the Liberals were back in office, Prime Minister Lester B. Pearson was having the broadcasting act redrafted for the fourth time in a little more than thirty years.

The BBG was to be greatly strengthened and turned into the Canadian Radio Television Council—later "Council" was to be changed to "Commission" because this was considered to be a more bilingual name. The CRTC was to have five full-time members on its board instead of the three that the BBG had, and it would be given more staff and more money. There was also to be some reorganisation of the top management of the CBC. Those who drew up the act were overcome with the spirit of the centennial and Confederation, as they wrote that the objective of the Canadian Broadcasting Corporation was "to contribute to the development of national unity and provide for a continuing expression of Canadian identity." While the House of Commons was in the midst of debating the new act, Judy LaMarsh got into an unseemly row with the CBC president, Alphonse Ouimet. This public quarrel did not enhance her relations with Mike Pearson who, as she indicated, had become very tired of her disruptions, but it may have helped in the passage of the legislation.

JUDY LaMARSH

I was on a television show with Pierre Berton, who wasn't paying much attention to the answers anybody gave. He was reading the questions. And I said something about "rotten management" in the CBC, and he said "Yeah, that's probably why we haven't been able to get our set for *Front Page Challenge*." He completely missed the fact that I'd said the management was rotten, and it was from a typescript that the press picked that up later on, which caused a great row.

At any rate, Ouimet got a resolution passed by the board of directors calling on the Prime Minister for my resignation. You know, it was really the wrong way around. You don't do that. But he was pretty arrogant and he was determined to get where he wanted to go. That lost him the support of the House.

Before this the House was against me and Mike was against me. He was sitting in front of me. He said, "I want to say something." I said, "I can end this trouble. You let me get out [of this mess] or else I get out. Don't worry about it." So I restrained him from getting into the debate at all. And the mood in the House began to change after three or four days. After they had jumped all over me, then they started jumping all over Ouimet—who the hell do these people think they were, attacking the Minister and a Member of Parliament? Then I got kind of concerned because it looked to me as if they were in the way of destroying public broadcasting, which I very strongly support.

Although Judy LaMarsh was not the first woman in a Canadian Cabinet—Ellen Fairclough was the first and had been a Minister in the Diefenbaker Government for almost six years—there were really no facilities for women in the Parliament Buildings. If she wanted to go the lavatory, she had to leave the Cabinet room, walk the length of a long corridor, down a flight of stairs to the secretaries' can, as she put it, on the next floor. Once, when she was caught short, she went to the men's room while one of the Ministers stood guard, and was astonished at all the marble fittings. The House of Commons was a private men's club, and there was no changing it. Judy also became aware of how few women got appointments, and she made a nuisance of herself asking about women and why they were not given jobs.

Pauline Jewett said that Mike Pearson was a traditionalist who didn't really believe that women should be in government, but the fact that there were so few women M.P.s was not his fault but the fault of the Liberal Party and all political parties who did not encourage women to run. When she suggested at a Liberal Party meeting in the mid-'60s that there should be a policy target of fifty women candidates in the next election, she could not even get a seconder.

PAULINE JEWETT

I remember on one occasion wanting to be one of the Liberal representatives on a parliamentary committee that was being planned to look into the conditions in penitentiaries. The guys

who were selecting people, the Whip and the Parliamentary
Assistant to the Minister of Justice and so on, said that they
thought this would be awkward because we'd be having to
examine things that would offend my sensibilities, and perhaps
even have to go into a men's washroom or something. Incredible.
Maybe they wanted me off for other reasons, but these were the
ones that were given.

Judy LaMarsh proposed a Royal Commission on the Status of Women
shortly after becoming a Minister, but it took her years to sell it to Prime
Minister Pearson. Judy suggested that Florence Bird, a journalist who
worked under the nom de plume *of Anne Frances, should head the*
commission.

JUDY LaMARSH

I insisted that there be a woman senator, and Pearson appointed Mary Kinnear. I said, "It's almost better to have nobody than Mary Kinnear." Later on they picked some woman in
B.C. that nobody in B.C. even knew. I saw her quoted as saying
that she hadn't understood going to the Senate meant she had to be
in Ottawa, and she didn't intend to be in Ottawa very often. Just
dismal, some of the people that they chose.

I made a couple of speeches and flew a few kites [about women].
I think what sparked me finally was that I had read something in
the paper that President Kennedy had set up an inquiry into the
status of women. I thought, "Boy, what a great idea." So I wrote
the States and we dragged around through the embassies and got
some of the information on it. Then we drafted an order-in-
council and I took it to Mike, and he didn't seem to be opposed.
He didn't treat it very seriously, but at some time he must have
given it a whirlaround because he told me that Jean Lesage snorted
about it and said that it was an invasion of the provincial
jurisdiction. Well, the B and B Commission wasn't and I don't
know how the hell the status of women could be.

Then I made a speech [on women's rights] during the 1965
election campaign. I really chose a great audience, a group of
Ukrainian women, the last and least liberated of all. There was one
woman there who worked for the provincial Citizenship
Department who was young, and she was the only person who

didn't think I was right out of my skull, making this speech. One of the Vancouver papers came out with a really snide editorial about "the next thing, we'll have to have is a Status of Men Commission." It wouldn't be a bad idea now either. But it must have been a year and a half or two years that I beat Mike over the head with that proposal.

Now I don't know where Laura Sabia got her idea; she may have got it as I did from seeing that Kennedy had done something. But Laura did a fabulous thing. She got the women's organisations in this country to come into Ottawa to speak with one voice. And Mike had been quite impressed by some briefs of the national women's organisations; there was one on clean water and one on energy that really impressed him. Well, the whole Cabinet was supposed to meet with these women when they came up to talk about the status of women. It must have been two years after I'd tried to get Mike to appoint a status of women commission. Sabia was smart enough not to speak because she turns a lot of people off, but there was a very clever woman who made the pre-sentation, Réjeanne Colas from Montreal—later she was the first woman to be appointed a Supreme Court judge in Quebec. She was very impressive. And I think Pearson was convinced then. At any rate, he took my draft and tore it all up and mishmashed it around.

When it came to naming the members of the commission, I wanted all women and he wouldn't go for that, and he had a number of Quebeckers in mind. I suggested the chairman, and it was kind of dumb of me because I really didn't know Florence Bird very well, but I had seen her on television a lot and met her several times. She was my suggestion, and I didn't know that she wasn't bilingual—it never occurred to me that she wouldn't be able to speak French.

FLORENCE BIRD

I wanted to get an interview with Mike. There was something —I can't quite remember what the issue was that I wanted to interview him about. And I was a bit annoyed that I was being given the run-around. So when the phone rang in my apartment, and a secretarial voice said, "This is the Prime Minister's office,

Mrs. Bird. The Prime Minister would like to speak to you," I wasn't surprised. Mike Pearson came on the line, and he said, "Florence, I guess you think I'm phoning you about that interview you've been trying to get." I said, "Yes, I hope you'll give it to me." He said, "No, I'm not going to give it to you. What I want you to do is to be chairman of a Royal Commission on the Status of Women." And I said, "My God!" which was probably not the best thing to have said, but I was really stunned. And then I said, in a sort of an insecure voice, "Do you think I can do it?" And he said, "Sure you can do it. I wouldn't ask you if I didn't think you could. Come up tomorrow morning to the office and look at the terms of reference. Good-bye."

The next morning I went to the Prime Minister's office and Mary Macdonald was there with the terms of reference. Mike came in and said, "I hope you're going to do it. I think you must do it, you know, and I hope you will do it. We haven't decided yet who to put on the commission, but you decide." I looked at the terms of reference and I can assure you that if I had realised how difficult and how widespread [they were, I wouldn't have undertaken it]. I can still recite them: "to enquire, report and make recommendations to the federal government as to what steps it can take to give women equal opportunities with men in every aspect of Canadian society"—*every* aspect of Canadian society. Then there was a list of about nine different areas: criminal law, family law, the training of women to return into the labour force, the political position of women in the country, taxation, marriage, and divorce. It was a sociological study of the entire society. I was so upset by the thought that I would really have to do it because I kept thinking of all the women whom I've known who needed help.

So there I was. I was really caught on this, that I had to do it. I had a great sense of obligation. You have to pay off somewhere in your life the tremendous opportunity that's been given to you. I looked at the list and I said, "All right, I'll do it." And I said, "Who are the other commissioners?" "Well," they said, "the Cabinet would have to decide on them but if there were any persons you didn't want, you could refuse to have them on the commission." I was the first woman ever to be chairman of a federal royal commission. I was appointed February 2, 1967.

The Royal Commission on the Status of Women did not begin its public hearings until the spring of 1968, which was well after Prime Minister Pearson had resigned. Florence Bird thought that he might have planned it that way.

FLORENCE BIRD

We asked for briefs in the spring of 1967, and we wanted to give people plenty of time to prepare them because the preparation is in itself an education. If you have the hearings too soon, you rush people, and a lot of women didn't know exactly how to prepare a brief. So we made up a small pamphlet which we distributed, 50,000 of them, in supermarkets and in libraries saying what was needed in a brief and asking some sort of key questions. We also wrote letters or telephoned to all the larger organisations like the CLC [Canadian Labour Congress], the Canadian Bar Association, and other big women's organisations and men's organisations, and gave them time, really, to do a good job. You see, we were getting into the summer when nobody does anything.

So that by the time the following spring came we had a chance to read those briefs. We gave them till the first of March—they had to be in then. We started out then on nine weeks of hearings—we went out for three weeks, then came back for a couple of weeks, and then went out again. I went up to the Arctic with one other commissioner.

The change in the attitude of the newspapers and the media was very interesting, because they'd laughed at us: who needs a Royal Commission? Ha, ha, ha. Women had never had it so good. Ha, ha, ha. Let women by all means make advances to men, but do it slyly and surreptitiously as they always have, you know. I was really horrified by the sort of inbred chauvinism of my colleagues. Very saddening. I was horrified by it, but I didn't show it, I think. I kept my cool, which is the thing you have to do if you're chairman of a royal commission. And as the public hearings went on, and they saw what widows felt, what was happening to widows, what was happening to the poor, what was happening under property rights, the attitude in the press began to change.

On the morning of July 23, 1967, President Charles de Gaulle arrived in Quebec City aboard the French cruiser, Colbert. The Canadian government had wanted him to come to Ottawa first, as all other heads of state did, but he told Paul Martin, who saw him in Paris a couple of months before his visit, that he was coming by boat, which meant that he would land in Quebec. Léo Cadieux, who was the Canadian Defence Minister by then, felt that it was awkward and old-fashioned to travel by warship, and too much a reminder of gunboat diplomacy. But, Cadieux said, De Gaulle had made a trip to South America in the same cruiser — and that was his style. Governor-General Roland Michener received the French president when he stepped ashore at Wolfe's Cove, and External Affairs Minister Martin represented the federal government at the ceremonies in Quebec City.

There was no doubt that General de Gaulle was not just like any other of the score or more heads of state who visited Canada during the centennial year. The Quebec government of Premier Daniel Johnson regarded him as their own special guest and believed, as one provincial official stated, that his visit would be a recognition of the state of Quebec in international diplomacy. Premier Johnson had said, on the eve of his arrival, that it would make both French and English Canadians more conscious of the French Fact in Canada. Some 300,000 fleur-de-lis and tricolour flags had been handed out to the populace, but not a single Canadian maple leaf flag.

PAUL MARTIN

I had gone to see General de Gaulle two months before he came to Canada, and discussed his visit with him. There were certainly no indications that he wasn't looking forward to coming to Ottawa. He gave no indication that he wanted to speak about Quebec in a way that would prejudice Canadian unity. I'm sure that if he had come to Ottawa he would not have spoken against Confederation. He would have emphasised the French Fact, he would have demonstrated his great partial interest in Canadian French culture.

ROLAND MICHENER

The government, after some negotiation with the province of Quebec, established a routine for receiving De Gaulle properly. The Governor-General of Canada should receive him first when he set foot on Canadian soil—it was a little sticky, but finally they agreed—Danny Johnson would be second, and they would take him off my hands immediately. He would finally come back to me and to the government of Canada in Ottawa, after opening the French pavilion [at Expo in Montreal] and touring the province of Quebec. That was the routine.

So I went down to Anse Au Foulon—it's the ancient name for what some irreverent people call Wolfe's Cove—where the big ships come in. He was aboard the *Colbert,* a French cruiser. We received him there. It was quite early in the morning, and about 5,000 people gathered in a sort of stadium that had been constructed for the purpose underneath the cliff. Half of them, I think, were American tourists.

I stood in line at the foot of the gangplank, my wife next, then Johnson and his wife.

Incidentally, the *Colbert* was not flying the Canadian flag, as she ought to have been. She was flying only the tricolour. So that was a mark against our visitor, but I don't think anybody complained. I don't know why it was because it is a courtesy to always put the host country's flag at one end of the ship and your own at the other. I don't know which is which.

De Gaulle marched down the aisle and down the gangplank, and was received and went along. No sign of Madame de Gaulle until my wife gave me a kick in the shin and I turned around to see, and there was Madame de Gaulle coming down the gangplank about a full minute and a half in arrears. I don't know why he did that—he was to have the full glory of the reception or something of the kind, or perhaps she might have been late that morning.

Then we went up to the speaking area and I read him a good lengthy address of welcome in which I explained everything, as it were, for about ten minutes. The only problem I had was that a helicopter kept coming down and drowning me out. It was a press helicopter and I could never make up my mind whether it was by design or by—the timing was good anyway. I had to stop at one stage, it was so noisy. However, I got through. Then Johnson made an address of welcome and President de Gaulle spoke.

Afterwards, we all got into cars in two cavalcades, one federal and one provincial, but my wife got in the wrong car. She got in the provincial one due to some error of a protocol officer, and she found herself sitting in there with Madame de Gaulle—and she thought that was quite proper, that's the way it should be—and Mrs. Johnson, who seemed a bit surprised that my wife was there instead of with me. The agreement was that we were to dash up to the Citadelle, my wife and I, and to receive the General there. The Johnsons would take the De Gaulles—Mrs. Johnson, the wife, Danny Johnson, the General—and they'd go on the separate cavalcade and around the longer route and give us time to get in and change. I went on, wondering what had happened to my wife. She finally turned up with President de Gaulle.

In the meantime, we'd got into the Citadelle and were ready to receive the great man, and we did. He came up to the salon, and we had a very representative group there, I remember. Paul Martin was there, and our Ambassador to France and a few others. Perhaps twenty people. We gave some refreshment and had twenty minutes' talk and then they all left.

PAUL MARTIN

When De Gaulle arrived in Quebec City on the Sunday morning, I was there to greet him on behalf of the federal government along with the Governor-General, and then I saw him in the afternoon on board the boat, had twenty minutes with him. This followed my having seen him two months before in France. When he spoke that night at the Quebec government dinner at the Chateau Frontenac, it wasn't from the Canadian point of view the best speech, but there was nothing that was deliberately offensive. What he did in that speech was to emphasise his support for French culture as it existed in Quebec and elsewhere, and when he finished his speech, he said, *"Vive le Canada, vive le Québec, vive la France."* But he said, *"Vive le Canada."*

I reported to Pearson that night, called him on the phone and told him about the day, told him about that speech. We laughed at some points in it. I forget exactly what they were, but perhaps more De Gaulle mannerisms than anything else.

There wasn't very much about Canada in the speech. Remember, he was speaking in the capital of the province of Quebec, and he had reserved that for his speech in Ottawa. Now, I never saw that [Ottawa] speech. I did try to get a text before he arrived, and I tried to get one when he was in Quebec. But I had discussed it with him in Paris and he gave me a general indication of the line that he would take. I don't know whether there was a text. De Gaulle was a very great speaker and he was capable of making the greatest speech without a text, and it may be that there wasn't [a text]. But he was going to repeat basically what he had said in Toronto when he went to Toronto in the days of John Diefenbaker as Prime Minister. He made a speech in Toronto in which he talked about Canada, Confederation, and the place of French Canada in it. That was the theme that he was going to incorporate among other things.

LÉO CADIEUX

If you look at the film of the so-called spur-of-the-moment phrase, *vive le Québec libre,* you will see that in the afternoon De Gaulle is surrounded by only activists of the separatist movement. They kept close to him with the banners and the posters and everything, and showing the slogan all the time. For a man who does not know that this slogan is the slogan of the separatists, and who uses it as a general expression, there is some measure of—I don't say excuse, because I don't think you can use the word *libre* in the sense that he used it, because the implication was *libre* from the rest of Canada—but some measure of explanation.

*When he came ashore at Quebec City, President de Gaulle ended his first short speech by saying, "*Vive le Canada dans son ensemble." *That was to be the last time that he was to greet Canada in its entirety, or as we might say, "Long live Canada, from sea to sea." He did say "*Vive le Canada" *after the state banquet tendered him by Premier Johnson, but by the time he reached Montreal, he had stopped saluting Canada. There was no doubt that De Gaulle was impressed by the enthusiastic welcome he received all along the Chemin du Roy and in Montreal. The huge crowds waving blue Quebec banners and tricolours and carrying placards proclaiming a Free Quebec and a Free France must have had an effect on him. On the balcony of the Montreal City Hall, he said that the atmosphere he had found along the route that he had travelled was similar to that of Liberation Day in Paris. Then, he cried out, "*Vive Montréal, vive le Québec, vive le Québec libre ..." *The view expressed in the French-language paper* La Presse *was that De Gaulle had offered himself as a liberator and had been accepted as such, and that the General had perhaps changed the course of history.*

There was an immediate and angry reaction in English Canada, and the government was faced with yet another crisis. Paul Martin said that there had never been an occasion when there had been such an avalanche of protests. A Cabinet meeting was hastily called for the next morning, July 25, 1967. By all accounts, Prime Minister Pearson was furious. There is some uncertainty as to whether he came to the Cabinet with a draft of the telegram that he was going to send to De Gaulle, but this may have been due to the fact that some Ministers arrived after the meeting had begun. Afterward, Mr. Pearson issued a statement in which he said that "certain statements by the President tend to encourage the small minority of our population whose aim is to destroy Canada, and as such are unacceptable to the Canadian people and its government." Canadians did not need to be liberated, and the Prime Minister reminded General de Gaulle that many thousands of Canadians had given their lives in the liberation of France. The next day the French president cancelled his visit to Ottawa and flew back to France.

JEAN MARCHAND

It's the only time that I saw Mr. Pearson behaving like Jean Marchand. That's the worst thing I can say. He was really scandalised, because this was part of his former job, and he knew that those things were not done in international life. He was really, really angry, as I never saw him before. "What are we going to do?" He had the Cabinet working on statements of all kinds. I never saw him as much disturbed as that. And we were all disturbed, actually. But he was more disturbed than I was. He felt very strongly about it, and he was right. He was thinking of all kinds of things, including inviting Mr. de Gaulle to go home. And of course we were supporting him. We never blamed him for his reaction; we just tried to see how we could prevent worsening the situation.

Personally, I didn't think that the statement would have this kind of impact [on De Gaulle]. But he did. He told me after, "I knew that he wouldn't stand that for a minute."

LAWRENCE PENNELL

It was one of the few times I'd seen Mr. Pearson really exercised, that is, manifesting his deep concern, and he made it very clear that he was going to respond. When I came into the picture, he had pretty well resolved it himself and indicated to us what he proposed to do.

J. R. NICHOLSON

I'll never forget the De Gaulle incident. *"Vive le Québec libre!"* This is no secret—we were in Cabinet discussing what action we should take for between two and three hours, and really all we were doing was drafting a telegram. But that was important—important to Canada, particularly to French Canada, and it was important to our relationship with France. De Gaulle never got over that telegram. He cancelled his proposed visit to Ottawa, the state dinner in his honour, and everything else. Pearson was really up in arms over that incident, and so were all my French Canadian colleagues in the Cabinet just as incensed as Pearson. Perhaps this is not the word to say, but Mike was going to discipline De Gaulle for acting out of turn on Canadian soil. It was bad enough for him to say it in France, but to say it on Canadian soil—Mike didn't hesitate to take a stand on that issue.

WALTER GORDON

Pearson was just first-class. He had complete confidence in himself in a matter of that kind. Here, the head of another state, France, came to Canada and behaved in an absolutely inexcusable fashion. Pearson, as the Prime Minister of Canada, responded immediately. I am sure he didn't hesitate for a minute on that. He may have gotten some advice—not from me but other people—but he spoke with confidence and very well. We were all proud of him.

PAUL MARTIN

The criticism that came in to Pearson and to all Members of the Cabinet was unusual in its immensity. Obviously, Pearson had to do something, the Cabinet had to do something. My own view was that it was important to try and get an explanation from De Gaulle before taking precipitous action. The Cabinet felt otherwise, and Mike felt otherwise.

The telegram saying that his remarks were unacceptable was delivered to his [De Gaulle's] place of residence in Quebec—he wasn't staying in an hotel—it was sent to a house where he was staying. He didn't see the telegram until late that night, at midnight as a matter of fact, and he left the next morning. I had hoped that we would have been able to contact De Gaulle or his foreign minister, which I had tried to do myself without any luck, to give him a chance of explaining what he meant by these remarks. That's what I wanted to have done, because it was a serious thing to have the matter develop as it did. However, I couldn't persuade my colleagues, and the telegram was sent, and when De Gaulle received it, he took that as an indication from the Prime Minister and the government that he was not wanted.

ROLAND MICHENER

We were having a big dinner party for President de Gaulle, 120 people. He was to occupy the Queen's Suite, as we called it, and the bed had been extended so that he could lie his full six feet seven in comfort. We didn't know until the morning whether he was coming.

I had the pretty shrewd suspicion that he wouldn't come after the events of the day before, but I never heard from General de Gaulle that he wasn't coming. It filtered through External Affairs, and at nine o'clock we were told that he was going home—nine o'clock in the morning of the day of the dinner, which was pretty well advanced. The chef was working on the puddings, which were fancy ones with magnificent big cherries in them and cream. He was decorating the silver dishes in which these should sit, round silver dishes, with great thick ribbons of tricolour in sugar. He had about eight or ten of them there, all spun and hardening. And he'd been very sensitive.

He was a Vichy man, a native of Vichy, who had worked at Government House for seventeen years altogether before he went home. His legs gave out. But he'd been rather touchy about the events of De Gaulle's journey across the province and his address in Montreal. He was quite irascible. One of the aides told me that he went down to ask him something and Zonda threw an egg at him. He was fortunate it wasn't a plate. My wife went down to see him and said, "I'm sorry to have to tell you that the President is not coming to dinner. He's decided to go home."

So Zonda said, "Alors ..." I don't know what else. But he took his big hand and he smashed the first one of these things, and he smashed the next one; but that seemed to relieve his feelings. Anyway, we made plans and we divided all the fish which was being cooked among the household staff—they enjoyed Arctic char that day. The meat wasn't cooked, the puddings were not finished.

Mr. and Mrs. Pearson and my wife and I went through the ceremony of eating the dinner, the full dinner, alone in the dining room of Government House. Just the four of us. No attendants. Sort of a personal affair. We drowned our sorrows in the champagne that we might otherwise have served at the De Gaulle dinner.

PAUL MARTIN

I called Drapeau. I hadn't heard Drapeau's speech, when he explained to De Gaulle over the television at that banquet [that French Canadians had got along without any attention from France for 200 years and were able to look after themselves]. I called to congratulate him. He said, "Why didn't you call me yesterday, before you sent that telegram?" I said, "What would have been the point?"

He said, "You know, the moment he made that speech, Johnson and I spoke to De Gaulle. Johnson first of all said, 'The use of the phrase *vive le Québec libre*—that was the phrase used by my opponents in the election against me. I can't understand, Mr. President, why you used those words?' And I too said, 'Why did you use it?'"

Drapeau told me that De Gaulle was amazed at their reaction. He [De Gaulle] said, "Well, all I did, I saw this sign in front of me, *vive le Québec libre*—what is wrong with that?" He didn't fully understand the context of the phrase as had been explained by Johnson.

Well, that confirmed my view of really what was in the old

man's mind. But unfortunately he'd said it. It angered the rest of
the country. He should have explained then, he should have taken
the initiative himself and explained, "Now, no one is at all doubtful of my strong partiality for the French language and for French
culture. I want to encourage that in Quebec. But I don't want to
destroy Canada." He should have done that. That's what he'd told
me two months before was really in his mind; and that's what I
really believe was in his mind. But he was carried away by the tremendous reception that he got all along the King's Way.

It was a regrettable incident. Most people in France regretted it.
Most of his colleagues regretted it. André Malraux has written,
"*C'était un indiscretion.*" It *was* an indiscretion, but I don't think it
was a mischievous indiscretion. That's where I differ with so
many others. But I can't prove my point because, when he got
back to Paris, he repeated it again. But that, I think, was because he
was so angry at the reaction to what he had said.

LÉO CADIEUX

I tried later as Ambassador to France to find out what happened.
The version that I got was that most of the French cabinet
ministers were there to receive De Gaulle when he returned, and
everybody had a very worried look. They went into a *salon
d'honneur* at the airport, and no doubt had a briefing from the
General on what happened. According to the reports that I've got
from some newsmen who were there, they all came out laughing,
and there was a story saying that—but it was never confirmed.
No minister who was present could ever be made to admit that
this was what happened. So we don't know—but the story that
we got was that De Gaulle admitted that he had made a mistake,
but "having said that, what can I do? Maybe if I had to do it over
again, maybe I'd do it over again." So I don't know. What can you
do with a man like that? I suppose that he was not unhappy to
show that France felt a very special solicitude for what he thought
was the predicament of the French Canadians. It was his way of
seeing things and his way of trying to help.

*On August 1, 1967, a few days after President de Gaulle flew back to
France, the provincial premiers had their regular annual meeting. It was*

there that Premier John Robarts of Ontario proposed the Confederation of Tomorrow Conference, which he wanted to hold in Toronto toward the end of centennial year, and he got the tentative agreement of his fellow premiers to attend. Robarts had first raised the matter at a federal-provincial conference in 1966 when he said that, as the next year was Confederation Year, there should be a conference at which they could all sit around a table and review the past hundred years and talk about their aims and aspirations and what they thought the future held. There should be no talk of money. And he gave notice that Ontario might take the lead in calling such a conference. Everybody, including Mike Pearson, said it was a good idea, although the federal officials seemed less than enthusiastic.

Now that he had the agreement of the premiers, John Robarts went ahead with the planning of his conference.

JOHN ROBARTS

I sent members of my own staff to every provincial capital to see every provincial leader and ask them about what they wanted on the agenda and what their attitude toward it would be.

I went to see Danny Johnson in Montreal myself—he and I were not unused to meeting together if we felt so inclined to discuss anything we wanted to discuss. I had dinner with him in the Ritz Hotel and said, "Now, Danny, you've got some points of view you want to make to the rest of Canada about Quebec," and, as I recall my phraseology, I said, "I'll give you the best soapbox you can get in Canada, if you'd like to take it." And then I said, "Incidentally, if you don't come there won't be a conference," because the conference without Quebec would have been just not feasible. He said he would come, and he prepared a huge paper covering Quebec's position, and he was listened to from coast to coast. It worked.

It soon became apparent that the federal government and the federal bureaucracy did not like Ontario entering what they considered to be their domain and calling a confederation conference. Premier Robarts had been warned by his political advisors that Ottawa would scuttle the conference and that he would find himself in political difficulties. But he went ahead. The federal government only sent observers to the conference; none of

Pearson's Cabinet Ministers attended. In fact, Prime Minister Pearson was quoted as saying that he considered the whole procedure to be out of order.

JOHN ROBARTS

I didn't consider it out of order. I wasn't trying to upset the federal government, but I was trying to demonstrate to them that there were some points of view other than the one that they were trying to force down everybody's throat, if you want to put it that way, and that the various areas of Canada had varying points of view.

I thought is was kind of bush-league for the federal government to object to it, and I think in the event it proved so to be. They didn't make any marks objecting. We did no harm, and we did a lot of good. I thought it was rather small-minded to take that attitude, but men don't relinquish any iota of power easily. That's what you find out in the political game. And they were deathly afraid that someone was going to impinge upon their God-given right to govern us with a firm hand from far away.

I don't know that Mike Pearson personally objected so much. I have an idea that it was his advisors. Mike Pearson wasn't the kind of man that would inherently object to that conference. He was a much bigger man than that. I mean, he saw the big picture.

The Confederation of Tomorrow Conference opened on November 27, 1967. That was the day that President de Gaulle held a press conference in which he reaffirmed his support for the separatists. He said that Quebec was bound to be free, that his visit had shown that the nationalist movement there would be victorious, the situation was irreversible, and he demanded that the province be raised to the rank of a sovereign state. This became known as the Second Declaration of Paris; the First Declaration of Paris was the statement he made on returning from Montreal in which he repeated his call for a free Quebec. As might be expected, English Canada was up in arms over this latest intervention by De Gaulle. The next day Prime Minister Pearson tried to calm an enraged Parliament; he said that it was "intolerable" that the head of a foreign government should recommend action that would destroy Canadian Confederation and the unity of the Canadian state.

At the Confederation of Tomorrow Conference, which was held in the topmost floor of the then tallest tower in Toronto, Premier Daniel Johnson of Quebec asserted that there should be a new constitution, one that would acknowledge "the existence in Canada of two nations, bound together by history, each enjoying equal collective rights." This would mean that Quebec would have a veto on all national decisions and would have the power of an independent sovereign state. Premier Joey Smallwood of Newfoundland cried out that if one province were to be the equivalent of the nine other provinces, then "you wouldn't have Canada, you would have something else." The conference ended on November 30, 1967, with the decision to set up a four-man committee of premiers to be called the Continuing Committee on Confederation.

JOHN ROBARTS

In the first place, we weren't there to reach any decisions — and this was made very clear in the preliminary material. We were there to discuss Canada. We were there to give people a forum for their point of view. We wanted the people of Canada to hear everything about everything; we wanted the people in British Columbia to hear the man from Quebec, we wanted the people in Nova Scotia to hear the man from Ontario, and so on. And by Jove, we achieved this. It was quite remarkable. I mean the amount of mail that came in from all over Canada [was phenomenal]. Although I don't suppose you can write down what it did, it took a lot of steam out of some of the conflicts that were brewing at the time.

Then the Toronto press was in full cry, and the three papers did their best to screw it up by getting everything dramatic they could out of it, all the fights. I'll never forget Joey Smallwood standing up on television holding up a newspaper — I forget which one it was — pointing to the headline that quoted him and saying, "This is wrong! I did not say this!" This sort of thing made it very dramatic and very interesting. The *Globe and Mail* wrote an editorial which was headed "Mea Culpa," and they admitted something that somebody had accused them of. Well, this got the whole thing down to a pretty human level.

People were able to see their provincial leaders, hear them, hear what they had to say. The Maritimes were very anxious to speak about economic opportunity and so on, and their problems there.

Danny Johnson had the whole position of Quebec to put, the cultural position and the language question, and the feeling of the French Canadian that he didn't have a proper place in the total Confederation. This received a very sympathetic response from people generally. But that's all it was intended to do.

The success of the Confederation of Tomorrow Conference was due to the fact that it was fully covered by television. The participants, who might have been well known in their own particular provinces, became national figures, and Premier Robarts found that wherever he went in Canada, he was recognised and people stopped him on the street to talk to him about the conference. Although the federal authorities did not appreciate the provincial initiative in calling the Confederation of Tomorrow Conference, they were obviously impressed by its impact. At any rate, as soon as they could afterward, they called a federal-provincial conference on the constitution and threw the meeting open to television. It was that televised constitutional conference in early February, 1968, that made a relatively new Member of Parliament and the recently appointed Justice Minister, Pierre Elliott Trudeau, a national figure. It could be said that John Robarts and his Confederation of Tomorrow Conference were responsible for Trudeau's becoming Liberal Leader and Prime Minister, to which Robarts replied, "The Lord works in mysterious ways his wonders to perform."

14 The Trudeau Succession

THE OLD ORDER was changing. John Diefenbaker had been replaced as Progressive Conservative Leader and Leader of the Opposition by Robert Stanfield, the former premier of Nova Scotia, in September 1967. Lester Pearson was expected to resign at the end of that year, but when he did announce his resignation at a press conference in Ottawa on December 14, 1967, it came as a surprise. There had been so much speculation about his quitting that it had been largely discounted, although the politicians were taking no chances and those with aspirations for the Liberal leadership had been off and running for months. In fact, it was said that the unification of the armed forces was meant to project Paul Hellyer as a stern, decisive successor. The way that some of his Ministers were campaigning for his job before he had given it up was the subject of caustic comments in Parliament and the press. Now it was official: Mr. Pearson said that he had resigned the leadership of his party and would turn over the prime ministership when his successor was chosen at the forthcoming convention. However, it would be some time before that could happen, and, meanwhile, the nation's business suffered as the candidates, now openly declared, beat the boondocks for supporters and jockeyed for position. The Cabinet, which had never been watertight, now leaked like a sieve. As Ben Benson said, all that a reporter had to do in those days was to stand outside the door of the Cabinet room, and the first person who came out would tell him what had gone on, especially if that person were a *candidate for the leadership—and almost all the candidates were members of the Cabinet.*

The first to declare was the only serious candidate* who was not a Cabinet Minister: Eric Kierans, a former Quebec minister (the Lesage government had been defeated in June of 1966 by the Union Nationale led by Daniel Johnson) told a televised press conference on January 9, 1968, that it was time for new people to guide the destiny of Canada. On January 11, Paul Hellyer, who was then Minister of Transport, made it official; he had really been the first in the field. The following day, Allan MacEachen, Minister of National Health and Welfare, announced his candidacy. On January 17, John Turner, the new Minister of Consumer and Corporate Affairs, entered the leadership race; at age thirty-eight, he was the youngest candidate and emphasised the potential of youth. On January 19, three more Cabinet Ministers, External Affairs Minister Paul Martin, Finance Minister Mitchell Sharp, and Agriculture Minister J. J. Greene, held the usual TV press conferences to make it official that they were in the running. In the meantime, Robert Winters, the Minister of Trade and Commerce, decided not to be a candidate, which dismayed his supporters, who had taken it for granted that he had returned to Parliament in 1965 with the idea of becoming Prime Minister. While Paul Martin claimed to be French Canadian, he was never considered such, and the Liberals who believed in alternating the party leadership between French-speaking and English-speaking Canadians†—and they included Prime Minister Pearson—kept looking to Manpower Minister Jean Marchand and Pierre Trudeau, the Justice Minister. On February 16, Trudeau, who had become the darling of the media, was given an extravagant send-off. Just three days after he announced his candidacy, the government was defeated on a money bill in the House of Commons; the resulting turmoil had an effect on the leadership race.

After the 1965 election Pearson had discussed his intention of retiring with reporters and had even advised members of his Cabinet who were interested in succeeding him how they should behave. And there were times when Pearson had wanted to quit and let Paul Martin take over the government.

---

*Lloyd Henderson, the nuisance candidate, was the first to enter the race; he got No votes at the convention.

†In practice, the leadership alternated between Quebec and Ontario.

PAUL MARTIN

I know that there were three different occasions when Mike told me he was going to quit. One was shortly after the election in '65, and one was when there seemed to be no particular problem. He called me in one night and said that he thought he had better quit, and that he had actually been discussing with some of his colleagues as to who should replace him, and that he was going to go to the Governor-General the next day, and suggest that I be called upon to form a government. Well, I was so amazed at this. He had suggested it once before, not as definitely, and I told him, "That isn't the way things happen. The Governor-General isn't necessarily obliged to pick someone because the Prime Minister suggests it." And I said, "I don't really think that you're looking at this thing objectively enough. The people want you to stay, I think you should stay." I think perhaps he was doing this because he wanted some encouragement.

There was another occasion when Ben Benson came to me and said, "Well, you're going to have some heavy responsibility, aren't you?" I said, "What do you mean?" He said, "Mike is going to quit and he wants you to take over and he's going to recommend this to the Governor-General." Well, I sort of smiled because I knew that that isn't the way these things happen, you see. But he obviously had been discussing that with a number of people. And I think at the time he was tired. He likely had been worried about his problems, maybe with Walter, and with others. I don't know. Why does a man do the things that he sometimes does?

JEAN MARCHAND

Mr. Pearson spoke to me once; it was the shortest meeting I had with him. It was in his library, and he said, "Jean, you should take over right away." It was as simple as that. I said, "No, I'm not going to take over right away . . ." That was in May of '67, something like that.

JUDY LaMARSH

When he had talked about quitting—and we saw a lot of one another in centennial year during those state visits—I had decided that I wanted to get out at the end of '67; it would be a sensible break. I went out to see him at Harrington Lake, and his wife was there at the interview. I said I would like to go in the court, and I thought the Court of Appeal in Ontario because it might not have been accepted to have a woman judge travelling around as a high court judge on circuit. He listened very thoughtfully and then he never answered.

Then, one day I was out talking about something else and I said, "You haven't answered me about the court." And he said, "I don't think that's the place for you. I think that you shouldn't go yet," and this and that. He had been talking about his own resignation. I said, "Are you saying you won't appoint me?" And he said, "Yes," which really shocked me because Larry Pennell was appointed and had been there [in Parliament] much less time than I had—and didn't have any better reputation as a lawyer than I had. That really disaffected me quite a bit.

Then he announced that he was going to leave the Cabinet. He didn't do it at first and the Cabinet was very tough on him. It had begun to disintegrate because he had talked in a loose way about leaving at the end of centennial year, he hadn't said it was positive, and half the Cabinet Ministers had started going out campaigning for leadership. So we put it to him and in effect made him make the announcement.

PAUL HELLYER

Some time in '66, he [Pearson] spoke to me, and I would guess he spoke to two or three other people like Martin and Sharp, and told us that it was his intention to quit in '67. It was really on the basis of that inside information that we began to do some of the things toward the next convention that later got us into a certain amount of trouble.

At some stage he actually said that if he were in my position there were certain things he would begin to do. I would guess this was early in '67. And I think I wrote down somewhere what he said. But the purport of it was that if the roles were reversed, that he would begin to look around for some confidantes that he could use as the embryo of an organisation.

MAURICE SAUVÉ

During '67 we had the regular Quebec Ministers' meeting once a week. I tried to raise the problem of the succession of Mr. Pearson. I said, "We should discuss this amongst ourselves. My views are that we should probably have an Anglophone to succeed Mr. Pearson. We could negotiate our support for this Anglophone, and we could negotiate better Cabinet jobs, good appointments as Deputy Ministers of major departments and secretary of the Cabinet, and appointments to major crown corporations over a period of years. And then in exchange for the agreement by the man that we're ready to support, we'll give him the support of Quebec, and we could deliver practically all the votes of Quebec."

Every time I was bringing this up, Marchand would always say to me, "It's not time; next time, next time," and I could never discuss this. Finally Pearson resigned, and I said to Marchand, "We want to discuss this. "Oh, another time, another time." I said, "I don't understand."

On the day Mr. Pearson announced his resignation in the House, a reporter asked me, "Mr. Sauvé, do you intend to run?" I said, "No, my view is that it's not time for a French Canadian to succeed Mr. Pearson, and because of this I have no intention of running."

CHRISTOPHER YOUNG

Mr. Pearson would have been seventy in 1967, and he apparently came to the conclusion—although I don't recall him saying it at the time—that he would resign in '67 when he was seventy. He would have gone in the spring on his seventieth birthday, but since it was centennial year he decided to stay on through the centennial, and in fact announced his retirement in December by error—to his horror, he found that it was going to take four months to set up a convention. He thought that it would take a month or two.

It's unusual though. Even when people say that [they are going to resign] they don't often do it. I think Sir Robert Borden and Mackenzie King were the only other Canadian Prime Ministers who actually resigned voluntarily as opposed to being either defeated or kicked out or whatever.

VICTOR MACKIE

I made a practice of seeing Pearson as much as I could because I wanted to keep in touch with him—to see what was happening with the government. At the same time I saw Diefenbaker as much as I could; I tried to keep in touch with both sides. I respected their confidences; I never, ever betrayed a confidence from Dief or a confidence from Mike. He had told me that one of these days he was going to be stepping down and he said, "I will let you know in advance. I don't want you to write it until I tell you to write it, because I don't want it to get out before I tell the caucus, before I tell my own people."

He was as good as his word; he called me one day and asked me to drop into 24 Sussex for lunch. I drove out to his house and he took me into his study and said, "I am just telling you that I am going to retire. I have made the decision and I am telling you in advance but don't write it until I give you the word. But I am letting you know now so that you can be ready for it as I told you I would." At that time I asked him who did he think would succeed him and he said, "I have no idea."

JOHN TURNER

I told Mr. Pearson that I was going to stand for the leadership. He told me that he was sorry he couldn't wait two or three years longer to give me more chance to prepare myself, that he thought it was probably premature, but he'd see that I got a fair run.

JOHN NICHOL

For a long time the only people who knew were Paul Lafond at the Liberal Federation and myself. Paul had worked on the Mackenzie King resignation. He worked on the St. Laurent resignation. In fact, he had written the letters. He had the files on how these other fellows had done it. So Paul was my great confidante in the Liberal Party, and we worked together. No one else knew about it. No one on our staff knew about it. There was no stationery, no memos, no nothing. I'm convinced no Cabinet Ministers knew about it. And it stayed that way right up until the day he resigned.

I had a journalist in my office who had come up from the Washington *Post* or the Washington *Star*. Mr. Pearson was holding a press conference at noon that day to announce his resignation. This guy was in my office talking about Canadian politics, and he had a flight out of Ottawa at one o'clock, and he said he was going to catch it. I said, "Listen, I think you'd be very unwise to take that flight. The Prime Minister's having a press conference at twelve o'clock, and I think you'd be wise to catch a later flight and stay for the press conference."

He said, "Why? What's going to happen?" And I said, "Well, I don't know if anything particular is going to happen, but it will be very interesting, and you've come a long way, and I think you'd be very foolish not to stay for it. Have some lunch, go up there and catch a plane at three o'clock." He said, "Oh, I don't want to. I've been to these things before." I said, "Look, take my advice. I'm trying to be helpful to you. Come to the press conference."

Anyway he did. He came up to me afterwards, and his eyes were sticking out like organ stops, and he said. "Thank you very much!" He had an all-American scoop.

PAUL MARTIN

Pearson felt very strongly about the principle of alternation. He felt that one time it should be Quebec's turn to be leader of the Liberal Party; the next time it should be English-speaking Canada. I didn't subscribe to that. And the time will come when that view will not prevail. But that was the picture in 1968. Mike told me frankly that it had to be somebody from Quebec. He said, "Otherwise I would strongly encourage you to do what you're doing, even though I think it's coming to you rather late in life."

Well, I reminded him how old Mr. St. Laurent was when he'd become Leader. I reminded him of the things that he had told me when he had become Leader. But I understood his point of view.

The timing of the federal-provincial conference on the Constitution could not have been better for a prospective candidate, as the conference was held from February 5 to 7, 1968, just three months before the Liberal Party's leadership convention. As Justice Minister, Pierre Trudeau was bound to play a leading role at the conference, so that all the cameras and cables and paraphernalia of television might have been laid on by his campaign committee, as one of the officially declared candidates noted. Yet Lester Pearson had nothing to do with all this. The Prime Minister had told Jean Marchand and Pierre Trudeau on the day of his resignation that one of the two of them should run for the leadership, but, at the time, he wanted Marchand, who was his Quebec lieutenant, as his successor.

Actually, Mr. Pearson was somewhat alarmed that Pierre Trudeau took such a hard line at the conference: he refused to give in to Quebec Premier Daniel Johnson's demands for more power. Tom Kent, who was a delegate, said that the Prime Minister was a little worried at the Justice Minister's style, which was so different from his own. Mr. Pearson agreed that the federal government's main thrust at the meeting should be the entrenchment in the Constitution of a Bill of Rights, which would mean the entrenchment of language rights. There was no mention of co-operative federalism at this conference, and Pierre Trudeau spoke of equal language rights as being the basis for what he called a genuine federalism. The Quebec premier repeated the two-nation claim that he had made at the Confederation of Tomorrow Conference and said that a new Constitution should be drawn up as a result of agreement between the two nations. He added that it was not necessary to break up the ten-partner Canada to make a two-partner Canada, but it was necessary to create a two-partner Canada to maintain a ten-partner Canada. However, special powers for Quebec were anathema to Trudeau, who said they would weaken the position of the Quebec Members of Parliament in Ottawa and would lead inexorably to separation. He put forward bilingualism as the real answer. There were some sharp exchanges between the two French Canadians, and during one of them Johnson complained that the Quebec delegation had not come to the federal-provincial conference to be cross-examined. The end came with a compromise resolution which acknowledged that French-speaking Canadians should have the same language rights outside Quebec that English-speaking Canadians had inside Quebec—it was the work of Prime Minister Pearson.

Pierre Trudeau was criticised by writers such as Claude Ryan for being adamant and inflexible, but to the vast majority in English Canada he was a hero, a French Canadian spokesman who would keep the Quebeckers in their place. Before the conference began, the Justice Minister crossed the country, explaining to the provincial premiers the federal government's stand on the constitution.

J. R. SMALLWOOD

As Minister of Justice, Trudeau came to see me, as he did all the premiers, on the constitution matter, the French thing — "what do they feel about it?" He had lunch with me, brought [Senator] Carl Goldenberg and some executive assistant along. He came in this big long leather coat and leather cap. I helped him off with it, hung it up, and I said, "Have a sherry." He had a sherry, and I said, "What are you doing down here, Minister?"

"Oh," he said, "I'm seeing all the premiers." I said, "What about?" He said, "Well, you know this conference coming up in February on the constitutional problem. I just wanted to find out how the premiers feel and how the provinces feel." I said, "I'm willing to do that, but not unless I can be very frank and very blunt." "Please," he said, "please, that's what I want." I said, "Now, I don't want to offend you." He said, "No, not at all. Just tell me the truth."

I said, "Okay. For the province of Quebec, for the legislature of Quebec, for the government of Quebec, nothing except what there will be for the province of Prince Edward Island and the legislature of Prince Edward Island and the government of Prince Edward Island, or Newfoundland or Nova Scotia or Manitoba or any province. For the province of Quebec and the legislature of Quebec and the government of Quebec, the same as for any other in Canada."

He said, "I see." "But for Canadians who are French," I said, "whether they be in Quebec or anywhere else in Canada, absolutely equal rights, absolutely equal. I wouldn't agree to an iota less than complete equality." He said, "That's plain enough." I said, "Well, I hope I haven't offended you." "No, no," he said, "I wish I could state my views as clearly as you've done." I said, "Well, you can state yours just as clearly as I've stated mine." "Oh, no," he said, "you misunderstand me. You have stated *my* views." I said, "You agree with what I've just said?" He said, "Completely. That's exactly what I think and believe."

We talked then about economic disparity and so on. When that luncheon was over—we talked for a couple of hours, I had three or four ministers there—and we came out into the lobby there were newspaper fellows waiting. We chatted with them and he went off. I said, "This man is an outstanding man in the world today. He's got ability and talent that's on a world scale. Myself, I feel like a clumsy elephant with arthritis." That went all across Canada.

I said, "Gentlemen, you've just met the next Prime Minister of Canada," and I came out for Trudeau.

On February 19, 1968, the Pearson Government was defeated on a tax bill in the House of Commons. It was a Monday night, and on the weekend before there had been all the headlines and the media-inspired excitement over Pierre Trudeau entering the Liberal leadership race. There was a certain amount of in-fighting going on between the candidates, three of whom were away campaigning. However, it was not so much the leadership race that brought the government down as it was a miscalculation on the part of the chief government Whip, Bernard Pilon, a Quebec Member whom the Opposition had dubbed "Miracle Whip" because of his uncanny ability, up to then, of judging when the minority government was safe, and a lot of Ministers being at sixes-and-sevens and giving counter-orders.

The purpose of the bill on which the government was defeated that night was to impose a surtax —according to Tommy Douglas, the surtax would have been 5 percent on low income wage earners but only 2 percent on businesses. However, it was not only the left-wing New Democrats and the Opposition generally who were opposed to the bill but there were some Liberals including Walter Gordon who were against it, which complicated matters but apparently did not faze Bernard Pilon, the Whip. However, when the House rose for dinner, Hédard Robichaud, the Minister of Fisheries, was heard to complain about the way things were being run and to say that he wouldn't be surprised to see the government defeated before the day was over.

WALTER GORDON

I was a member of the Cabinet with no duties, and, in the normal course, I might not have gone down to Ottawa on a

Monday, but I went this Monday, fortuitously. When I walked into the House, about five-thirty, somebody came running over and asked me if I would make a speech on the bill so that it would keep things going until the six-o'clock adjournment. I said yes, I would be glad to if I could speak about economic conditions in general, but as I had been opposing this particular item so strenuously in Cabinet right along, I didn't feel that I could suddenly turn around and support it. Well, word came back, "That's perfectly all right. Just keep the thing going until six o'clock."

I know that I didn't have to make a speech. They had a vote, which the government won by just a few. It was very dangerous. So we all sighed a sigh of relief and went up to dinner.

ALLAN MACEACHEN

I was Leader of the House at the time, and I certainly did everything possible to avoid a vote that night because I knew things were very, very close. I remember particularly the Minister of Fisheries, Mr. Robichaud, who was in the House, and with whom I had talked on this matter, and we both agreed that in no way should there be a vote. It was unnecessary to have a vote. But the fact is that I was overruled by the Acting Prime Minister, who was Mr. Winters, and he was encouraged by Mr. Hellyer. I was telling Paul [Hellyer] after the decision was made to have the vote, that if he wanted to lead the House it was fine with me, that all he had to do was go to the Prime Minister and take on the job.

I realised at the time that we were in trouble. But anyway, Mitchell [Sharp] was the Minister who wanted to get his bill through and the Whip said it was okay. But we lost the vote.

MITCHELL SHARP

We had got through second reading,* and this particular day we were taking the committee-of-the-whole stage of this finance bill. Before that day began, I saw Allan MacEachen, who was the House Leader, and he and I agreed that we would do only the

---

*All bills go through first reading, second reading (agreement in principle), committee of the whole (clause-by-clause examination), and third reading for final approval or defeat.

committee-of-the-whole stage that day. So I took this bill through committee clause by clause, and it was a very, very difficult exercise because we were in the minority and in committee of the whole the bells do not ring. So I had to be very sure, every time a clause was put before the House, that we'd enough Members sitting behind me who could carry each clause, and this I managed.

It came to the end of the committee-of-the-whole stage, and we didn't have the Speaker in the Chair, we had the Deputy Speaker, Herman Batten, a Newfoundland Member who had no experience with the House at all. He had some notes in front of him. He said, "When shall this bill be read a third time?" Allan MacEachen, who was the House Leader, said "Next sitting of the House." The Speaker didn't hear him, and he went on reading from this sheet of paper, and he said, "Moved by Mr. Sharp, seconded by Mr. Benson, this bill will now be read a third time."

I got to my feet, and I said, "Mr. Speaker, I didn't move third reading." The Opposition then began to bait me, and to say, "Why don't we get it over with now?" And Paul Hellyer said, "Sure, go ahead, this is fine." The reason I say that is that Allan MacEachen was very angry at Paul for having said that to me.

But what finally convinced me was the Whip, who passed me a piece of paper, which said, "We have enough Members. Go ahead." I said, "Well, Mr. Speaker, if the House wishes to proceed, I have no objection." Those were fatal words. So the bells rang and rang and rang and rang, and the Conservatives managed to bring in some Members the Whip didn't know were in the vicinity. They brought them from all over the place and defeated the third reading of the bill by two votes. So the House adjourned.

ROBERT STANFIELD

We were always trying to get the best vote, and I can recall that night we kept the bells ringing a long, long time. In fact I think I said something to Mike Starr [Opposition House Leader] about "Don't you think you've left the bells ringing long enough?" and he said, "Well, there are one or two more fellows to come and we think it's going to be close and we'd like to get them in."

It wasn't that we were trying to catch them unawares. They knew they were in a minority position. They had a Whip at that time—a fine man, he seemed to have such an instinct, such a faculty of judging when his minority was safe. Well, he misjudged things a little and they were defeated. I was enormously surprised that night and had not prepared myself for any particular reaction but the government was defeated.

It was a comedy of errors. Pearson was on holiday in Jamaica and there was a hastily called Cabinet meeting in the office of Robert Winters, who was Acting Prime Minister. The assembled Ministers knew they had to telephone Mr. Pearson and tell him that his government had been defeated and that he would have to return to Ottawa. Finally Robert Winters made the call.

WALTER GORDON

We didn't know what the vote was on. When we went down to the House we found that against the advice of Allan MacEachen, the House Leader, Sharp had asked for third reading, and he thought he would get it as a matter of course. Well, the bells rang for an hour or an hour and a half, and he lost. The government was defeated on a money bill. We found out later there were some Liberals in town. They wouldn't come down because they were against the bill. But that was incidental.

Poor Mr. Stanfield, who I think is a great guy—all he had to do in my opinion was to get up and walk out of the House: "The government is defeated; there is nothing more to do here." But he didn't do that. We had some sort of rump Cabinet meeting right afterward, and somebody telephoned Pearson in Jamaica and he came right back.

BRYCE MACKASEY

We fell asleep at the switch, thanks to the knack of Mike Starr—who gambled and caught us cold, no argument about it—forced a vote and we were in the embarrassing situation of losing a vote on a money bill. We all retreated into Bob Winters' office. Now that I look back, it's like something from Gilbert and Sullivan. We were all, twenty-odd Cabinet Ministers, in this little room, all determining what we should do, and none of us knowing what. Somebody was saying, "I wish Pickersgill* was here." And someone saying, "Well, he's not; he's independent now so we shouldn't bother him." Whether anyone did or not, I don't know. But it was ironic to see all the people asking what we should do, and nobody seemed to know.

Mr. Winters kept saying, "I want you all to know that I'm not running for Leader." He'd periodically say this, and I could never understand what it had to do with it all. I don't think it had anything, but emotionally he was upset at this disturbance.

J. W. PICKERSGILL

I was very tired that day, and at about nine o'clock I went to bed, and I was reading or watching the television. No, I must have been listening to the radio, or turned the radio on at ten o'clock. I heard the news, and the first item was that the government had been defeated, and they said the tax bill had been defeated. I think they said on third reading. At any rate, I thought that they must have got it all mixed up, that what happened was some clause had been defeated, which would not have been fatal to the government.

However, I was a little uneasy. I listened to the rest of the news, and it was barely over when the telephone rang. One of the Ministers, who shall be nameless—why nameless? Because, after all, it's bad enough for me to reveal the secrets of the Cabinet when I was there, but to reveal the secrets of the Cabinet when I wasn't present ... I really shouldn't tell the story at all, in a way, but there's nothing to it.

The Cabinet had met under Bob Winters' direction, because under the system we had in Mr. St. Laurent's time and in Mr. Pearson's, whoever was the senior Minister available in Ottawa was Acting Prime Minister when the Prime Minister was away. It happened because Paul Martin was away, that Winters was the Acting Prime Minister. They'd had a meeting to decide what to do, and somebody said they ought to call me. Apparently it was

*In September 1967 Jack Pickersgill resigned as Minister of Transport to become chairman of the new Canadian Transport Commission.

thought that I knew more about parliamentary procedure than some of the Ministers.

At any rate, I said, "Do absolutely nothing. Don't commit yourself to anything. Don't say anything in public at all. This is a problem for the Prime Minister and the Prime Minister alone, and wait till he gets home."

LAWRENCE PENNELL

It's really an amusing story, because after it was over we decided we'd have to call Mr. Pearson, so the question was who's going to call him. It's his first holiday in two or three years, and he had just arrived. And so we sat in Bob Winters' office, wondering who was to make the phone call. Finally Mr. Winters makes the call, he elected to do it, he gets on the phone and I can just sit back and hear it now—I could only hear one side of the conversation.

"Well, there was a vote tonight on the budget, Mr. Prime Minister." "Yes?" "It was 84 to 82." "No, no, we had the 82" "Yes." "No, they had the 84 and we had the 82." Anyway, it ended up that he was to come back. And he came back. I guess he flew back that night.

My office was directly opposite the Cabinet room in the Centre Block. I just happened to come out heading for the emergency Cabinet meeting, and I met Mr. Pearson coming down the hallway. He was obviously tired from being up all night. And with typical Pearson humour and wit, he said, "By the way, did anything happen when I was away on my holidays, Larry?" To which I replied in the same spirit, "Nothing that I can think of, Mr. Prime Minister."

Lester Pearson returned to Ottawa shortly after noon on Tuesday, February 20, and the first thing he did, after meeting briefly with his Cabinet, was to telephone Robert Stanfield and ask for a twenty-four-hour adjournment of the House of Commons. Stanfield agreed to this but was upset that Pearson would not let him say a few words of explanation when the adjournment motion was put—it is not normally debatable. Then the Prime Minister approved a motion that Allan MacEachen had devised, which was to the effect that the vote on February 19 should not be regarded as a vote of confidence in the government. The strategy having been set, Pearson then took to the air waves, accusing the Conservatives of having "manufactured" the parliamentary crisis; he asserted that he would not allow their trickery, as he put it, to plunge the country into another election.

A Tory front bencher, Davie Fulton, protested at Pearson's campaign of vilification but his Question of Privilege was considered a tactical error because it spoiled the Opposition argument that there could be no legal session of the House after the defeat of the tax bill. Paul Martin and Jean Marchand worked on Réal Caouette to get him to change his vote. There were reports that Pearson had sent the Governor of the Bank of Canada, Louis Rasminsky, to see the Opposition Leader to warn him the Canadian dollar was under pressure, but Stanfield denied that he had backed down as a patriotic gesture. He said that he had done so because his mail showed that the public did not want an election.

This was a masterly performance on the part of Mike Pearson, and it was acknowledged as such by his friends and political opponents. Once again, he had shown how he could rise to a crisis, but never before had he demonstrated such confidence in his ability to control the parliamentary process. However, there were many who felt that he could not have got away with this if Diefenbaker had been Opposition Leader. These critics asserted that Pearson had taken advantage of Stanfield's decency, as they put it, as well as his naïveté, in outmanoeuvring him. Gordon Churchill, a hard-line Tory, resigned from the Conservative Party in disgust. There were others too, including Liberals, who believed the government should have resigned, and there were some who thought that if there had been an election, Stanfield would have become Prime Minister and the whole course of Canadian history changed.

T. C. DOUGLAS

When Pearson came back and met Mr. Sharp who said, "Sorry about this, Chief," which I thought was the understatement of Canadian history, he called Bob Stanfield and he didn't call me. I don't know whether he called [Réal] Caouette or not—I doubt it. He certainly didn't call me, which in parliamentary circles, is considered pretty sneaky. If you talk to the party Leader of one party, you talk to them all. When he was in trouble during the flag debate, he never talked to one of us, he talked to all of us. But on this thing, he called Bob Stanfield and said that he needed a little time to decide what to do. Will you give us an adjournment?

Before that, he had others call Stanfield, including the Governor of the Bank of Canada. That, I can't verify. But certainly I know from Bob Stanfield's own statement that he was called by certain people in influential circles in the government, in Finance particularly, saying that there's a very critical situation on right now about the Canadian dollar, etc., etc., and if an election were suddenly called, this could be disastrous for the country.

After all the build-up, then comes Pearson, saying will you at least agree to an adjournment. Well, it doesn't seem very bad to have an adjournment and Stanfield agrees. There was no debate, there can't be a debate on an adjournment motion. Pearson picked up his papers and [was] out of the House like a shot—to do what? To go on radio that night, on a national hook-up, which the rest of us don't get, to tell people that it would never do to have an election. After all, it was just a little routine money bill that wasn't very important and it would be ridiculous to put the country to the expense of an election over this minor matter. As a matter of fact, it was not a minor bill—it was an expression by the Members of the House of Commons who were there that they were opposed to a fundamental principle in the budget, a principle affecting the distribution of the tax burden of this country, an unfair and unjust distribution.

I thought it was a very discreditable performance. Pearson played on the decency of an honest man.

ROBERT STANFIELD

We felt that the government had no alternative but to resign. That is the position that we maintained. Now, Mr. Pearson and Mr. Trudeau, who was then the Minister of Justice, and Mr. Forsey, who was a constitutional expert in quotation marks, had a different opinion; they took the position that the government had the right to seek the confidence of the House. In order to do this they drafted a resolution of confidence, which we proceeded to debate.

We were quite confident at the outset that we could fight this off, but it became very apparent that public opinion was running very strongly against us. The public obviously could not understand why the government was not entitled to bring a vote of confidence—to bring a motion of confidence before the House to see whether the government still enjoyed the confidence of the House, despite this defeat. The public obviously didn't appreciate or didn't care about the Constitution or the niceties to which we were referring. The others were able to refer to instances at Westminster where governments had been defeated, perhaps not on things as basic as the money bill, but had not felt it necessary to resign. In any case, my telegrams and my mail became very heavy and running each day strongly against our position, and I came to the conclusion as did my staff—Lowell Murray and others who were working with me—that we were getting hurt on this, that the government had the public on its side in terms of having the right to seek a vote of confidence.

I know there are a lot of stories around that, as a great patriotic gesture, I backed off because Mr. Pearson or somebody had persuaded me that the country was having a foreign-exchange emergency of some sort and it was in the public interest this controversy quiet down. I was aware that the country was in financial difficulties as the dollar was in difficulty, but I am afraid I couldn't take the credit of having been motivated by patriotic reasons particularly. Day after day I became more and more convinced that we would get slaughtered if we had to fight Mike Pearson in these circumstances, and that he would finally be able to get the clear majority he hadn't been able to get in '63 and '65 campaigns against us, in these circumstances.

Now, you can say that was a right judgement or a wrong judgement, but that was the basis of my judgement. I'm afraid I cannot take the credit for patriotic attitudes that have frequently been ascribed to me in this connection.

GORDON CHURCHILL

When the House opened on Tuesday, MacEachen moved the adjournment and Stanfield had no opportunity to speak, and so nothing occurred. This was very, very disturbing indeed.

Then Mr. Pearson went on television and appealed to the public and said, "We don't want an election, it would be terrible, and it was just trickery that caused all this" and things of this nature. He made a very effective public appeal. And nothing was said on the other side. If the Leader of the Opposition had been someone other than Mr. Stanfield, none of this could have occurred. It could not have happened with Mr. Diefenbaker as Leader. He would have pressed him right to the bitter end. But Mr. Stanfield was a different type, and he should have immediately gone on television and rebutted what Mr. Pearson had to say, which he didn't.

ALLAN MacEACHEN

We put a motion of confidence. Pierre Trudeau was Minister of Justice at the time and the Prime Minister said to me, "You'd better get the Minister of Justice and a few other Ministers, and work on this motion." Pierre and the others came up to my office and it was the first time I really had a conversation with him, and I was saying to myself, "I wonder what help he can be to me in this crisis. After all he's just arrived."

It was very important what motion we would put, how we would draft the motion, particularly the effect it would have on Réal Caouette and the Social Crediters. When that vote was lost, as I remember, Réal Caouette was very much against the government. However, there were two or three days of cooling off. He cooled off, so he supported that motion.

I went to Pearson's office with my final draft and he took his pencil and he put the finishing touches, and I still have that somewhere, his revised motion that went on the order paper.

I think the greatest blunder ever made was Davie Fulton getting up on a question of privilege on the use by the Prime Minister of the television. That broke the log jam. That meant that I was able to get up and reply. The House was back in business—the Opposition recognised its existence as a viable being.

JUDY LaMARSH

In my view what we did was completely unconstitutional, and I said, "We don't have any choice but to resign." Then Mike came back. And it was just incredible what he did. He buffaloed poor Stanfield into having the House rise for a couple of days and then going back in and letting the Socreds and the others say, "We didn't mean what we did." To be defeated on a tax bill—that should have been the end and we should have quit. That would have been the honourable thing to do.

PAUL MARTIN

The fact that we'd been defeated on that bill didn't mean that the government would have had to resign. That is something that should have been emphasised right away, and it wasn't. It was an embarrassing experience, of course: no government likes to be defeated. But it has long been established in British parliamentary practice that the government decides what is a vote of confidence.

JOHN TURNER

Mr. Pickersgill is convinced, so am I, that had Mr. Stanfield filibustered the third reading of that tax bill of Mitchell Sharp's, forced us into an election, even in the middle of a leadership contest, Mr. Stanfield would have been Prime Minister. He had his chance and he lost it. I might say that Mr. Diefenbaker and Alvin Hamilton and Gordon Churchill also gave Mr. Stanfield that same advice, and I know that.

WALTER GORDON

The government had lost on a money bill, and if the Opposition had walked out, I think that would have been the end of it. Now, I don't know if that would have been all that fatal. The government didn't have to go to the country the following morning. They could have had their leadership convention and then gone. You know, you don't have to have an election the day after the House is dissolved. But it would have put Stanfield in a much better position.

GORDON CHURCHILL

On Monday [February 26] we caucused on the matter twice, and there was a report over the radio or in the paper that Mr. Stanfield had capitulated. In caucus I asked him about this, and how he would explain it, and he said that he would deal with it and explain it without any trouble when the time came, and that he thought that the party should not any longer oppose the propositions put forward by Mr. Pearson.

There was another caucus on that Monday, at which I sat silent. I'd made up my mind what I was going to do. At the caucus people talked in glowing terms about supporting the Leader, and the various things that we should do, and keeping a united party and all the rest of it. One or two objected but we broke up with the understanding that we'd have to go ahead with the proposition. Well, I couldn't go ahead with it. So, without apprising anyone of what I intended to do, I rose in the House on the next day and withdrew from the Conservative Party and sat as an independent.

Subsequently we discovered that Mr. Stanfield had been approached by Mr. Pearson and informed that if the government were upset on this occasion or if an election were called, that the financial circumstances in Canada would be appalling. The Bank of Canada head, Rasminsky, had a meeting with Mr. Stanfield. And the appeal made to Mr. Stanfield was that, in the national interest, obstruction should cease in the House of Commons, the bill should be passed and the Prime Minister permitted to carry on. Well, Stanfield told us nothing of this at all; none of us knew this.

ROBERT STANFIELD

Mr. Pearson called me—I think it was on a Sunday—and said Mr. Rasminsky would like to give me a briefing on the Canadian dollar, and he did come around that evening. He chatted with me for an hour and he was concerned. He thought things were under control, but did note a substantial depletion in Canadian foreign reserves. They had gone down considerably. He was frank enough to indicate what he thought the real danger line would be, which was some distance below where it had gotten, but he thought I ought to know that there was a position of some real concern to the Bank at that time.

As I say, I'm not sure whether that meeting took place after the defeat of the tax bill or before. I would say quite frankly that during the parliamentary crisis, I was aware that the dollar was in difficulty.

Although Lester Pearson had saved his government from the defeat of the tax bill, the resulting parliamentary crisis, together with the parlous state of the dollar and the Canadian economy, made some Liberals look for a strong man. A committee to draft Robert Winters for the leadership was set up in Nova Scotia, and similar organisations were established in Toronto and Winnipeg. The fact that the Trade Minister had been Acting Prime Minister and therefore responsible for the shambles in the House of Commons did not seem to affect his supporters, who were impressed by the strong stand he had taken against the budget deficits. On February 28, 1968, Robert Winters resigned from the Cabinet and announced his candidacy the following day. However, it was too late since Premier Smallwood of Newfoundland had made up his mind to support Trudeau and even his good friend Jack Nicholson was committed to Hellyer.

J. R. SMALLWOOD

I got a phone call from somebody in Nova Scotia. He said, "Mr. Premier, you're a friend of Bob Winters?" "Yes." And he said, "Some of his friends, some of us have been talking and we think he should be in this fight. We want to encourage him to come back in again. How do you feel about that? Would you join us?" I said, "Well, I don't know; I'd have to think about that." I said, "It was a pretty grievous thing. I came out publicly [for Winters]. I was the first man in Canada. And then he saws me off on the end of the limb and withdraws. I don't know. Let me think about it."

They called me back some days later, and I said, "No, I've decided no, I can't support Bob. I just can't do it." It may be that around that time there was beginning to be talk about this man Trudeau. Pickersgill and I talked about it, and I said, "Jack, it's the turn of a French Canadian if we're going to follow the Liberal tradition, and this man Trudeau . . ." But Pickersgill thought that Marchand would be better. I said, "I don't know either one of them."

At any rate, Bob changed his mind and asked his friends to work up a movement to get him back so that it would be in response to a demand that he came back. I hadn't joined in it, and soon after I came out firmly in support of Trudeau. I was the only premier in Canada who did. Ever afterwards, Bob Winters and his friends said that I'd ratted on him. The fact is, he ratted on me. I had found a Leader. Now mind you, if Bob Winters had become the Leader he would have won Newfoundland. And Trudeau lost it.

J. R. NICHOLSON

If [Winters] had declared himself in early January instead of taking off for India, he could well have won [the Liberal leadership]. I know from a personal conversation I had with Joey Smallwood how disappointed he was that Winters had refused to run for the leadership. He referred to him as "the son of a fishboat captain from Nova Scotia with a good army record and a great academic record at the university, and success in politics, and a success in business later after he left politics. He's the ideal man; we should have him." And he said, "I can't guarantee him all the votes, but I can give him most of the votes in Newfoundland, I'm sure of it."

Now that was in early January in '68. [After the parliamentary crisis], I was sitting in the House with Winters. He had several books of letters from all over Canada encouraging him to run for the leadership. I said, "Have you made a decision, Bob?" He said, "Yes, I think I have. It's pretty well made up. And I assume I'll have your support in the light of our conversation?" I said, "Unfortunately you won't. I am committed. If there's a show-down after the first ballot I could switch back to you if I can." I said, "You're going to have trouble not only with the group that will support me—and I had about 65 to 80 votes— but you're going to have trouble with Joey Smallwood." "I'll have no trouble with Joey." I said, "You will."

Joey had never met Trudeau at the time that he had this conversation with me and was trying to get Winters to run. But Trudeau, when he was Minister of Justice, visited all the provinces of Canada to talk to the heads of provincial governments on the patriation of the Constitution, the B.N.A. Act, and he made a very profound impression on Joey Smallwood. Joey had assured Trudeau of his support, and Joey couldn't back out of it. And it was the Newfoundland vote that went with Trudeau that was the difference between the Trudeau and the Winters vote.

The government's defeat damaged the leadership prospects of Mitchell Sharp; he was regarded as the dupe who had allowed the vote to be called. It was not a good image for a Finance Minister. After the parliamentary crisis was resolved, Sharp spoke to Prime Minister Pearson.

MITCHELL SHARP

I said, "What do you think I should do? In view of this I have to devote a lot of time on negotiations with the United States to be sure that we're not going to suffer and that they don't take actions which will precipitate a crisis in Canada." I said, "Effectively I cannot campaign. I wouldn't dare leave Ottawa. But do you think I should withdraw?" He said, "No, I don't think you should. I think, however, that you should not campaign. Leave that other question open as to whether you will remain in the race or not. One can never tell what will happen, and there's no point in making premature decisions. Just see how things go." That was my view too.

We also discussed Mr. Trudeau at the time of [that] conversation. I said, "I must say I'm very attracted by Trudeau, and I'm not quite sure what I should do, but I'm inclined to think he's the best of the candidates." Mr. Pearson at that time had the same view, however, as I did—that Mr. Trudeau was somewhat of an unknown quantity. He had been in the Cabinet for a short time. We'd been very impressed by him. I had particularly been impressed with him because he had taken a very similar view to mine on questions of relations with the provinces. And this gave me some confidence in his attitude on the questions of federation and so on. However, I agreed then that I would withdraw from the campaigning but would not withdraw my candidature.

The defeat of the government and the resulting parliamentary crisis did not sully Pierre Trudeau's leadership campaign. His bandwagon kept rolling along, picking up younger Liberals across the country who saw in him a break with the past and a champion against the party's Old Guard.

It was Jean Marchand who was really the king-maker—this was after he had decided that he didn't want to be Leader, if he ever wanted to be. He did tell a small committee of the Cabinet which included Lawrence

Pennell, Ben Benson, Walter Gordon, and Trudeau that if they couldn't get anyone else, he would run. That was before Trudeau was even thought of. Marchand said that he never really wanted to be Leader: his English wasn't good enough and then he wished to remain identified with Quebec. Tom Kent, who got to know him very well as his Deputy Minister, said that his lifestyle was against being Prime Minister. Although Lester Pearson and many other English-speaking Liberals thought at first of Marchand as the French Canadian candidate, Mitchell Sharp was not enthusiastic. He said that he couldn't see him as a potential Prime Minister. Furthermore, Sharp felt that the Liberals would not do particularly well with Marchand in an election campaign.

Jean Marchand began to look on Pierre Trudeau as a likely leadership candidate when the Justice Minister introduced amendments to the criminal code and said that the state had no business in the bedrooms of the nation.

JEAN MARCHAND

It was the first time that Pierre became a public figure. And the people were struck by the intelligence of the man, his knowledge of this subject, his personality and so forth. Before the Christmas holiday of 1967 I remember having a discussion with Pierre and I said, "I think it's possible that you could be a candidate because look at the reaction of the press and the people. They said, 'Gee, this guy is bright.' And I think that you can do it." "Oh," he said, "let's go and have a rest and we'll talk about that when I come back." He said, "Why don't we go on holiday together. I'm going to the South Pacific, to Tahiti." I think that this was where he met Margaret for the first time. I didn't go.

After he came back we met and he said, "No, it's not possible. There is a convention of the Quebec Liberal Federation at the end of the month. After that—I think it was on the fifth of February—"there is a federal-provincial conference, and as Minister of Justice I have to deal with those problems. It's very important for Quebec. Daniel Johnson will be there." And he went on: "If I announce now or if it's indicated that I have even an interest in that, it will spoil the whole thing." So I said, "Let's proceed gradually."

I arranged for him to be the speaker at the federal Liberal Convention in Montreal. It was a real hit. People said, "Oh, he's a very good man and we didn't know that he was that kind of a man." And he created a good impression. After that, well, the February conference was televised, and he was very successful. This is where he had a very strong debate with Johnson on the Constitution, very intelligent and aggressive, and he really got through. At the beginning of February he was really created.

He's one of the politicians in Canada, at least at the federal level, who was created in the shortest time that I know of—I would say between the 8th of December and the 5th of April, this man became a possible Prime Minister of Canada. Of course, I didn't know that he would make it, but I knew that he was possible. And the group agreed that Trudeau was really somebody to consider.

Trudeau said no up to the end. It was only on the 10th of February or around that time that he said, "Well, if you insist . . . We didn't come here for that. Why not back another one—like Paul Hellyer? He's interested and he's young." I said to Pierre, "In this business this is an opportunity. If you miss it, you don't know when it's going to come back. Hellyer is in his early forties and can last twenty years, and you wouldn't be here at that time." I didn't think that Hellyer was the kind of man that we should have. So I was having this kind of discussion with him. And he said, "Well, we didn't come here for that. . . " Because he was never anxious to have any job, not even in the Cabinet. I had to fight with him the first time Pearson asked me if I could convince him to become Parliamentary Secretary to the Prime Minister. "Oh," he said, "come on. I'll be a prisoner here in Ottawa." He wanted to stay free.

Finally, he said, "Well, okay let's try," and the committee approved. We started around the 15th of February. At the beginning of April he was Prime Minister of Canada.

One of the members of the original group or committee that had supported first Jean Marchand for the leadership of the Liberal Party and then Marchand's choice, Pierre Trudeau, was Ben Benson; he became co-chairman of the campaign committee with Marchand. They ran a good campaign, but it was really too easy. On April 3, 1968, just as the 2,500 delegates to the Liberal leadership convention were swarming into Ottawa, Mitchell Sharp announced that he was withdrawing from the contest and would be supporting Mr. Trudeau. Then it became apparent that Prime Minister Pearson, who made no secret about the fact that he wanted a French Canadian successor, was backing his former Parliamentary Secretary. There was, as the reporters said, a laying on of hands as there had been at the last Liberal leadership convention, and Pierre Elliott Trudeau was the anointed son.

MITCHELL SHARP

As the campaign went on and Mr. Trudeau was obviously a very attractive candidate to many people, and my own count of delegate support was neither here nor there. I was probably equal to some of the others, but I didn't see much chance that I could win. I was concerned because the race was turning into the people who supported Trudeau and those who didn't. And my view was increasingly that Trudeau was the best man that we could have, and I didn't want my continuation in the race to seem that I was opposed to him. Indeed, I rather supported him.

So I went to see Mr. Pearson again, a few days before I actually withdrew, and I gave him my view that I thought I should withdraw and come out in favour of Trudeau, and he said, "I entirely agree. I have come to the same conclusion. I will support Trudeau." I held a meeting of my team of supporters and we debated it and, with one exception, they all agreed with my judgement and said they would work for Trudeau.

I phoned Mr. Trudeau after this meeting and I said—I don't remember whether I called him Pierre then or not—but at any rate, I told him that I had decided to withdraw and that I would announce immediately that I was withdrawing and throwing my support behind him. He had never asked for it or anything like that, and he said he was very grateful. And I said, "I want nothing from you. I'm telling you what my action is so that you won't be surprised when it happens."

Then I had to get in touch with Claude Ryan because I had heard through my team that *Le Devoir* was going to come out for me as their favourite candidate. I had to get a message through to *Le Devoir* so they were not embarrassed by having an editorial appear the day that I withdrew.

Mr. Pearson's attitude toward the leadership was that at no time did he ever indicate publicly any preference. But he did indicate to me, at the time that I withdrew, his preference was the same as mine. At one time, apparently, he favoured me as candidate. And I'd heard also Mr. Trudeau did, before he decided [to run]. I've never asked Pierre anything about that. That is for him to disclose if he ever wishes to, and it may not be true; it's just what I've heard.

JEAN-LUC PEPIN

I was quite undecided. I was considered by everybody as a supporter of Mitchell Sharp, and I had great admiration and respect for Mr. Sharp, but really I couldn't be very enthusiastic about him. I began to waver, and I couldn't be very enthusiastic about Mr. Trudeau either. So I was there, halfway between, uncertain, uneasy, unsure, to the point where I said, "Well, I don't have to make up my mind; I'll just stay out of it." Then I received a phone call from Mr. Pearson at about that time, and I went to see him. And he said, "That wouldn't be very, very wise not to take part," implying that this was a position that was good for the Prime Minister but not necessarily [for me] and intimated that I should rally to Mr. Trudeau.

BRUCE HUTCHISON

Mr. Pearson told me that Trudeau was not his choice. He told me definitely that he did *nothing* to arrange or to promote the candidacy of Mr. Trudeau as Leader. He made no effort on behalf of any candidate, none. All he insisted on was that there must be a credible and prominent French-Canadian candidate for the leadership. He wanted that. But his own personal inclination, he said, was for Marchand, which in my view was a very poor piece of judgement. Mr. Pearson was never in a personal sense very close to Mr. Trudeau. This notion that he'd got Mr. Trudeau in and groomed him as a successor, there's no truth in that at all. He recognised that Mr. Trudeau, after he'd made him Minister of Justice, was an extraordinarily able man, a man of great brilliance. He understood that, but he disagreed with a lot of Mr. Trudeau's views, especially on foreign policy.

PAUL HELLYER

Pearson did everything he could to help Trudeau without public endorsement. He appointed a Cabinet Minister on the understanding that he would support Trudeau—Bryce Mackasey. He appointed to the Senate Richard Stanbury so that he wouldn't be able to support me, and made him president of the convention. He did all sorts of things, including having breakfast with his delegates from Algoma East riding and saying, "Now, let there be no mistake about it, this is what we're doing."

There's no doubt that he had considerable influence ... most of it done indirectly, but a lot of it done very effectively nevertheless. He could still pretend publicly to have been impartial. He could have the public image of impartiality while in fact being very much behind a particular candidate. I'm not faulting that—don't get me wrong—because I think any Leader is inclined to do that. They know who they would like to succeed them. And I think also that they have to be very careful to give the appearance of impartiality in case the guy doesn't get it. Because that could compromise the situation, split a party. So I'm not attempting to say that what he did was wrong. The whole purpose is to say that what he did can be documented, and it was very effective as well.

The withdrawal of Mitchell Sharp from the Liberal Party's leadership race left eight candidates in the running: Pierre Trudeau, Robert Winters, Paul Hellyer, Paul Martin, John Turner, J. J. "Joe" Greene, Allan MacEachen, and Eric Kierans. For some time at the end of 1967 and in the early days of 1968, the public opinion polls had shown Paul Martin well ahead of the other likely contestants, but the veteran campaigner, who had been defeated by Lester Pearson in the 1958 Liberal leadership convention, had suffered badly from the entry of Pierre Trudeau and Robert Winters. So had Allan MacEachen. Eric Kierans had put his name forward for the fun of it; he knew that he had no future in provincial politics because he had been president of the Quebec Liberal Party when René Lévesque had been ousted for separatist sympathies, but enjoyed public life and this was his way of making the federal scene. Jean Lesage, like his assistant in the Quiet Revolution, Maurice Sauvé, did not believe the time was ripe for a French Canadian successor to Prime Minister Pearson; he supported Martin at first and then switched to Winters. Sauvé stayed with Martin although he knew his prospects were hopeless.

MAURICE SAUVÉ

Why did I support Paul Martin? I looked around and said, "I don't want a French Canadian as Prime Minister. I don't think it's good. So who are the other candidates? What is the situation in the party?" I took all the names, and I gave them marks for ability to negotiate, knowledge of the party, good House debater, and so on. And bringing it all together, Martin had the largest number of marks. At the same time, I was convinced that we would not win the election in '68, so I said, "It doesn't matter who is there, Martin is going to be the interim Leader, we'll reorganise the party, and after that it's going to be the real cast." And I said, "I'm not in favour of a French Canadian. I don't think it's good for the country. I'm a very old friend of Trudeau, I've known him since I was a boy scout, socially and everything," but I said, "I can't okay him."

Then, of all the others, this one I didn't like and so on. So it was a rational decision, and Paul Martin was after me, so I said, "Fine, I'm going to support you, Paul."

PAUL MARTIN

I decided to run. Looking back on it now, perhaps it was a mistake. I think the times were out of joint, as far as I was concerned. Obviously, the people were looking for a younger person. The Kennedy influence persisted. Unlike Aristotle, the modern generation believed that the guardians of the faith shouldn't be the philosophers and the old men. I think they're gradually becoming reconciled to a contrary view now. Just before I had announced it, the Gallup polls showed me way ahead, even though I hadn't declared. And in three Gallup polls that were held, before Mr. Trudeau finally decided to come in, I was always ahead. But when he came into the picture, the situation changed. He took over, and for a while he and I began to polarise one another. He won.

ALLAN MacEACHEN

I think at one point I was serious, but there were two developments in the campaign. One, of course, was the emergence of Trudeau as a candidate, who obviously would compete for the type of support that I might be competing for. And the second development was the entry of Bob Winters, who ate up a lot of support in the Atlantic provinces. So these were two developments that occurred that really disabled, to put it mildly, my candidacy. If it ever had a chance, that meant it was [finished].

ERIC KIERANS

First of all, it was something to do. I'd liked public life, and I must say that all of my years in Quebec were entrancing—that's about the only word to describe them. I thought that public life generally offered that kind of excitement and feeling of accomplishment and of achievement. I simply knew that there was no longer any future within the provincial party because I would always be remembered as the person that had driven—or who had been president when René was driven out of the Quebec Liberal Party.

But I guess the fundamental reason was that I despised some of the basic elements of Canadian economic policy and I decided that, if for nothing else, I would try to make a frontal attack on this, our reliance since Confederation, on two things. To secure a rate of economic growth is one, selling any resource the day you find it or the day before if you can possibly arrange the contract. And the second thing is the capital investment—you know, borrow money not only for what we need ourselves but in order to build up industries that can then export abroad. There are only two pillars to the Canadian economic policy, both of which are going to cause us serious problems in the not-so-long run.

JOHN TURNER

Had I been given two or three more years in office, and been over forty, I might have made a better go at it. Had I achieved thirty more votes on the first ballot and been ahead of Winters, it might have been different. I might have gone down to the wire. But as for the rest, yes, I am satisfied. I'd made a commitment to my people, and to the delegates, that I would allow the delegates to decide, and that there would be no deals and no premature withdrawals, and that's the way it was.

J. J. GREENE

Marchand tried to persuade me to support Trudeau, and I said, "Well, I'll support him ahead of the other three." But I had people working for me, collecting money and I said, "It wouldn't be fair to them. I'm not kidding myself. I've got no more chance than a snowball in hell. When the time comes I'll support you, Jean, but only when I think I've done the right thing by my own people." I had no regrets about that. I maybe made a damned fool of myself, I don't know. Sharp had switched before the convention—and one of his people said to me, "Joe, I have no complaint, but I kicked in five grand, and I didn't mind if he lost, but I thought for my five grand I was entitled to have a horse in the race." Well, this is the kind of thing that persuaded me I'd better keep going.

On Thursday, April 4, 1968, the Liberal Party's leadership convention was formally opened in the recently completed Civic Centre at Ottawa's Lansdowne Park. That night Lester Pearson made his farewell speech. It was an emotional occasion, and Jim Coutts, the Prime Minister's former appointments secretary, said that he cried with everybody else. Coutts, who was not a delegate, had come up from Harvard University to pay his respects to his old boss on his retirement; he sat with Pearson during much of the convention. Keith Davey, now a Senator, wept too during the address and when they sang "Auld Lang Syne"; he was terribly embarrassed, as he said, but relieved to find that his good friend, Larry Pennell, who was next to him, was crying like a kid.

The next day, Friday, April 5, was nomination day, when the candidates at a Canadian political convention make their pitch. As might have been expected, the centre of interest was Pierre Trudeau, not so much for what he would say but for the reception that he would receive—and, as he approached the podium, hundreds of banners and placards were raised in a well-organised demonstration, and a chant of "Tru-deau, Tru-deau, Tru-deau" rolled across the arena. At most conventions the speeches have little or no effect, but on this occasion Joe Greene's great stump oratory certainly won him votes and may have extinguished the chances of one of the leading candidates.

J. J. GREENE

I think I helped to knock off Hellyer, if nothing else—to the good service of our party, as it turned out. I spoke just before him, and his speech was about as bad as his speech at the Conservative convention,* and mine went well. It was no Adlai Stevenson masterpiece, but it went well. Many delegates said, "We were going to go for Hellyer, but . . . "

PAUL HELLYER

What went wrong? Mostly my speech. It lost me, I think, about 130 first-ballot votes. We had someone polling people on the way in, and on the way out, and the difference was just dramatic. The difference was heightened by Joe Greene's great stump speech just ahead of me. And then for me to come on and read this speech mechanically was just too much, even for some of my very good supporters. So they left me temporarily, a lot of them going to Greene and intending to come back, but they were never able to come back because Winters overtook me in the second ballot. If MacEachen had stayed in one more round, and I had been in number-two position on the second ballot, I would probably have won if I had made a decent speech.

The last day of the convention, Saturday, April 6, 1968, saw the election of the new Leader. Voting began in the afternoon. The results of the first ballot were: Trudeau, 752; Hellyer, 330; Winters, 293; Martin, 277; Turner, 277; Greene, 169; MacEachen, 165; Kierans, 103. Martin, MacEachen, and Kierans dropped out. In the second ballot, Trudeau got 964 votes, a little over 200 short of the over-all majority, but Winters with 475 went ahead of Hellyer who had 465, Turner increased to 347, Greene went down to 104, while 11 votes were cast for MacEachen. Now the strategy was to form an alliance to stop Trudeau but Hellyer refused to step down in favour of Winters despite the pleading of Judy LaMarsh and other supporters. It was only after the third ballot, which showed Trudeau 1,051, Winters 621, Hellyer down to 377, Turner to 279, and Greene to 29, that Paul Hellyer put on a Winters sign and withdrew, while Greene joined MacEachen in Trudeau's box.

---

*Paul Hellyer quit the Trudeau government in 1969 and later joined the Progressive Conservative Party; he was a candidate at the 1976 P.C. leadership convention.

JUDY LaMARSH

I was on the floor, and mad because a lot of people who'd worked at the time Hellyer and I did had just suddenly left him and gone haring off after this guy [Trudeau] who'd called the party a garbage can and everything else. I felt that there was not any real appreciation of the people who'd been there in the tough days.

I thought Paul [Hellyer] should get out, and I was talking to people on the floor about it. Somebody said, "Come on, he won't get out; you come up and try and persuade him." I said, "I've got nothing to do . . . I'm not one of his advisors." "Come on and try to." So I went up the stairs to try and do it, and that's when they had these boom mikes for the first time, directional mikes. They'd put one in behind and picked up our conversation. I had no awareness that there was anyone even there from radio or television or anything else.

I wanted him to make a deal with Winters. I said, "Winters is a lot older and you're still young, and you can wait for the next time, and let's all get together and go and beat that bastard." It was as simple as that. And I didn't know how people knew about this, but it was on live on television. And it was in the papers the next day. I was kind of surprised when that came about.

PAUL HELLYER

There are a lot of people who disagree with my analysis, but it is based on a very methodical polling of all the delegates, not only on their first and second preferences but on who they did not want. As of that day, there were more people who did not want Trudeau than who did not want me. But there were more people who did not want Winters than who did not want Trudeau. So as soon as he [Winters] passed me it was all over for both of us. Had things gone differently, it would have been very close. I think our estimate was that I would have won by something between forty-five and seventy-five votes. Now, in retrospect I'm not sure that that would have been a good thing, but that is still my analysis of what would have happened under different circumstances.

You can transfer votes from right to centre, but you can't transfer votes from centre to right. So that there were more Winters people who could have supported me than my people who could support Winters, right? And this, in fact, happened. So that people who supported me like Keith Davey and [Senator] Doug Everett went to Trudeau when the choice was between Trudeau and Winters. Because they were amongst this group who, faced with this choice of Winters and Trudeau, did not want Winters more than they did not want Trudeau.

The results of the fourth ballot: Trudeau 1,203; Winters 954; Turner 195.

On April 20, 1968, just two weeks after the Liberal leadership convention, Lester Pearson resigned from the government, and Pierre Elliott Trudeau was sworn in as Prime Minister of Canada. Parliament returned from a four-week Easter recess on April 23, and shortly after 2:30 P.M. the new Prime Minister rose while the old Prime Minister looked on from a front-row seat; Trudeau expressed a few words of thanks for the congratulations he had received and then announced that he had called on the Governor-General (Roland Michener) that afternoon and that Parliament was dissolved and the writs issued for an election to be held on June 25, 1968. Just a couple of minutes after the sitting began, it was over.

T. C. DOUGLAS

It was a sad day in many ways. It may not have been deliberate. It may have been purely the result of inexperience. But all of us were ready for that day when the new Prime Minister was to take his seat. We all had little speeches congratulating him, and then each of the party Leaders was going to rise and introduce a motion of good wishes to the retiring Prime Minister. I don't know who told Mike, but somebody told him, probably Mitchell Sharp, because the House Leaders had all worked out the details of it, and the Speaker knew about it. So we were all in the House and the new Prime Minister came in and got up and said he wanted to express the appreciation of the House to the deputy clerk who was retiring, or something of that sort, and everybody agreed to that. Then, he said he wanted to let them know that he had been out to Government House and Parliament was dissolved.

I walked across the floor to Mike and I said, "Mike, I'm terribly sorry. We were expecting a chance to express our affection and our high regard for you." And he pulled his speech out and he said, "I had a speech," he said. "I think it was a good one. I never got a chance to use it."

I find it difficult to believe that Mr. Trudeau didn't know that this was in the wind. The fact is that the man who had served this country so well in the public service, at the United Nations, and as its Prime Minister walked out of Parliament without the Members having a chance to express to him the affection that most of them felt for him, whether they agreed with him, or even whether they thought he was a good Prime Minister, or not. And he, himself, had no opportunity to say a last word to the Parliament in which he had been the first minister for a number of years. I think that's rather sad.

Epilogue

IN THE ROTUNDA of Ottawa's Parliament Buildings hang paintings of the two Prime Ministers of the tenth decade of Confederation; they are on your left as you enter under the Peace Tower, on either side of the corridor leading to the Commons Chamber and the Opposition and Government Lobbies. The picture of Diefenbaker is arresting: it is larger than life-size and shows him standing there, a magisterial figure in the red robes of an honorary doctor of laws from the University of Delhi in India. Across the way, the canvas is less than half the size, or seems to be: it shows Pearson in a business suit, sitting slouched in a chair with a quizzical look on his face. Larry Pennell said that he thought the picture demeaned Mr. Pearson and was always upset when he saw it. As he was one of the few Cabinet Ministers who had no leadership ambitions, Pennell became a close confidante of Prime Minister Pearson during his last year in office. He could not understand how anyone could have commissioned such a picture, and yet he supposed that it did reflect the modesty of the man in many ways.

However, modesty was only one facet of Mike Pearson's character, and not the most memorable. Above all, he is remembered by the many who liked him and revered him and the few who disliked him as a good companion, witty, cheerful, outgoing. Paul Hellyer called him a "great guy" and said that he

436

was fun to be with, and Paul Hellyer was not one of his greatest admirers. He was of a happy disposition, not given to fits of depression or anger, according to his nephew, Christopher Young, although he did admit that his uncle could be irascible at times. Young did not agree with Bruce Hutchison's view that he was a very complicated man: Hutchison described him as a mysterious fellow whose thoughts were shared with very few people, if anybody. Although Pearson had many acquaintances, some of whom undoubtedly considered themselves his friends, he had actually very few friends; he was a difficult man to get close to. He was certainly not the simple, guileless hero that some of his followers made him out to be; as the book has shown, he was much more emotional than the image of Mike Pearson as the wise-cracking sportsman-diplomat would lead one to believe.

At the same time, he was an elitist. Mitchell Sharp said that what Lester Pearson liked best of all was a conversation with old comrades, usually from the Department of External Affairs: they had more or less the same educational background, the universities of Toronto and Oxford, and they would delight in repartee and swapping witticisms. It was the sort of lively intellectual exchange of the college common room or the faculty club, and that was Pearson's milieu. He was best at meeting and talking to small groups in a university lecture hall, sitting on the edge of a desk, relaxed and comfortable. He was no good with a crowd. Christopher Young said that he had no "theatrical quality," and there was certainly little sense of drama or occasion when he got up to speak. He could not get the feel of an audience as his arch-rival, John Diefenbaker, could and draw inspiration from it: in fact, he seemed to be uneasy and somewhat embarrassed at a large rally. However, there was no doubt about his appeal to the elite. In Chapter 2, Pauline Jewett told how furious she was with the Liberals over the pipeline debate but nevertheless voted for them in the 1957 election because she had a vision of Mike Pearson in the polling booth. The top officials and other members of the Ottawa establishment had the highest regard for him, and when they learned that he was dying of cancer, they were so upset that, according to a local doctor, they came to him and asked for tranquillisers.

Pearson's relationship with Gordon was recognised as

something special. As one of the Prime Minister's aides said, "When Mike and Walter were together, all the rest of us were strangers." Partly, this was because they belonged to a different generation than most of the members of the Cabinet who were ten to twenty years younger. Although they continued to be close until the 1965 election, it was Gordon's first budget, for which Pearson had to admit some responsibility, that led to the estrangement.

It may have been due to his diplomatic training but Lester Pearson appeared to be too anxious to please people; Tom Kent said that he didn't like anyone to leave his office feeling that they were in disagreement or had quarrelled over anything. As Prime Minister, he was best at dealing with the big issues, the great affairs of state, but, according to Kent, he could not seem to concentrate on them and would let himself get distracted by some other matter until he became so exhausted that he could not continue. This was one of his weaknesses; another was accounting. Pearson himself admitted that he was no good at figures, and told the story of how he got through his university mathematics examination: he was in such a nervous state, he said, that he had a nose bleed and could not complete the paper, but the examiner, a fellow baseball fan, marked him on the two questions that he had answered. His wife, Maryon, kept the family books. Thus, there were no financial constraints on his enthusiasm for social reform, which was probably the reason why he was able to get so much done. As Paul Hellyer put it, he was the kind of person who had a big heart and turned outward toward the poor and the underprivileged and the linguistic minorities but who, at the same time, if he had a drink on a government plane, would have no idea how it got there or who paid for it.

There was no doubt that the Canada Pension Plan and the introduction of Medicare were great achievements, and it could be said that Lester Pearson rounded out the Canadian social security system, although he did nothing about rationalising it—but that was not his metier. He was not much interested in reorganisation or administration, although he did restructure some of the departments of the federal government. His real skills, which he acquired in the Department of External Affairs, were in negotiation and conciliation. He was, by all accounts, a magnificent chairman, be it of a federal-provincial first ministers' conference or the smallest Cabinet committee, and he had an extraordinary knack of bringing together contending parties and of resolving differences and disputes. As an experienced diplomat, he always sought a consensus and usually got it. Diplomacy was his strength, and yet it could be a weakness. As Robert Stanfield noted, Prime Minister Pearson was inclined to feel that reaching an agreement was important in itself, and the horrible example of this was the 30 percent increase in pay for the St. Lawrence Seaway workers, which was the match that lit the fires of inflation. Still, he did hold the country together, and some observers feel that his diplomatic skills could have overcome the later and more dangerous threats to the continuance of Confederation.

However, Jean Marchand did not think so. He pointed out that Pearson was dealing with Quebec governments, including Jean Lesage's government, which were not separatist, and so he could "play this kind of game [of conciliation]." But when you have to deal with real separatists, as Marchand said, "this is a different kind of game—and there is no room for conciliation."

It was said by many of his contemporaries that Lester Pearson was a great diplomat, a great statesman, but a poor politician— Tommy Douglas called him a "bumbling politician." Yet, anybody who becomes Prime Minister must surely be a good politician, and Mr. Pearson not only did that but he brought the Liberal Party back to power in five years after its overwhelming defeat in the 1958 election. However, he was a latecomer to politics, and, as a result, he leaned over backward to show what a practical politician he could be. His appointments to the Senate were not what people expected of a Nobel Peace Prize winner. Judy LaMarsh recalled one occasion when the Cabinet was so disgusted with the list of Senate appointments, which consisted of "bagmen and party dunderheads," that they refused to pass it. Pearson was away at the time, but when he returned and took the chair at the next Cabinet meeting, she said that she had never seen him so mad. He said that he was not going to be Prime Minister if he couldn't get such things as these appointments passed.

The fact that he was not prepared to defend his Ministers when they got into trouble, and the devious way he worked at times, made people compare him with Mackenzie King, which was a sign of what a good politician he had become. While Lester Pearson was always considered to be a small "l" liberal, he was actually a traditionalist and conservative, with a small "c" in many ways, particularly in his attitude toward women's rights. He saw nothing wrong with recruiting Robert Winters and Jean Marchand from opposite side of the ideological fence, which was in keeping with the spirit of Mackenzie King's power politics, as was his way of holding out great prospects to potential candidates without ever committing himself. Jack Pickersgill quoted Charley Granger, a Newfoundland Liberal M.P., as telling an Ontario audience that Mr. Pearson was "a nice Mackenzie King," and Pickersgill, who had been Mackenzie King's secretary, thought that was a "pretty good description."

Yet, he did not enjoy the House of Commons as John Diefenbaker did. Mike Pearson did not seem to understand the adversary system of responsible government and loyal opposition, and certainly did not appreciate the daily encounters with his accredited opponent or the confrontation of debate. For someone as uncertain of Parliament as he was, the lack of a majority was an added and intolerable burden. And so there was the search for security, the attempts, recounted in Chapter 4, to suborn the Social Crediters and the New Democratic Party with the object of providing him with the necessary extra votes. All of which finally led to his calling an election with the sole purpose of winning a majority, and when he failed to do this, he decided to leave politics and announced his retirement at the end of 1967, when the Centennial celebrations were over.

Lester Pearson's instincts and intuitions, his "gut reactions," were usually right, but having come lately into politics, he was unsure of himself and could be easily influenced. As Maurice Sauvé said, the times when he changed his mind and accepted the advice of someone whom he considered to be more experienced than himself were the times when his government got into trouble. He would never take a major decision without consultation, which was due to his diplomatic upbringing as well as the exigencies of the Prime Minister's office. Maurice Lamontagne, who joined his staff in 1958 when he was Opposition Leader, was the author of the 1962 bilingual pledge; he also wrote the terms of reference for the Royal Commission on

Bilingualism and Biculturalism and selected its members. Maurice Sauvé had an important connection with the Quiet Revolution, but he was brash and unpopular with the Quebec caucus and never gained the confidence of the Prime Minister although Mr. Pearson did use him to resolve the disagreement over the Canada Pension Plan, which was the worst crisis up to then in Ottawa's relations with Quebec City; however, it was not at his initiative but Sauvé's. The way that the Canada Pension Plan was revised and turned into a carbon copy of the Quebec Pension Plan was an example of co-operative federalism. Critics called it appeasement but Pearson was not afraid of that word, and Premier Lesage asserted that Pearson understood that Quebec's needs were mainly economic and that Quebec wanted a return of its constitutional rights.

However, Maurice Lamontagne and Guy Favreau became embroiled in the so-called scandals and had to be replaced, and, in the end, Lamontagne had little to do with the beginning of bilingualism in the federal public service and even protested some of its more extravagant features. Lester Pearson was coming to rely more and more on the advice of the Quebec triumvirate of Marchand, Trudeau, and Pelletier; Jean Marchand became his Quebec lieutenant, succeeding the ailing Guy Favreau, and Pierre Trudeau his Parliamentary Secretary. Maurice Sauvé claimed that Pearson interpreted his failure to win a majority in the 1965 election as a rebuke by the Canadian people for his policy of appeasing Quebec and the provinces. At any rate, the 1965 election marked a turning point in Ottawa's relations with Quebec. Marchand, Trudeau, and Pelletier were hard-line federalists who did not believe in returning any power to the provinces; instead of co-operative federalism, there was to be confrontation, as Trudeau demonstrated when he clashed with the Quebec premier, Daniel Johnson, at the February 1968 constitutional conference while Prime Minister Pearson sat in the chair, looking somewhat bemused. Even greater emphasis was to be put on bilingualism as the means of preserving Confederation.

Most of Mr. Pearson's colleagues believed that his greatest achievements as Prime Minister were in the realm of national unity rather than that of social security. Paul Martin put at the top of the list "the promotion of the bilingual idea," while Jack

Pickersgill opted for the flag. But what about Mike Pearson himself? What did he think? Pauline Jewett recalled having him out to Ottawa's Carleton University to talk to her M.A. students — this was just before he died in 1972. She said that the students wanted to know what Pearson felt were his greatest achievements, and they expected him to talk about Suez and the creation of UNEF, the United Nations Emergency Force, or social planning and social progress. Instead, he spoke to them about bilingualism and what he had done to strengthen relations between the federal and Quebec governments.

Yet, despite his great diplomatic skills and his best efforts at conciliation, about all that Lester Pearson had done was to put off the day of reckoning in Canada. Judy LaMarsh felt that he had postponed the ultimate crisis by "maybe" twenty years. He had bought time, which was a precious enough commodity, but as Walter Gordon asserted in Chapter 7, "we didn't put it to the best possible use because now we're back not only to where we were then but worse off."

Biographies of Contributors*

BENSON, Edgar John: b. May 28, 1923, at Cobourg, Ont. Chartered accountant. Elec. to H. of C. for Kingston, g.e. 1962; re-elec. 1963, 1965. Min. of National Revenue, June 29, 1964; Pres. of Treasury Board, Oct. 3, 1966. Lib.

BIRD, Florence Bayard: b. Jan. 15, 1908, at Philadelphia, Penna. News commentator and writer. Chairman, Royal Commission on the Status of Women in Canada, Feb. 2, 1967.

CADIEUX, Léo: b. May 28, 1908, at St. Jerome, Que. Newspaperman. Elec. to H. of C. for Terrebonne, g.e. 1962; re-elec. 1963, 1965. Assoc. Min. of National Defence, Feb. 15, 1965; Min. of National Defence, 1967. Lib.

CAOUETTE, Réal: b. Sept. 26, 1917, at Amos, Abitibi, Que. Garage proprietor. Chief of Ralliement des Créditistes (Quebec S.C. Party). Elec. for Témiscamingue, b.e. Sept. 16, 1946; defeated g.e. 1949; re-elec. g.e. 1962, 1963, 1965. S.C.

CARDIN, Lucien: b. March 1, 1919, at Providence, R.I. Barrister.

*Up to 1968.

KEY TO ABBREVIATIONS USED:

Lib.	Liberal Party	b.e.	by-election
P.C.	Progressive Conservative Party	g.e.	general election
S.C.	Social Credit Party	H. of C.	House of Commons
CCF	Co-operative Commonwealth Federation which became		
NDP	New Democratic Party		

443

Served with Canadian Navy, 1941-45. Elec. to H. of C. for Richelieu-Verchères, b.e. 1952; re-elec. g.e. 1953, 1957, 1958, 1962, 1963, 1965. Assoc. Min. of Defence, April 22, 1963; Min. of Justice, 1965. Lib.

CHEVRIER, Lionel: b. April 2, 1903, at Cornwall, Ont. Lawyer. Elec. to H. of C. for Stormont (Ont.), g.e. 1935; re-elec. 1940, 1945, 1949, 1953. Min. of Transport, Nov. 15, 1948; resigned when apptd. Pres. of St. Lawrence Seaway Authority, July 1, 1954. Re-elec. to H. of C. for Laurier (Montreal), g.e. 1957, 1958, 1962, 1963. Min. of Justice, April 22, 1963; resigned when apptd. High Commissioner of Canada in Great Britain, Jan. 1964. Lib.

CHRÉTIEN, Jean: b. Jan. 11, 1934, at Shawinigan, Que. Lawyer. Elec. to H. of C. for Saint-Maurice (Que.), g.e. 1963; re-elec. 1965. Min. Without Portfolio, April 4, 1967; Min. of National Revenue, Jan. 18, 1968.

CHURCHILL, Gordon Minto: b. Nov. 8, 1898, at Cold Water, Ont. Served overseas in both world wars; awarded D.S.O. Elec. to H. of C. for Winnipeg South Centre, b.e. June 25, 1951; re-elec. g.e. 1953, 1957, 1958, 1962, 1963, 1965. Min. of Trade and Commerce, June 21, 1957; Min. of Veteran Affairs, Oct. 11, 1960; Min. of National Defence, Feb. 11, 1963. P.C.

CONNOLLY, John Joseph: b. Oct. 31, 1906, at Ottawa, Ont. Barrister. Professor, Notre Dame University, 1928-31. Summoned to Senate, June 12, 1953. Min. Without Portfolio, Feb. 3, 1964. Lib.

COUTTS, James: b. May 16, 1938, at High River, Alta. Lawyer. Lib. candidate in McLeod (Alta.) defeated g.e. 1962. Secretary (Appointments) to Prime Minister, 1963-66. Lib.

COWAN, Ralph: b. May 6, 1902, at Ottawa, Ont. Newspaperman. Elec. to H. of C. for York-Humber (Toronto), g.e. 1962; re-elec. 1963. 1965. Lib.

DAVEY, Keith: b. April 21, 1926, at Toronto, Ont. Advertising salesman. National organiser of Lib. Party of Canada 1961-66; national campaign director 1962, 1963, 1965. Summoned to Senate, Feb. 24, 1966.

DOUGLAS, Thomas Clement: b. Oct. 20, 1904, at Falkirk, Scotland. Came to Canada 1910. Baptist minister. Elec. to H. of C., g.e. 1935; re-elec. 1940; resigned May 1944 to become candidate in Sask. election. Premier of Sask. 1944-61. Founder of CCF and its successor, NDP; leader NDP, 1961. Re-elec. to H. of C. for Burnaby-Coquitlam, B.C. b.e. Oct. 22, 1962; re-elec. g.e. 1963, 1965. NDP.

DRURY, Charles Mills: b. May 7, 1912, at Westmount, Que. Businessman. Dep. Min. of Dept. of National Defence 1949-55. Awarded D.S.O. World War II. Elec. for Saint Antoine-Westmount, g.e. 1962; re-elec. 1963, 1965. Min. of Industry, July 25, 1963. Lib.

DUPUIS, Yvon: b. Oct. 11, 1926, at Montreal, Que. Businessman. Elec. to H. of C. for Saint Jean-Iberville-Napierville, g.e. 1958; re-elec. 1962; 1963. Min. Without Portfolio, Feb. 3, 1964; resigned 1965. Lib.

FISHER, Douglas Mason: b. Sept. 19, 1919, at Sioux Lookout, Ont. News commentator and writer. Served overseas in World War II. Elec. to H. of C. for Port Arthur, g.e. 1957; re-elec. 1958, 1962, 1963. Did not run 1965. NDP.

FOWLER, Robert MacLaren: b. Dec. 7, 1906, at Peterborough, Ont. Barrister and executive. Chairman, Royal Commission on Broadcasting, 1956-57; chairman, Federal Government Committee on Broadcasting, 1964-65. Lib.

GORDON, Walter Lockhart: b. Jan. 27, 1906, at Toronto, Ont. Chartered accountant. Chairman of Royal Commission on Canada's Economic Prospects, 1955. Elec. to H. of C. for Davenport (Toronto), g.e. 1962; re-elec. 1963, 1965. Min. of Finance, April 22, 1963; resigned from Cabinet Nov. 9, 1965; Pres. of Privy Council, 1967; resigned from Cabinet, March 11, 1968. Lib.

GREENE, John James: b. June 24, 1920, at Toronto, Ont. Lawyer. Served RCAF 1941-45; awarded D.F.C. Elec. to H. of C. for Renfrew South (Ont.), g.e. 1963; re-elec. 1965. Min. of Agriculture, Dec. 18, 1965. Lib.

HAMILTON, Alvin: b. March 30, 1912, at Kenora, Ont. Schoolteacher. Navigator, RCAF 1941-45. Elec. to H. of C. for Qu'Appelle (Sask.), g.e. 1957; re-elec. 1958, 1962, 1963, 1965. Min. of Northern Affairs and National Resources, Aug. 22, 1957; Min. of Agriculture, Oct. 11, 1960. P.C.

HAYS, Harry William: b. Dec. 25, 1909, at Carstairs, Alta. Cattle breeder. Mayor of Calgary, 1959-63. Elec. to H. of C. for Calgary South, g.e. 1963. Min. of Agriculture, April 22, 1963. Defeated g.e. 1965. Summoned to Senate, Feb. 24, 1966. Lib.

HEES, George Harris: b. June 17, 1910, at Toronto, Ont. Businessman. Served overseas in World War II. Elec. to H. of C. for Broadview (Toronto), b.e. May 15, 1950; re-elec. g.e. 1953, 1957, 1958, 1962; did not run 1963; re-elec. for Prince Edward-Hastings (Ont.), 1965. Min. of Transport, June 21, 1957; Min of Trade and Commerce, Oct. 11, 1960. P.C.

HELLYER, Paul Theodore: b. Aug. 6, 1923, at Waterford, Ont. Businessman. Served with armed forces 1944-46. Elec. to H. of C. for Davenport (Toronto), g.e. 1949; re-elec. 1953; defeated 1957; re-elec. for Trinity (Toronto), b.e. Dec. 15, 1958; re-elec. 1962, 1963, 1965. Assoc. Defence Min., April 26, 1957; Min. of National Defence, April 22, 1963; Min. of Transport, 1967. Lib.

HUTCHISON, Bruce: b. June 5, 1901, at Prescott, Ont. Journalist. Editor, *Victoria Daily Times,* 1950-63; editorial director of Vancouver *Sun*, 1963 on. Author of several books including the *Unknown Country* and *Mr. Prime Minister.*

JEWETT, Pauline: b. Dec. 11, 1922, at St. Catharines, Ont. Professor of Political Science. Elec. to H. of C. for Northumberland (Ont.), g.e. 1963; defeated 1965. Lib.

KEATE, Stuart: b. Oct. 13, 1913, at Vancouver, B.C. Publisher and journalist. Served with Canadian Navy, 1942-45. Publisher, *Victoria Daily Times,* 1950-64; publisher, Vancouver *Sun*, 1964 on.

KENT, Thomas Worrall: b. April 3, 1922, at Stafford, Eng. Public servant and writer. Asst. editor, London *Economist,* 1950-53; editor, Winnipeg *Free Press,* 1954-59. Policy Secretary to Prime Minister, 1963-65; Dep. Min., Dept. of Manpower and Immigration, 1966-68. Lib.

KIERANS, Eric William: b. Feb. 2, 1914, at Montreal, Que. Professor of Economics. Served with armed forces, 1942-45. Quebec Min. of Revenue, 1963-65; Quebec Min. of Health, 1965-66. Candidate at 1968 Lib. leadership convention. Lib.

KNOWLES, Stanley Howard: b. June 18, 1908, at Los Angeles, Calif. Printer and minister. Exec. vice-pres., Canadian Labour Congress, 1958-62. Elec. to H. of C. for Winnipeg North Centre, b.e. Nov. 30, 1942; re-elec. g.e. 1945, 1949, 1953, 1957; defeated 1958; re-elec. 1962, 1963, 1965. NDP.

LaMARSH, Judy Verlyn: b. Dec. 20, 1924, at Chatham, Ont. Barrister. Elec. to H. of C. for Niagara Falls, b.e. Oct. 31, 1960; re-elec. g.e. 1962, 1963, 1965. Min. of National Health and Welfare, April 22, 1963; Secretary of State, Dec. 18, 1965. Lib.

LAMONTAGNE, Maurice: b. Sept. 7, 1917, at Mont-Joli, Que. Professor of Economics. Asst. Dep. Min. of Northern Affairs and National Resources, 1954. Elec. to H. of C. for Outremont-Saint-Jean (Montreal), g.e. 1963; re-elec. 1965. Pres. of Privy Council, April 22, 1963; Secretary of State, Feb. 3, 1964. Lib.

LANGLOIS, Raymond: b. April 10, 1936, at Wolseley, Sask. Schoolteacher. Elec. to H. of C. for Megantic (Que.) g.e. 1962; re-elec. 1963, 1965. S.C.

LESAGE, Jean: b. June 10, 1912, at Montreal, Que. Barrister. Elec. to H. of C. for Montmagny-L'Islet, g.e. 1945; re-elec. 1949, 1953, 1957, 1958. Min. of Northern Affairs and National Resources, Dec. 16, 1953. Resigned from H. of C. June 13, 1958, to become leader of Quebec Lib. Party. Premier of Quebec, July 5, 1960, to 1966. Lib..

LEWIS, David: b. June 23, 1909, at Swislocz, Poland. Barrister. National secretary-pres. of CCF, 1936-61. Federal vice-pres. of NDP. Elec. to H. of C. for York South (Toronto), g.e. 1962; defeated 1963; re-elec. 1965. NDP.

MACDONALD, Mary: b. April 18, 1918, at Cobalt, Ont. Served overseas with Canadian Red Cross Corps during World War II. Officer, External Affairs, 1946. Executive Asst. to Prime Minister, 1963-68. Lib.

MacEACHEN, Allan Joseph: b. July 6, 1921, at Inverness, N.S. Professor of Economics. Elec. to H. of C. for Inverness-Richmond (N.S.). g.e. 1953; re-elec. 1957; defeated 1958; re-elec. 1962, 1963, 1965. Special Asst. to Leader of Opposition, 1958-62. Min. of Labor, April 22, 1963; Min. of National Health and Welfare, Dec. 18, 1965. Lib.

MACKASEY, Bryce Stuart: b. Aug. 25, 1921, at Quebec City, Que. Manufacturer. Elec. to H. of C. for Verdun (Montreal), g.e. 1962; re-elec. 1963, 1965. Min. Without Portfolio, Feb. 9, 1968. Lib.

MACKIE, Victor John : b. Feb. 12, 1918, at Moose Jaw, Sask. Journalist. Member of Parliamentary Press Gallery, 1951 on. Parliamentary correspondent of Winnipeg *Free Press* and Associated FP publications.

MACNAUGHTON, Alan Aylesworth: b. July 30, 1903, at Napanee, Ont. Barrister and solicitor. Elec. to H. of C. for Mount Royal (Montreal) g.e. 1949; re-elec. 1953, 1957, 1958, 1962, 1963. First Opposition Chairman of Public Accounts Committee, 1958-63. Speaker, May, 16, 1963, to Jan. 18, 1966. Summoned to Senate, July 8, 1966. Lib.

MARCHAND, Jean: b. Dec. 20, 1918, at Quebec City, Que. Labour organiser. Pres., Confederation of National Trade Unions, 1961. Elec. to H. of C. for Langelier (Que.), g.e. 1965. Min. of Citizenship and Immigration, Dec. 18, 1965; Quebec leader, 1966; Min. of Manpower and Immigration, Oct. 3, 1966. Lib.

MARCOUX, Guy: b. Feb. 21, 1924, at Beauport, Que. Physician. Elec.

to H. of C. for Quebec-Montmorency, g.e. 1962; re-elec. 1963; defeated 1965. S.C.

MARTIN, Paul Joseph James: b. June 23, 1903, at Ottawa, Ont. Barrister. Delegate to both League of Nations, Geneva, and United Nations, New York. Elec. to H. of C. for Essex East (Ont.), g.e. 1935; re-elec. 1940, 1945, 1949, 1953, 1957, 1958, 1962, 1963, 1965. Min. of National Health and Welfare, Dec. 17, 1946, to June 1957; Sec. of State for External Affairs, April 22, 1963. Lib.

MATHESON, John Ross: b. Nov. 14, 1917, at Arundel, Que. Barrister. Wounded in Italy during World War II. Elec. to H. of C. for Leeds (Ont.), g.e. 1962; re-elec. 1963, 1965. Lib.

McDONALD, Alexander Hamilton: b. March 16, 1919, at Fleming, Sask. Farmer. Served overseas with RCAF, 1940-45. Leader of Sask. Lib. Party, 1954-59. Deputy Premier of Sask. May 22, 1964. Summoned to Senate, Aug. 13, 1965. Lib.

McILRAITH, George James: b. July 29, 1908, at Lanark, Ont. Barrister. Elec. to H. of C. for Ottawa West, g.e. 1940; re-elec. 1945, 1949, 1953, 1957, 1958, 1962, 1963, 1965. Min. of Transport, April 22, 1963; Pres. of Privy Council, Feb. 3, 1964; Min. of Public Works, July 7, 1965. Government House Leader, Oct. 1964-May 1967. Lib.

MICHENER, Roland: b. April 19, 1900, at Lacombe, Alta. Lawyer. Served with RAF, 1918. Rhodes Scholar for Alberta, 1919. Elec. to H. of C. for St. Paul's (Toronto), g.e. 1953; re-elec. 1957, 1958; defeated 1962. Speaker, Oct. 14, 1957-62. High Commissioner to India, 1964-67. Sworn Governor-General of Canada, April 17, 1967. P.C.

NICHOL, John Lang: b. Jan. 7, 1924, at Vancouver, B.C. Businessman. Served with Canadian Navy during World War II. Pres. of Lib. Federation of Canada. Summoned to Senate, Feb. 24, 1966. Lib.

NICHOLSON, John Robert: b. Dec. 1, 1901, at Newcastle, N.B. Businessman. Gen. Mgr., Polymer Corporation, 1942-51. Elec. to H. of C. for Vancouver Centre, g.e. 1962; re-elec. 1963, 1965. Min. of Forestry, April 22, 1963; Postmaster General, Feb. 3, 1964; Min. of Citizenship and Immigration, Feb. 15, 1965; Min. of Labor, Jan. 4, 1966. Lib.

NIELSEN, Erik: b. Feb. 24, 1924, at Regina, Sask. Lawyer. Won D.F.C. on ultra-secret operations during World War II. Elec. to H. of C. for Yukon, b.e. Dec. 16, 1957; re-elec. g.e. 1958, 1962, 1963, 1965. P.C.

PELLETIER, Gérard: b. June 21, 1919, at Victoriaville, Que. Newspaperman. Editor, *La Presse,* Montreal, 1961-65. Elec. to H. of C., g.e. 1965. Lib.

PENNELL, Lawrence: b. March 11, 1915, at Brantford, Ont. Lawyer. Elec. to H. of C. for Brant-Haldimand (Ont.), g.e. 1962; re-elec. 1963, 1965. Solicitor General, July 7, 1965. Lib.

PEPIN, Jean-Luc: b. Nov. 1, 1924, at Drummondville, Que. Professor and political commentator. Elec. to H. of C. for Drummond-Arthabaska, (Que.), g.e. 1963; re-elec. 1965. Min. of Mines of Technical Surveys, July 7, 1965; Min. of Energy, Mines and Resources, Oct. 3, 1966. Lib.

PICKERSGILL, John W.: b. June 23, 1905, at Wyecombe, Ont. Lecturer in history. Secretary to Prime Minister, 1937-52. Clerk of Privy Council, 1952-53. Elec. to H. of C. for Bonavista-Twillingate (Nfld.), g.e. 1953; re-elec. 1957, 1958, 1962, 1963, 1965. Secretary of State, June 12, 1953; Min. of Citizenship and Immigration, July 1, 1954; resigned with Lib. admin. June 21, 1957; Secretary of State, April 22, 1963; Min. of Transport, Feb. 3, 1964. Pres. of Canadian Transport Commission, Sept. 19, 1967. Lib.

O'HAGAN, Richard: b. March 23, 1928, at Woodstock, N.B. Communicator. Special Asst. to Leader of Opposition, Jan. 1961; press secretary to Prime Minister, April 22, 1963. Minister-counsellor, Washington, Nov. 1966. Lib.

ROBARTS, John Parmenter: b. Jan. 11, 1917, at Banff, Alta. Barrister. Served with Canadian Navy, 1940-45. Premier of Ontario, Nov. 8, 1961-Feb. 12, 1971. P.C.

SAUVÉ, Maurice: b. Sept. 20, 1923, at Montreal, Que. Economist. Elec. to H. of C. for Iles-de-la-Madeleine, g.e. 1962; re-elec. 1963, 1965. Min. of Forestry, Feb. 3, 1964; Min. of Forestry and Rural Development, Oct. 3, 1966. Lib.

SÉVIGNY, Pierre: b. Sept. 17, 1917, at Quebec City, Que. Industrialist. Elec. to H. of C. for Longeuil (Montreal), g.e. 1958; re-elec. 1962. Assoc. Defence Min., Aug. 20, 1959; resigned before g.e. 1963 where defeated. P.C.

SHARP, Mitchell William: b. May 11, 1911, at Winnipeg, Man. Economist. Assoc. Deputy Min. of Trade and Commerce, 1951-58. Elec. to H. of C. for Eglinton, (Toronto), g.e. 1963; re-elec. 1965. Min.

of Trade and Commerce, April 22, 1963; Min. of Finance, Dec. 18, 1965. Lib.

SMALLWOOD, Joseph: b. Dec. 24, 1900, at Gambo, B.B., Nfld. Journalist and author. Mem. Newfoundland del. which negotiated and signed terms of union, 1949. Premier of Nfld. 1949 on. Lib.

STANFIELD, Robert Lorne: b. April 11, 1914, at Truro, N.S. Lawyer. Premier of N.S. 1956-67. Resigned to become National Leader of P.C. Party, Sept. 9, 1967. Elec. to H. of C. for Halifax, b.e. Nov. 6, 1967. Leader of Opposition, Nov. 15, 1967. P.C.

THOMPSON, Robert Norman: b. May 17, 1914, at Duluth, Minn. Educator. Served with RCAF, 1941-43. Advisor to Imperial Ethiopan government, 1945-51. National Leader of S.C. Party, 1961. Elec. to H. of C. for Red Deer (Alta.), g.e. 1962; re-elec. 1963, 1965. S.C.

TURNER, John Napier: b. June 7, 1929, at Richmond, Eng. Lawyer. Elec. to H. of C. for St. Lawrence-St. George (Montreal), g.e. 1962; re-elec. 1963, 1965. Min. Without Portfolio, Dec. 18, 1965; Registrar General, April 1967; Min. of Consumer and Corporate Affairs, Jan. 1968. Lib.

WALKER, James Edgar: b. July 21, 1911, at Vegreville, Alta. Insurance agent. Elec. to H. of C. for York Centre (Toronto), g.e. 1962; re-elec. 1963, 1965. Lib.

WRIGHT, Maurice: b. May 19, 1915, at Winnipeg, Man. Lawyer. Counsel for the Canadian Labour Congress at (Norris) Industrial Inquiry Commission on the Disruption of Shipping, 1962-63.

YOUNG, Christopher: b. July 9, 1926, at Accra, Gold Coast (Ghana), where Can. father taught. Journalist. Parliamentary correspondent, Southam News Service, Jan. 1960; editor, Ottawa *Citizen,* Nov. 1961 on.

ZINK, Lubor: b. Sept. 20, 1920, at Klapy, Czechoslovakia. Journalist. Fled from Nazis, 1939. Served with Czechoslovak armoured brigade in World War II. Press Officer to Jan Masaryk, Czech Foreign Minister. Fled from Communists, 1948. Editorial page editor, Brandon *Sun,* 1958-62; Ottawa columnist, Toronto *Telegram,* 1962 on.

Index

(Excerpts from contributors are in italics.)

451